# Forms under Revised Article 9

## Uniform Commercial Code Committee

Task Force on Forms under Revised Article 9

Jonathan C. Lipson, editor

Section of Business Law
American Bar Association

Defending Liberty
Pursuing Justice

The materials contained herein represent the opinions of the authors and editors and should not be construed to be the action of either the American Bar Association or the Section of Business Law unless adopted pursuant to the bylaws of the Association.

Nothing contained in this book is to be considered as the rendering of legal advice for specific cases, and readers are responsible for obtaining such advice from their own legal counsel. This book and any forms and agreements herein are intended for educational and informational purposes only.

The Introduction, Summary of Revised Article 9 and Commentary to the Forms under Revised Article 9 are protected under the United States copyright law and may not be reproduced in any manner without express permission. The Forms themselves may be reproduced by the original purchaser (or single transferee) in conjunction with his or her individual professional practice. No part of the Forms may be republished in any form without express permission of the American Bar Association.

The set of files in the software accompanying this book may only be used on a single computer or moved to and used on another computer. Under no circumstances may the set of files be used on more than one computer at one time. If you are interested in obtaining a license to use the set of files on a local network, please contact: Director, Copyrights and Contracts, American Bar Association, 750 N. Lake Shore Drive, Chicago, IL 60611, (312) 988-6101.

Copyright 2002 by the American Bar Association.
All rights reserved.
Printed in the United States of America.

Library of Congress Cataloging-in-Publication Data

Forms under Revised Article 9 / editor, Jonathan C. Lipson.
    p. cm.
ISBN 1-59031-081-0 (pbk.)
1. Security (Law)—United States—Forms. 2. Security (Law)—United States—States—Forms. I. Lipson, Jonathan C.
    KF1048.5 .F67 2002
    346.7307'4'0269—dc21                                                 2002004854

Cover design by Catherine Zaccarine.

Discounts are available for books ordered in bulk. Special consideration is given to state bars, CLE programs, and other bar-related organizations. Inquire at Publications Planning & Marketing, American Bar Association, 750 North Lake Shore Drive, Chicago, Illinois 60611

07  06  05  04  03  02    6  5  4  3  2

# Summary Table of Contents

# Contents

# Introduction

## WHY THIS BOOK?

In the menagerie of legal literatures, form books are strange and unloved beasts. While practitioners frequently stock their libraries with form books, they rarely use them. Most large firms have their own forms of security (and other) agreements, developed over years of painstaking practice and departmental lunches. Practicing attorneys rarely turn to form books, except, perhaps in desperation, or for the dyspeptic task of demonstrating that someone has made a mistake. And, if practitioners pay form books little heed, at least they have heard of them. Many law professors enjoy long and fruitful careers in the academy blissfully ignorant of the existence of form contracts, much less whole books of them.

At least part of the problem may be that form books are neither fish nor fowl. They undoubtedly aim to be useful. Yet, form books often sacrifice analysis for endless raw examples, intermittently (if sparsely) annotated with applicable statutory or other citations. Form books often leave the more intensive analysis of the relevant topic to other works (hornbooks, treatises, and so on).[1] Yet, hornbooks and treatises also leave gaps. While they sometimes contain forms, the forms usually appear to be an afterthought, and rarely incorporate the meatier analysis of the text.

This book aspires to be better. It is a collection of many forms likely to be useful to attorneys who practice commercial law in general, and who provide financial transactions services, in particular. Yet, unlike many simple collections of forms, this book offers what we hope will be helpful (perhaps even thoughtful) analyses of the role of the form in the larger context of Revised Article 9 of the Uniform Commercial Code and other applicable law. Indeed, half of the first chapter of the book—"Getting Started"—is not forms at all, but materials designed to aid the practitioner attempting to understand the many intricacies of Revised Article 9.

---

1. Notable recent exceptions are the ABA's *Model Asset Purchase Agreement with Commentary* and *Model Stock Purchase Agreement with Commentary.*

The balance of the book proceeds in more traditional terms, and includes a series of annotated security agreements, financing statements, other perfection-related documents, enforcement documents and miscellaneous documents (including opinion letters) that we hope will aid the practitioner and, perhaps, the academic. These forms have been annotated fairly closely, with statutory and other citations, comparisons to prior law and practice and discussions of what might be considered better practice under Revised Article 9. In this way, we hope this book will offer the best of traditional form books and treatises.

## WHY THESE FORMS?

Critics may observe the large number of forms in this book approvingly, and yet ask, Where are the rest? Should there not be a specialized form of security agreement for fixtures? Elecronic chattel paper? What about consumer materials? Surely, the critic would argue, consumer secured financing, with its special considerations, warrants attention here.

The response to these and probably many other criticisms would be—Agreed. Nevertheless, in the interest of getting the forms likely to be of the greatest use to the largest number of practitioners most quickly, judgments were made about which forms to develop immediately and which to consider in the future. We believe, in any case, that the basic tools exist in this volume to craft virtually any other form that might be necessary or proper in practice. And, after you've built upon these forms, to create your own, we invite you to share your improvements with us, so that we may share them with other practitioners.

## HOW TO USE THIS BOOK

Form books are not literature. Thus, it is not likely that anyone (except, perhaps, the insomniac) will read this book from cover to cover. Rather, it is more likely that this form book will be treated as a reference. It may be most useful for those new to Revised Article 9 to start with the summary of Revised Article 9, in Part 1. For those more familiar with the statute, it will probably be most useful as a check against forms currently in use. You may wish to use all of the forms for a given secured transaction; or, you may wish to extract portions of the forms, as appropriate to the deal.

These forms are not intended to be adhesion contracts. We understand—and expect—that they will be subject to negotiation and modification in due course. We have thus tried to indicate matters that might be subject to negotiation with [*italicized text in brackets*]. There will, of course, be many provisions that are up for grabs in addition to, or lieu of, those so indicated.

Accompanying this book is an electronic version of the forms unadorned by annotations. The purpose of the electronic version is obvious: Load it onto the computer, and begin to draft. The electronic versions should be accessible on most computers.

## WHO ARE WE?

The Task Force on Forms under Revised Article 9 was formed in 2000 under the aegis of Corinne Cooper. Her hard work and good planning brought together some of the nation's top commercial finance practitioners, all seeking to prepare a useful guide to practice under Revised Article 9. In 2001, Jonathan Lipson became chair of the Task Force and editor of the forms in this volume.

This project has benefitted from the contributions of many generous and talented people. The members of the Task Force that contributed to this volume are: Kathi Allen, Michael Avidon, Paul Barkes, E. Carolan Berkley, William Boston, Linda Chang, Penny Christophorou, Bennett Cohen, Corinne Cooper, Charles Cottam, Tinna Damaso, John C. Deal, Michelle Druce, Howard Darmstadter, R. Marshall Grodner, Russell Hakes, David Hamilton, Gail Hillebrand, Dick Hills, Kevin Hochberg, Kathleen Hopkins, Robert Ihne, Jennifer Jordan, Phil Karasik, David V. Kenner, Kraig Kohring, John Krahmer, Dana Kull, Phil Kunkel, Earl Leitess, Steve Leitess, Jonathan C. Lipson, John T. McGarvey, Thomas S. Marrion, David M. Mason, John Mazey, Juliet Moringiello, Carol Morrison, Peter S. Munoz, Daniel Murray, Ruth Olson, Sandra M. Rocks, Jeffrey Rosentahl, Yvonne Rosmarin, Mathew S. Rotenberg, Shelly Rothschild, Frederick Runge, Linda Rusch, Marsha Simms, Edwin E. Smith, David Snyder, Lynn Soukup, Andrew M. Toft, Jeffrey S. Turner, Paul S. Turner, Steven O. Weise, W. Joe Wilson, and Bob Wood.

Special credit goes to Ed Smith, Jeff Turner, and Steve Weise, who contributed many of the most important forms in this volume, and who indicated what would be considered "best practice," and to Corinne Cooper, who got the process rolling. Last, but certainly not least, is the terrific staff of the ABA—Jacqueline McGlamery, Judy Stofko, and Genevieve Canceko—who worked hard and well to complete this book.

## NEXT STEPS

No form book worth its salt is ever finished. Rather, the forms in this book should evolve to respond to the needs of practitioners, to address unforeseen changes in law or practice, and to correct errors. If you would like to participate in this on-going process, you may contact Jonathan Lipson, at jlipson@ubmail.ubalt.edu.

Jonathan C. Lipson
Editor

# PART 1

# Getting Started

# Summary of Revised Article 9 of the Uniform Commercial Code (2001)

## SCOPE OF REVISED ARTICLE 9

Revised Article 9—entitled *Secured Transactions*—generally applies to any interest (regardless of form) created by agreement in personal property or fixtures and which secures payment or other performance of an obligation.[1] This interest is referred to as a ***security interest***,[2] and the property subject to the security interest is referred to as ***collateral***.[3] Revised Article 9 also generally applies to sales of accounts, chattel paper, promissory notes, payment intangibles,[4] agricultural liens,[5] and all consignments,[6] even true consignments, within its scope.[7]

## Parties

### Debtor and Obligor

Revised Article 9 refers to the ***debtor*** as the person who has a property interest in the collateral other than a security interest or other lien.[8] The debtor is often—but not always—the "owner" of the collateral. The term "debtor" also includes a seller of accounts, chattel paper, promissory notes or payment intangibles,[9] a person who has a property

---

1. Rev. § 9-109(a)(1).
2. *See* UCC § 1-201(37) (defining "security interest").
3. *See* Rev. § 9-102(a)(12) (defining "collateral").
4. Rev. § 9-109(a)(3).
5. *See* Rev. § 9-102(a)(5) (defining "agricultural lien").
6. *See* Rev. § 9-102(a)(20) (defining "consignment").
7. Rev. § 9-109(a)(2) & (4).
8. Rev. § 9-102(a)(28)(A).
9. Rev. § 9-102(a)(28)(B).

interest in collateral subject to an agricultural lien,[10] and a consignee.[11] Revised Article 9 refers to the person who owes the secured obligation as the ***obligor***.[12]

### Secured Party

The person in whose favor a security interest is granted is defined in Revised Article 9 as the ***secured party***.[13] The term "secured party" also includes a buyer of accounts, chattel paper, promissory notes or payment intangibles, the person who holds an agricultural lien, and a consignor.[14] A secured party may be a "representative" for holders of secured obligations, such as an indenture trustee or collateral agent, where the security interest is granted to the secured party as representative.[15]

## Form of Transaction Is Irrelevant

The form of the transaction or the label which the parties give to the transaction is irrelevant for purposes of determining whether Revised Article 9 applies. Rather, Revised Article 9 applies to a transaction—regardless of labels—if, in economic reality, the transaction is a secured transaction. For example, the parties may characterize a transaction as a sale or a lease of goods. If, however, in economic reality a security interest is being created, Revised Article 9 will nevertheless apply.[16] It follows that the parties need not refer in their documents to a "security interest" or a "security agreement." Even if the parties use other terms, such as "assignment," "hypothecation," "conditional sale," "trust deed" or the like, Revised Article 9 still applies whenever a security interest in personal property is being created.[17] Similarly, it is generally irrelevant whether title to the collateral is in the name of the debtor or the secured party.[18]

## Exclusions

### Generally

Although Revised Article 9 covers most security interests in personal property and fixtures, certain interests in personal property collateral are outside of the scope of Revised Article 9. These interests include common law bailments and true leases, the latter being governed by UCC Article 2A.

### Specific Exclusions

Rev. §§ 9-109(c) & (d) exclude certain transactions and types of personal property collateral from Revised Article 9's scope. These specific exclusions encompass transactions preempted by federal law, landlords' liens, and certain of the following transactions or liens: statutory and common law liens, wage claims, security interests created by governments and governmental subdivisions and agencies, sales of accounts and chattel paper as part of a sale of the business out of which they arose, insurance claims, judgment claims,

---

10.    Rev. § 9-102(a)(28)(A); *see also* Rev. § 9-102(a)(5) (defining "agricultural lien").
11.    Rev. § 9-102(a)(28)(C); *see also* Rev. § 9-102(a)(20) (defining "consignment").
12.    Rev. § 9-102(a)(59).
13.    Rev. § 9-102(a)(72)(A).
14.    Rev. § 9-102(a)(72)(D), (B), & (C) respectively.
15.    Rev. § 9-102(a)(72)(E); *see also* Rev. § 9-102 cmt. 3.b.
16.    UCC § 1-201(37) & Rev. § 9-109(a)(10).
17.    Rev. § 9-109(a)(1)("regardless of its form").
18.    Rev. § 9-202.

rights of set-off, real estate interests, tort claims, and deposit accounts. The extent of some of these specific exclusions is further discussed below:

- *Non-Possessory Liens Other Than Agricultural Liens.* Revised Article 9 excludes from its scope landlords' liens and, generally, other nonpossessory liens arising by statute or common law. But **agricultural liens** are included within Revised Article 9's scope. "Agricultural liens" are generally nonpossessory statutory liens on a debtor's farm products in favor of a landlord or supplier of goods or services to the debtor in connection with the debtor's farming operations.[19]
- *Security Interest Granted by a State, Foreign Government, or State or Foreign Governmental Unit under Another Statute.* A security interest created by a state government, foreign government or state or foreign governmental unit is not included within Revised Article 9's scope to the extent that another state or foreign governmental statute governs security interests created by that state government, foreign government or state or foreign governmental unit.[20]
- *Certain Sales of Accounts, Chattel Paper, Promissory Notes and Payment Intangibles.* There are limited exclusions from Revised Article 9's scope for sales of accounts, chattel paper, promissory notes and payment intangibles arising out of the sale of the business out of which they arose. This is also true for assignments of accounts, chattel paper, promissory notes and payment intangibles for collection only. Similarly, there are limited exclusions for an assignment of a right to payment under a contract to an assignee that is obligated to perform under the contract, and an assignment of a single account, promissory note or payment intangible in full or partial satisfaction of pre-existing indebtedness.[21]
- *Insurance Claims Other Than Health-Care-Insurance Receivables.* While Revised Article 9 generally excludes assignments of insurance claims as original collateral, Revised Article 9 does include within its scope assignments of insurance claims, as original collateral, relating to the provision of health-care goods and services.[22] Assignments of insurance claims may also be within Revised Article 9's scope if they are proceeds of Revised Article 9 collateral.[23]
- *Tort Claims Other Than Commercial Tort Claims.* Revised Article 9 includes within its scope commercial tort claims.[24] "Commercial tort claims" are generally defined as claims in tort where the claimant is an organization, or where the claimant is an individual, and the claim arose from the individual's business or profession.[25] Other tort claims, such as tort claims by an individual arising out of personal injury, are excluded.
- *Consumer Deposit Accounts.* Assignments of *commercial* deposit accounts are included within the scope of Revised Article 9. Assignments of consumer deposit accounts in a consumer transaction are excluded.[26]

---

19.  Rev. § 9-102(a)(5)(defining "agricultural lien"), 9-109(a)(2) & 9-109(d)(2).
20.  Rev. § 9-109(c)(2) & (3); see also Rev. § 9-102(a)(45)(defining "governmental unit") & (76)(defining "State").
21.  Rev. § 9-109(d)(4), (5), (6) & (7).
22.  Rev. § 9-102(a)(46)(defining "health-care-insurance receivable") & 9-109(d)(8).
23.  *See* Rev. § 9-102(a)(64)(E), 9-315 & 9-312 & discussion of "Claimants as to Proceeds" under "Priority" below.
24.  Rev. § 9-102(a)(13)(defining "commercial tort claim") & 9-109(d)(12).
25.  Rev. § 9-102(a)(13) (defining "commercial tort claim").
26.  Rev. § 9-102(a)(26)(defining "consumer transaction"), 9-102(a)(29)(defining "deposit account") & 9-109(d)(13).

- *Real Estate Interests.* Revised Article 9 does not generally apply to security interests in real estate interests as such, including rents under real estate leases.[27] Even so, Revised Article 9 does apply to transactions affected by real estate in several circumstances:

  - If the secured party is granted a security interest in a promissory note or other right to payment within the scope of Revised Article 9, which note is secured by a real estate mortgage or other real estate interest, Revised Article 9 applies to the promissory note or other right to payment.[28]
  - If the debtor has an interest in a contract relating to real estate, such as a purchase and sale agreement, option agreement or the like, the debtor's rights to payment under the contract are likely to be considered accounts under Revised Article 9 rather than real estate interests excluded from the scope of Revised Article 9.[29]
  - If a secured party is taking a security interest in goods which are or are to become fixtures, both Revised Article 9 and real estate law may apply to the fixtures.[30]
  - Revised Article 9 addresses the priority conflict between a secured party claiming a security interest in fixtures, crops or a manufactured home[31] and the interest of an owner or a mortgagee or other encumbrancer claiming an interest in that collateral under real estate law.[32]

### Effect of Exclusion

Even though a type of assignment or a type of property may be excluded from Revised Article 9's scope, it is still often possible for a secured party to obtain a security interest in that type of property under other federal or state statutes, or under common law.

## REVISED ARTICLE 9 COLLATERAL CATEGORIES

Revised Article 9 classifies collateral into different categories, based largely on the debtor's use of the collateral. It is important for the secured party to determine the type of collateral in which the secured party is taking a security interest, since that determination will in turn guide the secured party in, among other things, deciding how to perfect the security interest. Collateral types under Revised Article 9 may be discussed broadly as comprising personal property consisting of goods, investment property, semi-intangible property, and other intangible property.

---

27.   Rev. § 9-109(d)(11).
28.   Rev. § 9-109(d)(11)(A); *see* Rev. § 9-203(g) & 9-308(e) & UCC § 9-308 cmt. 6.
29.   *See* Rev. § 9-102(a)(2)(defining "accounts" to include rights to payment arising from real property sold or otherwise disposed of).
30.   *See* "Revised Article 9 Collateral Categories" & discussion of "Fixtures" under "Priority" below.
31.   *See* Rev. § 9-102(a)(53) (defining "manufactured home").
32.   *See* discussion of "Priority" below.

## Goods

"Goods" are all things which are movable at the time the security interest attaches and include fixtures.[33] Goods *do not*, however, include money, documents, instruments, investment property, accounts, chattel paper, general intangibles or minerals before extraction. Nor do goods include deposit accounts or letter-of-credit rights (discussed below). Software embedded in goods and customarily viewed as a part of the goods (e.g., the computer chip in the automatic brakes on an automobile) is considered as part of the goods. Goods themselves are divided into four subcategories: consumer goods, inventory, farm products and equipment.

### Consumer Goods

"Consumer goods" are goods used or bought for use primarily for personal, family or household purposes[34]

### Inventory

"Inventory" consists of goods, other than farm products, held by a person for sale or lease, or consisting of raw materials, work in process, or materials consumed in business.[35]

### Farm Products

"Farm products" are crops, livestock or other supplies produced or used in farming operations. Farm products include products of crops or livestock in their unmanufactured state. For the goods to be farm products, the debtor must be engaged in a farming operation with respect to the goods.[36] A farming operation includes aquatic farming operations, and farm products include aquatic goods produced in aquacultural operations.[37]

### Equipment

"Equipment" is a residual subcategory of goods. It consists of goods which are not consumer goods, inventory or farm products.[38]

## Investment Property

"Investment property" is comprised of certificated and uncertificated securities, securities accounts and security entitlements, all of which are defined in UCC Article 8.[39] Investment property also includes commodity contracts and commodity accounts.[40]

## Semi-intangibles

There are certain movables which are conventional tangible embodiments of intangible rights of the debtor. These are defined in Revised Article 9 as instruments, chattel paper, documents and letter-of-credit rights.

---

33.   Rev. § 9-102(a)(44).
34.   Rev. § 9-102(a)(23).
35.   Rev. § 9-102(a)(48).
36.   Rev. § 9-102(a)(34).
37.   Rev. § 9-102(a)(35); *see also* Rev. § 9-102(a)(34).
38.   Rev. § 9-102(a)(33).
39.   Rev. § 9-102(a)(49); *see also* UCC §§ 8-102(a)(15)(defining "security"), 8-501(a)(defining "securities account") & 8-102(a)(17)(defining "security entitlement").
40.   Rev. § 9-102(a)(15) & (14) respectively. *See also* Rev. § 9-102(a)(49).

### Instrument

An "instrument" is a negotiable instrument governed by UCC Article 3 or another writing evidencing a right to the payment of money which, in the ordinary course of business, is transferred by delivery with any necessary indorsement or assignment. However, a negotiable instrument or other writing will not qualify as an instrument if it is included in the definition of chattel paper or investment property.[41] A credit card slip also does not qualify as an "instrument."[42] Within the category of instrument, Revised Article 9 provides a subcategory of "promissory note."

- *Promissory Note.* A "promissory note" is an instrument evidencing only a promise to pay (rather than an order to pay, such as a check). The term "promissory note" does not, however, include an instrument, such as a certificate of deposit, containing an acknowledgement of receipt of funds by a bank.[43]

### Chattel Paper

"Chattel paper" refers to any writing or writings or other records which evidence both a monetary obligation and a security interest in or a lease of specific goods.[44] A charter for the lease or hire of a vessel, however, is not chattel paper.[45] If the chattel paper writings or other records also include a monetary obligation secured by a security interest in or lease or license of software used in the chattel paper specific goods, those writings or other records relating to the software are included in the chattel paper relating to the goods. Revised Article 9 further divides chattel paper into two subcategories: tangible chattel paper and electronic chattel paper.

- *Tangible Chattel Paper.* If the chattel paper is evidenced by a record consisting of information inscribed on a tangible medium, such as a writing, then the chattel paper is "tangible chattel paper."[46]
- *Electronic Chattel Paper.* If the chattel paper is evidenced by records stored in an electronic medium, the chattel paper is "electronic chattel paper."[47]

### Document

A "document" is a document of title, such as a bill of lading or warehouse receipt.[48]

### Letter-of-Credit Right

A "letter-of-credit right" is a right to payment or performance under a letter of credit, whether the letter of credit is written or is evidenced electronically. The term does not include the debtor's drawing rights as beneficiary under the letter of credit.[49]

---

41.   Rev. § 9-102(a)(47).
42.   Rev. § 9-102(a)(47)(iii).
43.   Rev. § 9-102(a)(65).
44.   Rev. § 9-102(a)(11) & 9-102(a)(69)(defining "record").
45.   Rev. § 9-102(a)(11).
46.   Rev. § 9-102(a)(78).
47.   Rev. § 9-102(a)(31).
48.   Rev. § 9-102(a)(30); UCC §§ 1-201(15) & 7-102(1)(e).
49.   Rev. § 9-102(a)(51).

## Other Intangibles

Under Revised Article 9 pure intangibles that are not investment property are accounts, deposit accounts, commercial tort claims or general intangibles.

### Accounts

An "account" is any right to payment, whether or not it has been earned by performance, for property sold or leased or for services rendered and which is not evidenced by an instrument or chattel paper. A charter for the lease or hire of a vessel is an account. The term also includes a right to payment, whether not earned by performance, for real property sold, intellectual property licensed, the incurrence of a suretyship obligation, a policy of insurance, use of a credit card, and government sponsored or licensed lottery winnings. In addition, a health-care-insurance receivable is a subcategory of account.[50]

- *Health-Care-Insurance Receivable.* A "health-care-insurance receivable" is an interest in or claim under a policy of insurance which is a right to payment of a monetary obligation for health-care goods or services provided.[51]

### Deposit Account

A "deposit account" is a demand, time, savings, passbook or similar account maintained with a bank,[52] but does not include investment property or an account evidenced by an instrument.[53] Accordingly, a deposit account would include an uncertificated certificate of deposit, where there is no separate writing evidencing the bank's obligation to pay, as well as a nonnegotiable certificate of deposit, if the certificate does not qualify as an instrument.[54]

### Commercial Tort Claim

A "commercial tort claim" is a claim of an organization[55] arising in tort. It is also a claim of an individual arising in tort if the claim arises out of the individual's business or profession and does not include damages for death or personal injury.[56] If, however, a commercial tort claim is contractually settled, it may cease to be a claim arising in tort and may become a payment intangible as described below.[57]

### General Intangibles

"General intangibles" is a residual category for intangible property. The term comprises any personal property other than goods, accounts, chattel paper, documents, instruments, investment property, letter-of-credit rights, commercial tort claims, deposit

---

50.　Rev. § 9-102(a)(2).
51.　Rev. § 9-102(a)(46). *See also* Rev. § 9-102(a)(2).
52.　Rev. § 9-102(a)(8)(defining "bank").
53.　Rev. § 9-102(a)(29).
54.　*See* Rev. § 9-102 cmt. 12.
55.　*See* UCC § 1-201(2) (defining "organization").
56.　Rev. § 9-102(a)(13)(B).
57.　*See* Rev. § 9-109 cmt. 15.

accounts and money.[58] Within the category of general intangibles are two special subcategories: payment intangibles and software.

- *Payment Intangible.* A "payment intangible" is a general intangible under which the principal obligation of the account debtor[59] is to pay money, such as a loan not evidenced by an instrument or chattel paper.[60]
- *Software.* "Software" is a computer program and includes related supporting information. However, software embedded in goods and customarily viewed as a part of the goods is considered part of the goods and not software.[61]

## Other Terms Relating to Revised Article 9 Types of Collateral

Certain other terms are important to know as they relate to Revised Article 9 types of collateral:

### As-extracted Collateral

"As-extracted collateral" are oil, gas or other minerals that are subject to a security interest created by a debtor having an interest therein before extraction and that attaches to the minerals as extracted.[62] It also includes accounts arising out of the sale at the wellhead or minehead of oil, gas or other minerals in which the debtor had an interest before extraction.[63]

### Fixtures

"Fixtures" are goods that have become so related to particular property that an interest in them arises under real property law.[64]

### Supporting Obligation

A "supporting obligation" is a letter-of-credit right or secondary obligation that supports the payment or performance of an account, chattel paper, a document, a general intangible, an instrument or investment property.[65] Suretyship law, as explained by the RESTATEMENT (3d), SURETYSHIP AND GUARANTY § 1 (1996), determines whether an obligation is "secondary."[66] The most common secondary obligation is a guaranty by one party of payments to be made by another.

## ATTACHMENT

Revised Article 9 uses the term ***attachment*** to describe the moment at which a security interest becomes enforceable against the debtor.[67] For a security interest to attach, three

---

58. Rev. § 9-102(a)(42).
59. *See* Rev. § 9-102(a)(3) (defining "account debtor").
60. Rev. § 9-102(a)(61).
61. Rev. § 9-102(a)(75).
62. Rev. § 9-102(a)(6)(defining "as-extracted collateral").
63. Rev. § 9-102(a)(6).
64. Rev. § 9-102(a)(41).
65. Rev. § 9-102(a)(77).
66. *See* Rev. § 9-102 cmt. 2.a.
67. Rev. § 9-203(a).

(3) things must occur: (1) value must be given; (2) the debtor must have rights in the collateral; and (3) either (i) the collateral must be in possession of the secured party by agreement of the debtor or, if the collateral is investment property, a deposit account, electronic chattel paper or a letter-of-credit right, the secured party must have "control" of the collateral; or (ii) the debtor must have "authenticated" (*i.e.*, executed) a security agreement that describes the collateral.[68] A *security agreement* is the agreement under which a security interest is granted or provided for.[69] The following discussion provides a description of these elements of attachment.

## Value

In general, value is given for any consideration sufficient to support a simple contract. Some examples of value include a loan of money, a binding commitment to lend money, the issuance of a guarantee, or acting as an accommodation party. Value also includes whole or partial satisfaction of a pre-existing claim.[70]

## Rights in the Collateral

As a general matter, the debtor can only grant a security interest in whatever ownership or other rights it has. Similarly, the secured party can generally enjoy no greater rights in the collateral than the debtor itself holds unless the UCC provides otherwise.[71] Note, however, that a mere power of the debtor to transfer collateral is sufficient to satisfy the "rights in the collateral" requirement.[72] Thus, a seller of accounts may have the power again to transfer rights in the sold accounts where the interest of the buyer in the accounts is unperfected, and a consignee may have the power to transfer rights in consigned goods where the consignor's interest in the consigned goods is unperfected.[73]

## Possession of or Control by the Secured Party or Security Agreement

The secured party must either possess the collateral, or, in case of investment property, a deposit account, electronic chattel paper or a letter-of-credit right, the secured party must have "control" of the collateral; or the debtor must have authenticated a security agreement describing the collateral.[74] The description of the collateral in the security agreement must be sufficient reasonably to identify the collateral.[75] These requirements are further discussed below.

### Possession

A secured party may satisfy the possession requirement by using a third party who possesses the collateral, if the collateral is in possession of the third party by agreement of the debtor and the third party acknowledges in a signed writing or other authenticated

---

68.   Rev. § 9-203(b).

69.   Rev. § 9-102(a)(73). Various forms of security agreements appear as Forms 2.1–2.5.

70.   UCC § 9-201(44)(b).

71.   Rev. § 9-203(b); *see also* Rev. § 9-203 cmt. 6.

72.   Rev. § 9-203(b)(2).

73.   Rev. §§ 9-318 & 9-319.

74.   Rev. § 9-203.

75.   Rev. § 9-108.

record[76] that it holds for the benefit of the secured party.[77] If the collateral is a certificated security in registered form, there needs to be delivery to the secured party under UCC § 8-301.[78]

### Control

The concept of "control" applies to investment property, deposit accounts, electronic chattel paper and letter-of-credit rights.[79] The requirements for control are further discussed below under "Perfection."

### Security Agreement

A security agreement must be "authenticated" (*i.e.*, executed) by the debtor.[80] The term **authenticated** includes a signature on a written document or an authorized electronic transmission.[81]

### Reasonable Identification of the Collateral

The security agreement must "reasonably identify" the collateral.[82] "Reasonable identification" is a flexible concept, permitting identification in a variety of ways: a specific listing, a reference to a category, collateral type or quantity, or use of a computational formula. However, an "all assets"—also known as "super-generic"—description in a security agreement is insufficient.[83] Moreover, a description by collateral type alone is insufficient if the collateral is a commercial tort claim or, in a consumer transaction, if the collateral is consumer goods, a security entitlement, a securities account or a commodity account.[84] If the collateral is timber to be cut, a real estate description in the security agreement is required.[85]

## After-Acquired Property

Revised Article 9 permits a security agreement to contain an after-acquired property clause.[86] The secured party cannot, however, obtain a security interest in after-acquired consumer goods as original collateral unless the debtor acquires rights in the consumer goods within ten days after the secured party gives value.[87] Moreover, a security interest in a commercial tort claim will attach only to a tort claim existing at the time that the security agreement is signed or otherwise authenticated. The security interest will not attach as original collateral to an after-acquired commercial tort claim.[88]

## Future Advances and Cross-Collateralization

A security interest under Revised Article 9 may secure future advances and provide for cross-collateralization of various obligations.[89] Official Comment 5 to § 9-204 expressly

---

76.  *See* Rev. § 9-102(a)(7) (defining "authenticate") & (69) (defining "record").
77.  Rev. §§ 9-203(b)(3)(B) & 9-313(c)(1).
78.  Rev. § 9-203(b)(3)(C).
79.  Rev. § 9-203(b)(3)(D).
80.  Rev. § 9-203(b)(3)(A).
81.  Rev. § 9-102(a)(7).
82.  Rev. §§ 9-108(a) & 9-203(b)(3)(A).
83.  Rev. § 9-108(c).
84.  Rev. § 9-108(e).
85.  Rev. § 9-203(b)(3)(A).
86.  Rev. § 9-204(a).
87.  Rev. § 9-204(b)(1).
88.  Rev. § 9-204(b)(2).
89.  Rev. § 9-204(c).

rejects the holdings of cases under former Article 9 which require that future advances be of the same type or otherwise related to the original advance for the future advances to be secured by the collateral securing the original advance.

## Agricultural Liens

The concept of attachment does not apply to an agricultural lien. Revised Article 9 merely refers to the agricultural lien becoming "effective" under the statute giving rise to it.[90]

# PERFECTION

A security interest that has attached will generally prevail over a creditor using judicial process to obtain a lien on the collateral, including a trustee in bankruptcy having the status of a lien creditor under § 544(a) of the Bankruptcy Code, if it is **perfected**. Only a security interest that *has attached* can be perfected.[91] There are three principal ways in which an attached security interest may be perfected. First, the secured party may file a properly completed financing statement in the appropriate filing office.[92] Second, the secured party may take possession of the collateral or, in the case of investment property, a deposit account, electronic chattel paper or a letter-of-credit right, may obtain "control" of the collateral. Third, in a few cases, the security interest may be perfected automatically upon attachment. Depending upon the category of collateral, there may be only one method of perfection or several.

## Perfection by Filing

Security interests in most types of collateral may—and some must—be perfected by filing a properly completed financing statement in the appropriate filing office.[93]

### Contents of Financing Statement

To be legally sufficient, a financing statement must provide the debtor's name (the legal name),[94] the name of the secured party or its representative, and indicate the collateral covered by the financing statement.[95] Where the collateral is timber to be cut, as-extracted collateral or fixtures (in the case of a fixture filing), additional information is required for the financing statement to be sufficient.[96] Moreover, while an "all-assets" collateral description is insufficient in a security agreement, it is sufficient in a financing statement.[97] A financing statement may still be effective even though it contains errors, so long as the errors are minor and are not "seriously misleading."[98] A debtor's name on a financing statement that

---

90.   Rev. § 9-308(b).
91.   Rev. § 9-308(a).
92.   *See* Rev. § 9-102(a)(39) (defining "financing statement") & (37) (defining "filing office").
93.   Rev. § 9-310(a). Various forms of financing statements and related documents appear as Forms 3.2.1–3.2.7.
94.   *See* Rev. § 9-503)
95.   Rev. § 9-502(a).
96.   Rev. § 9-502(b) & (c).
97.   Rev. § 9-504(2).
98.   Rev. § 9-506(a).

varies from the debtor's legal name is not seriously misleading if a search of the records of the filing office under the debtor's legal name would disclose the financing statement.[99]

### Authorization by the Debtor

Revised Article 9—unlike former Article 9—does not require a debtor's signature on a financing statement. The secured party may not, however, file a financing statement against the debtor unless the filing is "authorized" by the debtor.[100] If the debtor has authenticated a security agreement, the authorization is automatic, at least to the extent of the collateral described in the security agreement.[101] Absent an authenticated security agreement, however, a secured party will need an authorization authenticated by the debtor to pre-file a financing statement, or to file a financing statement with a collateral description broader than that contained in the debtor's authenticated security agreement.[102] A secured party that files a financing statement without the debtor's authorization may be liable to the debtor for actual or statutory damages.[103]

### Office in Which Filing Should be Made

Revised Article 9 contains choice of law rules that determine the jurisdiction in which to file a financing statement in order to perfect a security interest. These choice of law rules are discussed in further detail below. Once the jurisdiction in which the filing must be made is determined, the financing statement must be filed in the central filing office in that jurisdiction, typically the Secretary of State's office. For as-extracted collateral, timber to be cut or a fixture filing, however, the financing statement (or fixture filing) must be filed in the local real estate recording office, not the central filing office.[104]

### What Constitutes Filing

The financing statement is "filed" when it has been "communicated"[105]—sent or transmitted—to the filing office, with the correct filing fee.[106] Rev. § 9-516(b) sets forth the only grounds on which a filing office may refuse to accept a financing statement for filing, thereby rendering the filing ineffective even if it is otherwise sufficient. These reasons include the communication of the financing statement by a means not authorized by the filing office and the failure to tender a payment at least equal to the filing fee. They also include the failure to provide in the financing statement other information, such as a mailing address for the debtor, whether the debtor is an individual or an organization,[107] and, if the debtor is an organization, the debtor's type and jurisdiction of organization and the debtor's state organizational identification number or a statement that the debtor has none.[108] The reasons set forth in § 9-516(b) are the only grounds for filing office rejection.[109] If there are such grounds for the filing office to reject the filing but the filing office nevertheless accepts the filing, the filing is still effective so long as the financing statement is legally sufficient under Rev. § 9-502.

---

99.    Rev. § 9-506(c).
100.   Rev. § 9-509(a)(1).
101.   Rev. § 9-509(b).
102.   A form of pre-filing authorization letter appears as Form 1.3.
103.   *See* Rev. § 9-625(b) & (e)(3).
104.   Rev. § 9-501.
105.   *See* Rev. § 9-102(a)(18) (defining "communicate").
106.   Rev. § 9-516(a).
107.   *See* UCC § 1-201(28) (defining "organization").
108.   Rev. § 9-516(b); *see especially* Rev. § 9-516(b)(5).
109.   Rev. § 9-520(a).

### How Filings Are Indexed

Filings are to be indexed in the name of the debtor so that subsequent searchers can find them.[110] Once an initial filing is made, any amendment, including an assignment, continuation statement or termination statement, relating to the initial filing must be linked in the filing office records to the initial filing.[111] Moreover, the filing office may not delete its records pertaining to any financing statement until at least one year after the financing statement has lapsed.[112]

### Lapse; Continuation; Termination

Filings generally expire after five years. If the financing statement's effectiveness is to be continued thereafter, a continuation statement must be filed within six months prior to the end of the five-year period.[113] Revised Article 9 makes exceptions for initial financing statements filed in connection with a public-finance transaction or a manufactured-home transaction,[114] which have a thirty-year duration.[115] And, a financing statement that indicates that the debtor is a transmitting utility[116] has a duration that lapses only on the filing of a termination statement relating to that financing statement.[117] If a financing statement lapses, the security interest perfected by the filed financing statement becomes unperfected, and is also deemed never to have been perfected as against a purchaser for value (but not a lien creditor).[118] When the secured obligations have been satisfied and the secured party has no further obligation to extend credit, the secured party is obligated to file a termination statement or, in a commercial transaction, to provide to the debtor a termination statement.[119] The debtor may file a termination statement if the secured party was required to file or provide the termination statement and has failed to do so.[120] The termination statement filed by the debtor must indicate on it that the debtor authorized the filing of the termination statement.[121] In addition, a secured party that fails to file or provide a termination statement when required to do so may be liable to the debtor for actual or statutory damages.[122]

### "Bogus" Filings

Revised Article 9 permits a debtor, who believes that a filing record concerning the debtor is inaccurate or has been wrongfully filed, to file a corrective statement setting forth the basis of the debtor's belief that the record is inaccurate or has been wrongfully filed. The corrective statement becomes part of the filing record but does not impair the effectiveness of an initial financing statement or other filed record.[123] Revised Article 9

---

110.    Rev. § 9-519(c)(1) & (f)(1).
111.    Rev. § 9-519(c)(1) & (f)(2).
112.    Rev. § 9-522(a).
113.    Rev. § 9-515.
114.    *See* Rev. § 9-102(a)(67) (defining "public-finance transaction") & (54) (defining "manufactured-home transaction").
115.    Rev. § 9-515(b).
116.    *See* Rev. § 9-102(a)(80) (defining "transmitting utility").
117.    Rev. § 9-515(f).
118.    Rev. § 9-515(c).
119.    Rev. § 9-513.
120.    Rev. § 9-509(d)(2).
121.    Rev. § 9-509(d)(2).
122.    Rev. § 9-625(b) & (e)(4).
123.    Rev. § 9-518.

leaves to other law the availability of civil remedies, or the imposition of criminal penalties, against those who misuse the filing system.

### Other Provisions

Additional details concerning financing statements and the UCC filing system are contained in part 5 of Revised Article 9.

## Perfection by Possession

Certain types of collateral may or must be perfected by possession.

### Money

A secured party's security interest in money[124] must be perfected by possession by the secured party.[125]

### Instruments

A secured party may perfect a security interest in an instrument by either filing or possession.[126]

### Certificated Securities

A security interest in a certificated security may be perfected by filing, possession or control.[127] A secured party's perfection of a security interest in a certificated security by possession is accomplished by the secured party taking delivery of the certificated security under UCC § 8-301.[128] Delivery generally means that the secured party obtains possession of the security certificate even if lacking a necessary indorsement.[129]

### Chattel Paper

A security interest in tangible chattel paper may be perfected by filing or by the secured party's taking possession of the tangible chattel paper.[130]

### Other Collateral

A security interest in goods and negotiable documents may be perfected by filing or by the secured party's taking possession of the collateral.[131]

### Possession by Third Parties

Where the secured party wishes to perfect a security interest in collateral by possession but the collateral is in the possession of a third party "bailee," Revised Article 9 requires the third party in possession of collateral, other than goods covered by a document of title, to authenticate a record acknowledging that it holds the collateral for the benefit of the secured party.[132] The third party in possession may not be the debtor or a lessee in the

---

124.   *See* UCC § 1-201(24) (defining "money").
125.   Rev. § 9-312(b)(3).
126.   Rev. §§ 9-312(a) & 9-313(a).
127.   Rev. §§ 9-312(a), 9-313(a) & 9-314(a).
128.   Rev. § 9-313(a).
129.   *See* UCC § 8-301.
130.   Rev. §§ 9-312(a), 9-313(a) & 9-314(a).
131.   Rev. §§ 9-310(a), 9-312(a) & 9-313(a).
132.   Rev. § 9-313(c)(1); *cf.* UCC §§ 8-106(a) & (b), & 8-301(a)(2) (certificated securities). Forms of bailee acknowledgment appear as Forms 3.5.1 (non-farm products) and 3.5.2 (farm products).

ordinary course from the debtor.[133] A secured party in possession of collateral does not relinquish possession if the secured party delivers the collateral to a possible purchaser of the collateral (other than the debtor or an ordinary course lessee of the collateral) for inspection and return.[134]

## Perfection by Control

The concept of control applies to perfection of a security interest in investment property, deposit accounts, electronic chattel paper and letter-of-credit rights.[135]

### Investment Property

A security interest in investment property may be perfected by control or filing.[136] The concept of **control** is the same under Revised Article 9 as it is under UCC Article 8 and includes delivery, with indorsements, of certificated securities to the secured party, an agreement by the issuer of uncertificated securities that the issuer will honor instructions from the secured party without further consent of the debtor, and an agreement by a bank, broker or other securities intermediary holding a securities account, or by a commodity intermediary, that it will honor instructions from the secured party without further consent of the debtor. Control also includes registering the securities, the securities account or the commodity account in the name of the secured party. Where the secured party is the debtor's securities intermediary or commodity intermediary, the securities intermediary or commodity intermediary automatically has control.[137]

### Deposit Accounts

A security interest in a deposit account as original collateral (as opposed to proceeds of other collateral) may be perfected *only* by the secured party's obtaining control over the deposit account.[138] A secured party obtains control over a deposit account if it is the depositary bank or if the deposit account is in the secured party's name. A secured party also has control if the depositary bank enters into an agreement (known as a control agreement) with the secured party that the depositary bank will comply with instructions from the secured party as to the funds in the deposit account, without further consent from the debtor.[139]

### Electronic Chattel Paper

A security interest in electronic chattel paper may be perfected by control or by filing.[140] A secured party obtains control over electronic chattel paper if there is only one authoritative or identifiable copy of the electronic record of the chattel paper, the copy of the record identifies the secured party and its interest, the copy is communicated to and maintained by the secured party or its designated custodian, the copy is readily

---

133.    Rev. § 9-313(c).

134.    Rev. § 9-313(h).

135.    Rev. §§ 9-106, 9-104, 9-105, 9-107 & 9-314(a). Forms of deposit account and securities account control agreements appear as Forms 3.3.1 and 3.3.2, respectively.

136.    Rev. §§ 9-312(a) & 9-314(a).

137.    UCC §§ 8-106 & 9-106.

138.    Rev. §§ 9-312(b)(1) & 9-314(a).

139.    Rev. § 9-104(a).

140.    Rev. §§ 9-312(a) & 9-314(a).

identifiable as the authoritative copy and any revision of the authoritative copy is readily identifiable as authorized or unauthorized.[141]

### Letter-of-Credit Rights

A security interest in a letter-of-credit right may be perfected by the secured party obtaining control over the letter-of-credit right. Control is the sole method of perfection of a security interest in a letter-of-credit right unless the security interest in the letter-of-credit right is perfected as a supporting obligation.[142] A secured party has control over a letter-of-credit right if the issuer or nominated person has consented to an assignment of proceeds of the letter of credit under § 5-114(c) or other applicable law.[143]

## Automatic Perfection

In some situations, no additional steps beyond attachment are necessary to perfect a security interest.

### Generally

The following security interests under Revised § 9-309 are automatically perfected upon attachment: a purchase-money security interest in consumer goods, a sale of promissory notes or payment intangibles, an assignment of accounts or payment intangibles which does not alone or in conjunction with other assignments to the same assignee transfer a significant part of the outstanding accounts or payment intangibles of the assignor, a security interest arising under UCC Article 2, 2A or 4 or by delivery of a financial asset under Rev. § 9-206(c), a security interest in investment property created by a securities intermediary or commodity intermediary, an assignment of a health-care-insurance receivable to the health-care provider, a security interest in favor of an issuer or nominated person in documents presented to the issuer or nominated person for draw under a letter of credit,[144] an assignment for the benefit of creditors, and a security interest created by an assignment of a beneficial interest in a decedent's estate.

### Supporting Obligations

In addition, Revised Article 9 provides for automatic attachment of a security interest in a supporting obligation if the security interest in the supported collateral has attached and for automatic perfection of a security interest in a supporting obligation if the security interest in the supported collateral is perfected.[145]

### Temporary Automatic Perfection

A security interest in instruments, certificated securities and negotiable documents is temporarily perfected for a period of twenty days to the extent that it arises for new value given under an authenticated security agreement.[146] A security interest in proceeds is also temporarily perfected for a period of twenty days if the security interest in the original collateral was perfected.[147]

---

141.  Rev. § 9-105.
142.  Rev. §§ 9-312(b)(2) & 9-314(a).
143.  Rev. § 9-107. A form of assignment of proceeds of letter of credit appears as Form 3.4.
144.  *See* UCC § 5-118.
145.  Rev. §§ 9-203(f) & 9-308(d).
146.  Rev. § 9-312(e).
147.  Rev. § 9-315(d); see discussion below of "Claimants as to Proceeds" under "Priority."

## Other Methods of Perfection

Federal and state statutes may, of course, provide other methods of perfection of security interests (or their functional equivalent) in vessels, aircraft, intellectual property and titled goods (such as motor vehicles that are not inventory of a dealer). Compliance with these methods of perfection constitutes the equivalent of perfection by filing under Revised Article 9.[148] A security interest in titled goods that are inventory is generally perfected by filing, rather than by noting the security interest on the certificates of title.[149] A security interest in goods covered by a nonnegotiable document may be perfected by filing as to the goods, by issuance of the document in the name of the secured party, or by acknowledgment by the bailee of the secured party's interest.[150]

# PRIORITY

Even though a security interest has attached and become perfected, it will not prevail over other creditors and other interested parties if the security interest does not have *priority*. Priority is the ranking of various interests in the same collateral among the secured party and other claimants.

## Unsecured Creditors

A secured party will prevail over unsecured creditors with respect to collateral in which the secured party has a perfected security interest.[151] Even if the secured party fails to perfect its security interest, the secured party will still prevail over unsecured creditors with respect to collateral in which the secured party has an unperfected security interest, at least outside of the debtor's bankruptcy.[152]

## Lien Creditors

### Definition

A *lien creditor* is a creditor who has acquired a lien on the debtor's property by judicial process, and includes a trustee in bankruptcy.[153]

### Secured Party vs. Lien Creditor Generally

A perfected security interest will prevail over the lien of a lien creditor on the secured party's collateral so long as the secured party's security interest in the collateral is perfected at or before the time the lien arises.[154] Even if the security interest is not perfected, the secured party will prevail over the lien creditor so long as, before the lien arises, the secured party has filed a financing statement covering the collateral and, as set forth in

---

148.    Rev. § 9-311(b).
149.    Rev. § 9-311(d).
150.    Rev. § 9-312(d). Forms of bailee acknowledgment appear as Forms 3.5.1 (non-farm products) and 3.5.2 (farm products).
151.    Rev. §§ 9-201(a) & 9-317(a).
152.    Rev. § 9-201(a).
153.    Rev. § 9-102(a)(52).
154.    Rev. § 9-317(a)(2)(A).

Rev. § 9-203(b)(3), the debtor has authenticated a security agreement describing the collateral or the secured party has possession or control of the collateral.[155]

### Future Advances

Future advances by the secured party on collateral in which the secured party's security interest is superior to the lien of the lien creditor on the original advance will likewise be secured by the collateral in priority to the lien creditor's lien, so long as the future advances are made within the later of forty-five days after the lien arose and the time that the secured party obtained knowledge of the lien, or are made pursuant to a commitment[156] incurred without knowledge of the lien.

### Purchase-Money Security Interests

A secured party taking a purchase-money security interest[157] will also have priority over a lien creditor holding a lien on the purchase-money collateral so long as the secured party perfected its security interest by filing before the expiration of a period of twenty days after the debtor received possession of the collateral.[158]

## Other Non-Purchase Money Secured Parties

Absent another Revised Article 9 priority rule to the contrary, in cases in which there is more than one secured party claiming a security interest in the same collateral, the first secured party to file a financing statement or perfect its security interest has priority. This is the so-called "first-to-file-or-perfect" priority rule.[159] It follows that a perfected security interest in collateral prevails over an unperfected security interest in the collateral.[160] If both security interests are unperfected, the first security interest to attach has priority.[161]

## Purchase-Money Secured Parties

A *purchase-money security interest* is a security interest in collateral which is either taken by a vendor of that collateral to finance its purchase price or a security interest given to a third party lender in the collateral purchased with the proceeds of the lender's loan.[162] The purchase-money collateral must generally be goods. It may, however, also be software sold or licensed with goods which are themselves purchase-money collateral, if the software is acquired principally for use with the goods.[163] A holder of a perfected purchase-money security interest, who has taken certain applicable steps, achieves "super priority," *i.e.,* its security interest in the purchase-money collateral will rank ahead of any security interest which would otherwise be entitled to priority under the first-to-file-or-perfect priority rule. To achieve super priority, the purchase-money secured party must take the following steps:

---

155.    Rev. § 9-317(a)(2)(B).
156.    *See* Rev. § 9-102(a)(68) (defining "pursuant to commitment").
157.    *See* "Purchase-Money Secured Parties" (discussed below).
158.    Rev. § 9-317(e).
159.    Rev. § 9-322(a)(1).
160.    Rev. § 9-322(a)(2).
161.    Rev. § 9-322(a)(3).
162.    Rev. § 9-103.
163.    Rev. § 9-103(b)(3) & (c).

*Inventory Collateral*

If the collateral is inventory, the purchase-money secured party must perfect its security interest before the debtor receives possession of the inventory. In addition, the purchase-money secured party must notify existing holders of a security interest of record in the same type of inventory of the purchase-money lender's intention to take a purchase-money interest in the inventory in advance of the debtor receiving possession of the inventory.[164] The notice is effective for five years.[165] Purchase-money inventory advances may be cross-collateralized so that the total of the purchase-money inventory advances from the same supplier or lender may be secured by successive shipments of the purchase-money inventory collateral from the same supplier or financed by the same lender.[166]

*Farm Products Livestock Collateral*

Revised Article 9 contains analogous purchase-money priority rules for purchase-money security interest in farm products livestock.[167] The purchase-money priority also extends to products of the livestock in their unmanufactured state.

*Other Collateral*

If the security interest is in collateral other than inventory or farm products livestock, the purchase-money secured party must perfect its security interest before the expiration of a period of twenty days after the debtor obtains possession of the collateral.[168]

If two secured parties, one being a vendor and the other being a lender, each claim purchase-money priority over the same collateral, the vendor's purchase-money security interest prevails over that of the lender.[169] In addition, a purchase-money security interest in a commercial transaction does not lose its status as a purchase-money security interest merely because it also secures non-purchase-money obligations, the purchase-money obligations are also secured by non-purchase-money collateral, or the purchase-money obligations have been renewed or refinanced.[170]

## Consignors

Revised Article 9 treats all consignments, as defined in Rev. § 9-102(a)(20), whether "true" consignments or security consignments, as purchase-money security interests and requires consignors to comply with Revised Article 9 rules applicable to purchase-money secured parties in order to obtain priority.[171]

## Buyers, Lessees and Non-Exclusive Licensees in the Ordinary Course

Customers of the debtor who buy the debtor's goods in the ordinary course of the debtor's business take free of the security interest of the debtor's secured party even if they

---

164. A form of inventory purchase-money security interest notification appears as Form 3.5.3.
165. Rev. § 9-324(b).
166. Rev. § 9-103(b)(2).
167. Rev. § 9-324(d) & (e). A form of livestock purchase-money notification appears as Form 3.5.4.
168. Rev. § 9-324(a).
169. Rev. § 9-324(g)(1).
170. Rev. § 9-103(f)
171. *See* UCC § 1-201(37)(defining a consignment as a security interest) & Rev. § 9-103(d).

know of the security interest.[172] However, only a customer of the debtor that takes possession of the goods or has a right to recover the goods from the debtor under Article 2 will be an ordinary course buyer.[173] A buyer of consumer goods has a right to recover the goods from the debtor under Article 2 when the buyer acquires a "special property" in the goods.[174] The acquisition by a buyer of a special property in goods generally occurs at the time that the goods are identified to the sales contract.[175] In addition, a buyer of goods collateral from a debtor may not take free of the secured party's security interest as a buyer in ordinary course if the secured party is in possession of the goods.[176] Analogous rules for lessees and nonexclusive licensees in the ordinary course are set forth in Rev. § 9-321.

## Buyers and Other Transferees Not in the Ordinary Course

Generally, if the debtor sells or otherwise disposes of collateral not in the ordinary course and the disposition is not authorized by the secured party, the security interest continues in the collateral and continues perfected notwithstanding its disposition.[177] Future advances by the secured party will likewise be secured in priority over the interest of the buyer, so long as the future advance is made within the earlier of forty-five days after the sale occurred and the secured party learned of the sale, or the secured party makes the advance pursuant to a commitment[178] entered into without knowledge of the lien and before the expiration of a period of forty-five days after the buyer's purchase.[179] If the security interest is unperfected, the buyer gives value and the buyer has no knowledge of the security interest, the buyer acquires its interest in the collateral free of the secured party's security interest.[180]

## Negotiable Documents

While goods are in possession of a bailee who has issued a negotiable document covering the goods, a perfected security interest in the negotiable document has priority over a security interest perfected in the goods during that period.[181] In addition, where goods are evidenced by a negotiable document, a holder of the negotiable document to whom the negotiable document has been duly negotiated prevails over an earlier security interest in the goods to the extent provided in UCC Article 7.[182]

## Instruments

A security interest in an instrument perfected by filing is generally subordinate to the interest of another secured party or other purchaser if the other secured party or other

---

172.   UCC § 1-201(9)(definition of "buyer in ordinary course of business") & Rev. § 9-320(a).
173.   UCC § 9-201(9).
174.   UCC §§ 2-502(2) & 2-716(3).
175.   *See* UCC § 2-401(2).
176.   Rev. § 9-320(e).
177.   Rev. §§ 9-315(a)(1) & 9-507(a).
178.   *See* Rev. § 9-102(a)(68) (defining "pursuant to commitment").
179.   Rev. § 9-323(d) & (e).
180.   Rev. § 9-317(b).
181.   Rev. § 9-312(c)(2).
182.   Rev. § 9-331(a).

purchaser takes possession of the instrument for value, in good faith and without knowledge that the purchase violates the rights of the secured party that perfected by filing.[183] A holder in due course of a negotiable instrument has priority over an earlier secured party to the extent set forth in UCC Article 3.[184]

## Chattel Paper

### Generally

If a security interest in chattel paper is perfected only by filing, not by possession of tangible chattel paper or control of electronic chattel paper, an ordinary course new value purchaser of the chattel paper who takes possession of the tangible chattel paper or control of the electronic chattel paper in good faith has priority over the security interest perfected by filing so long as the purchaser is without knowledge that the purchase violates the filing secured party's rights.[185] If the secured party's interest is legended on the chattel paper, the purchaser is viewed as having knowledge that the purchase will violate the secured party's rights.[186]

### "Merely as Proceeds"

An ordinary course new value purchaser of chattel paper who takes possession of tangible chattel paper or control of electronic chattel paper in good faith will have priority over a security interest in the chattel paper claimed "merely as proceeds" of inventory perfected by filing, even if the purchaser knows of the security interest, so long as the filing secured party's interest is not legended on the chattel paper.[187]

### "New Value"

Revised Article 9 defines "new value," with one exception, to require additional monetary or other specific consideration.[188] The one exception is where an inventory secured party, by taking possession of tangible chattel paper or control of electronic chattel paper that is proceeds of its inventory collateral, would qualify for priority under Rev. § 9-330(a) or (b) but for its failure to provide "new value." In that situation, the inventory secured party need not make an additional advance for value previously given by it to constitute "new value" under Rev. § 9-330(a).[189]

## Investment Property

A security interest in investment property perfected by control is superior to a security interest in the same investment property perfected by filing, even if control occurs after the time of filing.[190] If competing security interests are each perfected by control,

---

183.    Rev. § 9-330(d).

184.    Rev. § 9-331(a); *see also* UCC § 3-306.

185.    Rev. § 9-330(b).

186.    Rev. § 9-330(f).

187.    Rev. § 9-330(a). For a discussion of when a security interest in chattel paper arises "merely as proceeds" see PEB Commentary No. 8.

188.    Rev. § 9-102(a)(57).

189.    *See also* Rev. § 9-330(e).

190.    Rev. § 9-328(1).

they rank in priority of the time of obtaining control.[191] Even so, a security interest perfected by control in favor of the debtor's securities intermediary has priority over a security interest perfected by filing or control by another secured party.[192] A secured party's possession by agreement of a security certificate in registered form, without any necessary indorsements, results in the secured party's security interest in the certificated security being superior to another secured party's security interest in the certificated security perfected by filing.[193] Where investment property collateral is transferred to a person protected under UCC Article 8's adverse claim cutoff rules, the transferee remains protected under UCC Article 8.[194]

## Deposit Accounts

A security interest in a deposit account perfected by control is superior to a security interest in the deposit account perfected by another method (*e.g.*, in the case where a security interest in original collateral, other than the deposit account, was perfected and the secured party holding that security interest has an automatically perfected security interest in the deposit account as proceeds of the original collateral).[195] If competing security interests are each perfected by control, they rank in priority of the time of obtaining control.[196] But a security interest perfected by control in favor of the debtor's depositary bank, and the depositary bank's right of recoupment or set-off, are superior to a security interest of a competing secured party perfected by control or another method unless the competing secured party obtained perfection by control by becoming the depositary bank's customer on the deposit account.[197] A transferee of funds from a deposit account in which the secured party has a security interest takes free of the secured party's security interest unless the transferee acts in collusion with the debtor in violating the rights of the secured party.[198]

## Letter-of-Credit Rights

A security interest in a letter-of-credit right perfected by control is superior to a security interest in a letter-of-credit right perfected automatically as a supporting obligation.[199] If competing security interests in the letter-of-credit right are each perfected by control, they rank in priority of the time of obtaining control.[200] A security interest in a letter-of-credit right is subordinate to the rights of a transferee beneficiary or nominated person under UCC § 5-114.[201] Although a secured party may become a transferee of a letter of credit, its rights as transferee will be derived from UCC Article 5 and letter of credit practice.[202]

---

191.    Rev. § 9-328(2).
192.    Rev. § 9-328(3).
193.    Rev. § 9-328(5).
194.    Rev. § 9-331(b).
195.    Rev. § 9-327(1).
196.    Rev. § 9-327(2).
197.    Rev. § 9-327(3) & (4) & 9-340.
198.    Rev. § 9-332(b).
199.    Rev. § 9-329(1).
200.    Rev. § 9-329(2).
201.    Rev. § 9-329(1).
202.    *See* Rev. §§ 9-109(c)(4) & 9-329 cmts. 3 & 4.

## Claimants as to Proceeds

### Definition

**Proceeds** are whatever is received upon the sale, exchange, or other disposition or collection of collateral.[203] Investment property distributions, partnership and limited liability company interest distributions, rentals for the lease of goods, and licensing royalties are all proceeds of the underlying collateral. Claims arising out of the loss or nonconformity of, or interference with, the collateral are also proceeds.[204]

### Attachment

Upon the sale, exchange or other disposition or collection of collateral, a secured party's security interest continues in any "identifiable" proceeds.[205] Common law tracing rules, such as the "lowest intermediate balance" test when cash proceeds are commingled with other funds in a deposit account, may be used to determine what proceeds are identifiable.[206]

### Perfection

The secured party's security interest in proceeds is automatically perfected for twenty days if the security interest in the original collateral was perfected. Unless the proceeds are identifiable cash proceeds, the secured party may be required to take additional steps during that twenty-day period to continue the perfection of its security interest beyond the twenty-day period.[207]

### Priority Generally

A secured party's priority in proceeds will usually date from the time of the secured party's priority in the original collateral for the purposes of applying the first-to-file-or-perfect priority rule.[208] However, an inventory purchase-money secured party entitled to priority over an earlier filed secured party has priority in proceeds of the inventory sold or otherwise disposed of only in limited circumstances:

- if the proceeds are identifiable cash proceeds received by the debtor on or before delivery of the inventory to the buyer,
- if the proceeds are instruments, chattel paper or proceeds of the chattel paper to which the purchase-money secured party, typically by taking possession of the instrument or chattel paper, is entitled to priority under Rev. § 9-330, or
- if the purchase-money security interest is in farm products livestock.[209]

A transferee of money[210]—whether or not proceeds—will take free of the interest of a security interest in the money unless the transferee has acted in collusion with the debtor in violating the rights of the secured party.[211]

---

203. Rev. § 9-102(a)(64).
204. Rev. § 9-102(a)(64).
205. Rev. §§ 9-203(f) & 9-315(a)(2).
206. Rev. § 9-315(b)(2); *see also* Rev. § 9-315 cmt. 3.
207. Rev. § 9-315(c) & (d).
208. Rev. § 9-322(b)(1).
209. Rev. § 9-324(a), (b) & (d).
210. *See* UCC § 1-201(24) (defining "money").
211. Rev. § 9-332(a).

### *Priority Where Certain Original Collateral Has Priority under a Non-Temporal Perfection Rule*

As discussed above, a perfected possessory or control security interest in a deposit account, investment property, a letter-of-credit right, chattel paper, an instrument or a negotiable document will typically have priority over a security interest perfected by an earlier filing. Such collateral is sometimes referred to as "non-filing" collateral, because secured parties generally neither expect nor need to file a financing to perfect a security interest in such collateral.[212] The secured party with priority as to the non-filing collateral, will also have priority in the proceeds if its security interest in proceeds is perfected, the proceeds are cash proceeds or are of the same type as the original collateral, and, in the case of proceeds that are proceeds of proceeds, any intervening proceeds are cash proceeds, are of the same type as the original collateral, or are an account relating to the collateral.[213] In addition, under certain circumstances, priority in the proceeds is based upon the first to file rather than under the "first-to-file-or perfect" priority rule. Those circumstances arise where:

- each secured party has a perfected security interest in a deposit account, investment property, a letter-of-credit right, chattel paper, an instrument or a negotiable document perfected by a method other than filing, and
- the proceeds are "filing collateral", (i.e., *not* cash proceeds or a deposit account, investment property, a letter-of-credit right, chattel paper, an instrument or a negotiable document).[214]

Otherwise, the "first-to-file-or-perfect" priority rule applies as to the proceeds.[215]

### *Returned or Repossessed Goods*

As Official Comments 9–11 to § 9-330 explain, Revised Article 9 treats returned or repossessed goods as proceeds of the accounts, chattel paper or other payment rights created when the goods were sold. Moreover, if a chattel paper purchaser has priority over a secured party claiming a security interest in the debtor's inventory, the chattel paper purchaser also has priority over the inventory secured party on returned or repossessed goods arising from the chattel paper.[216]

### *Agricultural Lien Proceeds*

Revised Article 9 does not address proceeds of an agricultural lien. Revised Article 9 leaves to other law, presumably the statute under which the agricultural lien is created, whether the agricultural lien extends to proceeds and, if so, whether the agricultural lien in proceeds is perfected and what priority it has over a competing claimant.[217]

## Statutory and Agricultural Liens

A possessory lien on goods for services and materials furnished in the ordinary course given by statute or common law has priority over a secured party's security interest in the

---

212.   Rev. § 9-322 cmt. 7.
213.   Rev. § 9-322(c).
214.   Rev. § 9-322(d).
215.   *See* Rev. § 9-322 cmt. 9.
216.   Rev. § 9-330(c)(2).
217.   *See* Rev. § 9-315 cmt. 9.

goods unless the lien is given by statute and the statute provides otherwise.[218] If the lien is an agricultural lien, the general Revised Article 9 priority rules apply unless the agricultural lien is given by statute and the statute provides otherwise.[219]

## Unpaid Sellers

An unpaid seller that has not taken a perfected purchase-money security interest entitled to priority in goods sold to a debtor will not usually prevail over a secured party of the debtor holding a perfected security interest in the goods acquired by the debtor. This is the case even if the unpaid seller has a reclamation claim to the goods under UCC Article 2.[220] But an unpaid seller that retains possession of the goods that it sells to the debtor will have priority over a secured party of the debtor holding a perfected security interest in goods acquired by the debtor.[221]

## Real Estate Claimants as to Fixtures

A security interest in fixtures may be perfected by a filing a UCC-1 financing statement as to the goods *or* by making a *fixture filing*[222] filed at the office in the jurisdiction where real estate mortgages are recorded, and which provides that it is being filed in the real estate records.[223] A fixture filing made before the interest of a competing real estate claimant is recorded will generally enable the secured party claiming a security interest in the fixtures to prevail over the real estate claimant if the secured party would have prevailed over the real estate claimant's predecessor in interest.[224] A purchase-money security interest in goods which become fixtures will generally prevail over an existing interest of record of a competing real estate claimant if a purchase-money fixture filing is made as to the goods within twenty days after the goods become fixtures.[225] A fixture security interest will, however, often be subordinate to the construction mortgage of a construction mortgagee where the goods become fixtures before completion of construction.[226] Even so, a security interest in certain readily removable goods perfected before the goods become fixtures has priority over a competing real estate claimant in the goods, including a construction mortgagee.[227] In addition, a secured party with a security interest in a manufactured home has priority over a competing real estate claimant if the security interest in the manufactured home was perfected in a manufactured-home transaction under an applicable certificate of title statute.[228]

---

218.   Rev. § 9-333.

219.   Rev. § 9-322(g); *see also* Rev. § 9-322 cmt. 12.

220.   UCC §§ 2-402(3)(a), 2-403(4), 2-702(3), 1-201(32) & 1-201(33).

221.   Rev. § 9-110.

222.   *See* Rev. § 9-102(a)(40) (defining "fixture filing").

223.   Rev. §§ 9-334(e)(3) & 9-501(a)(1) & (2).

224.   Rev. § 9-334(e)(1).

225.   Rev. § 9-334(d).

226.   Rev. § 9-334(h).

227.   Rev. § 9-334(e)(2); *see also* Rev. § 9-334(h).

228.   Rev. § 9-334(e)(4); *see also* Rev. § 9-102(a)(53) & (54) (defining "manufactured home" and "manufactured-home transaction," respectively).

## Crops

A perfected security interest in crops has priority over the interest of an owner or mortgagee of the real estate on which the crops are grown if the debtor is the owner of the real estate or is in possession of it.[229]

## Accessions

Under Rev. § 9-102(a)(1), an *accession* is goods that are "physically united" with other goods such that the identity of the original goods is not lost.[230] Priority in accessions is generally determined by the other priority rules set forth in part 3 of Revised Article 9, including as to priority disputes between a secured party holding a security interest in an accession and a secured party holding a security interest in the whole of the goods.[231] However, a security interest in an accession is junior to a security interest in the whole perfected by compliance with a certificate of title statute.[232] For example, in the event that a debtor grants to a secured party a security interest in a motor vehicle perfected by notation of the secured party's interest on the motor vehicle's certificate of title and the debtor also grants to a seller of tires to the debtor a security interest in the tires perfected automatically or by filing, the motor vehicle secured party will prevail as to the tires if the tires become accessions to the motor vehicle.[233]

## Commingled Goods

*Commingled goods* are essentially the opposite of accessions: Rev. § 9-336(a) defines "commingled goods" as goods that are "physically united" with other goods such that their identity *is* lost in a product or mass.[234] If goods in which one secured party has a perfected security interest are commingled with other goods in which another secured party has a perfected security interest, if neither secured party otherwise has a prior security interest in the other's goods, and if the identity of each secured party's collateral is lost in a product or mass, then each secured party's security interest attaches to the product or mass.[235] Their priority then ranks equally in proportion to the value of the collateral at the time that the collateral became commingled.[236]

## Filing Office Records

A financing statement that is improperly rejected by the filing office is nevertheless effective under Rev. § 9-520(c)'s "tender rule." The security interest subject to the rejected filing is, however, subordinate to the interest of a subsequent secured party or other purchaser giving value in reliance upon the clean record in the filing office.[237] In addition, a

---

229.   Rev. § 9-334(i).
230.   *See* Rev. § 9-102(a)(1) (defining "accession").
231.   *See* Rev. § 9-335 cmt. 6.
232.   Rev. § 9-335(d).
233.   *See* Rev. § 9-335 cmt. 7.
234.   Rev. § 9-336(a).
235.   Rev. § 9-336(d).
236.   Rev. § 9-336(f)(2) & cmt. 6.
237.   Rev. § 9-516(d).

secured party may, inadvertently or otherwise, file a financing statement containing information, required by Rev. § 9-516(b)(5), that is incorrect. For example, the secured party may incorrectly state in the financing statement the type of organization or mailing address of the debtor. In such a case, the secured party's security interest is perfected, but is subordinate to a later perfected secured party, and a purchaser, other than a secured party, of the collateral takes free of the earlier secured party's security interest, if the later secured party or other purchaser gives value in reliance upon the incorrect information.[238]

## Creditors Senior by Contractual Subordination

Any secured party may contractually subordinate its security interest to a secured party or other person whose interest would not otherwise have priority.[239]

## Production-Money Secured Parties (Optional)

Revised Article 9 contains an *optional* set of model provisions for those jurisdictions that wish to provide a priority security interest, referred to as a **production-money security interest**, for those who extend new credit enabling a debtor to produce crops if the proceeds of the credit are in fact used for the production of the crops. These provisions, set forth in Appendix II to Revised Article 9, are analogous to the purchase-money security interest provisions for inventory contained in Rev. §§ 9-103 & 9-324. In the event that a jurisdiction enacts the production-money security interest provisions, a holder of a production-money security interest in crops will prevail over an earlier filed secured party claiming a non-production-money security interest in the crops.[240] If the secured party holds both a production-money security interest and an agricultural lien on the crops, the priority rules applicable to the agricultural lien govern.[241]

## CERTAIN THIRD-PARTY RIGHTS

## Rights of Account Debtors

### Definition

An **account debtor** is someone who is obligated on an account, chattel paper or general intangible. An obligor on a negotiable instrument, however (*e.g.*, a maker or indorser), is not an account debtor, even though the negotiable instrument is otherwise part of chattel paper.[242]

### Account Debtor Discharge

An account debtor is obligated to pay the assignee of an account, chattel paper or general intangible when the account debtor is notified that the obligation has been assigned and that payments are to be made to the assignee. The account debtor is permitted to

---

238.  Rev. § 9-338.
239.  Rev. § 9-339.
240.  Model Rev. § 9-324A(a)
241.  Model Rev. § 9-324A(e).
242.  Rev. § 9-102(a)(3).

request the assignee to exhibit reasonable evidence that the assignment has been made; if the assignee fails to provide that evidence, the account debtor may continue to pay the assignor.[243]

### Claims and Set-Offs

Where a secured party has a security interest in an account, chattel paper or general intangible arising under a contract between the debtor and the account debtor, the account debtor may assert a claim or defense against the secured party arising under that contract.[244] The account debtor may also assert a claim or defense arising with respect to any other obligation of the debtor to the account debtor except for claims or defenses accruing on such other obligations after the account debtor has been notified of the security interest.[245] The secured party is not, however, generally subject to affirmative contract or tort liability to the account debtor merely because of the existence of the security interest.[246] Moreover, in a *commercial* transaction, a claim or defense of an account debtor may be asserted only to reduce the amount owed; it may not be asserted affirmatively against the secured party.[247] Nevertheless, the rules of Rev. § 9-404 are subject to any contrary *consumer* law.[248] Among other things, the consumer account debtor has the benefit of the notice required by Federal Trade Commission Rule 433,[249] to be stated on the evidence of an account or general intangible or upon chattel paper even if the notice is not so stated.[250] The obligations of an insurer under a health-care-insurance receivable are governed by other law.[251]

### Agreements Not to Assert Claims or Defenses

Subject to any contrary consumer law in a consumer transaction, an account debtor may agree generally not to assert personal claims or defenses against an assignee.[252] A consumer account debtor also has the benefit of the notice of the FTC Holder in Due Course Waiver required to be stated on the evidence of an account or general intangible or upon chattel paper even if the notice is not so stated.[253] The provisions of Rev. § 9-403 are otherwise a "safe harbor," *i.e.*, they are without prejudice to other circumstances where such agreements are effective under other law.[254]

### Anti-Assignment Clauses

Revised Article 9 renders ineffective a clause restricting the creation or enforcement of a security interest in an account or chattel paper, or, if it secures an obligation, a promissory note or a payment intangible.[255] Revised Article 9 also renders ineffective a rule of law that would prevent the attachment, perfection or enforcement of a security interest in

---

243.    Rev. § 9-406(c).
244.    Rev. § 9-404(a)(1).
245.    Rev. § 9-404(a)(2).
246.    Rev. § 9-402.
247.    Rev. § 9-404(b).
248.    Rev. § 9-404(c). *See also* Rev. § 9-207(b) & (c) (providing that consumer rules shall displace Revised Article 9).
249.    *See* 16 C.F.R. Part 433 (the so-called "FTC Holder in Due Course Waiver").
250.    Rev. § 9-404(d) & cmt 4.
251.    Rev. § 9-404(e).
252.    Rev. § 9-403.
253.    Rev. § 9-403(d).
254.    Rev. § 9-403(f).
255.    Rev. §§ 9-406(d) & 9-407.

an account or chattel paper.[256] Moreover, Revised Article 9 renders ineffective a clause in any promissory note or payment intangible, in the case of a sale of the promissory note or payment intangible, or in any other general intangible, as well as any rule of law, relating to a promissory note or payment or other general intangible, that prevents a security interest from attaching and becoming perfected, so long as the rights of the account debtor or other party favored by the anti-assignment clause or rule of law are not disturbed. A security interest in such a promissory note or payment or general intangible may attach and be perfected notwithstanding an anti-assignment clause or rule of law restricting assignment, but the secured party is not entitled to enforce the security interest without, if so permitted under other law, the consent of the account debtor or other party favored by the anti-assignment clause or rule of law.[257] For purposes of Rev. § 9-408, an assignment of a health-care-insurance receivable is treated as if it were a general intangible rather than an account governed by Rev. § 9-406.[258]

## Persons Obligated on Instruments

Under UCC Article 3, a person obligated on a negotiable instrument, such as a maker or indorser, when notified to pay a transferee of the instrument, may require the transferee to exhibit the instrument in order to demonstrate that the transferee is the person entitled to enforce the instrument.[259] Revised Article 9 does not change this rule, nor does it address whether a non-negotiable instrument must be exhibited by the transferee as a condition to payment by the obligated person.

## Securities Intermediaries

Revised Article 9 does not affect the rule in UCC Article 8 that a securities intermediary has no obligation to enter into a control agreement with a secured party claiming a security interest in a securities account, even if the debtor/entitlement holder so requests.[260]

## Depositary Banks

Unless a secured party has control over a deposit account, the depositary bank has no obligation to deal with the secured party with respect to the deposit account.[261] A depositary bank has no obligation to enter into a control agreement with the secured party relating to the deposit account even if the debtor customer so requests.[262]

## Letter of Credit Issuers

A clause in a letter of credit restricting its transfer is ineffective to prevent a security interest in a letter-of-credit right from attaching and being perfected as a supporting obligation, so long as the rights of the issuer or any nominated person are not disturbed.[263]

---

256.  Rev. § 9-406(f).
257.  Rev. § 9-408.
258.  Rev. §§ 9-406(i) & 9-408.
259.  UCC §§ 3-501(b)(2) & 3-602(a).
260.  UCC § 8-106(g).
261.  Rev. § 9-341.
262.  Rev. § 9-342.
263.  Rev. § 9-409.

# CERTAIN DUTIES OF SECURED PARTY

## Duty of Reasonable Care When Collateral Is in Possession or Control of Secured Party

A secured party generally has an obligation under Revised Article 9 to use reasonable care to preserve collateral in the secured party's possession. Unless otherwise agreed with the debtor, the secured party must take reasonable steps to preserve rights of the debtor in instruments and chattel paper in the secured party's possession against prior parties.[264] The secured party is entitled to charge the collateral in its possession for the secured party's reasonable expenses in preserving the collateral.[265] If the debtor agrees to the secured party's repledge of collateral in the secured party's possession or control, the debtor's right of redemption as a claim against the secured party is preserved even though a third party who took by repledge may have gained superior rights in the collateral, whether by law or by agreement with the debtor.[266] The secured party's duties under Rev. § 9-207 do not apply where the secured party is a buyer of accounts, chattel paper, promissory notes or payment intangibles or is a consignor unless, in the case of the duty of reasonable care, the buyer or consignor has recourse against the debtor or a secondary obligor based upon a credit or other default of the account debtor or other obligor on the collateral.[267]

## Duty to Account

Revised Article 9 permits a debtor to ask the secured party to approve or correct the debtor's statement of the amount of the secured obligation and the identity of collateral.[268] The secured party is required to respond within fourteen days or risk liability to the debtor for any loss to the debtor caused by the secured party's failure to respond.[269] If the secured party has sold its interest in the secured obligations and collateral, it must disclose the name and address of the secured party's successor, if known to the secured party.[270] The debtor also has the right to request an accounting of the unpaid secured obligations, with analogous provisions for the timeliness of the secured party's response, risk of the secured party's liability to the debtor for failure to respond, and required disclosure of any known transferee of the unpaid secured obligations.[271]

## Duty to Terminate or Release

Once the secured obligations have been paid and the secured party has no further commitment to extend credit or otherwise give value, the financing statement perfecting the security interest must be terminated by the filing of a termination statement.[272] If the

---

264.   Rev. § 9-207(a).
265.   Rev. § 9-207(b)(1).
266.   Rev. § 9-207(c)(3); *see also* Rev. §§ 9-207 cmts. 5 & 6 & 9-314 cmt. 3.
267.   Rev. § 9-207(d).
268.   Rev. § 9-210(a)(3) & (4) & (b)(2).
269.   Rev. §§ 9-210(b) & 9-625(b) & (f).
270.   Rev. § 9-210(d) & (e).
271.   Rev. §§ 9-210(a)(2), (b), & (e) & 9-625(b) & (f). Although Revised Article 9 does not appear to entitle parties other than the debtor to an accounting, best practice may suggest that it is appropriate to share the accounting with other parties asserting an interest in the collateral, *e.g.* junior secured parties or secondary obligors.
272.   Rev. § 9-102(a)(79)(defining "termination statement"). A form of termination statement is contained as Form 3.2.7.

financing statement covers consumer goods, the secured party must file the termination statement.[273] In other transactions, the secured party must, and otherwise within twenty days of a debtor's request, send the termination statement to the debtor to file, or file the termination statement itself.[274] If the secured party fails to do so in a timely manner, it risks liability to the debtor for any loss to the debtor caused by the secured party's failure.[275] Revised Article 9 provides analogous provisions, once the secured obligations have been paid and the secured party has no further commitment to extend credit or otherwise give value, for the secured party to release control of collateral and to release account debtors from any obligations to make payments to the secured party.[276]

## CHOICE OF LAW

When it is necessary to determine whether a security interest has attached, has or has not been perfected, or has priority over another interest, it is necessary to ask which jurisdiction's law applies. If a dispute occurs in a particular forum in a UCC jurisdiction, the first step is to look to the choice of law rules of the forum jurisdiction's UCC to determine which jurisdiction's laws the forum jurisdiction is required to apply. Several concepts should be kept in mind: (1) the security agreement's choice of law provisions, which governs the *contractual* agreement between the debtor and the secured party, (2) the law which will govern perfection (and, in particular, dictate where to file a financing statement), and (3) the law which will govern the effect of perfection or non-perfection, and the priority of the security interest.

### Contractual Choice of Law

The UCC typically respects the parties' contractual choice of law for purposes of determining the contractual rights and obligations of the debtor and the secured party to the other as long as the secured transaction bears a "reasonable relation" to the jurisdiction whose law was chosen.[277] The secured party and the debtor may not, however, vary by contract the mandatory choice of law rules in Revised Article 9, as discussed below, dealing with the perfection, the effect of perfection or nonperfection, and priority of security interests.[278]

### Perfection[279]

Choice of law regarding perfection usually—but not always—reduces to the question of the state (or other jurisdiction) in which to file a financing statement to perfect a security interest. "Perfection," as discussed in this section, is distinct from the effect of perfection or non-perfection, or priority, both of which may have different choice of law rules, and which are discussed in greater detail below.

---

273.   Rev. § 9-513(a).
274.   Rev. § 9-513(c).
275.   Rev. §§ 9-513 & 9-625(b) & (e)(4).
276.   Rev. §§ 9-208, 9-209 & 9-625(b) & (e)(1) & (2).
277.   UCC § 1-105(1).
278.   UCC § 1-105(2).
279.   A checklist that can be used to determine where to file a financing statement is contained as Form 3.1.

### General Rule: Location of the Debtor

Except as provided below, the local law of the jurisdiction where the debtor is located governs whether a security interest is perfected.[280] Given that choice of law generally turns on the debtor's location, Revised Article 9 provides special rules to determine that location.

**Registered organizations.**   A debtor may be a *registered organization*, which is defined under Revised Article 9 as an organization[281] organized solely under the law of a single State[282] or the United States, and for which the State or United States is required to maintain a public record showing it to have been organized.[283] A debtor which is a registered organization is located in the jurisdiction of its organization.[284] For example, if the debtor is a corporation, limited liability company or limited partnership organized under the laws of a particular state, the debtor is located in that state.[285]

**Other debtors.**   A debtor which is not a registered organization is located at the debtor's principal residence if he or she is an individual, at the debtor's place of business if the debtor is an organization that has only one place of business, or at the debtor's chief executive office if the debtor is an organization that has more than one place of business.[286]

**Foreign debtors.**   If the debtor is located in a jurisdiction outside of the United States which does not provide for a public filing system that enables a secured party to prevail over a subsequent lien creditor, then the debtor is deemed to be located in the District of Columbia.[287]

**Special rules.**   Special rules apply to determine the locations of federal registered organizations, certain foreign air carriers, and bank branches and agencies.[288]

### Possessory Security Interests

The local law of the jurisdiction where the collateral is located governs perfection by possession.[289]

### Fixtures

The local law of the jurisdiction where fixtures are located governs perfection by a fixture filing.[290]

### Timber to Be Cut

The local law of the jurisdiction where the timber is located governs perfection of a security interest in timber to be cut.[291]

---

280.   Rev. § 9-301(1).
281.   UCC § 1-201(28).
282.   Which is limited to jurisdictions in the United States & its territories & possession. *See* Rev. § 9-102(a)(76).
283.   Rev. § 9-102(a)(70).
284.   Rev. § 9-307(e).
285.   *See* Rev. § 9-102 cmt. 11.
286.   Rev. § 9-307(b).
287.   Rev. § 9-307(c).
288.   *See* Rev. § 9-307(f), (h), (i) & (j).
289.   Rev. § 9-301(2).
290.   Rev. § 9-301(3)(A).
291.   Rev. § 9-301(3)(B).

## As-extracted Collateral

The local law of the jurisdiction where the wellhead or minehead is located governs perfection of a security interest in as-extracted collateral.[292]

## Titled Goods

The local law of the issuing jurisdiction generally governs perfection of a security interest in goods subject to a certificate of title, assuming that the security interest is noted on the certificate of title.[293] However, the choice-of-law rule for determining perfection of a security interest in titled goods that also happen to be inventory held for sale or lease by a person in the business of selling goods of that kind is the debtor's location under Rev. § 9-301. That is because, under Rev. § 9-311(d), the security interest in titled goods that also happen to be inventory need not be noted on the certificate of title for the goods; instead, a security interest in titled goods inventory may be perfected by compliance with the ordinary filing rules.[294]

## Agricultural Liens

The local law of the jurisdiction where the relevant farm products are located governs perfection of an agricultural lien on farm products.[295]

## Investment Property

The local law of the jurisdiction in which the debtor is located governs perfection of a security interest in investment property perfected by filing.[296] If, however, perfection is not claimed by filing:

- the local law where the security certificate is located governs perfection,
- the local law of the issuer's jurisdiction[297] governs perfection of a security interest in an uncertificated security, and
- the local law of the securities intermediary's jurisdiction[298] or commodity intermediary's jurisdiction[299] governs perfection of a security interest in a security entitlement, securities account or commodity account.[300]

## Deposit Accounts

The local law of the jurisdiction of the depositary bank governs perfection of a security interest in a deposit account.[301] Revised Article 9 contains rules for determining where the depositary bank is located that closely follow the rules for determining the location of a securities intermediary.[302]

---

292.  Rev. § 9-301(4).
293.  Rev. § 9-303(c).
294.  *See* Rev. § 9-303 cmt. 5.
295.  Rev. § 9-302.
296.  Rev. § 9-305(c)(1).
297.  *See* UCC § 8-110(d) (setting forth applicable rules).
298.  *See* UCC § 8-110(e) (setting forth applicable rules).
299.  *See* Rev. § 9-305(b) (setting forth applicable rules).
300.  Rev. § 9-305(a).
301.  Rev. § 9-304(a).
302.  *See* Rev. § 9-304(b).

### *Letter-of-Credit Rights*

The law of the jurisdiction of the issuer or nominated person generally determines perfection of a security interest in a letter-of-credit right, other than a letter-of-credit right which is claimed merely as a supporting obligation. The issuer's or nominated person's jurisdiction is determined under UCC § 9-116.[303] If, however, the issuer's or nominated person's jurisdiction is not a State,[304] then the law of the debtor's location determines whether or not the security interest has been perfected.[305]

## Effect of Perfection or Non-Perfection and Priority

To determine the effect of perfection or non-perfection, and priority, Revised Article 9 at times requires the forum jurisdiction to look to the local law of a jurisdiction that is different from the jurisdiction whose law determines perfection:

### *Negotiable Documents, Goods, Instruments, Money or Tangible Chattel Paper*

The local law of the jurisdiction in which negotiable documents, goods, instruments, money or tangible chattel paper is located governs the effect of perfection or non-perfection and priority.[306]

### *Certificated Securities*

The local law of the jurisdiction where the security certificate is located governs the effect of perfection or non-perfection and priority.[307]

### *Uncertificated Securities*

The location of the issuer of uncertificated securities governs the effect of perfection or non-perfection and priority.[308]

### *Security Entitlements, Commodity Contracts, Securities Accounts and Commodity Accounts*

The local law of the jurisdiction where the securities intermediary or commodity intermediary is located governs the effect of perfection or non-perfection and priority as to security entitlements, commodity contracts, securities accounts and commodity accounts.[309]

### *Other Personal Property*

In all other cases, the effect of perfection or non-perfection and priority are governed by the law of the jurisdiction that governs perfection (*e.g.* the debtor's location).

---

303.  Rev. § 9-306.
304.  *See* Rev. § 9-102(a)(76) (defining "state")
305.  *See* Rev. § 9-306 cmts. 2 & 3.
306.  Rev. § 9-301(3)(C).
307.  Rev. § 9-305(a)(1).
308.  Rev. § 9-305(a)(2).
309.  Rev. § 9-305(a)(3) & (4).

# POST-CLOSING CHANGES

## Change of Debtor's Name

If a debtor changes its name so that an existing financing statement becomes "seriously misleading," the secured party must file an amendment to the existing financing statement to reflect the debtor's new name within four months following the name change, or the financing statement will not perfect the security interest as to assets the debtor acquires after that four-month period.[310]

## Change of Debtor's Location

If a debtor that is not a registered organization changes its location to another jurisdiction, the secured party must file a new financing statement in the new jurisdiction within four months following the change (or before the financing statement in the original jurisdiction lapses, if earlier) in order to maintain the perfection of its security interest by filing in collateral which must be perfected by filing where the debtor is located.[311] A debtor that is a registered organization will not typically be able to change its location. For example, a dissolved corporation will be considered as located in the jurisdiction in which it was organized prior to the dissolution.[312] Moreover, the attachment, perfection and priority of a security interest in the assets of a corporate debtor which reincorporates will likely be analyzed as if the new corporation were a new debtor under the "double debtor" provisions discussed below.

## Double Debtor Issues

Revised Article 9 offers some solutions to the "double debtor" problem—*i.e.*, how to treat security interests in collateral that becomes subject to a security interest created by another debtor.

### Transfer of Collateral to a Person Who Becomes a Debtor

If collateral in which a secured party has a security interest perfected by filing under the law of the jurisdiction of the location of the debtor is transferred to a person who thereby becomes a debtor,[313] the filing remains effective to continue the perfection of the security interest.[314] If, however, the transferee debtor is located in a jurisdiction different from that of the transferor debtor, the secured party has a period of one year (or until the expiration of any earlier period in which perfection would lapse under the law of the transferor debtor's jurisdiction) to perfect the security interest under the law of the jurisdiction of the location of the transferee debtor in order to maintain the perfection of its security interest beyond that period.[315] If the security interest is not perfected in that

---

310. Rev. § 9-507(c).
311. Rev. § 9-316(a).
312. *See* Rev. § 9-307(g).
313. *See* Rev. § 9-102(a)(28) (defining "debtor").
314. Rev. § 9-507(a).
315. Rev. § 9-316(a)(3). *See also* Rev. § 9-509(c) (secured party's authority to file financing statement in new jurisdiction).

jurisdiction during that period, it is deemed never to have been perfected against a purchaser for value.[316]

### Priority Dispute between Secured Party of Transferor and Secured Party of Transferee as to Transferred Collateral

A debtor may transfer collateral subject to a perfected security interest to a transferee who creates a security interest in favor of the transferee's secured party. In that case, the "first-to-file-or-perfect" priority rule is called off, and the transferor debtor's secured party will prevail as to the transferred collateral so long as its security interest in the transferred collateral remains perfected.[317]

### Priority Dispute between Secured Party of Transferor and Secured Party of Transferee when Transferee Becomes Bound by Transferor's Security Agreement

**New debtor.**    A debtor, whose assets are subject to a security interest under a security agreement in favor of its secured party, may merge with another entity, or may otherwise transfer its assets to another entity that generally becomes obligated for the debts of the transferor debtor. If the transferee becomes generally liable for the debts of the transferor debtor by law or by contract, the transferee becomes bound by the original debtor's security agreement, both for existing and, if applicable under the security agreement, after-acquired collateral.[318] Revised Article 9 refers to the transferor in such a case as the *original debtor*,[319] and the transferee as a *new debtor*.[320]

**Attachment.**    A new debtor is, by definition, bound by the original debtor's security agreement.[321] Accordingly, the security interest of the original debtor's secured party in the new debtor's collateral existing at the time of the transaction and, if applicable under the security agreement, after-acquired collateral attaches in the hands of the new debtor.[322]

**Perfection.**    A filing that would have been effective to perfect a security interest in the collateral of the original debtor's secured party under the security agreement had the original debtor not effected the transaction with the new debtor is generally effective to perfect the secured party's security interest in that collateral, both existing and after-acquired, in the hands of the new debtor.[323] But there are three important exceptions.

*Continuation of perfection as to transferred assets if the new debtor is located in a new jurisdiction.*    If collateral in which the original debtor's secured party has a security interest that is perfected under the law of the jurisdiction of the location of the original debtor but the new debtor is located in another jurisdiction, the secured party has one year (or the expiration of any earlier period in which the perfection of the security interest would lapse under the law of the original debtor's jurisdiction) to perfect the

---

316.    Rev. § 9-316(b).
317.    Rev. § 9-325.
318.    Rev. § 9-203(d).
319.    Rev. § 9-102(a)(60).
320.    Rev. § 9-102(a)(56).
321.    Rev. § 9-203(d).
322.    Rev. § 9-203(e).
323.    Rev. § 9-508(a).

security interest under the law of the jurisdiction of the location of the new debtor in order to maintain the perfection of its security interest.[324] If the security interest is not perfected in that jurisdiction during that period, it is deemed never to have been perfected against a purchaser for value.[325]

*Perfection as to after-acquired assets if the new debtor is located in a new jurisdiction.* If the new debtor is located in a jurisdiction different from that of the original debtor, the original debtor's secured party must perfect its security interest under the law of the new debtor's jurisdiction in order for the original secured party's security interest to be perfected in the new debtor's collateral acquired after the new debtor became bound by the original debtor's security agreement.[326] The secured party of the original debtor has no grace period to perfect its security interest in collateral acquired after the new debtor became bound by the original debtor's security agreement, if the location of the new debtor is in a jurisdiction different from that of the original debtor.

*Perfection as to after-acquired assets if the new debtor is located in same jurisdiction but its name is seriously misleading.* If the original debtor's secured party has perfected its security interest in the collateral of the original debtor by filing in the jurisdiction of the location of the original debtor and the new debtor is located in the same jurisdiction, but the name of the new debtor is seriously misleading when compared to the name of the original debtor, the original debtor's secured party has four months from the time that the new debtor became bound by the original debtor's security agreement to file a financing statement against the new debtor. If the original debtor's secured party fails to file a financing statement against the new debtor within that four month period, its security interest in collateral acquired by the new debtor after that four-month period will not be perfected by filing.[327]

**Priority as to existing collateral.** If the original debtor's secured party has a perfected security interest in the transferred collateral, the "first-to-file-or-perfect" priority rule is called off, and the original debtor's secured party will prevail over the secured party of the new debtor as to the transferred collateral.[328]

**Priority as to after-acquired collateral.** If the original debtor's secured party needs to rely upon perfection by filing against the original debtor to claim perfection of its security interest in collateral acquired by the new debtor after the new debtor became bound by the original debtor's security agreement, the original debtor's secured party's security interest in the after-acquired collateral is junior to a security interest created by the new debtor's secured party.[329]

---

324.   Rev. § 9-316(a)(3). *See also* Rev. § 9-509(c) (secured party's authority to file financing statement in new debtor's jurisdiction).

325.   Rev. § 9-316(b).

326.   *See* Rev. § 9-316(a)(3). This section provides a one-year grace period to continue perfection in a new debtor's location only for *collateral existing at the time that the new debtor becomes bound* under Rev. § 9-203(d). For authorization for the original debtor's secured party to file a financing statement against the new debtor, *see* Rev. § 9-509(b).

327.   Rev. § 9-508; *see* Rev. § 9-509(b) for the secured party's authorization to file the financing statement.

328.   Rev. § 9-325.

329.   Rev. § 9-326.

## Titled Goods

A secured party may have perfected its security interest in titled goods by having its security interest noted as lienholder on the certificate of title for the goods. If the debtor obtains a certificate of title for the goods in a new jurisdiction, and the secured party's security interest is not noted on the new certificate of title, the secured party's security interest continues to be perfected, despite the coverage under the new certificate of title, so long as the security interest would have remained perfected if the goods had not been covered by the new certificate of title.[330] However, that security interest becomes "unperfected" as against a purchaser of the goods for value unless, during the four-month period commencing from the time of coverage under the new certificate of title, the secured party's security interest is noted on the new certificate of title or the secured party has repossessed the goods.[331] Absent perfection by either method within that four-month period, a buyer may take free of the security interest under Rev. § 9-317(b).[332] Even during the four-month period, an innocent buyer, other than a dealer, that buys in reliance upon a new "clean" certificate of title will take free of the security interest.[333] Likewise, even during the four-month period, an innocent secured party that extends credit in reliance upon a new "clean" certificate of title, takes a security interest in the titled goods and perfects the security interest under the issuing state's certificate of title statute, has priority over the earlier security interest.[334]

## Proceeds

Additional steps may be required to maintain the perfection of its security interest in proceeds.[335]

## ENFORCEMENT

Revised Article 9 sets forth various rights and remedies of a secured party with respect to the collateral upon the debtor's default. Revised Article 9 also requires that the secured party proceed to enforce its security interest in ways that protect the debtor and certain other interested parties.

## Default

Upon a debtor's "default," a secured party has the rights and remedies under part 6 of Revised Article 9. Revised Article 9 does not define the word "default." A default will instead be determined by the security agreement or other agreements between the debtor and the secured party. Events of default contained in loan agreements, promissory notes and security agreements typically include the debtor's nonpayment, misrepresentations,

---

330.   Rev. § 9-316(d).
331.   Rev. § 9-316(e).
332.   *See* Rev. § 9-316 cmt. 5.
333.   Rev. § 9-337(1).
334.   Rev. § 9-337(2).
335.   Rev. § 9-315(d).

failure to comply with covenants, cross-defaults and the debtor's bankruptcy. A default occurs under an agricultural lien when the secured party has the right to enforce the lien.[336]

## Secured Party's Options after Default

The remedies of a secured party are not exclusive, and the secured party may resort to any one remedy without losing rights under the others.[337] Upon the debtor's default, the secured party may take possession of collateral, but only if doing so will not result in a breach of the peace.[338] The secured party may collect the collateral from account debtors and other persons obligated on collateral.[339] The secured party may also, subject to certain debtor and third party protections, either sell or otherwise dispose of the collateral and apply the proceeds to the satisfaction of the secured debt or retain the collateral in satisfaction of the secured debt.[340] In addition, the secured party may judicially foreclose on the collateral under local judicial foreclosure procedures.[341] Below is a discussion of the secured party's options of collection, disposition and retention relating to the collateral.

### Collection

When agreed between the debtor and the secured party, but in any event upon the debtor's default, the secured party may collect payments directly from account debtors and other persons obligated on collateral by notifying the account debtors and obligated persons to pay the secured party directly.[342] If there is credit recourse to the debtor (as in the case of a full or partial recourse loan to the debtor), the collection must be made in a commercially reasonable manner.[343] Revised Article 9 provides a mechanism by which a secured party that is an assignee of an obligation secured by a real estate mortgage may become the mortgagee of record upon the debtor's default in order to foreclose nonjudicially on the mortgage.[344] The secured party may receive and apply against the secured debt funds in a deposit account over which the secured party has control.[345] Furthermore, the secured party may deduct the secured party's collection expenses from collections made by it in a commercially reasonable manner.[346]

### Disposition

The secured party may sell or otherwise dispose of the collateral by public or private sale and apply the proceeds of the disposition towards the satisfaction of the secured debt. The following discussion highlights the requirement of the commercial reasonableness of the disposition, the requirement of notification of the disposition, provisions of Revised Article 9 relating to the disposition itself, and a special provision that adjusts a secured party's deficiency claim in the event of a disposition to an insider for low value.

---

336. Rev. § 9-606.
337. Rev. § 9-601(c).
338. Rev. § 9-609(a) & (b).
339. Rev. § 9-607.
340. Rev. §§ 9-610 & 9-620.
341. Rev. § 9-601(f).
342. Rev. § 9-607(a).
343. Rev. § 9-607(c).
344. *See* Rev. § 9-607(b).
345. Rev. § 9-607(a)(4) & (5).
346. Rev. § 9-607(d).

**Requirement of commercial reasonableness.** Every aspect of the disposition must be *commercially reasonable.*[347] The obligation of the secured party to exercise commercial reasonableness may not be waived by the debtor or an obligor.[348]

**Requirement of notification of disposition.** Unless the collateral is perishable or threatens to decline speedily in value or is of a type customarily sold on a recognized market, the secured party must send the debtor and certain other persons reasonable authenticated notification of the time and place of any public disposition or reasonable authenticated notification of the time after which any private disposition is to take place.[349] The notification must be given not only to the debtor and any secondary obligor, but also to all persons who have given to the secured party an authenticated notification of an interest in the collateral and to all secured parties and other lienholders of the collateral disclosed on a search of the proper filing office within certain time parameters.[350] In a commercial transaction, ten days prior notification of disposition is *per se* reasonable.[351] Revised Article 9 also sets forth "safe harbor" disposition notification forms in commercial and consumer transactions.[352] The debtor or any secondary obligor may waive its right to receive the disposition notice, but only in an authenticated agreement made after default.[353]

**The disposition itself.** The secured party may disclaim or modify disposition warranties otherwise given to a foreclosure transferee.[354] The secured party may purchase the collateral at a public disposition. The secured party may not purchase collateral at a private disposition unless the collateral is of a kind customarily sold on a recognized market or is the subject of standard price quotations.[355] A secured party's disposition generally discharges the security interest under which the disposition is made and all subordinate interests in the collateral.[356] Furthermore, Revised Article 9 provides a title clearing mechanism for the secured party to effect a transfer of record title to titled collateral to the foreclosure purchaser of that collateral.[357]

**Insider dispositions for low value.** If a secured party, a person related to a secured party[358] or a secondary obligor acquires collateral at a foreclosure disposition and the amount of the foreclosure proceeds so paid is significantly below the range of proceeds that a complying disposition to an unrelated purchaser would have brought, any deficiency calculation will be adjusted to reflect a credit to the debtor for the higher amount of disposition proceeds that would have been paid to the secured party by such a hypothetical unrelated purchaser.[359]

---

347.   Rev. § 9-610 & 9-615.
348.   Rev. § 9-602(7).
349.   Rev. § 9-611, 9-612 & 9-613. Forms of notification of disposition are contained as Forms 4.1.3 & 4.1.4.
350.   Rev. § 9-611(b), (c) & (e).
351.   Rev. § 9-612(b).
352.   Rev. § 9-613 & 614.
353.   Rev. § 9-624(a).
354.   Rev. § 9-610(e).
355.   Rev. § 9-610(c).
356.   Rev. § 9-617(a)(2) & (3).
357.   Rev. § 9-619.
358.   *See* Rev. § 9-102(a)(62) & (63) (defining "person related to" for individuals and organizations, respectively).
359.   Rev. § 9-615(f).

### Retention of Collateral in Satisfaction of the Secured Debt

The secured party may under some circumstances retain the collateral in total satisfaction or, in the case of a commercial transaction, partial satisfaction of the secured debt. The following discussion highlights certain limitations of the retention remedy, the requirement that the secured party send to the debtor and others an advance notice of the secured party's proposal to retain collateral, the effect of a person entitled to receive the proposal objecting to the proposal, and the effect of acceptance of retention.

**Limitations on retention remedy.** If the collateral is consumer goods, the debtor may not propose to retain collateral which is not in the possession of the secured party. Otherwise, a secured party may propose to retain any collateral, whether tangible or intangible and even tangible collateral that is at the time in the debtor's possession.[360] A secured party in a commercial transaction may propose to retain collateral in partial satisfaction, rather than total satisfaction, of the secured debt. But in a consumer transaction, the secured party may only propose to retain collateral in total satisfaction of the secured debt.[361] Moreover, the remedy of retaining the collateral in satisfaction of the secured obligation is not available for certain consumer goods where a significant portion of the purchase price of the goods or of the secured debt has already been paid.[362]

**Requirement to send a proposal of retention.** The secured party must send a proposal to retain the collateral not only to the debtor but also to all persons who have given to the secured party an authenticated notification of an interest in the collateral and to all secured parties and other lienholders of the collateral disclosed on a search of the proper filing office.[363] If the secured party proposes to retain the collateral in partial satisfaction of the secured debt, the secured party must also send the proposal to any secondary obligor.[364] The debtor or a secondary obligor may waive its right to receive a retention notice, or agree to the secured party's retention, but only after default.[365]

**Effect of objection to retention.** If the secured party receives an objection from the debtor, a secondary obligor or another secured party or lienholder entitled to notice and the objection is received within twenty days after the notice was sent, the secured party may not retain the collateral in satisfaction of the secured debt.[366]

**Effect of acceptance of retention.** Acceptance of retention of the collateral generally discharges the debtor's obligation to the extent the debtor has consented to the acceptance, and all subordinate interests in the collateral.[367]

---

360.　*See* Rev. § 9-620(a)(3).

361.　Rev. § 9-620(g).

362.　Rev. § 9-620(e).

363.　Rev. § 9-621(a). Forms of notification of proposed retention of collateral in satisfaction of the secured obligation are contained as Forms 4.1.1 & 4.1.2.

364.　Rev. § 9-621(b).

365.　Rev. §§ 9-602(10) & 9-620(c)(1).

366.　Rev. § 9-620(a) & (d). The debtor must affirmatively consent to a proposal for a secured party's retention in partial satisfaction of the secured obligation. Rev. § 9-620(c)(1).

367.　Rev. § 9-622.

## Application of Noncash Proceeds

If the secured party receives noncash proceeds[368] by collection or disposition of the collateral, the secured party may value the noncash proceeds and apply them to the secured obligation, but the secured party must do so in a commercially reasonable manner. Alternatively, unless the secured party's failure to value and apply the noncash proceeds to the secured debt is commercially unreasonable, the secured party may reduce and collect or dispose of the noncash proceeds, as collateral, until the noncash proceeds have been converted to cash for application to the secured debt.[369]

## Surplus or Deficiency

If the collateral secures an obligation, unless otherwise agreed, the secured party is to account to the debtor for any surplus in the collection or disposition of collateral, and the debtor is liable for a deficiency. In a secured transaction which is a sale of accounts, chattel paper, promissory notes or payment intangibles, unless otherwise agreed, the debtor is neither entitled to a surplus nor liable for a deficiency.[370]

## Redemption

The debtor may redeem the collateral by paying off the secured debt any time before the secured party has disposed, or is contractually committed to dispose, of the collateral, or has retained the collateral in satisfaction of the secured debt.[371] The debtor may waive its right of redemption in a commercial transaction, but only after default.[372]

## Non-compliance

Revised Article 9 provides that the secured party is generally liable to the debtor for any loss caused by the secured party's failure to comply with the enforcement provisions of part 6 of Revised Article 9.[373] Revised Article 9 adopts a rebuttable presumption rule for commercial transactions where an improper foreclosure or other enforcement results in a deficiency claim: in a commercial transaction, the value of the collateral is presumed to have equaled the entire secured debt (thus eliminating the deficiency claim) unless the secured party is able to show otherwise.[374] Revised Article 9 does not address which measure of damages should be applied in a consumer transaction. A specific penalty, however, may be imposed, regardless of any damages being shown, on a non-complying secured party where the collateral is consumer goods.[375] In some circumstances, a secured party who does not comply with the enforcement provisions of part 6 of Revised Article 9, whether in a commercial or consumer transaction, may be liable for statutory damages as well.[376]

---

368.    *See* Rev. § 9-102(a)(58) (defining "non cash proceeds").
369.    Rev. §§ 9-608(a)(3) & 9-615(c). *See also* Rev. § 9-608 cmt. 4 & Rev. § 9-615 cmt. 3.
370.    Rev. §§ 9-608(b) & 9-615(e).
371.    Rev. § 9-623.
372.    Rev. § 9-624(c).
373.    Rev. § 9-625(b).
374.    Rev. § 9-626(a)(3).
375.    Rev. § 9-625(c)(2).
376.    Rev. § 9-625(e)(5) & (6).

## Status of Guarantors

A guarantor or other secondary obligor[377] of the secured obligations is entitled to many of the same rights and protections as is the underlying debtor. Revised Article 9 requires disposition notifications to be given to guarantors and other secondary obligors, and it provides that a guarantor or other secondary obligor may not waive such notification unless the waiver is given after default.[378] A secured party is not, however, liable for failure to provide a disposition notification to a guarantor or other secondary obligor unknown to the secured party.[379]

## Certain Consumer Provisions

Although ten days advance notice of a disposition will be *per se* reasonable in a commercial transaction, no similar safe harbor applies to notification of dispositions in a consumer transaction.[380] A secured party must, following disposition of collateral, provide a consumer debtor with an explanation of the calculation of any deficiency claim before making demand upon the debtor for payment of that deficiency.[381] In a consumer transaction, a secured party may not retain collateral that is in the possession of the debtor and may not retain collateral in partial satisfaction of the secured debt.[382] A consumer debtor may not waive his or her right of redemption, even after default.[383] Revised Article 9 leaves the courts to fashion an appropriate damage rule (*e.g.* rebuttable presumption, absolute bar, or offset) in the case of a secured party's non-compliance with part 6 of Revised Article 9.[384]

## Certain Exclusions

The enforcement provisions in part 6 of Revised Article 9 do not apply to true consignors. Nor do these provisions apply to buyers of accounts, chattel paper, promissory notes or payment intangibles except for the buyer's obligation to use commercial reasonableness in the collection of collateral where the buyer has a right of chargeback on uncollected collateral or full or limited credit recourse to the debtor.[385]

# DEFINITION OF "GOOD FAITH"

Consistent with revisions to other UCC Articles, Revised Article 9 has its own definition of "good faith" as "honesty in fact *and the observance of reasonable commercial standards of fair dealing.*"[386]

---

377.   *See* Rev. § 9-102(a)(71) (defining "secondary obligor").
378.   Rev. §§ 9-611(c)(2) & 624(a).
379.   Rev. § 9-628(a) & (b).
380.   Rev. § 9-612(b).
381.   Rev. § 9-616.
382.   Rev. § 9-620(a)(3) & (g).
383.   Rev. § 9-624(c).
384.   Rev. § 9-626(b).
385.   Rev. §§ 9-601(g) & 9-607(c).
386.   Rev. § 9-102(a)(43)(italics added).

## TRANSITION PROVISIONS

Part 7 of Revised Article 9 contains provisions to assist in the transition from former Article 9 to Revised Article 9. These transition provisions are summarized below.

### Effective Date

In order to minimize choice of law issues arising on the effective date of Revised Article 9 in a particular jurisdiction, Revised Article 9 provides a uniform effective date of July 1, 2001.[387] Unless otherwise provided in part 7 of Revised Article 9, Revised Article 9 applies, as of its effective date, to all transactions within its scope, even if the transaction was entered into prior to that date at a time when former Article 9 or other law applied.[388]

### Pre-Effective-Date Causes of Action

Revised Article 9 does not affect causes of action in litigation pending on Revised Article 9's effective date.[389]

### Pre-Effective-Date Collateral Description in Security Agreement

Official Comment 3 to the § 9-703 makes clear that, as a matter of customary contract interpretation, former Article 9 terms used in a collateral description in a security agreement executed prior to Revised Article 9's effective date should not normally be interpreted as requiring, after Revised Article 9's effective date, that the terms be interpreted as if defined in Revised Article 9. Instead, the terms should generally be interpreted as they were defined in former Article 9 when the security agreement was executed.

### Pre-Effective-Date Security Interests Created Outside of Former Article 9 but within Revised Article 9

Unless otherwise provided in part 7 of Revised Article 9, a security interest in collateral outside of the scope of former Article 9 but included within the scope of Revised Article 9 remains valid under Revised Article 9 and may be enforced after Revised Article 9's effective date under Revised Article 9 or under the law governing the transaction prior to Revised Article 9's effective date.[390]

### Pre-Effective-Date Security Interests Perfected under Former Article 9

A security interest that is enforceable and perfected under former Article 9 or other law may or may not meet the requirements for enforceability and perfection under Revised Article 9.

---

387.    Rev. § 9-701. Certain states (Alabama, Connecticut, Florida and Mississippi) have delayed the effectiveness of Revised Article 9. Care should always be taken to confirm the effective date of Revised Article 9 in any given jurisdiction.

388.    Rev. § 9-702(a).

389.    Rev. § 9-702(c).

390.    Rev. § 9-702(b).

### Requirements Met under Revised Article 9

A security interest that is enforceable and perfected under former Article 9 or other law, and for which the requirements for enforceability and perfection are met under Revised Article 9 on Revised Article 9's effective date, remains enforceable and perfected under Revised Article 9.[391]

### Requirements Not Met under Revised Article 9: Generally

If the security interest is enforceable and perfected under former Article 9 or other law, but the requirements for enforceability or perfection are not met under Revised Article 9 on Revised Article 9's effective date, the security interest remains enforceable and, with one exception described below for a security interest perfected by filing under former Article 9, remains perfected for a period of one year following Revised Article 9's effective date. The security interest will no longer be enforceable, and its perfection will lapse, if the requirements for enforceability and perfection under Revised Article 9 have not been satisfied by the end of that one-year period.[392]

### Requirements Not Met under Revised Article 9: Perfection by Filing under Former Article 9

The one exception to the general rules for the continuation, on and after Revised Article 9's effective date, of perfection of a security interest perfected under former Article 9, but not under Revised Article 9, relates to a security interest perfected under former Article 9 by filing. In the case of a security interest perfected by filing under former Article 9, the one-year post-effective date grace period in Rev. § 9-703(b) for maintaining perfection under Revised Article 9 does not apply.[393] The maintenance of perfection, on and after Revised Article 9's effective date, of a security interest perfected by filing under former Article 9 is addressed separately in Rev. §§ 9-705 and 9-706, as discussed below.

## Pre-Effective-Date Unperfected Security Interests

A security interest that is enforceable but is unperfected under former Article 9 or other law may or may not meet the requirements for enforceability and perfection under Revised Article 9.

### Enforceability of Unperfected Security Interest

An unperfected security interest which is enforceable under former Article 9 or other law, but for which the requirements for enforceability are not met under Revised Article 9 on Revised Article 9's effective date, remains enforceable for a period of one year following Revised Article 9's effective date. The security interest will no longer be enforceable if the requirements for enforceability under Revised Article 9 have not been satisfied by the end of that one-year period.[394]

### Perfection of Unperfected Security Interest

A security interest which is enforceable but unperfected under former Article 9 or other law, and for which the requirements for perfection are not met under Revised

---

391.   Rev. § 9-703(a).
392.   Rev. § 9-703(b).
393.   Rev. § 9-703(b) ("Except as otherwise provided in Section 9-705"); *see also* Rev. § 9-705 cmt. 4.
394.   Rev. § 9-704(1) & (2).

Article 9 on Revised Article 9's effective date, does not achieve perfection under Revised Article 9 until Revised Article 9's perfection requirements are satisfied.[395]

## Perfection by Pre-Effective-Date Actions other than Filing for After-Acquired Collateral

If an action (exclusive of the filing of financing statements) under former Article 9 or other law is taken before Revised Article 9's effective date to perfect a security interest that attaches in collateral after Revised Article 9's effective date, and that action would have been sufficient to perfect the security interest under former Article 9 or other law, the security interest in that collateral becomes and remains perfected under Revised Article 9 for one year following Revised Article 9's effective date. The perfection will lapse if the requirements for perfection under Revised Article 9 have not been satisfied by the end of that one-year period.[396]

## Perfection by Pre-Effective-Date Filing

The filing of a financing statement that is effective to perfect a security interest in collateral under former Article 9 may or may not be effective to perfect a security interest in that collateral under Revised Article 9.

### Pre-Effective-Date Filing Effective under Revised Article 9

If a financing statement filed in a jurisdiction and office before Revised Article 9's effective date, whether or not effective under former Article 9, would, if filed in that jurisdiction and office on Revised Article 9's effective date, be effective to perfect a security interest under Revised Article 9, the filing is given effect under Revised Article 9.[397] Such a filing may be continued, after Revised Article 9's effective date, by the filing of a continuation statement in that jurisdiction and office only if the continuation statement, together with other filing office records relating to the financing statement, satisfies the requirements of part 5 of Revised Article 9 for an initial financing statement.[398] The continuation statement, to be effective, must be filed within the six-month period prior to the lapse of the financing statement.[399]

### Pre-Effective-Date Filing Not Effective under Revised Article 9

If a financing statement filed in a jurisdiction and office before Revised Article 9's effective date that is effective to perfect a security interest under former Article 9 would, if filed on Revised Article 9's effective date, be *ineffective* to perfect that security interest under Article 9, the filing is nevertheless given effect under Revised Article 9 until the earlier to occur of the financing statement's normal lapse (without regard to any continuation statement filed after Revised Article 9's effective date) and June 30, 2006.[400] To avoid lapse and in order to continue the original financing statement, an initial financing state-

---

395.    Rev. § 9-704(3)(B).
396.    Rev. § 9-705(a).
397.    Rev. § 9-705(b).
398.    Rev. § 9-705(d) & (f).
399.    Rev. § 9-515(d).
400.    Rev. § 9-705(c). Certain states (Alabama, Connecticut, Florida and Mississippi) have delayed the effective date of Revised Article 9. The cutoff date for financing statements filed under former Article 9 may also be extended.

ment (often called an *"in lieu" initial financing statement*), referring to the original financing statement to be continued, must be filed under Rev. § 9-706 in the jurisdiction and office required by Revised Article 9.[401]

### Continuation Where Revised Article 9 Changes the Meaning of a Collateral Description

If a financing statement filed before Revised Article 9's effective date is filed in the correct jurisdiction and office under Revised Article 9 but the meaning of the collateral description on the financing statement has changed under Revised Article 9 (*e.g.*, a general intangible under former Article 9 might be an account under Revised Article 9), any continuation statement filed on or after Revised Article 9's effective date must contain an amendment to the collateral description to comply with the meaning of the collateral description in Revised Article 9; otherwise, the continuation statement is not effective for the collateral for which the description should have been amended.[402] Similarly, any "in lieu" initial financing statement that is filed to continue under Rev. § 9-706 an original financing statement filed before Revised Article 9's effective date must contain a collateral description that complies with the meaning of the collateral description in Revised Article 9.[403] Upon Revised Article 9's effective date, the secured party is authorized by the debtor to make any such amendment necessary to continue the perfection of the secured party's security interest.[404]

### Continuation: Other Requirements

In addition to collateral description requirements, a continuation statement filed on or after Revised Article 9's effective date, together with any other records already on file in the filing office pertaining to the related financing statement, as well as an "in lieu" initial financing statement filed as a continuation under § 9-706, must generally satisfy the other requirements for an initial financing statement under part 5 of Revised Article 9. The continuation statement, or "in lieu" initial financing statement, may need to contain the requisite information set forth in § 9-516(b) to avoid filing office rejection.[405]

## Initial Financing Statement as a Continuation: the "In Lieu" Initial Financing Statement

If a financing statement filed before Revised Article 9's effective date remains effective on Revised Article 9's effective date although filed in a jurisdiction and office which would not otherwise be effective to perfect the security interest under Revised Article 9, that financing statement, to avoid lapse, must be continued as an "in lieu" initial financing statement in the jurisdiction and office required by Revised Article 9.[406]

### Requirements

An "in lieu" initial financing statement must satisfy the filing requirements of part 5 of Revised Article 9. In addition, in order to put subsequent searchers on notice that the "in

---

401.    A form of "in-lieu" financing statement appears as Form 3.2.1.
402.    Rev. § 9-705(f). *See also* Rev. § 9-504 (cross-referencing Rev. § 9-108).
403.    Rev. § 9-706(c)(1).
404.    Rev. § 9-708(2).
405.    *See* Rev. §§ 9-516(b), 9-705(f) & 9-706(c)(1).
406.    A form of "in-lieu" initial financing statement is contained as Form 3.2.1.

lieu" initial financing statement is intended to continue the original financing statement filed in a different jurisdiction and office, the "in lieu" initial financing statement must identify the original filing by filing office, dates of filing and filing numbers (both for original filing and the most recent continuation statement, if any, of the original filing) and must indicate that the original filing remains effective.[407] Upon the effective date of Revised Article 9, the secured party is authorized by the debtor to file any "in lieu" initial financing statement necessary to continue the perfection of the secured party's security interest created under former Article 9.[408]

### Pre-Effective-Date Filings Covered

The "in lieu" initial financing statement may continue more than one original financing statement filed before Revised Article 9's effective date.[409]

### Timing of Filing

The "in lieu" initial financing statement may be filed at any time before lapse of the original filing, even before the normal six-month period prior to lapse.[410] The secured party may make any "in lieu" initial financing statement filing even before the effective date of Revised Article 9 assuming that the filing office will accept the filing and that the debtor has signed the financing statement, as required under § 9-402(1) of former Article 9, or has otherwise authorized the filing.[411]

### Period of Effectiveness

An "in lieu" initial financing statement filed on or after Revised Article 9's effective date lapses upon the expiration of the period for the effectiveness of the financing statement set forth in Rev. § 9-515.[412] An "in lieu" initial financing statement filed before Revised Article 9's effective date lapses upon the expiration of the period for the effectiveness of a financing statement set forth in § 9-403 of former Article 9.[413]

## Amendments to Pre-Effective-Date Financing Statements

### Generally

An amendment, other than a termination, made on or after Revised Article 9's effective date to a financing statement filed before Revised Article 9's effective date, must generally be filed in the jurisdiction and office required by Revised Article 9.[414] If the financing statement was filed in the jurisdiction and office required under Revised Article 9, then the financing statement may be amended by the filing of an amendment in that office.[415] If, however, the financing statement was not filed in the jurisdiction and office required by Revised Article 9, the financing statement must be amended by means of the

---

407.    Rev. § 9-706(c).
408.    Rev. § 9-708(2).
409.    *See* Rev. § 9-706 cmt. 2.
410.    *See* Rev. § 9-706 cmt. 1.
411.    *See* Rev. § 9-706 cmt. 1.
412.    Rev. § 9-706(b)(2).
413.    Rev. § 9-706(b)(1).
414.    Rev. § 9-707(b)(first sentence).
415.    Rev. § 9-707(c)(1).

filing of an "in lieu" initial financing statement filed in the jurisdiction and office required by Revised Article 9. The amendment may be made by filing the "in lieu" initial financing statement with the modified information, or the "in lieu" initial financing statement may filed first and then amended to reflect the modified information.[416]

### Alternative Technique for Termination

As an alternative, it may be possible to file a termination statement in the office in which the related financing statement was filed before Revised Article 9's effective date.[417] If, however the financing statement was not filed in the jurisdiction and office required by Revised Article 9, the termination statement may be filed only if the financing statement has not already been continued by an "in lieu" initial financing statement filed in the jurisdiction and office required by Revised Article 9.[418] Moreover, the termination statement must be one that is effective under the law of the jurisdiction in which the financing statement filed before Revised Article 9's effective date was filed.[419] That requirement will usually mean that the financing statement may be terminated in this manner only if it is filed in an office of that jurisdiction referred to in the jurisdiction's Rev. § 9-501, *i.e.*, the statewide central filing office in the jurisdiction or a local filed office in the jurisdiction in which a financing statement was filed as fixture filing or covering timber to be cut or as-extracted collateral is filed.[420]

## Priority

Revised Article 9 determines priorities that were not established under former Article 9 before Revised Article 9's effective date. Accordingly, an attached security interest that was not perfected under former Article 9 may not, merely by Revised Article 9 becoming effective and causing that security interest to become perfected, obtain priority over a competing perfected security interest to which it was junior under former Article 9.[421] Moreover, the priority of a security interest that attaches after the effective date of Revised Article 9, and which is perfected by a financing statement filed before Revised Article 9's effective date, dates from Revised Article 9's effective date, not from the date of the earlier filing, if the earlier filing would have been ineffective to perfect the security interest under former Article 9.[422]

---

416.   Rev. § 9-707(c)(2) & (3).
417.   Rev. § 9-707(e).
418.   Rev. § 9-707(e)("unless…").
419.   Rev. § 9-707(b)(second sentence).
420.   *See* Rev. §§ 9-513(d)(termination statement effective when filed in the filing office) & 9-102(a)(37)(defining "filing office" as the place designated in Rev. § 9-501 as the place to file a financing statement).
421.   Rev. § 9-709(a).
422.   Rev. § 9-709(b).

# Comparative Security Agreement[*]

THIS SECURITY AGREEMENT ("Security Agreement") is made the ~~30th~~ 1st day of ~~June~~ July, 2001,[1] between Vending Machine Manufacturing Co., a Delaware corporation ("Debtor") and Finance Company, an Illinois corporation ("Secured Party")~~, as Agent for the lenders listed on Exhibit A~~.[2]

This Security Agreement is entered into with respect to:

(i)     a loan (the "Loan") to be made by Secured Party to Debtor[3] pursuant to a Loan Agreement (the "Loan Agreement") dated the same date as this Security Agreement;

(ii)    the sale by Debtor and the purchase by Secured Party of Accounts;[4]

(iii)   the sale by Debtor and the purchase by Secured Party of Chattel Paper;[5]

(iv)    the sale by Debtor and the purchase by Secured Party of Payment Intangibles;[6] and

(v)     the sale by Debtor and the purchase by Secured Party of Promissory Notes.[7]

Secured Party and Debtor agree as follows:

1.   **Definitions.**

1.1     *"Collateral."* The Collateral shall consist of all of the ~~following~~ personal property[8] of Debtor, wherever located, and now owned or hereafter acquired[9], including:

(i)     Accounts[, including health-care-insurance receivables][10] ~~all amounts owed to Debtor for the licensing of intellectual property rights~~;

---

[*]The following annotated comparative security agreement demonstrates how Revised Article 9 may affect the preparation of a security agreement. This security agreement is intended to provide a different way of thinking about Revised Article 9. This security agreement is not intended as a model form, *per se.* Form security agreements appear as Forms 2.1–2.5 in this book.

1. This Security Agreement, for discussion purposes, assumes that Revised Article 9 became effective in the relevant jurisdiction on July 1, 2001, as contemplated by Revised Article 9. Note that in many instances, different rules will apply in consumer transactions. See Rev. §§ 9-102(a)(26) & 9-201(b).

2. The "secured party" includes a "representative" of the "secured party." Rev. § 9-102(a)(72)(E). A financing statement may name a representative of the secured party without indicating that capacity. Rev. §§ 9-502(a)(2), 9-503(d). This rule should also apply to the security agreement if the obligations described cover those held by all participants.

3. If the "debtor" is a guarantor securing its obligations under a guaranty, the guarantor will have the rights of a "debtor" for the collateral that it supplies and also as an "obligor" if the primary obligor has also supplied collateral. Rev. §§ 9-102(28) & (59) & 9-602. Either way, it cannot waive its rights to the extent a debtor cannot waive its rights. Rev. § 9-602.

4. Revised Article 9, like former Article 9, applies to the sale of accounts. Rev. § 9-109(a)(3). Note the expanded definition of "accounts," described below. Rev. § 9-102(a)(2).

5. Revised Article 9, like former Article 9, applies to the sale of chattel paper. Rev. § 9-109(a)(3). The definition of "chattel paper" now includes transactions involving a combination of goods and software, to a limited extent. Rev. § 9-102(a)(11).

6. Revised Article 9, like former Article 9, applies to the sale of "payment intangibles." Rev. § 9-109(a)(3). The definition of "payment intangibles" is discussed below. Sales of payment intangibles are automatically perfected under Rev. § 9-309(a)(3). These changes are designed to facilitate securitization transactions without interfering with the sale of loan participations.

7. Revised Article 9 applies to the sale of "promissory notes." Rev. § 9-109(a)(3). The definition is discussed below. Rev. § 9-102(a)(65). Sales of promissory notes are automatically perfected under Rev. § 9-309(a)(4).

8. A financing statement may use a "supergeneric" description, such as "all [debtor]'s personal property." Rev. § 9-504(2). A security agreement, however, may not. Rev. § 9-108(c). Revised Article 9 provides a "safe-harbor" for describing collateral by an Article 9 type in a security agreement or in a financing statement. Rev. § 9-108(b)(3).

9. A security interest cannot attach to after-acquired commercial tort claims. Rev. § 9-204(b)(2).

10. "Accounts" include a wide variety of rights to payment arising out of the transfer of rights in tangible and intangible personal property, including credit card receivables and license fees. Rev. § 9-102(a)(2). Revised Article 9, unlike former Article 9, covers security interests in rights under an insurance policy if the right is a "health-care-insurance receivable." Rev. §§ 9-102(a)(46) & 9-109(d)(8). A separate reference to "health-care-insurance receivables" is not necessary.

(ii)    Chattel paper[11]~~, including equipment leases and conditional sales agreements~~;

(iii)   Inventory[12]~~, including property held for sale or lease and raw materials~~;

(iv)    Equipment[13]~~, including property used in the Debtor's business, machinery and production machines~~;

(v)     Instruments[, including Promissory Notes][14] ~~notes, negotiable instruments, and negotiable certificates of deposit~~;

(vi)    ~~Securities~~ Investment Property;[15]

(vii)   Documents ~~s, including a documents of title, a warehouse receipt, and a bill of lading~~;

(viii)  Deposit accounts;[16]

(ix)    Debtor's claim for interference with contract against Big Soda Pop Company;[17]

(x)     Letter-of-credit rights,[18]

(xi)    General intangibles[, including payment intangibles][19] licenses, ~~intellectual property, and tax returns~~;

(xii)   [Supporting obligations] Rights ancillary to, or arising in any way in connection with, any of the foregoing, including security ~~agreements securing any of the foregoing, guaranties guarantying any of the foregoing, documents, notes, drafts representing any of the foregoing, the right to returned goods, warranty claims with respect to any of the foregoing, amounts owed in connection with the short-term use or licensing of any of the foregoing, government payments in connection with the purchase or agreement not to produce any of the foregoing~~;[20]

(xiii)  ~~books and records pertaining to the foregoing and the equipment containing the books and records; and~~

•

11. "Chattel paper" includes tangible and electronic chattel paper. Rev. § 9-102(a)(11), (31) & (78). This results in some special perfection and priority rules discussed below. The definition of "chattel paper" now includes obligations arising from transactions involving a combination of goods and software, to a limited extent. Rev. § 9-102(a)(11).

12. "Goods," and therefore inventory, includes software "embedded" in goods that is customarily considered part of the goods (*e.g.*, the computer chip in a clock radio). Rev. § 9-102(a)(44) & (75).

13. "Equipment" no longer has its own definition. Rather, under Revised Article 9, "equipment" is the residual category of goods (goods that are not inventory, farm products, or consumer goods). Rev. § 9-102(a)(2). Like inventory and other categories of goods, equipment includes software embedded in the goods if the software is customarily considered part of the goods (*e.g.*, the computer chip in the automatic brake system in a car). Rev. § 9-102(a)(44) & (75).

14. "Instruments" continue to include non-Article 3 payment obligations that are "of a type that in ordinary course of business [are] transferred by delivery with any necessary indorsement or assignment." Rev. § 9-102(a)(47). A reference to "instruments" includes "promissory notes." *Id.*

A separate reference to "promissory notes" is not necessary. As noted above, Revised Article 9 applies to the sale of promissory notes. Rev. § 9-109(a)(3). A "promissory note" is an "instrument" that is not "order" paper (*e.g.*, a check) or a certificate of deposit. Rev. § 9-102(a)(65).

15. "Investment property" is a new term that covers property formerly defined as securities. *See also* new Article 8 and F. § 9-107. A reference to "general intangibles" (Rev. § 9-102(a)(42)) or "instruments" (Rev. § 9-102(a)(47)) will *not* include "investment property."

16. Unlike former Article 9, Revised Article 9 permits the creation of a security interest in a deposit account as original collateral. A reference to "general intangibles" will include "payment intangibles," but will not include a "deposit account." Rev. § 9-102(a)(42). Special perfection rules for deposit accounts are discussed below. A security interest in a deposit account as original collateral may be perfected only by "control," a method of perfection new under Revised Article 9. Rev. §§ 9-312(b)(1) & 9-314(a).

17. Article 9 covers a security interest in a tort claim if the claim is a "commercial tort claim." Rev. §§ 9-102(a)(13) & 9-109(d)(12). The security agreement must describe the commercial tort claim with greater specificity than simply the "type" or category of such claims (*i.e.*, "commercial tort claims"). Rev. § 9-108(e)(1). Nor can a security agreement create a security interest in after-acquired commercial tort claims. Rev. § 9-204(b)(2). A reference to "general intangibles" will *not* include a "commercial tort claim." Rev. § 9-102(a)(42).

18. Letter-of-credit rights are the right to payment under a letter of credit. Rev. § 9-102(a)(51). Article 5 controls the right to draw under a letter of credit. UCC § 5-114. A reference to "general intangibles" will *not* include letter-of-credit rights. Rev. § 9-102(a)(42). Special perfection rules for letter-of-credit rights are discussed below.

19. A reference to "general intangibles" under Revised Article 9 does *not* include some types of collateral that may sound like "general intangibles," such as commercial tort claims, deposit accounts, investment property, and letter-of-credit rights. The term "general intangibles" *does* include payment intangibles and software. Rev. § 9-102(a)(42). A separate reference to those types of collateral is not necessary. A "payment intangible" is a general intangible where the account debtor's principal obligation is the payment of money. Rev. § 9-102(a)(61).

20. "Supporting obligations" include guaranties and letter-of-credit rights that support payment of another obligation, such as an account or an instrument. Rev. § 9-102(a)(77). A security interest in a supporting obligation automatically attaches to a related supporting obligation. Rev. § 9-203(f). A security agreement does not need a separate reference to "supporting obligations." The security interest in the supporting obligation is automatically perfected if the security interest in the supported collateral is perfected. Rev. § 9-308(d). The same is true for a security interest in a security interest that secures an obligation that itself is collateral. Rev. §§ 9-203(g) & 9-308(e).

(xiv) [to the extent not listed above as original collateral, proceeds and products of the foregoing], ~~including money, deposit accounts, goods, insurance proceeds and other tangible or intangible property received upon the sale or other disposition of the foregoing.~~ [21]

1.2    *"Obligations."* This Security Agreement secures the following:

(i)    Debtor's obligations under the Loan, the Loan Agreement, and this Security Agreement;

(ii)    all of Debtor's other present and future obligations to Secured Party;[22]

(iii)    the repayment of (a) any amounts that Secured Party may advance or spend for the maintenance or preservation of the Collateral,[23] and (b) any other expenditures that Secured Party may make under the provisions of this Security Agreement or for the benefit of Debtor;

(iv)    all amounts owed under any modifications, renewals or extensions of any of the foregoing obligations;

(v)    all other amounts now or in the future owed by Debtor to Secured Party, ~~whether or not of the same kind or class as the other obligations owed by Debtor to Secured Party~~;[24] and

(vi)    any of the foregoing that arises after the filing of a petition by or against Debtor under the Bankruptcy Code, even if the obligations do not accrue because of the automatic stay under Bankruptcy Code § 362 or otherwise.

This Security Agreement does not secure any obligation described above which is secured by a consensual lien on real property.[25]

1.3    UCC. Any term used in the Uniform Commercial Code ("UCC") and not defined in this Security Agreement has the meaning given to the term in the UCC.[26]

## 2.    Grant of Security Interest.

Debtor grants a security interest in the Collateral to Secured Party to secure the payment or performance of the Obligations.[27]

## 3.    Perfection of Security Interests.

3.1    *Filing of financing statement.*

(i)    Debtor ~~shall sign~~ authorizes Secured Party to file[28] a financing statement (the "Financing Statement") describing the Collateral.

(ii)    Debtor authorizes Secured Party to file a financing statement (the "Financing Statement") describing any agricultural liens or other statutory liens held by Secured Party.[29]

21. "Proceeds" is broadly defined in Revised Article 9 to include whatever is acquired upon the sale, lease, license, exchange, or other disposition of collateral; rights arising out of collateral; and collections and distributions on collateral. Rev. § 9-102(a)(64). This is much broader than under former Article 9 (F. § 9-306). Like former Article 9, Revised Article 9 looks to non-UCC law for the method of tracing commingled proceeds. Rev. § 9-315(b)(2). It is expected that courts will use the lowest intermediate balance rule to trace a proceeds security interest in commingled cash proceeds. Rev. § 9-315 cmt. 3. A security interest in collateral automatically attaches to proceeds (Rev. § 9-203(f)), continues in the proceeds following its sale or other disposition (Rev. § 9-315(a)(1)), and is initially automatically perfected for 20 days, if the security interest in the original collateral was perfected. Rev. § 9-315(c) & (d). A security agreement does not need a separate reference to "proceeds."

22. A security agreement may provide that collateral secures future advances. Rev. § 9-204(c).

23. A security interest automatically secures expenses relating to the foreclosure sale, other than attorney's fees. The security interest secures reasonable attorney's fees if provided for by contract and permitted by applicable law. Rev. § 9-615(a)(1). The secured party is automatically entitled to reasonable attorney's fees incurred in enforcing collection from an account debtor or obligor on an instrument. Rev. § 9-607(d) & cmt. 10.

24. Revised Article 9 rejects decisions that have held that "other indebtedness" must be of the same "kind" or "class" or be "related" to the original debt secured. Rev. § 9-204 cmt. 5.

25. This provision is designed to avoid problems under state real property anti-deficiency laws, such as those that exist in California. *See generally* Rev. § 9-604.

26. Under former Article 9, there was some risk in using terms defined under the UCC because of the relatively narrow scope of those terms. These included "accounts" and "proceeds." The expansion of the definitions of those terms (as discussed above), among others, considerably reduces the risk of incorporating UCC-defined terms by reference. Care should continue to be taken that an incorporated definition has the meaning the parties intend to give to that word.

27. Like former Article 9, Revised Article 9 does not require the parties to use the word "grant" in order to create a security interest. Rev. §§ 9-102(a)(73), 9-203. Nevertheless, it is likely that practitioners will continue to use the term "grant."

28. The debtor does not have to sign the financing statement. Rev. § 9-502. Although former Article 9 probably permitted electronic filings, so long as the debtor "signed" an appropriate writing, this change will facilitate electronic filings. *See* PEB Commentary No. 15. The secured party will need the debtor to authorize the secured party to file a financing statement (or ratify it later). A form of "pre-filing" authorization letter appears as Form 1.3. The debtor's authentication of the security agreement "authorizes" the secured party to file a financing statement covering the collateral described in the security agreement. Rev. § 9-509(b)(1). The sample affirmative statement in paragraph 3.1(i) is not necessary.

29. An "agricultural lien" is a lien created by statute, involving agriculture and is not dependent on possession. Rev. § 9-102(a)(5). It is not a "security interest." Non-UCC law will continue to govern the creation and attachment of agricultural liens and thus govern their enforceability between the holder of the lien and the debtor. A "secured party" includes the holder of an agricultural lien. Rev. §§ 9-102(a)(72)(B), 9-109(a)(2). Perfection will occur under Article 9. Rev. §§ 9-308(b). Non-UCC law will govern the creation and perfection of other statutory liens. Rev. § 9-109(d)(2).

(iii) Secured Party shall receive prior to the Closing an official report from the Secretary of State of each Collateral State, ~~and the~~ Chief Executive Office State, <u>and the Debtor State</u>[30] (each as defined below) (the "SOS Reports") indicating that Secured Party's security interest is prior to all other security interests or other interests reflected in the report.

3.2  *Possession.*

(i)   Debtor shall have possession of the Collateral, except where expressly otherwise provided in this Security Agreement or where Secured Party chooses to perfect its security interest by possession <u>in addition to the filing of a financing statement.</u>[31]

(ii)  Where Collateral is in the possession of a third party, Debtor will join with Secured Party in notifying the third party of Secured Party's security <u>interest and obtaining an acknowledgment from the third party that it is holding the Collateral for the benefit of Secured Party.</u>[32]

3.3  <u>*Control.* Debtor will cooperate with Secured Party in obtaining control</u>[33]<u> with respect to Collateral consisting of:</u>

(i)   <u>Deposit Accounts;</u>[34] <u>and</u>

(ii)  <u>Investment Property;</u>[35]

(iii) <u>Letter-of-credit rights; and</u> [36]

(iv)  <u>Electronic chattel paper.</u>[37]

30. As defined below in the security agreement, the "Debtor State" is the state of the debtor's incorporation. Under Revised Article 9, a secured party will file a financing statement for all types of collateral in the state of the debtor's "location," except for fixture filings, to perfect a security interest in as-extracted collateral and in timber to be cut, and to perfect an agricultural lien (which is not a security interest). Rev. §§ 9-301 & 9-302. For debtors formed by a filing with a state, the debtor's "location" is the state of its organization. Rev. § 9-307(e). However, the secured party will need to continue to search in the applicable states under former Article 9 for five years after the effective date of Revised Article 9 (e.g., until July 1, 2006) because financing statements filed under former Article 9 remain effective until their former Article 9 lapse date (e.g., five years), but not for more than five years after the effective date of Revised Article 9. Rev. § 9-705(c).

31. Security interests perfected by possession will be governed by the law of the location of the collateral, rather than the location of the debtor. Rev. § 9-301(2). A security interest in an instrument may be perfected by filing. Rev. § 9-312(a). A security interest in an instrument (and other tangible property) may also be perfected by possession. Rev. § 9-313(a). Perfection by possession may confer priority over the claim of a purchaser (including a secured party). Possession of an instrument will eliminate the risk of a holder in due course defeating the rights of the secured party that perfects only by filing. Rev. § 9-331(a). In addition, a security interest in an instrument perfected by possession generally will prevail over one perfected only by filing. Rev. § 9-330(d). Similar rules apply to chattel paper. Rev. § 9-330. A security interest arising upon the sale of a promissory note is automatically perfected. Rev. § 9-309(4).

32. If a third party has possession of the collateral, perfection occurs when the third party "acknowledges" that it holds the collateral for the secured party's benefit. Rev. § 9-313(c)(1) & (2). A form of bailee acknowledgement for non-farm products collateral is contained in this book as Form 3.5.1. A lessee of collateral in the ordinary course of the debtor's business may not qualify as a third party in possession. The acknowledgment requirement changes former law, which required only that the third party receive notice of the security interest.

33. Revised Article 9 borrows the concept of "control" as a perfection device for investment property under former law for use in several circumstances under Revised Article 9. See F. §§ 8-106 & § 9-115.

34. A security interest in a deposit account as original collateral may be perfected only by "control." Rev. § 9-312(b). A form of deposit account control agreement appears as Form 3.3.1. "Control" occurs automatically when the depositary institution with respect to the deposit account is the secured party. For third parties, it occurs either (i) when the depositary institution has agreed with the secured party that the depositary will follow instructions from the secured party without further consent from the debtor, or (ii) the secured party becomes the bank's customer (UCC § 4-104(a)(5)) with respect to the deposit account. Rev. § 9-104. The existence of control does not of itself prevent the debtor from transferring funds from the account. See Rev. § 9-104(b). A transferee of money that does not act in "collusion" with the debtor will take the funds free of any security interest in the funds. Rev. § 9-332.

35. A security interest in investment property may be perfected by filing or control. Rev. §§ 9-312(a), 9-313(e), 9-314(a). Generally, "control" of investment property collateral other than a certificated security (e.g., a security entitlement) exists when (i) a securities intermediary has agreed with the secured party that the intermediary will follow entitlement orders from the secured party without further consent from the debtor, or (ii) the secured party puts the securities account in its name. Rev. § 9-106. Generally, control of a certificated security occurs by delivery with any necessary endorsement. Rev. § 9-106. "Delivery" (as defined in UCC § 8-301) without an endorsement (unless the certificate is endorsed in blank) will constitute perfection by possession, but not "control." Rev. § 9-313. A secured party with control of investment property will generally have priority over a secured party that perfects solely by the filing of a financing statement. Rev. § 9-328(1). A form of securities account control agreement appears as Form 3.3.2.

36. "Control" is the only way to perfect a security interest in letter-of-credit rights, Rev. § 9-312(b)(2), except to the extent the letter-of-credit rights are a supporting obligation for other collateral. Rev. § 9-308(d). Control requires the consent of the issuer of the letter of credit or compliance with other practice. UCC § 5-114(c), Rev. §§ 5-114(c), 9-107. A form of assignment of proceeds of letter of credit, which effects control, appears as Form 3.4

37. A security interest in electronic chattel paper may be perfected by filing or control. Rev. §§ 9-312(a), 9-314(a). "Control" requires compliance with special rules for the electronic identification of the secured party "on" the "original" of the electronic chattel paper. Rev. § 9-105. A secured party that perfects a security interest in electronic chattel paper by control will generally defeat a secured party that has perfected its security interest only by filing. Rev. § 9-330(b).

3.4   *Marking of Chattel Paper.* Debtor will not create any Chattel Paper without placing a legend on the Chattel Paper acceptable to Secured Party indicating that Secured Party has a security interest in the Chattel Paper.[38]

**4.   Post-Closing Covenants and Rights Concerning the Collateral.**

4.1   *Inspection.* The parties to this Security Agreement may inspect any Collateral in the other party's possession, at any time upon reasonable notice.

4.2   *Personal Property.* The Collateral shall remain personal property at all times. Debtor shall not affix any of the Collateral to any real property in any manner which would change its nature from that of personal property to real property or to a fixture.

4.3   *Secured Party's Collection Rights.* Secured Party shall have the right at any time to ~~notify any account debtors and any obligors under instruments to make payments directly to Secured Party. Secured Party may at any time judicially~~ enforce Debtor's rights against the account debtors and obligors.[39]

4.4   *Limitations on Obligations Concerning Maintenance of Collateral.*

(i)   *Risk of Loss.* Debtor has the risk of loss of the Collateral. ~~Secured Party shall not be responsible for any injury to, loss to, or loss in value of, the Collateral, or any part thereof, arising from any act of nature, flood, fire or any other cause beyond the control of Secured Party.~~ [40]

(ii)   *No Collection Obligation.* Secured Party has no duty to collect any income accruing on the Collateral or to preserve any rights relating to the Collateral.

4.5   *No Disposition of Collateral.* ~~Except as to inventory held for sale or lease in ordinary course of business, Debtor has no right to sell, lease or otherwise dispose of any of the Collateral.~~ Secured Party does not authorize, and Debtor agrees not to:

(i)   make any sales or leases of any of the Collateral,

(ii)   license any of the Collateral; or

(iii)   grant any other security interest in any of the Collateral.[41]

4.6   *Purchase Money Security Interests.* To the extent Debtor uses the Loan to purchase Collateral, Debtor's repayment of the Loan shall apply on a "first-in-first-out" basis so that the portion of the Loan used to purchase a particular item of Collateral shall be paid in the chronological order the Debtor purchased the Collateral.[42]

**5.   Debtor's Representations and Warranties.**

Debtor warrants and represents that:

5.1   *Title to and Transfer of Collateral.* ~~Its~~ It has rights in or the power to transfer the Collateral and its title to the Collateral is free of all adverse claims, liens, security interests and restrictions on transfer or pledge except as created by this Security Agreement.[43]

38. Purchasers of chattel paper will have priority in chattel paper over a security interest in chattel paper claimed "merely" as proceeds of inventory if the purchaser (i) purchases the chattel paper in the ordinary course of its business, (ii) acts in good faith, (iii) gives new value, and (iv) takes possession. In addition, the inventory secured party must not have marked the chattel paper (by "indicating" the security interest of that secured party). Rev. § 9-330. Marking tangible chattel paper does not operate to perfect the security interest, as does the electronic identification that a secured party can use to perfect a security interest in electronic chattel paper by obtaining "control" of the chattel paper.

39. A secured party may enforce all of the debtor's rights against an account debtor, including proceeding against collateral provided by the account debtor. Rev. § 9-607(a). The secured party may enforce claims against third persons obligated on the account debtor's obligation. A junior secured party that collects a check as proceeds of an account or inventory may defeat the senior secured party if the junior secured party qualifies as a holder in due course. Rev. § 9-331. The junior secured party would have even greater protection if the common debtor deposited the account debtor's check in the debtor's deposit account and then wrote its own check to the junior secured party. In that case, the junior would prevail unless it acted in "collusion" with the debtor to violate the rights of the senior secured party. Rev. § 9-332(b).

40. Revised Article 9 clarifies that the debtor generally bears most risks concerning the collateral. Rev. § 9-207. A secured party generally has an obligation under Revised Article 9 to use reasonable care to preserve collateral in the secured party's possession, although the secured party may charge the collateral for reasonable costs associated with preserving the collateral. Rev. § 9-207.

41. A transferee takes collateral free of a security interest if the secured party authorizes the disposition "free of the security interest." Rev. § 9-315(a). The statute makes clear that the secured party must intend to release its security interest in connection with its approval of the disposition. The express prohibition on transfer in the security agreement has been broadened to cover all types of collateral. Article 9 now protects ordinary course nonexclusive licensees of general intangibles and lessees of goods, as well as buyers of goods. Rev. §§ 1-201(a)(9), 9-320 & 9-321. The language in the security agreement is intended to create circumstances so that the debtor will "violate" the rights of the secured party if the debtor disposes of the collateral, thereby giving the secured party greater protection against certain transferees. As noted above, a junior secured party may under certain circumstances obtain priority in proceeds of collateral where the proceeds are negotiable instruments or money.

42. For inventory only, a PMSI in inventory remains a PMSI to the extent it secures a purchase money obligation for other inventory. Rev. § 9-103(b)(2). A secured party may have a PMSI in software to the extent the secured party finances the software in an "integrated" transaction with the goods in which the software will be used. Rev. § 9-103(c). "Embedded" software will constitute part of the "goods" themselves. Rev. § 9-102(a)(44) & (75). Revised Article 9 authorizes the parties to agree on a "reasonable" method of determining how much of the secured obligation is a "purchase money obligation." Rev. § 9-103(e). The PMSI for the price will have priority over an enabling loan. Rev. § 9-324(g). Multiple enabling PMSIs will rank in order of filing. Rev. §§ 9-322(a) & 9-324(g)(2).

43. A consignee of goods or seller of accounts or chattel paper does not have to have "rights in" the collateral to have the ability to grant another security interest or to make another sale if the consignor or the buyer has not perfected its security interest. Rev. § 9-203(b)(2). This recognizes that although the consignee or the seller may not "own" the property, those persons still have the "power" to grant an effective security interest in the property. See Rev. §§ 9-318 & 9-319. Generally, Rev. §§ 9-406–9-409 invalidate contractual and statutory restrictions on the transfer of contractual rights, to the extent those restrictions would impair the creation or perfection of the security interest in those rights or permit the creation or perfection to constitute a breach of the debtor's agreement with the other party to the agreement. For certain contract rights, such as the right to receive money, Revised Article 9 also in most instances disregards contractual or legal restrictions on the right to enforce the security interest.

5.2    *Location of Collateral.* All Collateral consisting of goods is located solely in the States (the "Collateral States") listed in **Exhibit []** ~~C~~.[44]

5.3    *Location, State of Incorporation and, Name* of Debtor. Debtor's:

(i)    chief executive office is located in the State (the "~~Debtor~~ Chief Executive Office State") identified in **Exhibit []**;

(ii)    state of incorporation is the State (the "Debtor State") identified in **Exhibit []; and**

(iii)    exact legal name is as set forth in the first paragraph of this Security Agreement.[45]

## 6.    Debtor's Covenants.

Until the Obligations are paid in full, Debtor agrees that it will:

6.1    preserve its corporate existence and not, in one transaction or a series of related transactions, merge into or consolidate with any other entity, or sell all or substantially all of its assets;[46]

6.2    not change the state ~~where any Collateral consisting of goods is located, except to another Collateral State;~~ where it is located;[47] and

~~6.3    not change the state of its chief executive office; and~~ [48]

6.3    not change its corporate name without providing Secured Party with 30 days' prior written notice.[49]

## 7.    Events of Default.

The occurrence of any of the following shall, at the option of Secured Party, be an Event of Default:

7.1    Any default,[50] Event of Default (as defined) by Debtor under the Loan Agreement or any of the other Obligations;

7.2    Debtor's failure to comply with any of the provisions of, or the incorrectness of any representation or warranty contained in, this Security Agreement, the Note, or in any of the other Obligations;

7.3    Transfer or disposition of any of the Collateral, except as expressly permitted by this Security Agreement;

7.4    Attachment, execution or levy on any of the Collateral;

7.5    Debtor voluntarily or involuntarily becoming subject to any proceeding under (a) the Bankruptcy Code or (b) any similar remedy under state statutory or common law; ~~or~~

7.6    Debtor shall fail to comply with, or become subject to any administrative or judicial proceeding under any federal, state or local (a) hazardous waste or environmental law, (b) asset forfeiture or similar law which can result in the forfeiture of property, or (c) other law, where noncompliance may have any significant effect on the Collateral; ~~or~~

44. As explained in the following note, Revised Article 9 generally provides for the filing of a financing statement in the state where the debtor is incorporated. However, the secured party will need to continue to search in the applicable states under former Article 9 for five years after the effective date of Article 9 (*i.e.* until July 1, 2006) because financing statements filed under former Article 9 remain effective until their former Article 9 lapse date (typically five years), but not for more than five years after the effective date of Revised Article 9. Rev. § 9-705(c).

45. All filings (except for fixture filings, and filings to perfect a security interest in as-extracted collateral and timber to be cut and to perfect and agricultural lien) are to be made at the "location" of the debtor. Rev. § 9-301(1). This replaces the former rule that provided for filing at the location of goods collateral. "Location" of the debtor means the state of formation for entities that register to come into existence. Rev. § 9-307(e). This replaces the former rule that looks to the state of the debtor's chief executive office. For a security interest perfected by possession, the location of the collateral determines the applicable law. Rev. § 9-301(2). The financing statement must use the registered name of the debtor if there is one; the use of an incorrect name is seriously misleading as a matter of law if a standard search does not find it. The statute confirms that trade names are neither sufficient nor necessary. Rev. §§ 9-502(a)(1), 9-503, 9-506(b). A secured party will probably want to obtain a formal certified copy of the debtor's articles of incorporation to confirm the state of incorporation and the exact name of the debtor. A financing statement does not have to indicate the representative capacity of the secured party. Rev. § 9-503(d). As noted above, for five years after the effective date of Revised Article 9, a secured party will want to conduct searches in the states that would have been appropriate under former Article 9.

46. Revised Article 9 contains a set of rules that concern when a "new debtor" becomes bound by the security agreement and when a financing statement naming the original debtor is effective to perfect a security interest in collateral acquired by the new debtor. *See* Rev. §§ 9-102(a)(56), 9-102(a)(60), 9-203(d), 9-326, 9-508. Generally, under these provisions, the security interest created by the new debtor in favor of its secured party will prevail over that created by the original debtor in favor of its secured party in collateral acquired by the new debtor.

47. If the debtor transfers the collateral to a person incorporated in another state (including in a "reincorporation" transaction) the secured party has one year to file a financing statement in that state. Rev. § 9-316(a)(3).

48. As noted above, Revised Article 9 does not require a filing in the state of the debtor's chief executive office, if the debtor is a "registered organization," and the office is in a state that is different from the state of formation. Rev. § 9-301(1).

49. The secured party has four months to file an amendment to the financing statement if the debtor changes its name in a manner that makes the financing statement "seriously misleading." Rev. § 9-507(b).

50. As with former Article 9, Revised Article 9 does not define "default."

7.7    Secured Party shall receive at any time following the Closing an SOS Report indicating that Secured Party's security interest is not prior to all other security interests or other interests reflected in the report.[51]

## 8. Default Costs.

8.1    Should an Event of Default occur, Debtor will pay to Secured Party all costs reasonably incurred by the Secured Party for the purpose of enforcing its rights hereunder, including:

   (i)    costs of foreclosure;[52]

   (ii)   costs of obtaining money damages; and

   (iii)  a reasonable fee for the services of attorneys employed by Secured Party for any purpose related to this Security Agreement or the Obligations, including consultation, drafting documents, sending notices or instituting, prosecuting or defending litigation or arbitration.[53]

## 9. Remedies Upon Default.

9.1    *General.* Upon any Event of Default, Secured Party may pursue any remedy available at law (including those available under the provisions of the UCC), or in equity to collect, enforce or satisfy any Obligations then owing, whether by acceleration or otherwise.[54]

9.2    *Remedies.* Upon any Event of Default, Secured Party shall have the right to pursue any of the following remedies separately, successively or simultaneously:

   (i)    File suit and obtain judgment and, in conjunction with any action, Secured Party may seek any ancillary remedies provided by law, including levy of attachment and garnishment.

   (ii)   Take possession of any Collateral if not already in its possession without demand and without legal process. Upon Secured Party's demand, Debtor will assemble and make the Collateral available to Secured Party as they direct. Debtor grants to Secured Party the right, for this purpose, to enter into or on any premises where Collateral may be located.[55]

   (iii)  Without taking possession, sell, lease or otherwise dispose of the Collateral at public or private sale in accordance with the UCC.

## 10. Foreclosure Procedures.

10.1   *No Waiver.* No delay or omission by Secured Party to exercise any right or remedy accruing upon any Event of Default shall: (a) impair any right or remedy, (b) waive any default or operate as an acquiescence to the Event of Default, or (c) affect any subsequent default of the same or of a different nature.

10.2   *Notices.* Secured Party shall give Debtor such notice of any private or public sale as may be required by the UCC.[56]

51. The filing office may reject a financing statement for a limited number of reasons stated in the statute (*e.g.* no filing fee; no debtor name). Rev. § 9-516(b). A refusal by a filing office to accept a financing statement for any other reason does not prevent the financing statement from being effective to perfect the security interest (§ 9-516(d)). Although the first secured party will have a perfected security interest, a subsequent purchaser (including a secured party) that gives value in reliance of the absence of the financing statement will have priority. Rev. § 9-516(d). Former law makes a filing effective if wrongfully refused. However, most decisions under former Article 9 protected the first filer against subsequent searchers, even if the subsequent searcher relied on the absence of a filing. In addition, a subsequent secured party bears the full risk of an indexing error by the filing office, even if the subsequent secured party relied on the absence of a financing statement as reflected in a search. Rev. § 9-517.

52. If the proceeds of a foreclosure sale (or other disposition) are sufficient, Revised Article 9 permits the secured party to recover these costs. Rev. § 9-615.

53. Revised Article 9 provides for the recovery of foreclosure costs, including reasonable attorney's fees (if the parties have so agreed). Rev. § 9-615.

54. The secured party's enforcement rights continue to be cumulative. Rev. § 9-601(c).

55. As under former Article 9, the secured party is subject to a nonwaivable obligation not to breach the peace in the course of attempting to take possession of the collateral. Rev. §§ 9-602 & 9-609.

56. The secured party must give notice of sale or other disposition to other secured parties of record. Rev. § 9-611(b). The statute provides practical rules indicating which secured parties of record are entitled to such notice. Rev. § 9-611(c)(3)(B). The statute provides a "safe harbor" form for giving notice to the debtor of a private or public sale. Rev. § 9-613(5). Forms of notification of proposed disposition appear as Forms 4.1.1–4.1.4.

10.3    *Condition of Collateral*. Secured Party ~~shall have~~ has no obligation to ~~give a notice to any other person.~~ clean-up or otherwise prepare the Collateral for sale.[57]

10.4    *No Obligation to Pursue Others*. Secured Party has no obligation to attempt to satisfy the Obligations by collecting them from any other person liable for them and Secured Party may release, modify or waive any collateral provided by any other person to secure any of the Obligations, all without affecting Secured Party's rights against Debtor. Debtor waives any right it may have to require Secured Party to pursue any third person for any of the Obligations.[58]

10.5    *Compliance With Other Laws*. Secured Party may comply with any applicable state or federal law requirements in connection with a disposition of the Collateral and compliance will not be considered adversely to affect the commercial reasonableness of any sale of the Collateral.[59]

10.6    *Warranties*. Secured Party may sell the Collateral without giving any warranties as to the Collateral. Secured Party may specifically disclaim any warranties of title or the like.[60] This procedure will not be considered adversely to affect the commercial reasonableness of any sale of the Collateral.

10.6    *Sales on Credit*. If Secured Party sells any of the Collateral upon credit, Debtor will be credited only with payments actually made by the purchaser, received by Secured Party and applied to the indebtedness of the Purchaser. In the event the purchaser fails to pay for the Collateral, Secured Party may resell the Collateral and Debtor shall be credited with the proceeds of the sale.[61]

10.7    *Purchases by Secured Party*. In the event Secured Party purchases any of the Collateral being sold, Secured Party may pay for the Collateral by crediting some or all of the Obligations of the Debtor.[62]

~~10.8    *Deficiency Judgment*. If it is determined by an authority of competent jurisdiction that a disposition by Secured Party did not occur in a commercially reasonable manner, Secured Party may obtain a deficiency from Debtor for the difference between the amount of the Obligation foreclosed and the amount that a commercially reasonable sale would have yielded.~~ [63]

10.8    *No Marshaling*. Secured Party have no obligation to marshal any assets in favor of Debtor, or against or in payment of:

(i)     the Note,

(ii)    any of the other Obligations, or

(iii)   any other obligation owed to Secured Party by Debtor or any other person.

~~10.10    *Retention of Collateral*. Secured Party will not be considered to have to have offered to retain the Collateral in satisfaction of the Obligations unless Secured Party has entered into a written agreement with Debtor to hat effect.~~[64]

57. The secured party "may" dispose of collateral "in its then condition or following any commercially reasonable preparation or processing." Rev. § 9-610(a) & cmt. 4. Although the language of the statute is permissive, the secured party should engage in a cost-benefit analysis to determine whether some preparation is appropriate, taking into account the secured party's risk of not being able to collect the preparation costs from the proceeds of the foreclosure sale or from the debtor.

58. The default rules of Revised Article 9 apply to secondary obligors. Rev. § 9-601(b). This continues the majority rule under former law. The debtor, secondary obligor, and other obligors may not waive most default rights. Rev. § 9-602(a). The "debtor" may be a "guarantor" to the extent it provides collateral to secure the obligation of another person. *See* the definition of "Obligations" in this Security Agreement. *See also* Rev. § 9-102(a)(59) & (71).

59. An Official Comment to Rev. § 9-610 addresses this issue. It notes that this would be an appropriate circumstance for the parties to agree on a "standard[] measuring the fulfillment of the … duties of a secured party" if the standard is "not manifestly unreasonable." Rev. § 9-603.

60. The secured party automatically gives "title" warranties when disposing of collateral, unless disclaimed. The statute provides sample disclaimer language. Rev. § 9-610(d), (e) & (f). The reference to other "like" warranties does not mean warranties of quality. A secured party gives implied warranties of quality only if they would arise under other law in the circumstances, such as UCC Article 2. *See* Rev. § 9-610 cmt. 11.

61. A secured party does not have to apply noncash proceeds unless the failure to do so would be commercially unreasonable. The secured party must apply any noncash proceeds in a commercially reasonable manner. Rev. § 9-615(c) & cmt. 3. This gives the secured party the ability to accept a note from a buyer at a foreclosure sale and establish a commercially reasonable discount value or credit the debtor as the secured party receives payments. A secured party that is in the business of accepting notes in the ordinary course of its business is more likely to have to apply the note at the time of sale. Hence, depending on the circumstances, paragraph 10.6 may be too aggressive. This may be an appropriate circumstance for the parties to agree on a "standard[] measuring the fulfillment of the…duties of a secured party" if the standard is "not manifestly unreasonable." Rev. § 9-603.

62. The secured party has a right to make a "credit bid" without this provision. As under former Article 9, a secured party may not purchase the collateral at a private sale unless the collateral has a readily determinable price. Rev. § 9-610(c). If there is a commercially reasonable sale of collateral to the secured party, a person "related" to the secured party, or a guarantor, for an amount that is "significantly below the range" of proceeds that would have been realized from a complying sale to an independent third person, the calculation of the deficiency will be based on the amount that would have been obtained from that third person. Rev. § 9-615(f).

63. The statute adopts the rebuttable presumption rule for non-consumer transactions. Rev. § 9-626(3)(B). This adopts the rule of a majority of the courts that have determined the issue under former Article 9.

64. The secured party may accept the collateral in satisfaction of the debt even if the secured party does not have possession of the collateral. Former Article 9 allowed retention only if the secured party had possession of the collateral. The secured party may accept collateral in partial satisfaction of the debt with the written consent of the debtor. Under Revised Article 9, the secured party may not make a "constructive" acceptance of collateral. This rejects those decisions under former law that permitted an implied acceptance, usually based on an extended retention of possession by the secured party without taking any action. Instead, the duration of any delay by the secured party will go to the question of the commercial reasonableness of the disposition. Rev. § 9-620. Forms of notification of full and partial strict foreclosure appear as Forms 4.1.1 & 4.2.2.

## 11. Miscellaneous

11.1   *Assignment.*

(i)   *Binds Assignees.* This Security Agreement shall bind and shall inure to the benefit of the heirs, legatees, executors, administrators, successors and assigns of Debtor and Secured Party and shall bind all persons who become bound as a debtor to this Security Agreement.[65]

(ii)   *No Assignments by Debtor.* Secured Party does not consent to any assignment by Debtor except as expressly provided in this Security Agreement.

(iii)   *Secured Party Assignments.* Secured Party may assign its rights and interests under this Security Agreement. If an assignment is made, Debtor shall render performance under this Security Agreement to the assignee. Debtor waives and[66] will not assert against any assignee any claims, defenses or set-offs which Debtor could assert against Secured Party except defenses which cannot be waived.

11.2   *Severability.* Should any provision of this Security Agreement be found to be void, invalid or unenforceable by a court or panel of arbitrators of competent jurisdiction, that finding shall only affect the provisions found to be void, invalid or unenforceable and shall not affect the remaining provisions of this Security Agreement.

11.3   *Notices.* Any notices required by this Security Agreement shall be deemed to be delivered when a record[67] has been (a) deposited in any United States postal box if postage is prepaid, and the notice properly addressed to the intended recipient, (b) received by telecopy, (c) received through the Internet, and (d) when personally delivered.

11.4   *Headings.* Section headings used this Security Agreement are for convenience only. They are not a part of this Security Agreement and shall not be used in construing it.

11.5   *Governing Law.* This Security Agreement is being executed and delivered and is intended to be performed in the State of Illinois and shall be construed and enforced in accordance with the laws of the State of Illinois, except to the extent that the UCC provides for perfection under the application of the law of another state.[68]

11.6   *Rules of Construction.*

(i)   No reference to "proceeds" in this Security Agreement authorizes any sale, transfer, or other disposition of the Collateral by the Debtor.

(ii)   "Includes" and "including" are not limiting.

(iii)   "Or" is not exclusive.

(iv)   "All" includes "any" and "any" includes "all."

65. A security agreement is operative with respect to a person that "becomes bound" as a "new debtor" to a security agreement entered into by another person (*e.g.*, an "original debtor" who merges with the new debtor). Under some circumstances, usually in an acquisition context, one person may "become bound" by a security agreement that an acquired person (*e.g.*, the "original debtor") has signed. Rev. §§ 9-102(a)(56), 9-203(d) & (e).

66. Neither the debtor nor a secondary obligor may waive certain enforcement rights under Revised Article 9. Rev. § 9-602. An account debtor may, in specified circumstances, agree not to assert against an assignee of the secured party any claims and defenses the account debtor may have against the secured party. Rev. § 9-403. *See also* Rev. §§ 9-340 & 9-404.

67. Revised Article 9 uses the term "record" generally to replace the concept of a "writing." Rev. § 9-102(a)(69).

68. For purposes of perfection and the effect of perfection, Revised Article 9 generally looks to the state of the debtor's formation when the debtor is a "registered organization" (*e.g.*, a corporation). Rev. § 9-301. There may be circumstances where the law of a state where goods are located or the debtor has its chief executive office governs questions of perfection and the effect of perfection. Rev. §§ 9-301(3) and 9-705(c).

11.7   *Integration and Modifications.*

(i)   This Security Agreement is the entire agreement of the Debtor and Secured Party concerning its subject matter.

(ii)   Any modification to this Security Agreement must be made in writing and signed by the party adversely affected.

11.8   *Waiver.* Any party to this Security Agreement may waive the enforcement of any provision to the extent the provision is for its benefit.

11.9   *Further Assurances.* Debtor agrees to execute any further documents, and to take any further actions, reasonably requested by Secured Party to evidence or perfect the security interest granted herein, to maintain the first priority of the security interests, or to effectuate the rights granted to Secured Party herein.[69]

The parties have signed this Security Agreement as of the day and year first above written at Los Angeles, California.

[DEBTOR]

Vending Machine Manufacturing Co.
a California corporation

By:_____
Jane Drink-Soft
President

By:_____
Bob Soft-Drink
Secretary

69. Paragraph 11.9 may be especially important in view of the complex transition rules. Rev. §§ 9-702 *et seq.*

Form 1.2

# Electronic Mail Protocol[1]

THIS ELECTRONIC MAIL PROTOCOL (as amended and in effect from time to time, this "Protocol") is dated as of _____ ____, 20___, among (i) _____ (the "Borrower"), (ii) _____ in its capacity as agent (the "Agent") for the lenders (the "Lenders") whose signatures appear below, and (iii) the Lenders.

WHEREAS, the Borrower, the Agent and the Lenders have entered[2] into a Credit Agreement dated as of _____ ____, 20___ (as amended and in effect from time to time, the "Credit Agreement"), which contemplates the making of amendments, waivers and other agreements, and the transmission of certain notices and other communications, among the parties hereto by electronic mail, if (but only if) the parties hereto agree in writing to an electronic mail protocol; and

WHEREAS, the parties hereto, having made such agreements and wishing to provide such communications from time to time by electronic mail, have agreed to enter in this Protocol as an electronic mail protocol;

---

1. To accommodate "the rapid development and commercial adoption of modern communication and storage technologies" (Rev. § 9-102 cmt. 9.a.), Revised Article 9 enables parties to enter into secured transactions wholly or partly in electronic media (*e.g.*, email communications). Best practice will dictate that parties to a transaction that occurs electronically may wish to establish protocols to determine when electronic communications are to be treated as authentic and authorized, and to allocate amongst themselves the risks of inauthenticity. This form may be used to establish such protocols. In this context, it will be important to consult not only Revised Article 9, but also the Uniform Electronic Transactions Act ("UETA") and the federal Electronic Signatures in Global Commerce Act ("E-Sign"). Pub. L. 106-229 (codified at 15 U.S.C. §§ 7001 to 7006, 7021 and 7031). These substantially similar laws are intended to enable parties to transact with electronic signatures. Although they both "step back" from Revised Article 9, they will continue to govern to the extent that Article 9 is inapplicable (*e.g.* as to a credit agreement to the extent it does not involve a secured transaction). Where applicable, this form contains references to particular provisions of UETA and E-Sign.

2. This agreement could also be used to establish procedures for entering into a credit (or other) agreement. It would have to be modified to do so.

NOW, THEREFORE, the parties hereto, intending to be legally bound, hereby agree as follows:

## § 1. DEFINITIONS AND RULES OF INTERPRETATION

1.1.  **Definitions.** Capitalized terms used herein without definition shall have the respective meanings provided therefor in the Credit Agreement. In addition, the following terms shall have the following meanings:

"Agreement" means any amendment, waiver or other modification to or under the Credit Agreement or any other Loan Document.[3] The term includes any security agreement, pledge agreement, mortgage, deed of trust or other agreement creating an interest in personal or real property to the extent that applicable law permits such agreement to be made by electronic means.

"Communication" means any notice or other communication required or permitted to be given or made under the Credit Agreement or any other Loan Document or an acknowledgement under § 3.3 hereof. The term does not include an Agreement.[4]

"Electronic" means relating to technology having electrical, digital, magnetic, wireless, optical, electromagnetic or similar capabilities. The term does not include facsimile technology.[5]

"Electronic record" means a record created, generated, sent, communicated, received or stored by electronic means.[6]

"Electronic signature" means an electronic sound, symbol, or process attached to or logically associated with an electronic record and executed or adopted by a person with the intent to sign the electronic record.[7]

"Information" means data, text, images, sounds, codes, computer programs, software, databases, or the like.[8]

"Information processing system" means an electronic system for creating, generating, sending, receiving, storing, displaying or processing information.[9]

"Record" means information that is inscribed on a tangible medium or which is stored in an electronic or other medium and is retrievable in perceivable form.[10]

---

3.    If the parties have not yet entered into the credit agreement (or other operative agreements), they should also be set forth here.

4.    Rev. § 9-102(a)(18)(B) defines "communicate" as meaning, in part, "to transmit a record by any means agreed upon by the persons sending and receiving the record...."

5.    The first sentence of this term is taken from the UETA and E-Sign definitions of the same term. *See* UETA § 2(5); E-Sign § 106(2).

6.    *See* UETA § 2(7); E-Sign § 106(4).

7.    *See* UETA § 2(8); E-Sign § 106(5).

8.    *See* UETA § 2(10); E-Sign § 106(7).

9.    *See* UETA § 2(11). E-Sign contains no similar term.

10.    *See* Rev. § 9-102(a)(69); UETA § 2(12); E-Sign § 106(9).

"Security procedure" means a procedure employed for the purpose of verifying that an electronic signature, record, or performance is that of a specific person authorized to act for the person or for detecting changes or errors in the information in an electronic record. The term includes a procedure that requires the use of algorithms or other codes, identifying words or numbers, encryption, or callback, or other acknowledgment procedures as determined in good faith, as defined in Section 9-102(a)(43) of the Uniform Commercial Code.

"Writing" means a notice or other communication, or a record, in paper form and includes a facsimile copy. The term does not include an electronic communication or an electronic record.

1.2. **Rules of Interpretation.** Terms defined in the Uniform Commercial Code of the State of _____ and not otherwise defined herein or in the Credit Agreement shall have the same meanings herein as specified therein. In the event that a term is defined in Article 9 of the Uniform Commercial Code but is defined differently in another Article of the Uniform Commercial Code, the definition used in Article 9 shall control.

# § 2.  PREREQUISITES

## 2.1.  Electronic Agreements and Communications Permitted but not Required.

(a)    Each party may, in accordance with the terms of this Protocol, make any Agreement with any other party, or transmit any Communication to any other party, by electronic means.

(b)    Nothing contained in this Protocol shall require any party to enter into any Agreement, or to transmit any Communication, by electronic means. Such party may at any time elect to enter into any Agreement, or to give or make any Communication, in writing instead of entering into such Agreement, or transmitting such Communication, by electronic means.

2.2.  **System Operations.** Each party, at its own expense, shall provide and maintain the equipment, software, services and testing necessary to perform under this Protocol.

2.3.  **Electronic Addresses.** Each party's electronic address for entering into Agreements, and sending and receiving Communications, by electronic means is set forth on the signature page hereto below such party's signature. Any party may from time to time change its electronic address for entering into Agreements, and sending and receiving Communications, by an authenticated notice in a writing sent to the other parties hereto or by an authenticated notice transmitted by electronic means to the other parties hereto and promptly confirmed in a writing.

2.4.  **Electronic Signatures.**

(a)    Each party has adopted, as its electronic signature, the electronic signature set forth on the signature page hereto below such party's signature. Any party may from time to time change its electronic signature by a notice in a writing sent to the other parties hereto marked "PRIVATE AND CONFIDENTIAL" and setting forth the new electronic signature of such party and the time of its effectiveness. The time of effectiveness for each receiving party may be no earlier than a time giving a reasonable opportunity for the receiving party to act on such notice following its receipt.

(b) Each party agrees that any electronic signature of such party contained in any Communication transmitted by electronic means shall be sufficient to verify that such party originated such Communication and to operate as a signature of such party for purposes of any provision of the Credit Agreement, the Security Agreement or any of the other Loan Documents that requires a signed writing.

(c) NONE OF THE PARTIES HERETO SHALL DISCLOSE TO ANY UNAUTHORIZED PERSON ITS ELECTRONIC SIGNATURE OR THE ELECTRONIC SIGNATURES OF THE OTHER PARTIES HERETO, EXCEPT AS REQUIRED BY LAW.

2.6.   **Record Retention.** Each party shall be responsible to retain electronic records of all Agreements made, and all Communications transmitted or received, by electronic means.

2.7.   **Security Procedures.** Each party shall use security procedures. The security procedures must be reasonably sufficient (a) to ensure that all Agreements made, and all Communications transmitted, by electronic means by or on its behalf are authorized by the transmitting party, (b) to protect against improper access to Agreements made, and Communications transmitted or received, by electronic means, (c) to protect against disclosure of any party's electronic signature except as provided in this Protocol, and (d) to ensure that all electronic records are unaltered from the original Agreement made, or the original Communication sent or received, electronically. Each party agrees to indemnify the other parties hereto and to hold such other parties harmless from and against any loss, cost or reasonable expense incurred or sustained by such other parties as a consequence of that party's failure to use reasonably sufficient security procedures.

## § 3.   TRANSMISSIONS

### 3.1.   **Proper Receipt; Effectiveness.**

(a)   An Agreement or Communication bearing the then-current electronic signature of the transmitting party is considered as properly received by the receiving party if and when it enters into the first information processing system operated by or on behalf of the receiving party.

(b)   Except as provided in § 3.3, an Agreement or Communication properly received by a receiving party during normal business hours at the office of the receiving party shall be effective upon such receipt and otherwise at the opening of business at such receiving party's office on the next Business Day.

(c)   For purposes of § 3.1(b), the office of the receiving party shall be that set forth on the signature page hereto below such party's signature. Any party may from time to time change its receiving party office by a notice in a writing sent to the other parties hereto or by notice transmitted by electronic means to the other parties hereto promptly confirmed in a writing.

3.2. **Verification; Functional Acknowledgment.** Except as otherwise provided in § 3.3, within one (1) Business Day after proper receipt of any Agreement or Communication by electronic means, the receiving party shall properly transmit a functional acknowledgment in return. A functional acknowledgement is a Communication that confirms that proper receipt of the Agreement or Communication has occurred and that all required portions of the Agreement or Communication have been received and are syntactically correct and are not garbled or unintelligible, but otherwise does not confirm the substantive content of the transmitted Agreement or Communication. Each functional acknowledgement shall contain a legend that puts the recipient of such acknowledgement on notice that it is for verification purposes only and should not be construed as an acceptance of the content of the originating party's Agreement or Communication. A functional acknowledgment is properly transmitted if it has been transmitted in a manner that complies with § 2. A functional acknowledgement shall constitute [**conclusive**] [**, save for manifest error, conclusive**] [**rebuttably presumptive**] evidence that an Agreement or Communication has been properly received.

3.3. **Garbled Transmissions.** If any transmitted Agreement or Communication is received in an unintelligible or garbled form, the receiving party shall notify the transmitting party (if identifiable from the received Agreement or Communication) in a reasonable manner promptly and in any event within one (1) Business Day after the receiving party first detects the error. Upon receipt of such notice, the transmitting party shall retransmit the Agreement or Communication. If the receiving party fails timely to inform the transmitting party of an error in the received, but garbled Agreement or Communication, the transmitting party's record of the contents of such Agreement or Communication shall control.

# § 4. TRANSACTION TERMS

4.1. **Terms.** Any Agreement made, or any Communication transmitted, by electronic means pursuant to this Protocol shall be construed in accordance with the terms of the Credit Agreement and the other Loan Documents. The terms of the Credit Agreement and the other Loan Documents shall prevail in the event of any conflict with the terms of this Protocol.

4.2. **Confidentiality.** All information contained in any Agreement made, or any Communication transmitted or received, by electronic means and that is confidential or proprietary shall be subject to any confidentiality terms of the Credit Agreement.

4.3. **Validity; Enforceability.**

(a) This Protocol has been executed by the parties hereto to evidence their mutual intent to create binding obligations pursuant to the electronic transmission and receipt of Agreements and Communications.

(b) Any Agreement or Communication properly received pursuant to this Protocol shall not be denied legal effect on the ground that the Agreement or Communication has been transmitted and received electronically and is not signed by way of a writing.

(c)   The parties agree not to contest the validity or enforceability of Agreements or Communications under the provisions of any applicable law relating to whether certain agreements are to be in a writing or signed by the party to be bound thereby if sent in accordance with this Protocol. Agreements or Communications received by electronic means hereunder and stored as electronic records, if introduced as evidence in any judicial, arbitration, mediation, or administrative proceedings, will be admissible as among the parties to the same extent and under the same conditions as other business records originated and always maintained in a writing. None of the parties shall contest the admissibility of electronic records maintained hereunder under either the business records exception to the hearsay rule or the best evidence rule on the basis that the Communications were not originated and always maintained in writing. However, nothing in this § 4.3(c) shall limit any party's right to contest whether an electronic record maintained hereunder has been altered.

[(d) The Credit Agreement provides that this Protocol and any amendment or modification to this Protocol must be in a writing and may not be executed and delivered or made by electronic means. Accordingly, the provisions of this § 4.3 shall not apply to any electronically received communications or electronic records purporting to amend or modify this Protocol itself.]

## § 5.  MISCELLANEOUS

5.1.   **Optional Termination.** Any party hereto may terminate this Protocol at any time by giving five (5) Business Days' prior notice of termination in an authenticated Writing or Record to the other parties hereto. Such termination notice shall specify the effective date of termination. Any termination shall not affect the respective rights and obligations of the parties arising prior to termination or affect any ongoing rights and obligations among the parties hereto which do not terminate under this Protocol.

5.2.   **Entire Agreement.** This Protocol is supplemental to the Credit Agreement and the other Loan Documents and, together with the Credit Agreement and the other Loan Documents, constitutes the complete agreement of the parties relating to the matters specified in this Protocol. No oral or electronic modification or waiver of any of the provisions of this Protocol shall be binding on any party hereto. This Protocol is for the benefit of, and shall be binding upon, the parties and their respective successors and assigns.

5.3.   **Force Majeure.** No party shall be liable for any failure to transmit or receive any Agreement or Communication by electronic means, where such failure results from any act of God or other cause beyond such party's reasonable control (including, without limitation, any mechanical, electronic or communications failure) which prevents such party from transmitting or receiving such Agreement or Communication.

5.4.   **Other Provisions Incorporated by Reference.** The notice provisions contained in §_____ of the Credit Agreement shall apply for purposes of giving any notices or other communications required or permitted to be given under this Protocol in a writing. [**The provisions of §§_____ (governing law, jurisdiction, etc.), _____ (third parties), _____ (counterparts), _____ (partial invalidity) and _____ (section headings) of the Credit Agreement shall apply mutatis mutandis to this Protocol.**]

IN WITNESS WHEREOF, each of the undersigned has executed this Protocol by its duly authorized representative as of the date first above written.

[BORROWER]

By: _____

Name: _____

Title: _____

Electronic address:

Receiving party location:

Electronic signature:

[AGENT]

By: _____

Name: _____

Title: _____

Electronic address:

Receiving party location:

Electronic signature:

[LENDER]

By: _____

Name: _____

Title: _____

Electronic address:

Receiving party location:

Electronic signature:

[LENDER]

By:_____

Name:_____

Title:_____

Electronic address:

Receiving party location:

Electronic signature:

[LENDER]

By:_____

Name:_____

Title:_____

Electronic address:

Receiving party location:

Electronic signature:

# Pre-Filing Authorization Letter[1]

[Date]

[Name and address of Secured Party]

   Re:   [Proposed Transaction Involving Article 9 Security Interest]

Dear:

   In connection with [insert proposed transaction involving Article 9 security interest], [insert name and address of debtor] ("Debtor") hereby authorizes [insert name of secured party] ("Secured Party") to file a financing statement (the "Financing Statement") naming Debtor as "debtor" and indicating the following collateral: [insert collateral description]. The Secured Party may file the Financing Statement in all offices it deems appropriate.[2]

            [DEBTOR]

            By: _____

            Name: _____

            Title: _____

---

   1.   Under certain circumstances, it may be appropriate to a file a financing statement prior to the consummation of the proposed secured transaction. This practice—often referred to as "pre-filing"—generally gives the filing party priority as of the date of filing under Rev. § 9-322. Under former Article 9, a debtor's signature was required on a financing statement. *See* F. § 9-402(1). Revised Article 9, by contrast, does not require a debtor to sign a financing statement. Rev. § 9-502 cmt. 3. A person may not, however, file a financing statement unless "authorized" by the debtor to do so, although the filing may later be ratified by the debtor. Rev. §§ 9-509(a) & 9-502 cmt. 3. A debtor that executes and returns this letter to the secured party will have authorized the "pre-filing" of a financing statement covering the indicated collateral.

   2.   The parties may wish to include language disclaiming a commitment to consummate the proposed transaction.

# PART 2

# Creating the Security Interest— The Security Agreement

# All Personal Property Assets Security Agreement[1]

SECURITY AGREEMENT, dated as of [insert date], between [insert debtor], a[n] [insert debtor's jurisdiction and form of organization] (the "Debtor"), and [insert secured party], a[n] [insert secured party's jurisdiction and form of organization] (the "Secured Party").

WHEREAS, the Debtor has entered into a[n] [insert agreement, *e.g.* credit agreement] dated as of [insert date of agreement] (as amended and in effect from time to time, the "Credit Agreement"), with the Secured Party, pursuant to which the Secured Party, subject to the terms and conditions contained therein, is to make loans [*or otherwise to extend credit*] to the Debtor; and

WHEREAS, it is a condition precedent to the Secured Party's making any loans [*or otherwise extending credit*] to the Debtor under the Credit Agreement that the Debtor execute and deliver to the Secured Party a security agreement in substantially the form hereof; and

WHEREAS, the Debtor wishes to grant a security interest in favor of the Secured Party as herein provided;

---

1.  This form is intended to be used where a debtor grants a security interest in all of its personal property assets. It may be used in addition to, or in lieu of, other specialized security agreements contained in this book, including those governing security interests in intellectual property. *See* Forms 2.2–2.5.

NOW, THEREFORE, in consideration of the promises contained herein and for other good and valuable consideration, the receipt and sufficiency of which are hereby acknowledged, the parties hereto agree as follows:

1.    **Definitions.**[2] All capitalized terms used herein without definitions shall have the respective meanings provided therefor in the Credit Agreement. The term "State," as used herein, means the [**State**] of [insert state]. [*All terms defined in the Uniform Commercial Code of the State and used herein shall have the same definitions herein as specified therein. However, if a term is defined in Article 9 of the Uniform Commercial Code of the State differently than in another Article of the Uniform Commercial Code of the State, the term has the meaning specified in Article 9.*] [*The term "Obligations," as used herein, means all of the indebtedness, obligations and liabilities of the Debtor to the Secured Party, individually or collectively, whether direct or indirect, joint or several, absolute or contingent, due or to become due, now existing or hereafter arising under or in respect of the Credit Agreement* [*, any promissory notes or other instruments or agreements executed and delivered pursuant thereto or in connection therewith*] *or this Agreement, and the term "Event of Default," as used herein, means the failure of the Debtor to pay or perform any of the Obligations as and when due to be paid or performed under the terms of the Credit Agreement*]. [Also, if not defined in the Credit Agreement or another document to which reference for defined terms is made, define "Default," "Event of Default," "Loan Documents" and "Security Documents" here].

---

2.    A general reference to UCC defined terms will clarify that the use in the security agreement of a UCC collateral type, such as "accounts," is intended to include all assets which fall into that collateral type as defined in the UCC. For further clarification, especially because some states have enacted non-uniform provisions in their UCC, the reference to the UCC should be a reference to the UCC of a particular state, which would typically be the state whose law governs the security agreement as a matter of contract between the debtor and the secured party (*see* § 22). When referring to the UCC for definitional terms, however, care should be taken to make sure that, if a term is defined in one Article of the UCC differently than in another Article, it is clear which Article's defined term is being referred to in the security agreement. Section 1 clarifies that the Article 9 definition of terms prevails over definitions of the same terms in other Articles. For example, the Article 9 definition of "instrument" includes a non-negotiable instrument as well as a negotiable instrument (*see* Rev. § 9-102(a)(47)), while the Article 3 definition of that term (*see* UCC § 3-104(b)) generally applies only to negotiable instruments. A security agreement should also clearly define the obligations that are secured and what event or condition constitutes a default by the debtor. Without a definition or other statement of the obligations secured, a security interest may not meet UCC § 1-201(37)'s definition of a security interest (*i.e.*, that the interest secures "payment or performance of an obligation"). The security interest may secure future advances, whether those advances are committed or discretionary. Rev. § 9-204(c). Be aware that some courts, in interpreting former Article 9, have been reluctant to enforce security agreement "dragnet" clauses by which all future obligations under unrelated credit facilities later established between the debtor and the secured party are also secured under the security agreement unless, at the time when those unrelated facilities are documented, they expressly provide that the obligations under them are secured by the security interest granted in the earlier security agreement. Although this interpretation is largely rejected by Article 9 (*see* Comment 5 of Rev. § 9-204), the better practice is for the secured party, in entering into a later, unrelated credit facility, to provide in the documentation authenticated by the debtor that the obligations under that credit facility are likewise secured upon the terms of the earlier authenticated security agreement. Without a definition or other statement in the security agreement of what constitutes a default, it may be unclear under what circumstances a secured party is entitled to exercise rights under part 6 of Article 9 of the UCC. This is because, although part 6 refers to the secured party's rights as secured party arising after "default" (*see* Rev. § 9-601(a)), neither Article 9 nor any other provision of the UCC defines what a default is.

2.    **Grant of Security Interest.**[3] The Debtor hereby grants to the Secured Party, to secure the payment and performance in full of all of the Obligations, a security interest in and so pledges and assigns to the Secured Party the following properties, assets and rights of the Debtor, wherever located, whether now owned or hereafter acquired or arising, and all proceeds and products thereof (all of the same being hereinafter called the "Collateral"): all personal and fixture property of every kind and nature including without limitation all goods (including inventory, equipment and any accessions thereto), instruments (including promissory notes), documents, accounts (including health-care-insurance receivables), chattel paper (whether tangible or electronic), deposit accounts, letter-of-credit rights (whether or not the letter of credit is evidenced by a writing), commercial tort claims [*include specific description of commercial tort claims existing at execution of security agreement*], securities and all other investment property, supporting obligations, any other contract rights or rights to the payment of money, insurance claims and proceeds, and all general intangibles (including all payment intangibles). The Secured Party acknowledges that the attachment of its security interest in any additional commercial tort claim as original collateral is subject to the Debtor's compliance with § 4.7.

---

3.    The better practice is for a security agreement to contain specific "granting" language evidencing the intent of the debtor to grant a security interest to the secured party. Words such as "grant a security interest," "pledge" and "assign" are considered synonymous under Revised Article 9 (*see* Rev. § 9-109(a)(1)("regardless of its form")) but may be useful additions or clarifications where non-Article 9 collateral, especially collateral excluded from Article 9 by Rev. § 9-109(c) & (d), is included within the collateral in which a security interest is being granted under the security agreement. Referring to collateral "wherever located" negates any implication that only collateral in one location or jurisdiction was intended to be included in the grant of the security interest and may also afford the secured party an opportunity to cause steps to be taken for the perfection of its security interest in foreign jurisdictions, if appropriate. The phrase "whether now owned or hereafter acquired" is a typical "after-acquired property clause" permitted by Rev. § 9-204(a). It is essential to include such a clause in any security agreement where after-acquired property is to be included in the collateral, especially where the collateral, such as inventory and accounts, turns over in the debtor's normal business cycle. Remember that, until the debtor has rights in the collateral or the power to transfer the collateral, the security interest in that collateral cannot attach at all. Rev. § 9-203(b)(2). A security interest in proceeds attaches automatically, even if not specifically mentioned in the security agreement. Rev. §§ 9-102(a)(12)(A), 9-203(f) & 9-315(a)(2). Similarly, if, as part of a manufacturing process, any goods comprised in the collateral become physically united with other goods so that their identity is lost, a security interest in the resulting "products" would normally be included in the collateral, even if not specifically mentioned in the security agreement. *See* Rev. § 9-336. The description of the collateral in the security agreement must "reasonably identify" the collateral. Rev. § 9-108(a). If the collateral does not consist of items that can be readily and easily identified by serial number or the like, it is often useful for the security agreement to describe the collateral by Article 9 collateral types (*e.g.*, "equipment", "inventory", "instruments," "chattel paper," "investment property" and the like). *See* Rev. § 9-108(b)(3). Investment property collateral may be described in the security agreement as investment property or by reference to a securities entitlement, securities account, commodity account, or the underlying financial asset or commodity contract. Rev. § 9-108(d). If a security interest in collateral excluded from Article 9 by Rev. §§ 9-109(c) or (d) (*e.g.*, an excluded insurance claim) is also being taken as collateral, the collateral description in the security agreement should specifically include a description of that collateral. Doing so would confirm that a security interest in the collateral is being granted even though the security interest may be governed under law other than Article 9. Collateral consisting of a commercial tort claim must, however, be described more specifically than merely by Article 9 collateral type. Rev. § 9-108(e)(1). Thus, the granting clause should include a specific description of the commercial tort claim collateral, as well as the commitment of the debtor contained in § 4.7 to amend the security agreement to include similarly specific descriptions of commercial tort claims that arise in the future. Finally, remember that an overly broad description, *i.e.* one that is a broader description than an Article 9 collateral type, such as "all assets" without further reference to Article 9 collateral types or a more specific description, is not a proper collateral description in a security agreement, and is invalid. Rev. § 9-108(c).

3.    **Authorization to File Financing Statements.**[4] The Debtor hereby irrevocably authorizes the Secured Party at any time and from time to time to file in any filing office in any Uniform Commercial Code jurisdiction any initial financing statements and amendments thereto that (a) indicate the Collateral (i) as all assets of the Debtor or words of similar effect, regardless of whether any particular asset comprised in the Collateral falls within the scope of Article 9 of the Uniform Commercial Code of the State or such jurisdiction, or (ii) as being of an equal or lesser scope or with greater detail, and (b) provide any other information required by part 5 of Article 9 of the Uniform Commercial Code of the State, or such other jurisdiction, for the sufficiency or filing office acceptance of any financing statement or amendment, including (i) whether the Debtor is an organization, the type of organization and any organizational identification number issued to the Debtor and, (ii) in the case of a financing statement filed as a fixture filing or indicating Collateral as as-extracted collateral or timber to be cut, a sufficient description of real property to which the Collateral relates. The Debtor agrees to furnish any such information to the Secured Party promptly upon the Secured Party's request. [*The Debtor also ratifies its authorization for the Secured Party to have filed in any Uniform Commercial Code jurisdiction any like initial financing statements or amendments thereto if filed prior to the date hereof.*]

4.    **Other Actions.**[5] To further the attachment, perfection and first priority of, and the ability of the Secured Party to enforce, the Secured Party's security interest in the

---

4.    A security interest in most collateral covered by Revised Article 9 may be perfected by the filing of a financing statement naming the debtor and the secured party or its representative and indicating the collateral. Rev. §§ 9-310(a) and 9-502(a). Financing statement forms, and related forms, are contained as Forms 3.2.1–3.2.7. The debtor's legal name should be inserted on the financing statement. Rev. § 9-503(a). The collateral should be indicated on the financing statement by a description that reasonably identifies the collateral for purposes of the security agreement or, in the case of an "all assets" security interest, which states "all assets", "all personal property" or the like. Rev. § 9-504. The financing statement should be filed in the state where the debtor is located, as determined under Rev. § 9-307, and in the central filing office of that state. Rev. §§ 9-301(1) & 9-501(a)(2). If, however, the financing statement covers timber to be cut or is as-extracted collateral or is filed as a fixture filing, the financing statement should be filed in the recording office in which a mortgage against the applicable real estate would be filed and should also contain additional information, including that relating to the real estate itself. *See* Rev. §§ 9-501(a)(1) & 9-502(b). Although there is no requirement that the financing statement be signed by the debtor, the financing statement will not be effective unless the debtor has authorized the filing. Best practice dictates that the authorization be in a record authenticated by the debtor. Rev. §§ 9-509(a)(1) & 9-510(a). Authorization is automatic for the secured party to file a financing statement indicating collateral that is described no more broadly than in the security agreement. Rev. § 9-509(b)(1). But, if the secured party wishes to use a broader collateral description in the financing statement, including an indication of the collateral as "all assets," "all personal property" or the like, the secured party will need an authorization from the debtor in an authenticated record for the secured party to file the financing statement. That authorization, as § 3 indicates, may be contained in the security agreement itself since the security agreement should be a record signed or otherwise authenticated by the debtor. In addition, if the secured party wishes to file a financing statement in advance of the closing, as permitted by Rev. § 9-502(d), the debtor's authorization in an authenticated record should be obtained by the secured party at or before the time when the filing is made. A form of pre-filing authorization letter, that would serve this purpose, appears as Form 1.3. The italicized language at the end of § 3 is intended as a precautionary ratification by the debtor of its authorization for any such pre-filing made by the secured party, and would not be necessary if the debtor executed an effective pre-filing authorization letter, as in Form 1.3. The secured party may be subject to certain liabilities to the debtor under Article 9 if the secured party files a financing statement against the debtor without the debtor's authorization. Rev. §§ 9-625(b) & (e)(3).

5.    A filed financing statement will not perfect a security interest in certain collateral (*e.g.*, money (Rev. § 9-312(b)(3)). Moreover, even where a filed financing statement would perfect a security interest in certain collateral, other methods of perfection may be required to assure priority of the security interest over the interests of another secured party or another competitor claiming an interest in the collateral, or to insure that the secured party will be able practically to realize the value of the collateral upon enforcement of the security interest. For example, a security interest in a deposit account perfected by control will have priority over a security interest in the deposit account claimed by another secured party as proceeds of other Article 9 collateral and not perfected by control. Rev. § 9-327(1). The provisions of this § 4 highlight additional steps the secured party may wish to consider.

Collateral, and without limitation on the Debtor's other obligations in this Agreement, the Debtor agrees, in each case at the Debtor's expense, to take the following actions with respect to the following Collateral:

4.1.   **Promissory Notes and Tangible Chattel Paper.**[6] If the Debtor shall at any time hold or acquire any promissory notes or tangible chattel paper, the Debtor shall forthwith endorse, assign and deliver the same to the Secured Party, accompanied by such instruments of transfer or assignment duly executed in blank as the Secured Party may from time to time specify.

4.2.   **Deposit Accounts.**[7] For each deposit account that the Debtor at any time opens or maintains, the Debtor shall, at the Secured Party's request and option, pursuant to an agreement in form and substance satisfactory to the Secured Party, either (a) cause the depositary bank to comply at any time with instructions from the Secured Party to such depositary bank directing the disposition of funds from time to time credited to such deposit account, without further consent of the Debtor, or (b) arrange for the Secured Party to become the customer of the depositary bank with respect to the deposit account, with the Debtor being permitted, only with the consent of the Secured Party, to exercise rights to withdraw funds from such deposit account. [*The Secured Party agrees with the Debtor that the Secured Party shall not give any such instructions or withhold any withdrawal rights from the Debtor, unless an Event of Default has occurred and is continuing, or would occur, if effect were given to any withdrawal not otherwise permitted by the Loan Documents.*] The provisions of this paragraph shall not apply to (i) any deposit account for which the Debtor, the depositary bank and the Secured Party have entered into a cash collateral agreement specially negotiated among the Debtor, the depositary

---

6.   A security interest in a promissory note or tangible chattel paper may be perfected by filing. Rev. § 9-312(a). But, unless the secured party has possession of the promissory note and all originals of the tangible chattel paper, it runs the risk that another secured party or other purchaser may obtain priority in such collateral by taking possession of the promissory note or originals of the tangible chattel paper priority over the secured party collateral. *See* Rev. §§ 9-330 & 9-331. So that the secured party may easily transfer the collateral to a foreclosure assignee, the secured party should not only take possession of the promissory notes and tangible chattel paper but also obtain instruments of transfer or assignment executed in blank by the debtor.

7.   A security interest in a deposit account as original collateral may be perfected only by "control." Rev. § 9-312(b)(1). Control is automatic if the secured party is the depositary bank for that deposit account. Rev. § 9-104(a)(1). Otherwise the secured party will need to enter into a control agreement with the depositary bank or to have the account transferred into the secured party's name. Rev. § 9-104(a)(2) & (3). A form of deposit account control agreement is contained as Form 3.3.1. The control agreement must provide that the depositary bank will comply with instructions from the secured party directing the disposition of funds in the deposit account without the further consent of the debtor. Rev. § 9-104(a)(2). As between the debtor and the secured party, the debtor may be permitted access to the deposit account until a default occurs and the secured party, if it is not itself the depositary bank, has notified the depositary bank, as provided in the control agreement or otherwise in an agreement with the depositary bank, not to permit further withdrawals or dispositions of funds in the deposit account by the debtor. The debtor's access to the deposit account under those circumstances will not result in loss of control. Rev. § 9-104(b). The secured party's security interest in the deposit account perfected by control will have priority over a security interest in the deposit account claimed by another secured party as proceeds of other Article 9 collateral. Rev. § 9-327(1). If, however, the secured party is not the depositary bank, the secured party's security interest will be junior to a security interest in favor of the depositary bank and to the depositary bank's rights of recoupment and setoff, unless the deposit account is in the name of the secured party or the depositary bank has subordinated its security interest and rights of recoupment and setoff in the control agreement or otherwise. Rev. §§ 9-327(3) & (4), & 9-340(c). The secured party should be cautious, for legal or reputational risk reasons, not to take a security interest in any payroll account or in any deposit account that is maintained by the debtor as a fiduciary account for others, such as payroll or sale or use tax accounts.

bank and the Secured Party for the specific purpose set forth therein, (ii) a deposit account for which the Secured Party is the depositary bank and is in automatic control, and (iii) deposit accounts specially and exclusively used for payroll, payroll taxes and other employee wage and benefit payments to or for the benefit of the Debtor's salaried employees [*Specify other fiduciary or escrow deposit accounts, if applicable.*]

4.3.    **Investment Property.**[8] If the Debtor shall at any time hold or acquire any certificated securities, the Debtor shall forthwith endorse, assign and deliver the same to

---

8.    A security interest in investment property may be perfected by filing. Rev. § 9-312(a). But, as with deposit accounts, unless the secured party has control of the investment property, it runs the risk that another secured party or other purchaser may, by taking control of the investment property, obtain priority over the secured party that perfected its security interest in this collateral merely by the filing. *See* Rev. § 9-328(1). A form of securities account control agreement is contained as Form 3.3.2.

If the investment property is a certificated security in bearer form, the secured party takes control of the certificated security by taking possession of the security certificate. UCC §§ 8-106(a), 8-301(a) & Rev. § 9-106(a). A form of pledge agreement that may be used to perfect a possessory security interest in a certificated security appears as Form 3.6.

If the investment property is a certificated security in registered form, the secured party takes control of the certificated security by taking possession of the security certificate and obtaining an indorsement on the security certificate or an accompanying stock power indorsed to the secured party or in blank or by arranging for the security certificate to be registered on the books of the issuer in the name of the secured party. UCC §§ 8-106(b), 8-301(a) & 9-106(a).

If the investment property is an uncertificated security, the secured party takes control of the uncertificated security by entering into a control agreement with the issuer or by arranging for the uncertificated security to be registered on the books of the issuer in the name of the secured party. UCC §§ 8-106(c), 8-301(b) & 9-106(a). The control agreement must provide that the issuer will comply with instructions from the secured party without the further consent of the debtor. UCC § 8-106(c)(2).

If the investment property comprises financial assets credited to a securities account, and the secured party is the securities intermediary, the securities intermediary automatically has control. UCC §§ 8-106(e) & Rev. § 9-106(a). Otherwise, the secured party will need to enter into a control agreement with the securities intermediary or to have the securities account transferred into the secured party's name as entitlement holder. UCC §§ 8-106(d), & Rev. § 9-106(a). The control agreement must provide that the securities intermediary will comply with entitlement orders from the secured party without the further consent of the debtor. UCC § 8-106(d)(2). As between the debtor and the secured party, the debtor may be permitted to deal with the securities account until a default occurs and the secured party, if it is not itself the securities intermediary, has notified the securities intermediary, as provided in the control agreement or otherwise in an agreement with the securities intermediary, not to deal with the securities account. The debtor's ability to deal with the securities account under those circumstances will not result in loss of control. UCC § 8-106(f). The secured party's security interest in the financial assets perfected by control will have priority over a security interest in the financial assets claimed by another secured party as proceeds of other Article 9 collateral (if not perfected by control). Rev. § 9-328(1). However, unless the secured party is the securities intermediary, the secured party's security interest will be junior to a security interest in favor of the securities intermediary unless the securities intermediary has subordinated its security interest in the control agreement or otherwise. Rev. § 9-328(3).

If the investment property is a commodity contract carried in a commodity account, and the secured party is the commodity intermediary, the commodity intermediary automatically has control. Rev. § 9-106(b)(1). Otherwise, the secured party will need to enter into a control agreement with the debtor and the commodity intermediary, and the control agreement must provide that the commodity intermediary will comply with directions from the secured party without the further consent of the debtor. Rev. § 9-106(b)(2). The secured party's security interest in the commodity contract perfected by control will have priority over a security interest in the commodity contract claimed by another secured party as proceeds of other Article 9 collateral. Rev. § 9-328(1). However, unless the secured party is the commodity intermediary, the secured party's security interest will be junior to a security interest in favor of the commodity intermediary, unless the commodity intermediary has subordinated its security interest in the control agreement or otherwise. Rev. § 9-328(4).

If the investment property is a certificated security in registered form, and the secured party takes possession of the security certificate but does not obtain an indorsement on the security certificate or an accompanying stock power indorsed to the secured party or in blank, the secured party has not obtained control. However, the security interest is perfected, and it prevails over another security interest in the certificated security perfected merely by filing. Rev. §§ 9-313 & 9-328(5).

the Secured Party, accompanied by such instruments of transfer or assignment duly executed in blank as the Secured Party may from time to time specify. If any securities now or hereafter acquired by the Debtor are uncertificated and are issued to the Debtor or its nominee directly by the issuer thereof, the Debtor shall immediately notify the Secured Party thereof and, at the Secured Party's request and option, pursuant to an agreement in form and substance satisfactory to the Secured Party, either (a) cause the issuer to agree to comply with instructions from the Secured Party as to such securities, without further consent of the Debtor or such nominee, or (b) arrange for the Secured Party to become the registered owner of the securities. If any securities, whether certificated or uncertificated, or other investment property now or hereafter acquired by the Debtor are held by the Debtor or its nominee through a securities intermediary or commodity intermediary, the Debtor shall immediately notify the Secured Party thereof and, at the Secured Party's request and option, pursuant to an agreement in form and substance satisfactory to the Secured Party, either (i) cause such securities intermediary or (as the case may be) commodity intermediary to agree to comply with entitlement orders or other instructions from the Secured Party to such securities intermediary as to such securities or other investment property, or (as the case may be) to apply any value distributed on account of any commodity contract as directed by the Secured Party to such commodity intermediary, in each case without further consent of the Debtor or such nominee, or (ii) in the case of financial assets or other investment property held through a securities intermediary, arrange for the Secured Party to become the entitlement holder with respect to such investment property, with the Debtor being permitted, only with the consent of the Secured Party, to exercise rights to withdraw or otherwise deal with such investment property. [*The Secured Party agrees with the Debtor that the Secured Party shall not give any such entitlement orders or instructions or directions to any such issuer, securities intermediary or commodity intermediary, and shall not withhold its consent to the exercise of any withdrawal or dealing rights by the Debtor, unless an Event of Default has occurred and is continuing, or, after giving effect to any such investment and withdrawal rights not otherwise permitted by the Loan Documents, would occur.*] The provisions of this paragraph shall not apply to any financial assets credited to a securities account for which the Secured Party is the securities intermediary.

4.4.    **Collateral in the Possession of a Bailee.**[9] If any Collateral is at any time in the possession of a bailee, the Debtor shall promptly notify the Secured Party thereof and, at the Secured Party's request and option, shall promptly obtain an acknowledgement from the bailee, in form and substance satisfactory to the Secured Party, that the bailee holds such Collateral for the benefit of the Secured Party, and that such bailee agrees to comply, without further consent of the Debtor, with instructions from the Secured Party as to such Collateral. [*The Secured Party agrees with the Debtor that the*

---

9.    Even if a security interest in collateral in possession of a bailee is perfected by filing, the secured party runs the risk that another secured party or other purchaser may, by taking possession of certain collateral, obtain priority in the collateral. *See, e.g.,* Rev. §§ 9-328(5)(certificated securities), 9-330 (tangible chattel paper and instruments) & 9-331 (negotiable collateral generally). If possession is a permitted method of perfection for a security interest in the collateral and the bailee acknowledges in an authenticated record that the bailee is holding the collateral for the benefit of the secured party, the secured party's security interest will be perfected by possession. Moreover, the bailee acknowledgement will also assure the secured party priority in the collateral over other secured parties who have perfected a security interest in the same collateral only by filing. Rev. §§ 9-310(b)(6) & 9-313.

*Secured Party shall not give any such instructions unless an Event of Default has occurred and is continuing or would occur after taking into account any action by the Debtor with respect to the bailee.*]

4.5.    **Electronic Chattel Paper and Transferable Records.**[10] If the Debtor at any time holds or acquires an interest in any electronic chattel paper or any "transferable record," as that term is defined in § 201 of the federal Electronic Signatures in Global and National Commerce Act, or in § 16 of the Uniform Electronic Transactions Act as in effect in any relevant jurisdiction, the Debtor shall promptly notify the Secured Party thereof and, at the request and option of the Secured Party, shall take such action as the Secured Party may reasonably request to vest in the Secured Party control, under § 9-105 of the Uniform Commercial Code, of such electronic chattel paper or control under § 201 of the federal Electronic Signatures in Global and National Commerce Act or, as the case may be, § 16 of the Uniform Electronic Transactions Act, as so in effect in such jurisdiction, of such transferable record. [*The Secured Party agrees with the Debtor that the Secured Party will arrange, pursuant to procedures satisfactory to the Secured Party and so long as such procedures will not result in the Secured Party's loss of control, for the Debtor to make alterations to the electronic chattel paper or transferable record permitted under UCC § 9-105 or, as the case may be, § 201 of the federal Electronic Signatures in Global and National Commerce Act or § 16 of the Uniform Electronic Transactions Act for a party in control to make without loss of control, unless an Event of Default has occurred and is continuing or would occur after taking into account any action by the Debtor with respect to such electronic chattel paper or transferable record.*]

4.6.    **Letter-of-Credit Rights.**[11] If the Debtor is at any time a beneficiary under a letter of credit, the Debtor shall promptly notify the Secured Party thereof and, at the request and option of the Secured Party, the Debtor shall, pursuant to an agreement in

---

10.  A security interest in electronic chattel paper may be perfected by filing. Rev. § 9-312(a). But, as with deposit accounts and investment property, unless the secured party has control of the electronic chattel paper, it runs the risk that another secured party or purchaser may, by taking control of it, obtain priority over the secured party that perfected its security interest in this collateral merely by the filing. *See* Rev. § 9-330. To obtain control, only one authoritative copy of the record constituting the intangible chattel paper must exist. Rev. § 9-105(1). That copy must identify the secured party of record, be maintained by the secured party or its designated custodian, and be capable of revision only with the participation of the secured party. Rev. § 9-105(2). Any copy that is not the authoritative copy must be identifiable as a copy that is not the authoritative copy, and any revision to the authoritative copy must be readily identifiable as authorized or unauthorized. Rev. § 9-105(5) & (6).

In addition, Section 201 of the federal Electronic Signatures in Global and National Commerce Act (Pub. L. 106-229, codified at 15 U.S.C. §§ 7001 to 7006, 7021 & 7031) ("E-Sign") contains a similar concept of control for certain electronic promissory notes secured by an interest in real property, and § 16 of the Uniform Electronic Transactions Act ("UETA") likewise contains a similar concept of control for certain electronic promissory notes, documents and chattel paper, whereby, in each case, the party in control of the so-called "transferable record" has priority. Since priority under E-Sign or UETA as against the interest of a perfected Article 9 secured party is unclear, a prudent secured party may wish to take control of any E-Sign- or UETA-defined "transferable record" comprising collateral as it would intangible chattel paper.

11.  Article 9 refers to a debtor's right as beneficiary of a letter of credit to receive the proceeds of the letter of credit if and when the debtor makes a complying draw on the letter of credit as a "letter-of-credit right." Rev. § 9-102(a)(51). If the letter of credit supports the payment or performance of an account, chattel paper, a document, a general intangible, an instrument or investment property (a "supported obligation"), the letter-of-credit right is also a "supporting obligation." Rev. § 9-102(a)(77). If the secured party's security interest in a supported obligation has attached, its security interest in the letter-of-credit right as a supporting obligation also attaches, automatically. Rev. § 9-203(f). If the secured party's security interest in the supported obligation is perfected, its security interest in the letter-of-credit right as a supporting obligation is likewise perfected, automatically. Rev. § 9-308(d). Although the secured party's security interest in a letter-of-credit right may be perfected as a supporting obligation, the secured party will have no right to receive the proceeds of a drawing under the letter of credit directly from the issuer or any

form and substance satisfactory to the Secured Party, either (i) arrange for the issuer and any confirmer or other nominated person of such letter of credit to consent to an assignment to the Secured Party of the proceeds of the letter of credit, or (ii) arrange for the Secured Party to become the transferee beneficiary of the letter of credit, with the Secured Party agreeing, in each case, that the proceeds of the letter to credit are to be applied [*as provided in the Credit Agreement*].

4.7 **Commercial Tort Claims.**[12] If the Debtor shall at any time hold or acquire a commercial tort claim [in addition to those listed in § 2], the Debtor shall immediately notify the Secured Party in a writing signed by the Debtor of the particulars thereof and grant to the Secured Party in such writing a security interest therein and in the proceeds thereof, all upon the terms of this Agreement, with such writing to be in form and substance satisfactory to the Secured Party.[13]

4.8. **Other Actions as to Any and All Collateral.**[14] The Debtor further agrees, at the request and option of the Secured Party, to take any and all other actions the Secured

---

confirmer without the consent of the issuer or such confirmer. Rev. § 9-409(b). In addition, the secured party's security interest in the letter-of-credit right as a supporting obligation will be junior to a security interest perfected by control or to the interest of a transferee beneficiary of the letter of credit. UCC § 5-114(e) & Rev. § 9-329(1). To protect itself against subordination to a control party, the secured party itself may wish to obtain control of the letter-of-credit right against the issuer and any confirmer. For the secured party to obtain control of a letter-of-credit right against the issuer or any confirmer, the issuer or such confirmer must consent to an assignment of the proceeds of a drawing under the letter of credit to the secured party. Rev. § 9-107. This step usually entails the completion of a standard assignment of proceeds form available from the issuer or confirmer and the payment of a small fee to the issuer or confirmer. A form of assignment of proceeds of letter of credit is contained as Form 3.4. However, even if the secured party obtains control of the letter-of-credit right, its interest will be junior to that of a transferee beneficiary of the letter of credit. UCC § 5-114(e). If the secured party is concerned about the risk that the debtor may transfer the letter to a transferee beneficiary, the secured party itself may wish to consider becoming a transferee beneficiary of the letter of the credit. To do so, the debtor must request the transfer from the issuer on the issuer's standard form and pay a small fee. The transfer may also require the issuer's consent, which the issuer may refuse if the letter of credit does not provide that it is transferable. *See* UCC § 5-112. There is, however, a disadvantage to the secured party becoming the transferee beneficiary. In order to draw under the letter of credit, the secured party itself will usually have to meet all of the conditions to draw, including obtaining all required documents and making all required warranties. UCC § 5-110. To avoid obtaining the documents required for presentation, assuming any endorsement or other signature liability on the documents presented, or assuming warranty liability, often the secured party will be content merely to become the assignee of the proceeds of the letter of credit.

12. If the collateral is to comprise a commercial tort claim as original collateral, the commercial tort claim must be described more specifically than by Article 9 collateral type. Rev. § 9-108(e)(1); *see also* the last sentence of § 2 of this Form. In addition, a mere after-acquired property clause in the security agreement is not sufficient to permit a security interest in the commercial tort claim to attach as original collateral. Rev. § 9-204(b)(2). A security agreement will, in general, cover a later-arising commercial tort claim only if the security agreement is amended or supplemented to describe the claim with requisite specificity. Section 4.7 contemplates such an amendment or supplement to the security agreement.

13. The secured party may wish to require that the notification be deemed an amendment to the security agreement so as to effect attachment at the time of notification.

14. The debtor should covenant to take any other action necessary or advisable for the security interest in the collateral to attach, become perfected, attain the agreed priority or be capable of being enforced. These actions may include compliance with requirements under former Article 9, if in effect in any applicable state; compliance with certificate of title statutes for titled goods (Rev. §§ 9-311(a)(2) & (3)); compliance with federal law, especially in the case of federally regulated intellectual property (*see* §§ 5.2 & 5.3 of this Form, below), or international treaties (Rev. §§ 9-109(c)(1) & 9-311(a)(1)); compliance with any statute, apart from Article 9, governing security interests granted by governments or governmental agencies (Rev. §§ 9-109(c)(2) & (3)); obtaining governmental and third party waivers, consents and approvals where still required notwithstanding the anti-assignment override provisions of Rev. §§ 9-406, 9-407 & 9-408 (*see, e.g.*, Rev. § 9-408(d)); obtaining waivers or subordinations from holders of liens excluded from Revised Article 9, such as landlord liens that are not agricultural liens; and complying with any filing requirement in a foreign jurisdiction, especially in the case of a foreign debtor (*see* Rev. § 9-307(c)) or collateral located in the foreign jurisdiction.

Party may determine to be necessary or useful for the attachment, perfection and first priority of, and the ability of the Secured Party to enforce, the Secured Party's security interest in any and all of the Collateral, including, without limitation, (a) executing, delivering and, where appropriate, filing financing statements and amendments relating thereto under the Uniform Commercial Code, to the extent, if any, that the Debtor's signature thereon is required therefor, (b) causing the Secured Party's name to be noted as secured party on any certificate of title for a titled good if such notation is a condition to attachment, perfection or priority of, or ability of the Secured Party to enforce, the Secured Party's security interest in such Collateral, (c) complying with any provision of any statute, regulation or treaty of the United States as to any Collateral if compliance with such provision is a condition to attachment, perfection or priority of, or ability of the Secured Party to enforce, the Secured Party's security interest in such Collateral, (d) obtaining governmental and other third party waivers, consents and approvals in form and substance satisfactory to Secured Party, including, without limitation, any consent of any licensor, lessor or other person obligated on Collateral, (e) obtaining waivers from mortgagees and landlords in form and substance satisfactory to the Secured Party and (f) taking all actions under any earlier versions of the Uniform Commercial Code or under any other law, as reasonably determined by the Secured Party to be applicable in any relevant Uniform Commercial Code or other jurisdiction, including any foreign jurisdiction.

5.    **Relation to Other Security Documents.**[15] The provisions of this Agreement supplement the provisions of any real estate mortgage or deed of trust granted by the Debtor to the Secured Party which secures the payment or performance of any of the Obligations. Nothing contained in any such real estate mortgage or deed of trust shall derogate from any of the rights or remedies of the Secured Party hereunder. [*In addition to the provisions of this Agreement being so read and construed with any such mortgage or deed of trust, the provisions of this Agreement shall be read and construed with the other Security Documents referred to below in the manner so indicated.*]

[5.1. **Pledge Agreement.** *Concurrently herewith the Debtor is executing and delivering to the Secured Party [pledge agreement(s)] pursuant to which the Debtor is pledging to the Secured Party all the shares of the capital stock [or other certificates securities] of [the Borrower's subsidiary or subsidiaries]. Such pledge(s) shall be governed by the terms of [such pledge agreement(s)] and not by the terms of this Agreement].*][16]

[5.2. **[Patent], [Trademark], [Copyright] Security Agreements.**[17] *Concurrently herewith the Debtor is [also] executing and delivering to the Secured Party the [Patent] [Trademark] [Copyright] Security Agreements pursuant to which the Debtor is granting to the Secured Party security interests in certain Collateral consisting of [patents and patent rights], [trademarks, service marks and trademark and service mark rights, together with the goodwill appurtenant thereto], [copyrights, and copyright registrations]. The provisions of*

---

15. If some of the collateral is covered by a more specific security agreement than the general security agreement, cross-references to the more specific security agreement are often appropriate to avoid conflicting provisions between the two security agreements. For example, forms of security agreement to be used with specific types of intellectual property are contained as Forms 2.2–2.4.

16. A form of pledge agreement appears as Form 3.6.

17. Forms of patent, trademark and copyright security agreements appear as Forms 2.2–2.4. They may be used in addition to, or in lieu of, this security agreement, to cover the applicable type of intellectual property collateral.

*the [Patent] [Trademark] [Copyright] Security Agreements are supplemental to the provisions of this Agreement, and nothing contained in the [Patent], [Trademark] [Copyright] Security Agreement[s] shall derogate from any of the rights or remedies of the Secured Party hereunder. Neither the delivery of, nor anything contained in, the [Patent] [Trademark] [Copyright] Security Agreement[s] shall be deemed to prevent or postpone the time of attachment or perfection of any security interest in such Collateral created hereby.]*

[5.3. **Copyright Memorandum.** *Concurrently herewith the Debtor is executing and delivering to the Secured Party for recording in the United States Copyright Office (the "Copyright Office") a Memorandum of Grant of Security Interest in Copyrights. The Debtor represents and warrants to the Secured Party that such Memorandum identifies all now existing material copyrights and other rights in and to all material copyrightable works of the Debtor, identified, where applicable, by title, author and/or Copyright Office registration number and date. [The Debtor represents and warrants to the Secured Party that it has registered all material copyrights with the Copyright Office, as identified in such Memorandum.] The Debtor covenants, promptly following the Debtor's acquisition thereof, to provide to the Secured Party like identifications of all material copyrights and other rights in and to all material copyrightable works hereafter acquired by the Debtor, to register such copyrights with the Copyright Office, and to execute and deliver to the Secured Party a supplemental Memorandum of Grant of Security Interest in Copyrights, in form and substance satisfactory to the Secured Party, modified to reflect such subsequent acquisitions and registrations.]*

6. **Representations and Warranties Concerning Debtor's Legal Status.** The Debtor has previously delivered to the Secured Party a certificate signed by the Debtor and entitled "Perfection Certificate" (the "Perfection Certificate").[18] The Debtor represents and warrants to the Secured Party as follows: (a) the Debtor's exact legal name is that indicated on the Perfection Certificate and on the signature page hereof, (b) the Debtor is an organization of the type, and is organized in the jurisdiction set forth in the Perfection Certificate, (c) the Perfection Certificate accurately sets forth the Debtor's organizational identification number or accurately states that the Debtor has none, (d) the Perfection

---

18. A form of perfection certificate is attached at the end of this form security agreement. The perfection certificate is designed to solicit from the debtor, well in advance of the closing of the credit transaction, the information that is necessary for the secured party to perfect its security interest by filing and to determine whether any earlier filings covering the same collateral exist. The perfection certificate solicits that information as required by parts 3 and 5 of Revised Article 9 and as required under the transition rules of part 7 of Revised Article 9. Those transition rules require, at least until June 30, 2006, that UCC searches continue to be made in the states and offices in which filings would have been made under former Article 9 to discover filings made before the effective date of Revised Article 9 (*e.g.*, July 1, 2001). *See* Rev. § 9-705(c). Section 6 of this form security agreement requires verification of the debtor's exact legal name since this is the name of the debtor that should be placed in the secured party's financing statement under the debtor name block and since the secured party would order UCC searches against the debtor under this name. *See* Rev. §§ 9-503(a) & 9-506. It requires verification also of the information required to determine in which state the secured party must file a financing statement against the debtor to perfect its security interest by filing and in which state to conduct a UCC search against the debtor under Revised Article 9 itself. For example, if the debtor is a corporation organized in a single state, or the debtor is another type of registered organization as defined in Rev. § 9-102(a)(70), the debtor will be located for purposes of Revised Article 9 in the state in which the debtor is organized. Rev. § 9-307(e). If, instead, the debtor is a general partnership, the debtor will be located in the state in which it has its chief executive office. Rev. § 9-307(b)(2) & (3). Perfection by filing is accomplished by filing a financing statement in the state in which the debtor is located unless the collateral is timber to be cut, as-extracted collateral or is a fixture filing and the applicable real estate is located in another state. Rev. § 9-301.

Certificate accurately sets forth the Debtor's place of business or, if more than one, its chief executive office, as well as the Debtor's mailing address, if different, (e) all other information set forth on the Perfection Certificate pertaining to the Debtor is accurate and complete, and (f) that there has been no change in any information provided in the Perfection Certificate since the date on which it was executed by the Debtor.

7.    **Covenants Concerning Debtor's Legal Status.**[19] The Debtor covenants with the Secured Party as follows: (a) without providing at least 30 days prior written notice to the Secured Party, the Debtor will not change its name, its place of business or, if more than one, chief executive office, or its mailing address or organizational identification number if it has one, (b) if the Debtor does not have an organizational identification number and later obtains one, the Debtor shall forthwith notify the Secured Party of such organizational identification number, and (c) the Debtor will not change its type of organization, jurisdiction of organization or other legal structure.

8.    **Representations and Warranties Concerning Collateral, etc.**[20] The Debtor further represents and warrants to the Secured Party as follows: (a) the Debtor is the owner of [*or has other rights in or power to transfer*] the Collateral, free from any right or claim or any person or any adverse lien, security interest or other encumbrance, except for the security interest created by this Agreement [*and other liens permitted by the Credit Agreement*], (b) none of the Collateral constitutes, or is the proceeds of, "farm products" as defined in § 9-102(a)(34) of the Uniform Commercial Code of the State, (c) [*except for*

---

19.  The debtor should covenant to provide to the secured party advance notice of the debtor's change of legal name, place of business or chief executive office (if the debtor's location is determined under Rev. § 9-307 by its place of business or chief executive office) or any change in the debtor's type of organization (*e.g.*, if the debtor is a limited partnership and converts to a limited liability company) or change of jurisdiction of organization (*e.g.*, if the debtor reincorporates in another state). In these situations, the secured party may need to take appropriate steps, such as amending its financing statement or filing a new financing statement in the destination location, in order to avoid the lapse of perfection or loss of priority of its security interest. *See* Rev. §§ 9-316(a)(2)(change of debtor's location when the security interest had attached and was perfected at the time of the change), 9-316(a)(3)(a transferee of the collateral becoming a debtor, or a new debtor becoming bound by the security agreement, when the security interest had attached and was perfected at the time of the transfer or the new debtor becoming bound), 9-507(c)(change of debtor's name) & 9-508 (assets acquired by a new debtor after the new debtor is bound by another debtor's security agreement). Other changes in status may not require an amendment of the financing statement for the secured party to preserve the perfection or priority of its security interest. *See* Rev. §§ 9-338 ("incorrect at the time the financing statement was filed") & 9-507(b). But prudence may suggest that the secured party amend that information.

20.  The debtor should represent and warrant to the secured party that the debtor has sufficient right in or power to transfer the collateral for the secured party's security interest to attach, Rev. § 9-203(b)(2), and that the collateral is either not encumbered or, if encumbered, the encumbrances have been approved by the secured party. If any of the collateral constitutes "farm products" as defined in Rev. § 9-102(a)(34), the debtor should inform the secured party, and the secured party may wish to take appropriate steps to obtain governmental consents under federal agricultural entitlement programs, to obtain waivers or subordinations from suppliers whose claims for unpaid agricultural supplies may have priority under federal law (*e.g.*, the Packers and Stockyards Act of 1921, 7 U.S.C. § 196, and the Perishable Agricultural Commodities Act, 1930, 7 U.S.C. § 499e(c)), or to preserve its security interest or the proceeds, following disposition of the farm product collateral, under the Food Security Act of 1985, 7 U.S.C. § 1631. If any of the accounts or other rights to payment comprised in the collateral are owed by governmental account debtors, the debtor should inform the secured party, and the secured party may wish to take steps under the federal Assignment of Claims Act of 1940, 31 U.S.C. § 3727 and 41 U.S.C. § 15, or any similar state statute to receive payments directly from the governmental account debtors. As a supplement to the secured party's due diligence, the debtor should represent and warrant that the debtor has complied with labor and environmental laws where failure of the debtor to comply may result in a governmental authority having priority in the collateral. *See, e.g.*, Mass. Gen. Laws ch. 21E, § 13 (environmental lien).

*[describe]]* none of the account debtors or other persons obligated on any of the Collateral is a governmental authority covered by the Federal Assignment of Claims Act or like federal, state or local statute or rule in respect of such Collateral, (d) the Debtor holds no commercial tort claim except as indicated on the Perfection Certificate, and (e) the Debtor has at all times operated its business in compliance with all applicable provisions of the federal Fair Labor Standards Act, as amended, and with all applicable provisions of federal, state and local statutes and ordinances dealing with the control, shipment, storage or disposal of hazardous materials or substances, (f) all other information set forth on the Perfection Certificate pertaining to the Collateral is accurate and complete, and (g) that there has been no change in any information provided in the Perfection Certificate since the date on which it was executed by the Debtor.

9.    **Covenants Concerning Collateral, etc.**[21] The Debtor further covenants with the Secured Party as follows: (a) the Collateral, to the extent not delivered to the Secured Party pursuant to § 4, will be kept at those locations listed on the Perfection Certificate and the Debtor will not remove the Collateral from such locations, without providing at least thirty days prior written notice to the Secured Party, (b) except for the security interest herein granted [*and liens permitted by the Credit Agreement*], the Debtor shall be the owner of [*or have other rights in*] the Collateral free from any right or claim of any other person, lien, security interest or other encumbrance, and the Debtor shall defend the same against all claims and demands of all persons at any time claiming the same or any interests therein adverse to the Secured Party, (c) the Debtor shall not pledge, mortgage or create, or suffer to exist any right of any person in or claim by any person to the Collateral, or any security interest, lien or encumbrance in the Collateral in favor of any person, other than the Secured Party [*except for liens permitted by the Credit Agreement*], (d) the Debtor will keep the Collateral in good order and repair and will not use the same in violation of law or any policy of insurance thereon, (e) [*as provided in the Credit Agreement,*] the Debtor will permit the Secured Party, or its designee, to inspect the Collateral at any reasonable time, wherever located, (f) the Debtor will pay promptly when due all taxes, assessments, governmental charges and levies upon the Collateral or incurred in connection with the use or operation of such Collateral or incurred in connection with this Agreement, (g) the Debtor will continue to operate, its business in compliance with all applicable provisions of the federal Fair Labor Standards Act, as amended,

---

21.   The debtor should covenant to maintain the collateral, to permit its inspection, to keep the collateral free of encumbrances, other than those permitted in the security agreement or other credit documents, and to comply with applicable law and the requirements of the debtor's insurers. The debtor should also covenant to keep collateral at locations known to the secured party so that the secured party may know where to investigate the existence of non-Article 9 liens on the collateral, such as judgment, tax and environmental liens and, in the case of collateral located in a former Article 9 state or in a foreign jurisdiction, the secured party may take the appropriate steps to perfect and insure the priority of its security interest in that collateral. The secured party would not normally prohibit sales of inventory by the debtor in the ordinary course of the debtor's business since typically such sales would be intended to generate the cash to pay the secured obligations. See Rev. § 9-320(a). Similarly, the secured party would not normally prohibit ordinary course leasing or licensing if the debtor were in the leasing or licensing business. See Rev. § 9-321. But other dispositions of collateral, particularly those outside of the debtor's ordinary course of business, should require the secured party's authorization for that collateral to be disposed of free of the secured party's security interest. Rev. § 9-315(a)(1). Specifying in advance in the security agreement or other credit documents what dispositions are permitted may avoid the annoyance to the secured party of routine collateral release requests by the debtor later, and, if such specifications are thoughtfully crafted, they may also minimize arguments by the debtor that the secured party had tacitly authorized a disposition not permitted by those specifications.

and with all applicable provisions of federal, state and local statutes and ordinances dealing with the control, shipment, storage or disposal of hazardous materials or substances, and (h) the Debtor will not sell or otherwise dispose, or offer to sell or otherwise dispose, of the Collateral or any interest therein except for [*(i)*] sales [*and leases*] of inventory [*and licenses of general intangibles*] in the ordinary course of business [*and (ii) so long as no Event of Default has occurred and is continuing, sales or other dispositions of obsolescent items of equipment consistent with past practices*] [*dispositions permitted by the Credit Agreement*].

### 10.   Insurance.

10.1.   **Maintenance of Insurance.**[22] The Debtor will maintain with financially sound and reputable insurers insurance with respect to its properties and business against such casualties and contingencies as shall be in accordance with general practices of businesses engaged in similar activities in similar geographic areas. Such insurance shall be in such minimum amounts that the Debtor will not be deemed a co-insurer under applicable insurance laws, regulations and policies and otherwise shall be in such amounts, contain such terms, be in such forms and be for such periods as may be reasonably satisfactory to the Secured Party. In addition, all such insurance shall be payable to the Secured Party as loss payee [*under a "standard" or "New York" loss payee clause*]. Without limiting the foregoing, the Debtor will (i) keep all of its physical property insured with casualty or physical hazard insurance on an "all risks" basis, with broad form flood and earthquake coverages and electronic data processing coverage, with a full replacement cost endorsement and an "agreed amount" clause in an amount equal to 100% of the full replacement cost of such property, (ii) maintain all such workers' compensation or similar insurance as may be required by law, and (iii) maintain, in amounts [*and with deductibles*] equal to those generally maintained by businesses engaged in similar activities in similar geographic areas, general public liability insurance against claims of bodily injury, death or property damage occurring, on, in or about the properties of the Debtor; business interruption insurance; and product liability insurance.

10.2.   **Insurance Proceeds.**[23] The proceeds of any casualty insurance in respect of any casualty loss of any of the Collateral shall, subject to the rights, if any, of other parties with an interest having priority in the property covered thereby, (i) so long as no Default or Event of Default has occurred and is continuing and to the extent that the amount of such proceeds is less than $_____, be disbursed to the Debtor for direct application by the Debtor solely to the repair or replacement of the Debtor's property so damaged or destroyed, and (ii) in all other circumstances, be held by the Secured Party as cash collateral for the Obligations. The Secured Party may, at its sole option, disburse from time to time all

---

22.   The secured party will want to verify that the collateral is adequately insured. The secured party should obtain certificates of insurance of the collateral; these certificates are issued by the insurance brokers or the insurers themselves. The secured party should be satisfied as to the risks, amounts of insurance, any applicable deductibles and the credit ratings of the insurers. The secured party should also consider supplemental mortgagee coverage whereby an insurer agrees that certain defenses which the insurer may be able to assert against the debtor, such as fraud or arson, the insurer cannot assert against the innocent secured party.

23.   Although insurance proceeds of casualty losses to Article 9 collateral ordinarily will constitute "proceeds" under Article 9 (Rev. § 9-102(a)(64)(E)) and the insurance claims themselves will be within the scope of Article 9 (Rev. § 9-109(d)(8)), the secured party should insist on being named an additional insured (where it has an ownership interest in the collateral) or loss payee (which is more typical) so that insurance proceeds are paid to the secured party directly.

or any part of such proceeds so held as cash collateral, upon such terms and conditions as the Secured Party may reasonably prescribe, for direct application by the Debtor solely to the repair or replacement of the Debtor's property so damaged or destroyed, or the Secured Party may apply all or any part of such proceeds to the Obligations [*with the Commitment (if not then terminated) being reduced by the amount so applied to the Obligations*].

10.3. **Continuation of Insurance.** All policies of insurance shall provide for at least _____ days prior written cancellation notice to the Secured Party.[24] In the event of failure by the Debtor to provide and maintain insurance as herein provided, the Secured Party may, at its option, provide such insurance and charge the amount thereof to the Debtor. The Debtor shall furnish the Secured Party with certificates of insurance and policies evidencing compliance with the foregoing insurance provision.

11. **Collateral Protection Expenses; Preservation of Collateral.**

11.1. **Expenses Incurred by Secured Party.** In the Secured Party's discretion, if the Debtor fails to do so, the Secured Party may discharge taxes and other encumbrances at any time levied or placed on any of the Collateral, maintain any of the Collateral, make repairs thereto and pay any necessary filing fees or insurance premiums. The Debtor agrees to reimburse the Secured Party on demand for all expenditures so made.[25] The Secured Party shall have no obligation to the Debtor to make any such expenditures, nor shall the making thereof be construed as the waiver or cure of any Default or Event of Default.

11.2. **Secured Party's Obligations and Duties.**[26] Anything herein to the contrary notwithstanding, the Debtor shall remain obligated and liable under each contract or agreement comprised in the Collateral to be observed or performed by the Debtor thereunder. The Secured Party shall not have any obligation or liability under any such contract or agreement by reason of or arising out of this Agreement or the receipt by the Secured Party of any payment relating to any of the Collateral, nor shall the Secured Party be obligated in any manner to perform any of the obligations of the Debtor under or pursuant to any such contract or agreement, to make inquiry as to the nature or sufficiency of any payment received by the Secured Party in respect of the Collateral or as to the sufficiency of any performance by any party under any such contract or agreement, to present or file any claim, to take any action to enforce any performance or to collect the payment of any amounts which may have been assigned to the Secured Party or to which the Secured Party may be entitled at any time or times. The Secured Party's sole duty with respect to the custody, safe keeping and physical preservation of the Collateral in its possession, under § 9-207 of the Uniform Commercial Code of the State or otherwise, shall

---

24. The secured party should also insist that it be given advance notice by the insurer or insurance broker of any impending cancellation, expiration or other coverage change in the insurance so that the secured party itself may, if necessary, make the premium payments to keep the policy in force. The amount of premiums paid by the secured party in that circumstance would be collateral protection expenses reimbursable to the secured party under § 11.1. Care should be taken that § 10.2 is consistent with any mandatory prepayment and commitment reduction provisions in any loan agreement or other credit document creating or evidencing the obligations secured.

25. The debtor should acknowledge in the security agreement that, if the secured party needs to incur expenses to protect the collateral, those expenses will be added to the secured debt. *See also* Commentary to § 21 of this form.

26. The foregoing language reaffirms that the secured party is assuming no obligation of the debtor to a third party contracting with the debtor merely because the secured party claims a security interest in the debtor's rights under the contract. *See* Rev. § 9-402. It also attempts to define the secured party's standard of care with respect to the collateral consistent with Rev. § 9-207. In particular situations, it may be useful to craft more specific language designed to amplify or limit the secured party's duty of care with respect to special or unusual collateral.

be to deal with such Collateral in the same manner as the Secured Party deals with similar property for its own account.

12. **Securities and Deposits.**[27] The Secured Party may at any time [*following and during the continuance of a Default and Event of Default*], at its option, transfer to itself or any nominee any securities constituting Collateral, receive any income thereon and hold such income as additional Collateral or apply it to the Obligations. Whether or not any Obligations are due, the Secured Party may [*following and during the continuance of a Default and Event of Default*] demand, sue for, collect, or make any settlement or compromise which it deems desirable with respect to the Collateral. Regardless of the adequacy of Collateral or any other security for the Obligations, any deposits or other sums at any time credited by or due from the Secured Party to the Debtor may at any time be applied to or set off against any of the Obligations [*then due and owing*].

13. **Notification to Account Debtors and Other Persons Obligated on Collateral.**[28] [*If [a Default or] an Event of Default shall have occurred and be continuing*], the Debtor

---

27. Cash distributions and other rights in respect of securities directly held by the debtor may be paid or made available directly to the debtor as registered owner of the securities unless the secured party or its nominee has become the nominal registered owner for that collateral. Rev. § 9-207(a). The security agreement should permit the secured party to become the nominal registered owner, either directly or through a nominee, of that collateral if the secured party determines that such an arrangement is necessary or advisable to protect its security interest in that collateral. Although generally contemplated as included in the secured party's collection right in Rev. § 9-607, the security agreement should also more specifically permit the secured party to settle or compromise claims with respect to the collateral. Many security agreements also contain clauses contractually preserving or expanding the secured party's common law rights of recoupment and setoff and for the debtor to waive any common law requirement that other collateral be inadequate before the secured party exercises any right of recoupment or setoff. Often the debtor, in negotiations with the secured party, will request that the secured party not be permitted to exercise any of the rights set forth in § 12 unless the debtor is in default.

28. Many secured credit transactions are structured so that collections of the debtor's accounts and other rights to payment are applied directly to the debtor's loan account with the secured party, while additional advances, often limited under a borrowing formula, are made to the debtor by the secured party to provide funds for the debtor's checks to clear in, and payment orders to be debited to, the debtor's operating account, or otherwise for the debtor to meet its expenses. In these transactions the debtor either collects checks and other items and deposits them directly into a collection account with the secured party or a correspondent bank for transfer to the secured party, or arranges for its account debtors and other persons obligated on collateral to remit funds directly into such a collection account or to a postal lock box. Often payments directed to a postal lock box are sent to a collection account over which the secured party alone has control and from which the secured party applies the proceeds of checks and other items, and funds transfers, either directly against the loan account or into a collection account for later application to the loan account. Other secured credit transactions are structured so that the debtor retains control over its collections of accounts and other rights to payment and elects whether to apply collections against the loan account or not and when to ask for additional advances. In any case, the secured party should retain the right to notify account debtors and other persons obligated on collateral to make payments directly to the secured party upon default by the debtor. Many security agreements, especially those under demand/discretionary lines of credit, permit the secured party to send such notifications to account debtors and other persons obligated on collateral even prior to default as permitted, with the debtor's agreement, by Rev. § 9-607(a). One significant advantage to such pre- and post-default direct collections and loan account application arrangements is that the cash proceeds received and applied by the secured party, without those proceeds having been commingled with other funds of the debtor not constituting proceeds of the secured party's collateral, should be traceable to the secured party's original collateral under Rev. § 9-315. Such direct tracing should enable even an undersecured secured party to avoid a preference attack on "eve of bankruptcy" payments under these arrangements on the grounds the payments were from the secured party's own collateral and therefore had no preferential effect. *See* 11 U.S.C. § 547(b)(5). The secured party's position, of course, is even stronger to the extent that it takes a perfected security interest, as original collateral under Article 9, in the deposit accounts comprising the debtor's cash management system. *See* § 4.2 and commentary to this Form.

shall, at the request and option of the Secured Party, notify account debtors and other persons obligated on any of the Collateral of the security interest of the Secured Party in any account, chattel paper, general intangible, instrument or other Collateral and that payment thereof is to be made directly to the Secured Party or to any financial institution designated by the Secured Party as the Secured Party's agent therefor, and the Secured Party may itself, [*if a Default or an Event of Default shall have occurred and be continuing,*] without notice to or demand upon the Debtor, so notify account debtors and other persons obligated on Collateral. After the making of such a request or the giving of any such notification, the Debtor shall hold any proceeds of collection of accounts, chattel paper, general intangibles, instruments and other Collateral received by the Debtor as trustee for the Secured Party without commingling the same with other funds of the Debtor and shall turn the same over to the Secured Party in the identical form received, together with any necessary endorsements or assignments. The Secured Party shall apply the proceeds of collection of accounts, chattel paper, general intangibles, instruments and other Collateral received by the Secured Party to the Obligations, such proceeds to be immediately credited after final payment in cash or other immediately available funds of the items giving rise to them.

## 14. Power of Attorney.

### 14.1. Appointment and Powers of Secured Party.[29] The Debtor hereby irrevocably constitutes and appoints the Secured Party and any officer or agent thereof, with full power of substitution, as its true and lawful attorneys-in-fact with full irrevocable power and authority in the place and stead of the Debtor or in the Secured Party's own name, for the purpose of carrying out the terms of this Agreement, to take any and all appropriate action and to execute any and all documents and instruments that may be necessary or useful to accomplish the purposes of this Agreement and, without limiting the generality of the foregoing, hereby gives said attorneys the power and right, on behalf of the Debtor, without notice to or assent by the Debtor, to do the following:

> (a) upon the occurrence and during the continuance of [*a Default or*] an Event of Default, generally to sell, transfer, pledge, make any agreement with respect to or otherwise dispose of or deal with any of the Collateral in such manner as is consistent with the Uniform Commercial Code of the State and as fully and completely as though the Secured Party were the absolute owner thereof for all purposes, and to do, at the Debtor's expense, at any time, or from time to time, all acts and things which the Secured Party deems necessary or useful to protect, preserve or realize upon the Collateral and the Secured Party's security interest therein, in order to effect the intent of this Agreement, all at least as fully and effectively as the Debtor might do, including, without limitation, (i) the filing and

---

29. The power of attorney in § 14.1(a) may be particularly important for collateral disposition purposes following the debtor's default, in cases where the collateral is registered in the debtor's name or is in the possession of a third party. Although Article 9 does provide some assistance to the secured party to "clear title" to the collateral upon enforcement of its security interest (Rev. §§ 9-607(b) & 9-619), a power of attorney as such may be more familiar in some circumstances to the title-clearing officials than a reference to a commercial statute. Moreover, the power of attorney may be useful for the secured party to deal with the collateral generally for purposes of effecting its preservation prior to disposition. The power of attorney in § 14.1(b) would be relevant if action is required in a state in which former Article 9 is still in effect.

prosecuting of registration and transfer applications with the appropriate federal, state, local or other agencies or authorities with respect to trademarks, copyrights and patentable inventions and processes, (ii) upon written notice to the Debtor, the exercise of voting rights with respect to voting securities, which rights may be exercised, if the Secured Party so elects, with a view to causing the liquidation of assets of the issuer of any such securities, and (iii) the execution, delivery and recording, in connection with any sale or other disposition of any Collateral, of the endorsements, assignments or other instruments of conveyance or transfer with respect to such Collateral; and

(b)   to the extent that the Debtor's authorization given in §3 is not sufficient, to file such financing statements with respect hereto, with or without the Debtor's signature, or a photocopy of this Agreement in substitution for a financing statement, as the Secured Party may deem appropriate and to execute in the Debtor's name such financing statements and amendments thereto and continuation statements which may require the Debtor's signature.

14.2.  **Ratification by Debtor.** To the extent permitted by law, the Debtor hereby ratifies all that said attorneys shall lawfully do or cause to be done by virtue hereof. This power of attorney is a power coupled with an interest and is irrevocable.

14.3.  **No Duty on Secured Party.** The powers conferred on the Secured Party hereunder are solely to protect its interests in the Collateral and shall not impose any duty upon it to exercise any such powers. The Secured Party shall be accountable only for the amounts that it actually receives as a result of the exercise of such powers, and neither it nor any of its officers, directors, employees or agents shall be responsible to the Debtor for any act or failure to act, except for the Secured Party's own gross negligence or willful misconduct.

15.   **Rights and Remedies.**[30] If an Event of Default shall have occurred and be continuing, the Secured Party, without any other notice to or demand upon the Debtor have in any jurisdiction in which enforcement hereof is sought, in addition to all other rights and remedies, the rights and remedies of a secured party under the Uniform Commercial Code of the State and any additional rights and remedies which may be provided to a

---

30.  The secured party's rights and remedies upon the debtor's default are generally set forth in part 6 of Revised Article 9. Because Article 9 does not define a "default," it will important to define carefully those acts or omissions that give rise to a "Default" or an "Event of Default." Note that this security agreement does not define these terms, but instead defers to the credit (or other) agreement that would likely be entered into in connection with this security agreement, and which would define such terms. While part 6 of Revised Article 9 sets forth the secured party's rights and remedies on the debtor's default, it is often helpful, especially in the case of non-Article 9 personal property collateral, for the debtor to acknowledge in the security agreement what the secured party's rights and remedies are. The secured party in turn owes various duties to the debtor. *See* Rev. § 9-602 and the sections cited therein. Many of these duties may not be waived by the debtor, in the security agreement or otherwise, or may be waived by the debtor only after default. If the secured party has determined a "reasonably convenient" location where, after default, the debtor should assemble the collateral and make it available to the secured party and that determination is not "manifestly unreasonable," that location may be set forth in the security agreement. *See* Rev. §§ 9-603(a) & 9-609(c). Many security agreements set forth a period of time which the parties agree to be a "reasonable notification" period to the debtor in advance of a disposition of collateral by the secured party. Rev. § 9-612(a). Article 9 does provide a "safe harbor" that ten days' prior notice is *per se* reasonable in a transaction in which the debtor is not a consumer. Rev. § 9-612(b). Forms of notification and complaint to be used in connection with the enforcement of a security interest appear as Forms 4.1.1–4.2.

secured party in any jurisdiction in which Collateral is located, including, without limitation, the right to take possession of the Collateral, and for that purpose the Secured Party may, so far as the Debtor can give authority therefor, enter upon any premises on which the Collateral may be situated and remove the same therefrom. The Secured Party may in its discretion require the Debtor to assemble all or any part of the Collateral at such location or locations within the jurisdiction(s) of the Debtor's principal office(s) or at such other locations as the Secured Party may reasonably designate. Unless the Collateral is perishable or threatens to decline speedily in value or is of a type customarily sold on a recognized market, the Secured Party shall give to the Debtor at least five Business Days prior written notice of the time and place of any public sale of Collateral or of the time after which any private sale or any other intended disposition is to be made. The Debtor hereby acknowledges that five Business Days prior written notice of such sale or sales shall be reasonable notice. In addition, the Debtor waives any and all rights that it may have to a judicial hearing in advance of the enforcement of any of the Secured Party's rights and remedies hereunder, including, without limitation, its right following an Event of Default to take immediate possession of the Collateral and to exercise its rights and remedies with respect thereto.

16.   **Standards for Exercising Rights and Remedies.**[31] To the extent that applicable law imposes duties on the Secured Party to exercise remedies in a commercially reasonable manner, the Debtor acknowledges and agrees that it is not commercially unreasonable for the Secured Party (a) to fail to incur expenses reasonably deemed significant by the Secured Party to prepare Collateral for disposition or otherwise to fail to complete raw material or work in process into finished goods or other finished products for disposition, (b) to fail to obtain third party consents for access to Collateral to be disposed of, or to obtain or, if not required by other law, to fail to obtain governmental or third party consents for the collection or disposition of Collateral to be collected or disposed of, (c) to fail to exercise collection remedies against account debtors or other persons obligated on Collateral or to fail to remove liens or encumbrances on or any adverse claims against Collateral, (d) to exercise collection remedies against account debtors and other persons obligated on Collateral directly or through the use of collection agencies and other collection specialists, (e) to advertise dispositions of Collateral through publications or media of general circulation, whether or not the Collateral is of a specialized nature, (f) to contact other persons, whether or not in the same business as the Debtor, for expressions of interest in acquiring all or any portion of the Collateral, (g) to hire one or more professional auctioneers to assist in the disposition of Collateral, whether or not the collateral is of a specialized nature, (h) to dispose of Collateral by utilizing Internet sites that provide for the auction of assets of the types included in the Collateral or that have the reasonable capability of doing so, or that match buyers and sellers of assets, (i) to dispose

---

31.   Although many of the secured party's duties to the debtor may not be waived by the debtor, in the security agreement or otherwise, or may be waived by the debtor only after default, the parties may nevertheless agree in the security agreement to the standards for the secured party to fulfill those duties, so long as they are "not manifestly unreasonable." *See* Rev. § 9-603. Such standards may include setting forth the publications in which a public disposition of the collateral should be advertised, the identity and bidders to be solicited in a private sale, or particular markets in which collateral dispositions should be made. The provisions of § 16 are intended to illustrate how such standards might be crafted.

of assets in wholesale rather than retail markets, (j) to disclaim disposition warranties, (k) to purchase insurance or credit enhancements to insure the Secured Party against risks of loss, collection or disposition of Collateral or to provide to the Secured Party a guaranteed return from the collection or disposition of Collateral, or (l) to the extent deemed appropriate by the Secured Party, to obtain the services of other brokers, investment bankers, consultants and other professionals to assist the Secured Party in the collection or disposition of any of the Collateral. [*Specify other standards applicable to any specific type of Collateral.*] The Debtor acknowledges that the purpose of this § 16 is to provide non-exhaustive indications of what actions or omissions by the Secured Party would fulfill the Secured Party's duties under the Uniform Commercial Code or other law of the State or any other relevant jurisdiction in the Secured Party's exercise of remedies against the Collateral and that other actions or omissions by the Secured Party shall not be deemed to fail to fulfill such duties solely on account of not being indicated in this § 16. Without limitation upon the foregoing, nothing contained in this § 16 shall be construed to grant any rights to the Debtor or to impose any duties on the Secured Party that would not have been granted or imposed by this Agreement or by applicable law in the absence of this § 16.

17. **No Waiver by Secured Party, etc.** The Secured Party shall not be deemed to have waived any of its rights or remedies in respect of the Obligations or the Collateral unless such waiver shall be in writing and signed by the Secured Party. No delay or omission on the part of the Secured Party in exercising any right or remedy shall operate as a waiver of such right or remedy or any other right or remedy. A waiver on any one occasion shall not be construed as a bar to or waiver of any right or remedy on any future occasion. All rights and remedies of the Secured Party with respect to the Obligations or the Collateral, whether evidenced hereby or by any other instrument or papers, shall be cumulative[32] and may be exercised singularly, alternatively, successively or concurrently at such time or at such times as the Secured Party deems expedient.

18. **Suretyship Waivers by Debtor.**[33] The Debtor waives demand, notice, protest, notice of acceptance of this Agreement, notice of loans made, credit extended, Collateral received or delivered or other action taken in reliance hereon and all other demands and notices of any description. With respect to both the Obligations and the Collateral, the Debtor assents to any extension or postponement of the time of payment or any other indulgence, to any substitution, exchange or release of or failure to perfect any security interest in any Collateral, to the addition or release of any party or person primarily or secondarily liable, to the acceptance of partial payment thereon and the settlement, com-

---

32. A secured party's rights under Article 9 are cumulative. Rev. § 9-601(c). But, the secured party should investigate whether, especially when real property collateral in a particular jurisdiction is being taken as well, a "one form of action" or "antideficiency" statute in that jurisdiction is applicable. These statutes often require the secured party to proceed against the real property collateral before or contemporaneously with proceeding against personal property collateral. *Cf.* Rev. § 9-604(a).

33. The debtor may be acting as a surety for a principal obligor. For example, the debtor may be granting a security interest in collateral to the secured party to secure the loan obligations owed to the secured party by a subsidiary of the debtor. In that case, it would be advisable for the secured party to require the debtor, as surety, to waive all suretyship defenses that are capable of being waived under Article 9. *See* RESTATEMENT OF SURETYSHIP AND GUARANTY § 48 (1996).

promising or adjusting of any thereof, all in such manner and at such time or times as the Secured Party may deem advisable. The Secured Party shall have no duty as to the collection or protection of the Collateral or any income therefrom, the preservation of rights against prior parties, or the preservation of any rights pertaining thereto beyond the safe custody thereof as set forth in § 11.2. The Debtor further waives any and all other suretyship defenses.

19. **Marshalling.**[34] The Secured Party shall not be required to marshal any present or future collateral security (including but not limited to the Collateral) for, or other assurances of payment of, the Obligations or any of them or to resort to such collateral security or other assurances of payment in any particular order, and all of its rights and remedies hereunder and in respect of such collateral security and other assurances of payment shall be cumulative and in addition to all other rights and remedies, however existing or arising. To the extent that it lawfully may, the Debtor hereby agrees that it will not invoke any law relating to the marshalling of collateral which might cause delay in or impede the enforcement of the Secured Party's rights and remedies under this Agreement or under any other instrument creating or evidencing any of the Obligations or under which any of the Obligations is outstanding or by which any of the Obligations is secured or payment thereof is otherwise assured, and, to the extent that it lawfully may, the Debtor hereby irrevocably waives the benefits of all such laws.

20. **Proceeds of Dispositions; Expenses.**[35] The Debtor shall pay to the Secured Party on demand any and all expenses, including reasonable attorneys' fees and disbursements, incurred or paid by the Secured Party in protecting, preserving or enforcing the Secured Party's rights and remedies under or in respect of any of the Obligations or any of the Collateral. After deducting all of said expenses, the residue of any proceeds of collection or sale or other disposition of the Collateral shall, to the extent actually received in cash, be applied to the payment of the Obligations in such order or preference as the Secured Party may determine [*or in such order or preference as is provided in the Credit Agreement*], proper allowance and provision being made for any Obligations not then due. Upon the final payment and satisfaction in full of all of the Obligations and after making any payments required by §§ 9-608(a)(1)(C) or 9-615(a)(3) of the Uniform Commercial

---

34. The equitable doctrine of marshalling appears inconsistent with the cumulative nature of the secured party's rights, as contemplated by Rev. § 9-601(c). Nevertheless, UCC § 1-103 sometimes invites courts to apply equitable principles if not expressly displaced by the particular provisions of the UCC. Moreover, marshalling principles have a greater likelihood of being applied where real property collateral is also being taken. Accordingly, it may be desirable to have the debtor expressly waive any right of marshalling.

35. The provisions of this § 20 constitute in effect an acknowledgment of the application of collection and disposition proceeds under the provisions of Rev. §§ 9-608 & 9-615. However, it is often advisable for the security agreement to address, after payment of the secured party's collection and disposition enforcement expenses, the order of application of the balance of the collateral proceeds to the secured obligations, especially where different credit facilities (*e.g.*, revolving credit, term loan, letter of credit facility, derivative transactions) are part of the obligations secured. For the secured party to collect legal fees and expenses from the collateral proceeds, the debtor's agreement to pay those fees and expenses must be set forth in the security agreement or other credit documents. Rev. §§ 9-608(a)(1)(A) & 9-615(a)(1). In addition, noncash proceeds need not be applied to the secured obligations unless failure to do so would be commercially unreasonable. If the noncash proceeds are applied, they must be applied in a commercially reasonable manner. Rev. §§ 9-608(a)(3) & 9-615(c). If they are not applied, they should be held by the secured party as additional collateral and applied to the secured obligations when reduced to cash.

Code of the State, any excess shall be returned to the Debtor. In the absence of final payment and satisfaction in full of all of the Obligations, the Debtor shall remain liable for any deficiency.

21.   **Overdue Amounts.** Until paid, all amounts due and payable by the Debtor hereunder shall be a debt secured by the Collateral and shall bear, whether before or after judgment, interest at the rate of interest [*for overdue principal set forth in the Credit Agreement*].[36]

22.   **Governing Law; Consent to Jurisdiction.** THIS AGREEMENT IS INTENDED TO TAKE EFFECT AS A SEALED INSTRUMENT AND SHALL BE GOVERNED BY, AND CONSTRUED IN ACCORDANCE WITH, THE LAWS OF THE STATE OF [insert].[37] The Debtor agrees that any action or claim arising out of, or any dispute in connection with, this Agreement, any rights, remedies, obligations, or duties hereunder, or the performance or enforcement hereof or thereof, may be brought in the courts of the State or any federal court sitting therein and consents to the non-exclusive jurisdiction of such court and to service of process in any such suit being made upon the Debtor by mail at the address [*specified in §_____ of the Credit Agreement*]. The Debtor hereby waives any objection that it may now or hereafter have to the venue of any such suit or any such court or that such suit is brought in an inconvenient court.

23.   **Waiver of Jury Trial.** THE DEBTOR WAIVES ITS RIGHT TO A JURY TRIAL WITH RESPECT TO ANY ACTION OR CLAIM ARISING OUT OF ANY DISPUTE IN CONNECTION WITH THIS AGREEMENT, ANY RIGHTS, REMEDIES, OBLIGATIONS, OR DUTIES HEREUNDER, OR THE PERFORMANCE OR ENFORCEMENT HEREOF OR THEREOF. Except as prohibited by law, the Debtor waives any right which it may have to claim or recover in any litigation referred to in the preceding sentence any special, exemplary, punitive or consequential damages or any damages other than, or in addition to, actual damages. The Debtor (i) certifies that neither the Secured Party nor any representative, agent or attorney of the Secured Party has represented, expressly or otherwise, that the Secured Party would not, in the event of litigation, seek to enforce the foregoing waivers or other waivers contained in this Agreement, and (ii) acknowledges that, in entering into the Credit Agreement [*and the other Loan Documents to which the Secured Party is a party*], the Secured Party is relying upon, among other things, the waivers and certifications contained in this § 23.

---

36.  Collateral protection and enforcement expenses can be significant in many cases. The security agreement should not only provide that these expenses constitute a debt secured by the collateral but should also provide for interest to be required to be paid on the incurrence of these expenses on the grounds that their incurrence is in effect an involuntary advance by the secured party.

37.  The governing law clause of the security agreement, in so far as the security agreement relates to a secured transaction governed by Revised Article 9, should be honored so long as the secured transaction bears a "reasonable relation" to the state whose law is chosen. UCC § 1-105(1). Although that governing law may provide the rules for the resolution of contract issues between the debtor and the secured party (*e.g.*, when attachment takes place, the rights of the secured party upon the debtor's default, or the rights of the debtor if the secured party were to fail to comply with a provision in Article 9), the choice of law rules governing the perfection of Article 9 security interests, the effect of perfection and non-perfection, and priority will be determined not by the chosen law governing the security agreement but by subpart 1 of part 3 of Article 9.

24. **Miscellaneous.** The headings of each section of this Agreement are for convenience only and shall not define or limit the provisions thereof. This Agreement and all rights and obligations hereunder shall be binding upon the Debtor and its respective successors and assigns, and shall inure to the benefit of the Secured Party and its successors and assigns.[38] If any term of this Agreement shall be held to be invalid, illegal or unenforceable, the validity of all other terms hereof shall in no way be affected thereby, and this Agreement shall be construed and be enforceable as if such invalid, illegal or unenforceable term had not been included herein. The Debtor acknowledges receipt of a copy of this Agreement.

IN WITNESS WHEREOF, intending to be legally bound, the Debtor has caused this Agreement to be duly executed as of the date first above written.

\*\*\*

By:[39] _____

Title: _____

Accepted:

\*\*\*

By:[40] _____

Title: _____

---

38. The language in § 24 binding the debtor's successors and assigns may be helpful if, without the secured party's consent, the debtor merges with another organization (*see* UCC § 1-201(28)) or is acquired by another organization. In that case, the successor entity may qualify as a "new debtor" (Rev. § 9-102(a)(56)) under Rev. § 9-203(d) and thereby be bound by the security agreement, including any after-acquired property clause contained in the security agreement. The secured party may, however, be required to take additional steps to maintain the perfection or priority of its security interest in collateral existing at the time that the new debtor becomes bound or in assets acquired by the new debtor after that time. *See* Rev. §§ 9-316(a)(2), 9-316(a)(3), 9-325, 9-326 & 9-508.

39. To verify that the debtor, if an organization (*see* UCC § 1-201(28)), is signing or otherwise authenticating the security agreement, the representative capacity of the person signing or otherwise authenticating on behalf of the debtor should be set forth under the individual's signature or other authentication and it should be clear that the individual is signing or otherwise authenticating in such a capacity.

40. Even though only the debtor needs to sign or otherwise authenticate the security agreement (Rev. § 9-203(b)(3)(A)), it is not unusual for the secured party to sign or otherwise authenticate the security agreement as well in order to indicate the secured party's acceptance of the terms of the security agreement.

# CERTIFICATE OF ACKNOWLEDGMENT[41]

COMMONWEALTH OR STATE OF * _____ )
)   ss.
COUNTY OF * _____ )

Before me, the undersigned, a Notary Public in and for the county aforesaid, on this _____ day of _____, 20____, personally appeared _____ to me known personally, and who, being by me duly sworn, deposes and says that [s]he is the _____ of _____, and that said instrument was signed and sealed on behalf of said [type of organization] by authority of its Board of Directors, and said _____ acknowledged said instrument to be the free act and deed of said [type of organization].


_____
Notary Public
My commission expires: _____

---

41. Although notarization of the debtor's signature or other authentication is not required on the security agreement under Revised Article 9, notarization of the debtor's signature is often required in the case where the secured party, following the debtor's default, needs to have the secured party's own signature notarized when it is signing a document in the debtor's name under the power of attorney given by the debtor in favor of the secured party in the security agreement.

# PERFECTION CERTIFICATE

## (UCC Financing Statements)[42]

The undersigned, the _____ and _____ of _____, a[n] _____ (the "Debtor"), hereby certifies, with reference to a certain _____ dated as of _____ (terms defined in such Security Agreement having the same meanings herein as specified therein), between the Debtor and _____, a[n] _____ (the " Secured Party"), to the Secured Party as follows:

1. **Name.** The exact legal name of the Debtor as that name appears on its [*Certificate of Incorporation*] is as follows:[43]

2. **Other Identifying Factors.**

(a)   The following is a mailing address for the Debtor:[44]

(b)   If different from its indicated mailing address, the Debtor's place of business or, if more than one, its chief executive office is located at the following address:[45]

| Address | County | State |
|---|---|---|
| | | |

(c)   The following is the type of organization of the Debtor:[46]

(d)   The following is the jurisdiction of the Debtor's organization:[47]

(e)   The following is the Debtor's state issued organizational identification number [*state "None" if the state does not issue such a number*]:[48]

3. **Other Names, etc.**

(a)   The following is a list of all other names (including trade names or similar appellations) used by the Debtor, or any other business or organization to which the Debtor became the successor by merger, consolidation, acquisition, change in form, nature or jurisdiction of organization or otherwise, now or at any time during the past five years:[49]

(b)   Attached hereto as Schedule 3 is the information required in § 2 for any other business or organization to which the Debtor became the successor by merger, consoli-

---

42. This form perfection certificate should be modified if farm products or as-extracted collateral are included in the collateral.

43. Rev. § 9-503(a).

44. Rev. § 9-516(b)(5)(A).

45. Rev. §§ 9-301(1) & 9-307; F. §§ 9-103(3), 9-103(4) & 9-401(6).

46. Rev. § 9-516(b)(5)(C).

47. Rev. § 9-516(b)(5)(C).

48. Rev. § 9-516(b)(5)(C).

49. Rev. § 9-507(c); F. § 9-402(7) (second and third sentences).

dation, acquisition of assets, change in form, nature or jurisdiction of organization or otherwise, now or at any time during the past five years:[50]

### 4. Other Current Locations.

(a)  The following are all other locations in the United States of America in which the Debtor maintains any books or records relating to any of the Collateral consisting of accounts, instruments, chattel paper, general intangibles or mobile goods:[51]

| Address | County | State |
|---------|--------|-------|
|         |        |       |

(b)  The following are all other places of business of the Debtor in the United States of America:[52]

| Address | County | State |
|---------|--------|-------|
|         |        |       |

(c)  The following are all other locations in the United States of America where any of the Collateral consisting of inventory or equipment is located:[53]

| Address | County | State |
|---------|--------|-------|
|         |        |       |

(d)  The following are the names and addresses of all persons or entities other than the Debtor, such as lessees, consignees, warehousemen or purchasers of chattel paper, which have possession or are intended to have possession of any of the Collateral consisting of instruments, chattel paper, inventory or equipment:[54]

| Name | Mailing Address | County | State |
|------|-----------------|--------|-------|
|      |                 |        |       |

---

50.  Rev. § 9-316; F. § 9-402(7) (second and third sentences).
51.  Rev. §§ 9-301(2) & (3); F. §§ 9-103(3), 9-103(4), 9-401(6).
52.  Rev. §§ 9-301(2) & (3); F. §§ 9-103(1) & 9-401(1) (Third Alternative).
53.  Rev. §§ 9-301(2) & (3); F. § 9-103(1).
54.  Rev. §§ 9-301(2) & (3), 9-312 & 9-313; F. §§ 9-103(1), 9-103(4), 9-304(2) & 9-304(3); *see also* F. §§ 9-326(3), 9-114, 9-305, 9-308 & 9-408.

5. **Prior Locations.**

(a)   Set forth below is the information required by § 4 (a) or (b) with respect to each location or place of business previously maintained by the Debtor at any time during the past five years in a state in which the Debtor has previously maintained a location or place of business at any time during the past four months:[55]

| Address | County | State |
|---------|--------|-------|
|         |        |       |

(b)   Set forth below is the information required by § 4(c) or (d) with respect to each other location at which, or other person or entity with which, any of the Collateral consisting of inventory or equipment has been previously held at any time during the past twelve months:[56]

| Name | Mailing Address | County | State |
|------|-----------------|--------|-------|
|      |                 |        |       |

6. **Fixtures.** Attached hereto as **Schedule 6** is the information required by UCC § 9-502(b) or F. § 9-402(5) of each state in which any of the Collateral consisting of fixtures are or are to be located and the name and address of each real estate recording office where a mortgage on the real estate on which such fixtures are or are to be located would be recorded.[57]

7. **Unusual Transactions.** Except for those purchases, acquisitions and other transactions described on **Schedule 3** or on **Schedule 7** attached hereto, all of the Collateral has been originated by the Debtor in the ordinary course of the Debtor's business or consists of goods which have been acquired by the Debtor in the ordinary course from a person in the business of selling goods of that kind.[58]

8. **File Search Reports.** Attached hereto as **Schedule 8(A)** is a true copy of a file search report from the Uniform Commercial Code filing officer (or, if such officer does not issue such reports, from an experienced Uniform Commercial Code search organization acceptable to the Secured Party) (i) in each jurisdiction identified in § 2(d) or in § 4 or 5 with respect to each name set forth in § 1 or 3, (ii) from each filing officer in each real estate recording office identified on **Schedule 6** with respect to real estate on which Collateral consisting of fixtures are or are to be located and (iii) in each jurisdiction in which any of the transactions described in **Schedule 3** or **7** took place with respect to the

---

55. F. §§ 9-103(3)(e) & 9-401(3).
56. Rev. §§ 9-301(2) & (3) & 9-316(a); F. §§ 9-103(1)(d) & 9-401(3).
57. Rev. §§ 9-502(b) & 9-516(b)(3)(D); F. §§ 9-401(1) & 9-402(5).
58. Rev. §§ 9-102(a)(64), 9-203(f), 9-301(2), 9-315(a)& 9-316; F. §§ 1-201(9), 9-306(2) & 9-402(7) (third sentence); *see also* F. § 9-301(1)(c).

legal name of the person from which the Debtor purchased or otherwise acquired any of the Collateral. Attached hereto as **Schedule 8(B)** is a true copy of each financing statement or other filing identified in such file search reports.

9.   **UCC Filings.** A duly authorized financing statement, in a form acceptable to the Secured Party and containing the indication of the Collateral set forth on **Schedule 9(A)** has been duly filed in the central Uniform Commercial Code filing office in the jurisdiction identified in § 2(d) and in each real estate recording office referred to on **Schedule 6** hereto. Attached hereto as **Schedule 9(B)** is a true copy of each such filing duly acknowledged or otherwise identified by the filing office.

10. **Termination Statements.** A duly signed or otherwise authorized termination statement in form acceptable to the Secured Party has been duly filed in each applicable jurisdiction identified in § 2(d), 3, 4 and 5 or on **Schedule 3** or **7** hereto [*or, in the case of* **Schedule 3** *or* **7,** *a release acceptable to the Secured Party from the secured party of the person from which the Debtor purchased or otherwise acquired the Collateral identified on* **Schedule 3** *or* **7**], has been delivered to the Secured Party. Attached hereto as **Schedule 10** is a true copy of each such filing duly acknowledged or otherwise identified by the filing office [*and of each such release*].

11. **Schedule of Filing.** Attached hereto as **Schedule 11** is a schedule setting forth filing information with respect to the filings described in §§ 9 and 10.

12. **Filing Fees.** All filing fees and taxes payable in connection with the filings described in §§ 9 and 10 have been paid.

IN WITNESS WHEREOF, we have hereunto signed this Certificate on _____ _____, 20____.

_____

Title:_____

_____

Title:_____

# Copyright Security Agreement[1]

SECURITY AGREEMENT, dated as of [*insert date*], between [*insert debtor*], a[*n*] [*insert debtor's jurisdiction and form of organization*] (the "Debtor"), and [*insert secured party*], a[*n*] [*insert secured party's jurisdiction and form of organization*] (the "Secured Party").

Debtor and Secured Party hereby agree as follows:

SECTION 1. **Definitions; Interpretation.**

(a)  **Terms Defined in Credit Agreement.** All capitalized terms used in this Agreement and not otherwise defined herein shall have the meanings assigned to them in the Credit Agreement.

(b)  **Certain Defined Terms.** As used in this Agreement, the following terms shall have the following meanings:

"Collateral" has the meaning set forth in § 2.

"Copyright Office" means the United States Copyright Office.

---

1.  This security agreement is intended to be used in cases where copyrights are collateral. It may be used in addition to or in lieu of the general, all personal property assets security agreement contained as Form 2.1. It may be advisable to use this separate copyright security agreement in addition to the all personal property assets security agreement (Form 2.1), as this form may be recorded as a copyright mortgage with the Copyright Office.

Special consideration should be given to perfecting a security interest in copyright and the proceeds thereof. Under cases such as *National Peregrine, Inc. v. Capital Fed. Sav. & Loan Ass'n* (*In re Peregrine Entertainment, Ltd.*), 116 B.R. 194 (C.D.Cal.1990) (Kozinski, J., sitting by designation), a secured party that filed only a financing statement in the appropriate state office was treated as unperfected as to both the copyrights and the proceeds thereof (royalty payments from the license of copyrighted movies). According to the District Court for the Central District of California, the secured party in that case should have recorded its security interest in the United States Copyright Office.

"Credit Agreement" means that certain Credit Agreement, dated as of the date hereof, between Debtor and Secured Party.

"UCC" means the Uniform Commercial Code as in effect in the State of [_____].

(c)    **Terms Defined in UCC.** Where applicable in the context of this Agreement and except as otherwise defined herein, terms used in this Agreement shall have the meanings assigned to them in the UCC.

(d)    **Construction.** In this Agreement, the following rules of construction and interpretation shall be applicable: (i) no reference to "proceeds" in this Agreement authorizes any sale, transfer, or other disposition of any Collateral by Debtor; (ii) "includes" and "including" are not limiting; (iii) "or" is not exclusive; and (iv) "all" includes "any" and "any" includes "all." To the extent not inconsistent with the foregoing, the rules of construction and interpretation applicable to the Credit Agreement shall also be applicable to this Agreement and are incorporated herein by this reference.

SECTION 2.  **Security Interest.**

(a)    **Grant of Security Interest.** As security for the payment and performance of the Obligations, Debtor hereby assigns, transfers and conveys to the Secured Party, and grants a security interest in and mortgage to the Secured Party of, all of Debtor's right, title and interest in, to and under the following property, in each case whether now or hereafter existing or arising or in which Debtor now has or hereafter owns, acquires or develops an interest and wherever located (collectively, the "Collateral"):

(i) All of Debtor's present and future United States registered copyrights and copyright registrations, including Debtor's United States registered copyrights and copyright registrations listed in **Schedule A** to this Agreement, all of Debtor's present and future United States applications for copyright registrations, including Debtor's United States applications for copyright registrations listed in **Schedule B** to this Agreement, and all of Debtor's present and future copyrights that are not registered in the Copyright Office including, without limitation, derivative works (collectively, the "Copyrights"),[2] and any and all royalties, payments, and other amounts payable to Debtor in connection with the Copyrights, together with all renewals and extensions of the Copyrights, the

---

2.    In order to perfect a security interest in copyrights, a secured party must follow the federal rules on the mortgage or hypothecation of copyright. 17 U.S.C. § 101 (1994). The Copyright Act makes recording priority applicable between conflicting "transfers of copyright ownership" under § 205. *Id.* §§ 205(a)&(d). A copyright mortgage may only be effectively recorded, however, if the copyright has been "registered." *Id.* § 205(c)(2) ("Recordation...gives all persons constructive notice...only if...registration has been made for the work."). Section 408 of the Copyright Act provides that "the owner of the copyright claim...may obtain registration of the copyright claim by delivering to the Copyright Office" a "deposit" of the work, *id.* § 408(b), and an application for registration that includes the name and address of the copyright claimant, the title of the work, *id.* § 409(6), and certain other information, as proscribed by the Copyright Act and the Register of Copyrights. Upon determining that "the material deposited constitutes copyrightable subject matter" and that the other requirements of the Copyright Act have been met, "the [Copyright] Register shall register the claim and issue to the applicant a certificate of registration under the seal of the Copyright Office." *Id.* § 410(a).

right to recover for all past, present, and future infringements of the Copyrights, and all manuscripts, documents, writings, tapes, disks, storage media, computer programs, computer databases, computer program flow diagrams, source codes, object codes and all tangible property embodying or incorporating the Copyrights, and all other rights of every kind whatsoever accruing thereunder or pertaining thereto;

(ii) All of Debtor's right, title and interest in and to any and all present and future license agreements with respect to the Copyrights;

(iii) All present and future accounts and other rights to payment arising from, in connection with or relating to the Copyrights; and

(iv) All cash and non-cash proceeds of any and all of the foregoing.

(b) **Continuing Security Interest.** Debtor agrees that this Agreement shall create a continuing security interest in the Collateral which shall remain in effect until terminated in accordance with § 11.

SECTION 3. **Supplement to Credit Agreement.** This Agreement has been entered into in conjunction with the security interests granted to Secured Party under the Credit Agreement or other security documents referred to therein. The rights and remedies of Secured Party with respect to the security interests granted herein are without prejudice to, and are in addition to those set forth in the Credit Agreement or any other security documents referred to therein, all terms and provisions of which are incorporated herein by reference.

SECTION 4. **Representations and Warranties.** Debtor represents and warrants to Secured Party that:

(a) **Copyright Registrations.** A true and correct list of all of Debtor's United States registered copyrights and copyright registrations is set forth in **Schedule A**.

(b) **Applications for Copyright Registration.** A true and correct list of all of Debtor's United States applications for copyright registrations is set forth in **Schedule B**.

SECTION 5. **Further Acts.** On a continuing basis, Debtor shall make, execute, acknowledge and deliver, and file and record in the proper filing and recording places, all such instruments and documents, and take all such action as may be necessary or advisable or may be requested by Secured Party to carry out the intent and purposes of this Agreement, or for assuring, confirming or protecting the grant or perfection of the security interest granted or purported to be granted hereby, to ensure Debtor's compliance with this Agreement or to enable Secured Party to exercise and enforce its rights and remedies hereunder with respect to the Collateral, including any documents for filing with the Copyright Office or any applicable state office. Secured Party may record this Agreement, an abstract thereof, or any other document describing Secured Party's interest in the Copyrights with the Copyright Office, at the expense of Debtor. In addition, Debtor authorizes Secured Party to file financing statements describing the Collateral in any UCC filing office deemed appropriate by Secured Party. If the Debtor shall at any time hold or acquire a commercial tort claim arising with respect to the Collateral,[3] the Debtor shall immediately notify Secured Party in a writing signed by the Debtor of the brief details thereof and grant to the Secured Party in such writing a security interest therein and in the proceeds thereof, all upon the terms of this Agreement, with such writing to be in form and substance satisfactory to the Secured Party.

SECTION 6. **Authorization to Supplement.** Debtor shall give Secured Party prompt notice of any additional United States copyright registrations or applications therefor after the date hereof. Debtor authorizes Secured Party unilaterally to modify this Agreement by amending **Schedule A** or **B** to include any future United States registered copyrights or applications therefor of Debtor. Notwithstanding the foregoing, no failure to so modify this Agreement or amend **Schedules A** or **B** shall in any way affect, invalidate or detract from Secured Party's continuing security interest in all Collateral, whether or not listed on **Schedule A** or **B.**

SECTION 7. **Binding Effect.** This Agreement shall be binding upon, inure to the benefit of and be enforceable by Debtor, Secured Party and their respective successors and assigns. Debtor may not assign, transfer, hypothecate or otherwise convey its rights, benefits, obligations or duties hereunder except as specifically permitted by the Credit Agreement.

SECTION 8. **Governing Law.** This Agreement shall be governed by, and construed in accordance with, the law of the State of [_____], except as required by mandatory provisions of law or to the extent the perfection or priority of the security interests hereunder, or the remedies hereunder, in respect of any Collateral are governed by the law of a jurisdiction other than [_____].

SECTION 9. **Entire Agreement; Amendment.** This Agreement and the Credit Agreement, together with the Schedules hereto and thereto, contains the entire agreement of the parties with respect to the subject matter hereof and supersedes all prior drafts and communications relating to such subject matter. Neither this Agreement nor any provision hereof may be modified, amended or waived except by the written agreement of the parties, as provided in the Credit Agreement. Notwithstanding the foregoing, Secured Party unilaterally may re-execute this Agreement or modify, amend or supplement the Schedules hereto as provided in § 6 hereof. To the extent that any provision of this Agreement conflicts with any provision of the Credit Agreement, the provision giving Secured Party greater rights or remedies shall govern, it being understood that the purpose of this Agreement is to add to, and not detract from, the rights granted to Secured Party under the Credit Agreement.

---

3.    A commercial tort claim is defined in Rev. § 9-102(a)(13) as "a claim arising in tort with respect to which: (A) the claimant is an organization, or (B) the claimant is an individual and the claim: (i) arose in the course of the claimant's business or profession; and (ii) does not include damages arising out of personal injury to or the death of an individual." If the collateral is to comprise a commercial tort claim as original collateral, the commercial tort claim must be described more specifically than by Article 9 collateral type. Rev. § 9-108(e)(1). In addition, an after-acquired property clause alone is not sufficient to permit a security interest in the commercial tort claim to attach as original collateral. Rev. § 9-204(b)(2). This provision permits future amendments to the security agreement that would provide the required specificity.

SECTION 10. **Counterparts.** This Agreement may be executed in any number of counterparts and by different parties hereto in separate counterparts, each of which when so executed shall be deemed to be an original and all of which taken together shall constitute but one and the same agreement. Delivery of an executed counterpart of this Agreement by facsimile shall be equally as effective as delivery of a manually executed counterpart. Any party hereto delivering a counterpart of this Agreement by facsimile shall also deliver a manually executed counterpart, but the failure to so deliver a manually executed counterpart shall not affect the validity, enforceability, or binding effect hereof.

SECTION 11. **Termination.** Upon payment and performance in full of all Obligations, the security interests created by this Agreement shall terminate and Secured Party (at Debtor's expense) shall promptly execute and deliver to Debtor such documents and instruments reasonably requested by Debtor as shall be necessary to evidence termination of all such security interests given by Debtor to Secured Party hereunder, including cancellation of this Agreement by written notice from Secured Party to the Copyright Office.

SECTION 12. **No Inconsistent Requirements.** Debtor acknowledges that this Agreement and the other documents, agreements and instruments entered into or executed in connection herewith may contain covenants and other terms and provisions variously stated regarding the same or similar matters, and Debtor agrees that all such covenants, terms and provisions are cumulative and all shall be performed and satisfied in accordance with their respective terms.

SECTION 13. **Severability.** If one or more provisions contained in this Agreement shall be invalid, illegal or unenforceable in any respect in any jurisdiction or with respect to any party, such invalidity, illegality or unenforceability in such jurisdiction or with respect to such party shall, to the fullest extent permitted by applicable law, not invalidate or render illegal or unenforceable any such provision in any other jurisdiction or with respect to any other party, or any other provisions of this Agreement.

SECTION 14. **Notices.** All notices and other communications hereunder shall be in writing and shall be mailed, sent or delivered in accordance with the Credit Agreement.

[Remainder of page intentionally left blank.]

IN WITNESS WHEREOF, the parties hereto have duly executed this Agreement, as of the date first above written.

[DEBTOR]

[————————————————],

a [————————————————]

By:————————————————

Title:————————————————

[SECURED PARTY]

[————————————————],

a [————————————————]

By:————————————————

Title:————————————————

## SCHEDULE A
to the Copyright Security Agreement

Debtor: [ _____ ]

## Registered Copyrights

| Title of Work | Registration Number | Date of Registration |
|---|---|---|
| | | |
| | | |
| | | |
| | | |
| | | |
| | | |
| | | |
| | | |
| | | |
| | | |
| | | |
| | | |
| | | |
| | | |
| | | |
| | | |
| | | |
| | | |
| | | |
| | | |
| | | |
| | | |
| | | |
| | | |

## SCHEDULE B
to the Copyright Security Agreement

Debtor: [_____]

## Copyright Applications

| Title of Work | Application Number |
|---|---|
|  |  |
|  |  |
|  |  |
|  |  |
|  |  |
|  |  |
|  |  |
|  |  |
|  |  |
|  |  |
|  |  |
|  |  |
|  |  |
|  |  |
|  |  |
|  |  |
|  |  |
|  |  |
|  |  |
|  |  |
|  |  |
|  |  |
|  |  |
|  |  |
|  |  |

# Patent Security Agreement[1]

SECURITY AGREEMENT, dated as of [insert date], between [insert debtor], a[an] [insert debtor's jurisdiction and form of organization] (the "Debtor"), and [insert secured party], a[an] [insert secured party's jurisdiction and form of organization] (the "Secured Party").

Debtor and Secured Party hereby agree as follows:

SECTION 1. **Definitions; Interpretation.**

(a)  **Terms Defined in Credit Agreement.** All capitalized terms used in this Agreement and not otherwise defined herein shall have the meanings assigned to them in the Credit Agreement.

(b)  **Certain Defined Terms.** As used in this Agreement, the following terms shall have the following meanings:

"Collateral" has the meaning set forth in § 2.

---

1.    This security agreement is intended to be used in cases where patents are collateral. It may be used in addition to or in lieu of the general, all personal property assets security agreement contained as Form 2.1. It may be advisable to use this separate patent security agreement in addition to the all personal property assets security agreement (Form 2.1), as this form may be recorded as a patent mortgage with the Patent and Trademark Office.

    Special consideration should be given to perfecting a security interest in patents. Unlike copyright, where some courts have held that the Copyright Act wholly preempts the Article 9 filing system, courts have developed what may be called a "straddle" approach to the perfection of a security interest in patents: A secured party may perfect a security interest as against a lien creditor or trustee by filing a UCC-1 financing statement. If, however, the secured party also seeks priority over later assignees of title to the patent, it may need to file a patent mortgage in the Patent and Trademark Office. *See, e.g., Moldo v. Matsco, Inc.* (*In re Cybernetic Servs.*), 252 F.3d 1039 (9th Cir. 2001).

"Credit Agreement" means that certain Credit Agreement, dated as of the date hereof, between Debtor and Secured Party.

"PTO" means the United States Patent and Trademark Office.

"UCC" means the Uniform Commercial Code as in effect in the State of [————].

(c)   **Terms Defined in UCC.** Where applicable in the context of this Agreement and except as otherwise defined herein, terms used in this Agreement shall have the meanings assigned to them in the UCC.

(d)   **Construction.** In this Agreement, the following rules of construction and interpretation shall be applicable: (i) no reference to "proceeds" in this Agreement authorizes any sale, transfer, or other disposition of any Collateral by Debtor; (ii) "includes" and "including" are not limiting; (iii) "or" is not exclusive; and (iv) "all" includes "any" and "any" includes "all." To the extent not inconsistent with the foregoing, the rules of construction and interpretation applicable to the Credit Agreement shall also be applicable to this Agreement and are incorporated herein by this reference.

SECTION 2. **Security Interest.**

(a)   **Grant of Security Interest.** As security for the payment and performance of the Obligations, Debtor hereby assigns, transfers and conveys to Secured Party, and grants to Secured Party a security interest in and mortgage to, all of Debtor's right, title and interest in, to and under the following property, in each case whether now or hereafter existing or arising or in which Debtor now has or hereafter owns, acquires or develops an interest and wherever located (collectively, the "Collateral"):

(i)   all patents and patent applications, domestic or foreign, all licenses relating to any of the foregoing and all income and royalties with respect to any licenses (including such patents and patent applications as described in **Schedule A**), all rights to sue for past, present or future infringement thereof, all rights arising therefrom and pertaining thereto and all reissues, divisions, continuations, renewals, extensions and continuations-in-part thereof;

(ii)   all general intangibles and all intangible intellectual or other similar property of Debtor of any kind or nature, associated with or arising out of any of the aforementioned properties and assets and not otherwise described above; and

(iii)   all proceeds of any and all of the foregoing Collateral (including license royalties, rights to payment, accounts and proceeds of infringement suits) and, to the extent not otherwise included, all payments under insurance (whether or not Secured Party is the loss payee thereof) or any indemnity, warranty or guaranty payable by reason of loss or damage to or otherwise with respect to the foregoing Collateral.

(b)   **Continuing Security Interest.** Debtor agrees that this Agreement shall create a continuing security interest in the Collateral which shall remain in effect until terminated in accordance with § 11.

SECTION 3. **Supplement to Credit Agreement.** This Agreement has been entered into in conjunction with the security interests granted to Secured Party under the Credit

Agreement or other security documents referred to therein. The rights and remedies of Secured Party with respect to the security interests granted herein are without prejudice to, and are in addition to those set forth in the Credit Agreement or any other security documents referred to therein, all terms and provisions of which are incorporated herein by reference.

SECTION 4. **Representations and Warranties.** Debtor represents and warrants to Secured Party that a true and correct list of all of the existing Collateral consisting of U.S. patents and patent applications or registrations owned by Debtor, in whole or in part, is set forth in **Schedule A**.

SECTION 5. **Further Acts.** On a continuing basis, Debtor shall make, execute, acknowledge and deliver, and file and record in the proper filing and recording places, all such instruments and documents, and take all such action as may be necessary or advisable or may be requested by Secured Party to carry out the intent and purposes of this Agreement, or for assuring, confirming or protecting the grant or perfection of the security interest granted or purported to be granted hereby, to ensure Debtor's compliance with this Agreement or to enable Secured Party to exercise and enforce its rights and remedies hereunder with respect to the Collateral, including any documents for filing with the PTO or any applicable state office. Secured Party may record this Agreement, an abstract thereof, or any other document describing Secured Party's interest in the Collateral with the PTO, at the expense of Debtor.[2] In addition, Debtor authorizes Secured Party to file financing statements describing the Collateral in any UCC filing office deemed appropriate by Secured Party. If the Debtor shall at any time hold or acquire a commercial tort claim arising with respect to the Collateral,[3] the Debtor shall immediately notify Secured Party in a writing signed by the Debtor of the brief details thereof and grant to the Secured Party in such writing a security interest therein and in the proceeds thereof, all upon the terms of this Agreement, with such writing to be in form and substance satisfactory to the Secured Party.

---

2.    The Patent Act does not expressly permit a patent holder to record a security interest in a patent in the Patent and Trademark Office. 35 U.S.C. § 261 governs assignments of patents, but only deals with outright assignments of title, not conditional assignments, such as security interests. Nevertheless, 37 CFR § 3.56 administratively permits a patent holder to record a security interest in a patent in the Patent and Trademark Office. This section provides that:

> Assignments which are made conditional on the performance of certain acts or events, such as the payment of money or other condition subsequent, if recorded in the [Patent and Trademark] Office, are regarded as absolute assignments for office purposes until canceled with the written consent of all parties or by the decree of a court of competent jurisdiction. The Office does not determine whether such conditions have been fulfilled.

3.    A commercial tort claim is defined in Rev. § 9-102(a)(13) as "a claim arising in tort with respect to which: (A) the claimant is an organization, or (B) the claimant is an individual and the claim: (i) arose in the course of the claimant's business or profession; and (ii) does not *include* damages arising out of personal injury to or the death of an individual." If the collateral is to comprise a commercial tort claim as original collateral, the commercial tort claim must be described more specifically than by Article 9 collateral type. Rev. § 9-108(e)(1). In addition, an after-acquired property clause alone is not sufficient to permit a security interest in the commercial tort claim to attach as original collateral. Rev. § 9-204(b)(2). This provision permits future amendments to the security agreement that would provide the required specificity.

SECTION 6. **Authorization to Supplement.** If Debtor shall obtain rights to any new patentable inventions or become entitled to the benefit of any patent application or patent for any reissue, division, or continuation, of any patent, the provisions of this Agreement shall automatically apply thereto. Debtor shall give prompt notice in writing to Secured Party with respect to any such new patent rights. Without limiting Debtor's obligations under this § 6, Debtor authorizes Secured Party unilaterally to modify this Agreement by amending **Schedule A** to include any such new patent rights. Notwithstanding the foregoing, no failure to so modify this Agreement or amend **Schedule A** shall in any way affect, invalidate or detract from Secured Party's continuing security interest in all Collateral, whether or not listed on **Schedule A.**

SECTION 7. **Binding Effect.** This Agreement shall be binding upon, inure to the benefit of and be enforceable by Debtor, Secured Party and their respective successors and assigns. Debtor may not assign, transfer, hypothecate or otherwise convey its rights, benefits, obligations or duties hereunder except as specifically permitted by the Credit Agreement.

SECTION 8. **Governing Law.** This Agreement shall be governed by, and construed in accordance with, the law of the State of [_____], except as required by mandatory provisions of law or to the extent the perfection or priority of the security interests hereunder, or the remedies hereunder, in respect of any Collateral are governed by the law of a jurisdiction other than [_____].

SECTION 9. **Entire Agreement; Amendment.** This Agreement and the Credit Agreement, together with the Schedules hereto and thereto, contains the entire agreement of the parties with respect to the subject matter hereof and supersedes all prior drafts and communications relating to such subject matter. Neither this Agreement nor any provision hereof may be modified, amended or waived except by the written agreement of the parties, as provided in the Credit Agreement. Notwithstanding the foregoing, Secured Party unilaterally may re-execute this Agreement or modify, amend or supplement the Schedule hereto as provided in § 6 hereof. To the extent that any provision of this Agreement conflicts with any provision of the Credit Agreement, the provision giving Secured Party greater rights or remedies shall govern, it being understood that the purpose of this Agreement is to add to, and not detract from, the rights granted to Secured Party under the Credit Agreement.

SECTION 10. **Counterparts.** This Agreement may be executed in any number of counterparts and by different parties hereto in separate counterparts, each of which when so executed shall be deemed to be an original and all of which taken together shall constitute but one and the same agreement. Delivery of an executed counterpart of this Agreement by facsimile shall be equally as effective as delivery of a manually executed counterpart. Any party hereto delivering a counterpart of this Agreement by facsimile shall also deliver a manually executed counterpart, but the failure to so deliver a manually executed counterpart shall not affect the validity, enforceability, or binding effect hereof.

SECTION 11. **Termination.** Upon payment and performance in full of all Obligations, the security interests created by this Agreement shall terminate and Secured Party (at

Debtor's expense) shall promptly execute and deliver to Debtor such documents and instruments reasonably requested by Debtor as shall be necessary to evidence termination of all such security interests given by Debtor to Secured Party hereunder, including cancellation of this Agreement by written notice from Secured Party to the PTO.

SECTION 12. **No Inconsistent Requirements.** Debtor acknowledges that this Agreement and the other documents, agreements and instruments entered into or executed in connection herewith may contain covenants and other terms and provisions variously stated regarding the same or similar matters, and Debtor agrees that all such covenants, terms and provisions are cumulative and all shall be performed and satisfied in accordance with their respective terms.

SECTION 13. **Severability.** If one or more provisions contained in this Agreement shall be invalid, illegal or unenforceable in any respect in any jurisdiction or with respect to any party, such invalidity, illegality or unenforceability in such jurisdiction or with respect to such party shall, to the fullest extent permitted by applicable law, not invalidate or render illegal or unenforceable any such provision in any other jurisdiction or with respect to any other party, or any other provisions of this Agreement.

SECTION 14. **Notices.** All notices and other communications hereunder shall be in writing and shall be mailed, sent or delivered in accordance with the Credit Agreement.

[Remainder of page intentionally left blank.]

IN WITNESS WHEREOF, the parties hereto have duly executed this Agreement, as of the date first above written.

[DEBTOR]

[————————————————————————],

a [————————————————————————]

By: ——————————————————————

Title: ——————————————————————


[SECURED PARTY]

[————————————————————————],

a [————————————————————————]

By: ——————————————————————

Title: ——————————————————————

# SCHEDULE A
to the Patent Security Agreement

Debtor: [ _____ ]

## Issued U.S. Patents of Debtor

| Patent No. | Issue Date | Title |
|---|---|---|
| | | |
| | | |
| | | |
| | | |
| | | |
| | | |
| | | |
| | | |
| | | |
| | | |
| | | |
| | | |
| | | |
| | | |
| | | |
| | | |
| | | |
| | | |
| | | |
| | | |
| | | |
| | | |
| | | |
| | | |
| | | |
| | | |

## Pending U.S. Patent Applications of Debtor

| Serial No. | Filing Date | Title |
|---|---|---|
|  |  |  |
|  |  |  |
|  |  |  |
|  |  |  |
|  |  |  |
|  |  |  |
|  |  |  |
|  |  |  |
|  |  |  |
|  |  |  |
|  |  |  |
|  |  |  |
|  |  |  |
|  |  |  |
|  |  |  |
|  |  |  |
|  |  |  |
|  |  |  |
|  |  |  |
|  |  |  |
|  |  |  |
|  |  |  |
|  |  |  |
|  |  |  |
|  |  |  |
|  |  |  |
|  |  |  |
|  |  |  |
|  |  |  |
|  |  |  |
|  |  |  |

# Trademark Security Agreement[1]

SECURITY AGREEMENT, dated as of [insert date], between [insert debtor], a[n] [insert debtor's jurisdiction and form of organization] (the "Debtor"), and [insert secured party], a[n] [insert secured party's jurisdiction and form of organization] (the "Secured Party").

Debtor and Secured Party hereby agree as follows:

SECTION 1. **Definitions; Interpretation.**

(a) **Terms Defined in Credit Agreement.** All capitalized terms used in this Agreement and not otherwise defined herein shall have the meanings assigned to them in the Credit Agreement.

(b) **Certain Defined Terms.** As used in this Agreement, the following terms shall have the following meanings:

"Collateral" has the meaning set forth in § 2.

"Credit Agreement" means that certain Credit Agreement, dated as of the date hereof, between Debtor and Secured Party.

"PTO" means the United States Patent and Trademark Office.

"UCC" means the Uniform Commercial Code as in effect in the State of [_____].

---

1. This security agreement is intended to be used in cases where trademarks are collateral. It may be used in addition to or in lieu of the general, all personal property assets security agreement contained as Form 2.1.

Special consideration should be given to perfecting a security interest in trademarks. Unlike copyright, where some courts have held that the Copyright Act wholly preempts the Article 9 filing system, courts have consistently held that a security interest in a trademark may be perfected *only* by filing a UCC-1 financing statement. *See, e.g., In re Together Dev. Corp.*, 227 B.R. 439 (Bankr. D. Mass. 1998), *aff'd*, 255 B.R. 606 (D. Mass. 2000).

(c)    **Terms Defined in UCC.** Where applicable in the context of this Agreement and except as otherwise defined herein, terms used in this Agreement shall have the meanings assigned to them in the UCC.

(d)    **Construction.** In this Agreement, the following rules of construction and interpretation shall be applicable: (i) no reference to "proceeds" in this Agreement authorizes any sale, transfer, or other disposition of any Collateral by Debtor; (ii) "includes" and "including" are not limiting; (iii) "or" is not exclusive; and (iv) "all" includes "any" and "any" includes "all." To the extent not inconsistent with the foregoing, the rules of construction and interpretation applicable to the Credit Agreement shall also be applicable to this Agreement and are incorporated herein by this reference.

SECTION 2.  **Security Interest.**

(a)    **Grant of Security Interest.** As security for the payment and performance of the Obligations, Debtor hereby grants to Secured Party a security interest in, and a mortgage upon, all of Debtor's right, title and interest in, to and under the following property, in each case whether now or hereafter existing or arising or in which Debtor now has or hereafter owns, acquires or develops an interest and wherever located (collectively, the "Collateral"):

(i)    all state (including common law), federal and foreign trademarks, service marks and trade names, and applications for registration of such trademarks, service marks and trade names (but excluding any application to register any trademark, service mark or other mark prior to the filing under applicable law of a verified statement of use (or the equivalent) for such trademark, service mark or other mark to the extent the creation of a security interest therein or the grant of a mortgage thereon would void or invalidate such trademark, service mark or other mark),[2] all licenses relating to any of the foregoing and all income and royalties with respect to any licenses (including such marks, names and applications as described in **Schedule A**), whether registered or unregistered and wherever registered, all rights to sue for past, present or future infringement or unconsented use thereof, all rights arising therefrom and pertaining thereto and all reissues, extensions and renewals thereof;

(ii)    the entire goodwill of or associated with the businesses now or hereafter conducted by Debtor connected with and symbolized by any of the aforementioned properties and assets;[3]

(iii)    all general intangibles and all intangible intellectual or other similar property of Debtor of any kind or nature, associated with or arising out of any of the aforementioned properties and assets and not otherwise described above; and

(iv)    all proceeds of any and all of the foregoing Collateral (including license royalties, rights to payment, accounts receivable and proceeds of infringement suits) and, to

---

2.    The parenthetical language deals with problems raised by *Clorox Co. v. Chemical Bank*, 40 U.S.P.Q. (BNA) 1098 (T.T.A.B. 1996), which held that an intent-to-use application cannot be assigned prior to the filing of a statement of use except to a successor to the business of the applicant. In *Clorox*, the Trademark Trial and Appeal Board held that a prohibited assignment of an intent-to-use application invalidates the registration—not simply the assignment.

3.    A trademark cannot be assigned "in gross." Rather, it can only be assigned with the good will of the business. *See, e.g., Visa, U.S.A., Inc. v. Birmingham Trust Nat'l Bank*, 696 F.2d 1371, 1375 (Fed. Cir. 1982) ("[A] mark may be transferred only in connection with the transfer of the good will of which it is a part. A naked transfer of the mark alone—known as a transfer in gross—is invalid.").

the extent not otherwise included, all payments under insurance (whether or not Secured Party is the loss payee thereof) or any indemnity, warranty or guaranty payable by reason of loss or damage to or otherwise with respect to the foregoing Collateral.

(b)   **Continuing Security Interest.** Debtor agrees that this Agreement shall create a continuing security interest in the Collateral which shall remain in effect until terminated in accordance with § 11.

SECTION 3. **Supplement to Credit Agreement.** This Agreement has been entered into in conjunction with the security interests granted to Secured Party under the Credit Agreement or other security documents referred to therein. The rights and remedies of Secured Party with respect to the security interests granted herein are without prejudice to, and are in addition to those set forth in the Credit Agreement or any other security documents referred to therein, all terms and provisions of which are incorporated herein by reference.

SECTION 4. **Representations and Warranties.** Debtor represents and warrants to Secured Party that:

(a)   **Trademarks.** A true and correct list of all of the existing Collateral consisting of U.S. trademarks, trademark registrations or applications owned by Debtor, in whole or in part, is set forth in **Schedule A**.

SECTION 5. **Further Acts.** On a continuing basis, Debtor shall make, execute, acknowledge and deliver, and file and record in the proper filing and recording places, all such instruments and documents, and take all such action as may be necessary or advisable or may be requested by Secured Party to carry out the intent and purposes of this Agreement, or for assuring, confirming or protecting the grant or perfection of the security interest granted or purported to be granted hereby, to ensure Debtor's compliance with this Agreement or to enable Secured Party to exercise and enforce its rights and remedies hereunder with respect to the Collateral, including any documents for filing with the PTO or any applicable state office. Secured Party may record this Agreement, an abstract thereof, or any other document describing Secured Party's interest in the Collateral with the PTO, at the expense of Debtor. In addition, Debtor authorizes Secured Party to file financing statements describing the Collateral in any UCC filing office deemed appropriate by Secured Party. If the Debtor shall at any time hold or acquire a commercial tort claim arising with respect to the Collateral[4], the Debtor shall immediately notify Secured Party in a writing signed by the Debtor of the brief details thereof and grant to the Secured Party in such writing a security interest therein and in the proceeds thereof, all upon the terms of this Agreement, with such writing to be in form and substance satisfactory to the Secured Party.

---

4.   A commercial tort claim is defined in Rev. § 9-102(a)(13) as "a claim arising in tort with respect to which: (A) the claimant is an organization, or (B) the claimant is an individual and the claim: (i) arose in the course of the claimant's business or profession; and (ii) does not include damages arising out of personal injury to or the death of an individual." If the collateral is to comprise a commercial tort claim as original collateral, the commercial tort claim must be described more specifically than by Article 9 collateral type. Rev. § 9-108(e)(1). In addition, an after-acquired property clause alone is not sufficient to permit a security interest in the commercial tort claim to attach as original collateral. Rev. § 9-204(b)(2). This provision permits future amendments to the security agreement that would provide the required specificity.

SECTION 6. **Authorization to Supplement.** If Debtor shall obtain rights to any new trademarks, the provisions of this Agreement shall automatically apply thereto. Debtor shall give prompt notice in writing to Secured Party with respect to any such new trademarks or renewal or extension of any trademark registration. Without limiting Debtor's obligations under this § 6, Debtor authorizes Secured Party to modify this Agreement by amending Schedule A to include any such new patent or trademark rights. Notwithstanding the foregoing, no failure to so modify this Agreement or amend **Schedule A** shall in any way affect, invalidate or detract from Secured Party's continuing security interest in all Collateral, whether or not listed on **Schedule A.**

SECTION 7. **Binding Effect.** This Agreement shall be binding upon, inure to the benefit of and be enforceable by Debtor, Secured Party and their respective successors and assigns. Debtor may not assign, transfer, hypothecate or otherwise convey its rights, benefits, obligations or duties hereunder except as specifically permitted by the Credit Agreement.

SECTION 8. **Governing Law.** This Agreement shall be governed by, and construed in accordance with, the law of the State of [_____], except as required by mandatory provisions of law or to the extent the validity, perfection or priority of the security interests hereunder, or the remedies hereunder, in respect of any Collateral are governed by the law of a jurisdiction other than [_____].

SECTION 9. **Entire Agreement; Amendment.** This Agreement and the Credit Agreement, together with the Schedules hereto and thereto, contains the entire agreement of the parties with respect to the subject matter hereof and supersedes all prior drafts and communications relating to such subject matter. Neither this Agreement nor any provision hereof may be modified, amended or waived except by the written agreement of the parties, as provided in the Credit Agreement. Notwithstanding the foregoing, Secured Party unilaterally may re-execute this Agreement or modify, amend or supplement the Schedules hereto as provided in § 6 hereof. To the extent that any provision of this Agreement conflicts with any provision of the Credit Agreement, the provision giving Secured Party greater rights or remedies shall govern, it being understood that the purpose of this Agreement is to add to, and not detract from, the rights granted to Secured Party under the Credit Agreement.

SECTION 10. **Counterparts.** This Agreement may be executed in any number of counterparts and by different parties hereto in separate counterparts, each of which when so executed shall be deemed to be an original and all of which taken together shall constitute but one and the same agreement. Delivery of an executed counterpart of this Agreement by facsimile shall be equally as effective as delivery of a manually executed counterpart. Any party hereto delivering a counterpart of this Agreement by facsimile shall also deliver a manually executed counterpart, but the failure to so deliver a manually executed counterpart shall not affect the validity, enforceability, or binding effect hereof.

SECTION 11. **Termination.** Upon payment and performance in full of all Obligations, the security interests created by this Agreement shall terminate and Secured Party (at Debtor's expense) shall promptly execute and deliver to Debtor such documents and instruments reasonably requested by Debtor as shall be necessary to evidence termination of all such security interests given by Debtor to Secured Party hereunder, including cancellation of this Agreement by written notice from Secured Party to the PTO.

SECTION 12. **No Inconsistent Requirements.** Debtor acknowledges that this Agreement and the other documents, agreements and instruments entered into or executed in connection herewith may contain covenants and other terms and provisions variously stated regarding the same or similar matters, and Debtor agrees that all such covenants, terms and provisions are cumulative and all shall be performed and satisfied in accordance with their respective terms.

SECTION 13. **Severability.** If one or more provisions contained in this Agreement shall be invalid, illegal or unenforceable in any respect in any jurisdiction or with respect to any party, such invalidity, illegality or unenforceability in such jurisdiction or with respect to such party shall, to the fullest extent permitted by applicable law, not invalidate or render illegal or unenforceable any such provision in any other jurisdiction or with respect to any other party, or any other provisions of this Agreement.

SECTION 14. **Notices.** All notices and other communications hereunder shall be in writing and shall be mailed, sent or delivered in accordance with the Credit Agreement.

[Remainder of page intentionally left blank.]

IN WITNESS WHEREOF, the parties hereto have duly executed this Agreement, as of the date first above written.

[DEBTOR]

[————————————————],

a [————————————————]

By:————————————————

Title:————————————————

[SECURED PARTY]

[————————————————],

a [————————————————]

By:————————————————

Title:————————————————

# SCHEDULE A
to the Trademark Security Agreement

Debtor: [ _____ ]

## U.S. Trademarks of Debtor

| Registration No. | Registration Date | Registered Owner | Mark |
|---|---|---|---|
| | | | |
| | | | |
| | | | |
| | | | |
| | | | |
| | | | |
| | | | |
| | | | |
| | | | |
| | | | |
| | | | |
| | | | |
| | | | |
| | | | |
| | | | |
| | | | |
| | | | |
| | | | |
| | | | |
| | | | |
| | | | |
| | | | |
| | | | |
| | | | |

# Pending U.S. Trademark Applications of Debtor

Debtor: [_____]

| Application No. | Filing Date | Applicant | Mark |
|---|---|---|---|
|  |  |  |  |
|  |  |  |  |
|  |  |  |  |
|  |  |  |  |
|  |  |  |  |
|  |  |  |  |
|  |  |  |  |
|  |  |  |  |
|  |  |  |  |
|  |  |  |  |
|  |  |  |  |
|  |  |  |  |
|  |  |  |  |
|  |  |  |  |
|  |  |  |  |
|  |  |  |  |
|  |  |  |  |
|  |  |  |  |
|  |  |  |  |
|  |  |  |  |
|  |  |  |  |
|  |  |  |  |
|  |  |  |  |
|  |  |  |  |
|  |  |  |  |
|  |  |  |  |
|  |  |  |  |
|  |  |  |  |
|  |  |  |  |
|  |  |  |  |
|  |  |  |  |

# Farm Products Security Agreement[1]

SECURITY AGREEMENT, dated as of [insert date], between [insert debtor], a[n] [insert debtor's jurisdiction and form of organization] (the "Debtor"), and [insert secured party], a[n] [insert secured party's jurisdiction and form of organization] (the "Secured Party").

Debtor and Secured Party hereby agree as follows:

1.     SECURITY INTEREST. To secure the full, prompt and complete payment and performance of each and every debt, liability and obligation of every type and description which the Debtor may now or at any time owe to the Secured Party, whether now existing or hereafter arising, direct or indirect, due or to become due, absolute or contingent, primary or secondary, liquidated or unliquidated, independent, joint, several or joint and several (all such debts, liabilities and obligations being herein collectively referred to as the "Obligations"), the Debtor grants the Secured Party a security interest (the "Security Interest") in the following property (the "Collateral"):

All of the personal property of the Debtor, wherever located, and now owned or hereafter acquired, including, but not limited to:[2]

All Accounts and other rights to payment whether or not earned by performance, and including, but not limited to, payment for property or services sold, leased, rented, licensed or assigned; Chattel Paper; Inventory; Equipment; Instru-

---

1.   This form is intended to be used in connection with the grant of a security interest in farm products, defined in Rev. § 9-102(a)(34) as certain goods used in a "farming operation," which in turn is defined in Rev. § 9-102(a)(35) as "raising, cultivating, propagating, fattening, grazing, or any other farming, livestock, or aquacultural operation." Special forms of bailee acknowledgment (farm products) and livestock purchase-money security interest notice appear in this book as Forms 3.5.2 and 3.5.4, respectively, and may be used in connection with this farm products security agreement.

2.   Rev. § 9-108(b)(3) permits the use of the statutory classifications to describe the collateral covered by the security agreement. While this form of security agreement uses the statutory terms in the first paragraph, the agricultural lender may wish to include a more specific description of agricultural collateral, including good constituting farm products.

ments; Investment Property; Documents; Deposit Accounts; Money; Letter-of-Credit Rights; General Intangibles; Payment Intangibles; Software; Supporting Obligations; and to the extent not included in the foregoing as original collateral, the proceeds and products of the foregoing.

All Farm Products, including, but not limited to, all poultry and livestock and their young, together with all products and replacements for such poultry and livestock; all crops, annual or perennial, and all products of such crops; and all feed, seed, fertilizer, chemicals, medicines and other supplies used or produced in Debtor's farming operations, and to the extent not included in the foregoing as original collateral, the proceeds and products of the foregoing.

All payments, rights to payment whether or not earned by performance, accounts, general intangibles and benefits, including, but not limited to, payments in kind, deficiency payments, letters of entitlement, storage payments, emergency assistance, diversion payments, production flexibility contracts, contract reserve payments, under or from any preexisting, current or future federal or state government program and, to the extent not included in the foregoing as original collateral, the proceeds and products of the foregoing.[3]

2.    REPRESENTATIONS, WARRANTIES, COVENANTS AND AGREEMENTS. The Debtor represents, warrants, covenants and agrees as follows:

a.    The legal name of the Debtor is as set forth at the top of the first page of this Agreement. The Debtor has not used any trade name, assumed name or other name except the Debtor's name stated above. The Debtor shall give the Secured Party prior written notice of any change in its name or if the Debtor uses any other name.

b.    [If the Debtor is a registered organization] The Debtor is a _____ whose state of organization is _____. The Debtor shall not change its state of organization without the prior written consent of the Secured Party.[4]

c.    The address of the Debtor's chief executive office is shown at the beginning of this Agreement. The Debtor shall give the Secured Party prior written notice of any change in such address. The Debtor has authority to execute and perform this Agreement.

d.    The Debtor hereby authorizes the Secured Party to file all financing statements and amendments to financing statements describing the Collateral in any offices as Secured Party, in its sole discretion, may determine. The Debtor hereby further authorizes the Secured Party to file a financing statement

---

3.    Specifically describing government program benefits is recommended in light of the inconsistent case law relating to the classification of such benefits under former Article 9. *See, e.g., In re Nivens*, 22 B.R. 287 (Bankr. N.D. Tex. 1982); *In re Sunberg*, 729 F.2d 561 (8th Cir. 1984); *In re Bechtold*, 54 B.R. 318 (Bankr. D. Minn. 1985). Revised Article 9 does not clarify the issue. Comment 5.i to Rev. § 9-102 suggests such benefits may be an account, a payment intangible, a general intangible other than a payment intangible, proceeds of other collateral, or "another type of collateral" depending on the nature of the government program.

4.    If the debtor is a "registered organization," as defined in Rev. § 9-102(a)(70), it will be "located" in its jurisdiction of registration. Rev. § 9-307(e). It will therefore be important to set forth such information in the security agreement. Note, however, that the local law of the jurisdiction where the relevant farm products are located governs perfection of an agricultural lien on farm products. Rev. § 9-302.

describing any agricultural liens or other statutory liens held by Secured Party in any offices as Secured Party, in its sole discretion, may determine.[5]

e. The Debtor hereby authorizes the Secured Party to file all effective financing statements pursuant to 7 U.S.C. § 1631, and amendments to effective financing statements describing the Collateral in any offices as Secured Party, in its sole discretion, may determine. If requested by the Secured Party, the Debtor will provide the Secured Party with a list of the buyers, commission merchants and selling agents to or through whom the Debtor may sell Farm Products. The Debtor authorizes the Secured Party to notify all such buyers, commission merchants and selling agents, or any other person of Secured Party's security interest in Debtor's farm products unless prohibited by law.[6]

f. The Debtor is the owner of the Collateral, will be the owner of the Collateral hereafter acquired, or has sufficient rights in the Collateral to transfer an interest, free of all security interests, liens and encumbrances other than the Security Interest and any other security of the Secured Party. The Debtor shall not permit any security interest, lien or encumbrance, other than the Security Interest and any other security interest of the Secured Party, to attach to any Collateral without the prior written consent of the Secured Party. The Debtor shall defend the Collateral against the claims and demands of all persons other than the Secured Party, and shall promptly pay all taxes, assessments and other government charges upon or against the Debtor, any Collateral and the Security Interest. No financing statement covering any Collateral is on file in any public office. If any Collateral is or will become a fixture, the Debtor, at the request of the Secured party, shall furnish the Secured Party with a statement or statements executed by all persons who have or claim an interest in the real estate, in form acceptable to the Secured Party, which statement or statements shall provide that such persons consent to the Security Interest.[7]

---

5. Section 2.d authorizes secured party to file financing statements covering the collateral described in the security agreement. Since agricultural suppliers often provide financing to agricultural businesses, the security agreement also specifically authorizes the secured party to perfect any agricultural lien to which it may be entitled under applicable law. "Agricultural liens" are not "security interests," but instead are nonpossessory statutory liens on a debtor's farm products in favor of a landlord or supplier of goods or services to the debtor in connection with the debtor's farming operations. Rev. § 9-102(a)(5)(defining "agricultural lien"), 9-109(a)(2) & 9-109(d)(2). The concept of attachment does not apply to an agricultural lien. Revised Article 9 merely refers to the agricultural lien becoming "effective" under the statute giving rise to it. Rev. § 9-308(b). Revised Article 9's priority rules, however, do apply to agricultural liens unless the agricultural lien is given by statute and the statute provides otherwise. Rev. § 9-322(g); *see also* Rev. § 9-322 cmt. 12. Such liens may therefore provide the secured party with a priority lien on the commodities produced by the farm business. *See* Rev. § 9-322(g).

6. Section 2.e authorizes the secured party to file an effective financing statement, if necessary, under 7 U.S.C. § 1631, which provides protection for certain purchasers of farm products. Among other things, this provision of federal law requires a secured party that wishes to preserve its security interest in farm products to notify purchasers of their interest within one year of the purchase. *Id.* § 1631(e). This provision also requires the debtor to provide the secured party with a list of buyers, commission merchants and agents utilized by the debtor for the sale of its farm products, which can be especially important in states lacking a central filing system under the federal statute. Such a list enables the secured party to provide direct notice to such parties under the federal statute.

7. Section 2.f requires the debtor to keep the collateral free from other security interests or liens unless the secured party consents to such security interests or liens. Most states provide multiple agricultural liens for landlords, bailees, suppliers, etc. As noted above, Revised Article 9's choice-of-law rules provide that the law of the state in which farm products are located governs perfection, the effect of perfection or nonperfection and the priority of an *agricultural lien* on the farm products. Rev. § 9-302. Choice of law regarding perfection, the effect of perfection or nonperfection, and priority of a *security interest* in farm products will determined by the rules of Rev. § 9-301.

g.   The Debtor shall not sell or otherwise dispose of any Collateral or any interest therein without the prior written consent of the Secured Party, except
that, until the occurrence of any Event of Default or the revocation by the
Secured Party of the Debtor's right to do so, and subject to the provisions of
this Agreement, the Debtor may (1) sell or lease any Collateral constituting
Inventory or Farm Products in the ordinary course of business at prices constituting the fair market value thereof and (2) use feed, seed, fertilizer, chemicals, medicines and other supplies used or produced in Debtor's farming
operations in the ordinary course of business. For purposes of this
Agreement, a transfer in partial or total satisfaction of a debt, obligation or
liability shall not constitute a sale or lease in the ordinary course of business.

h.   The Debtor shall deposit all proceeds of all Collateral into the deposit
account established and maintained by the Debtor at _____, or in such
other deposit account as required by the Secured Party. The Debtor shall not
grant any other person a security interest, lien or other encumbrance in such
deposit account.[8]

i.   The Debtor shall execute and deliver to the Secured Party all assignments,
transfers and other documents required by the Secured Party to transfer,
convey and assign to the Secured Party all federal and state government program payments, rights to payment whether or not earned by performance,
accounts, general intangibles and benefits.[9]

j.   The Debtor shall not store, transfer, or consign any Farm Products without
the prior written consent of the Secured Party and without first obtaining a
written acknowledgment from any person to whom physical possession of
any such Farm Products are delivered (i) of the Secured Party's security
interest in such Farm Products; (ii) that it holds possession of such Farm
Products for the Secured Party's benefit; (iii) that it will not issue negotiable
documents with respect to such Farm Products; and (iv) that it agrees to follow the Secured Party's instructions as to disposition of the Farm Products

---

8.   Section 2.h requires the debtor to deposit all proceeds of collateral into a deposit account specified by the
secured party. Presumably, the secured party will perfect a security interest in the specified deposit account by obtaining "control" of the deposit account as provided in Rev. § 9-104. A form of deposit account control agreement appears
as Form 3.3.1 in this book. Since many suppliers of agricultural credit are not banks, the priority of their security
interest in proceeds of collateral may be affected if such proceeds are deposited into a deposit account over which
another lender has obtained control. The secured party whose proceeds have been commingled in a deposit account
will be subordinate to the security interest, if any, of the bank at which the deposit account is maintained, or any other
secured party which has perfected a security interest in the deposit account by control. Rev. § 9-327(1). In addition,
the depositary bank's right of recoupment or set-off will be superior to a security interest of a competing secured
party perfected by control or another method unless the competing secured party obtained perfection by control by
becoming the depositary bank's customer on the deposit account. Rev. §§ 9-327(3) & (4) & 9-340. *See also* Rev. § 9-
327 cmt. 4 (discussing priority of bank with security interest in deposit account).

9.   Section 2.i requires the debtor to provide the secured party with appropriate assignments of farm program
benefits and payments. Federal law restricts the participant in a federal farm program from assigning its rights to
payment. 16 U.S.C. § 590h(g). In order to obtain such an assignment, the secured party must comply with the applicable regulations. *See* 7 C.F.R. § 1404.1-.9. It is not necessary to comply with these regulations in order to perfect a
security interest in such benefits. *See, e.g., In re Sunberg*, 729 F.2d 561 (8th Cir. 1984). Unless the secured party complies with the regulations, however, it will likely be unable to obtain direct payments from the government.

upon its receipt of such instructions.[10] All chattel paper, contracts, warehouse receipts, documents of title, or other documents or agreements, and all other non-cash proceeds of such Farm Products shall be endorsed, assigned and delivered immediately to the Secured Party.

k.   Each account, instrument, chattel paper, other right to payment and general intangible constituting Collateral is, or will be when acquired, the valid, genuine and legally enforceable obligation of the account debtor or other obligor named therein or in the Debtor's records pertaining thereto as being obligated to pay such obligation, subject to no defense, setoff or counterclaim. The Debtor shall not, without the prior written consent of the Secured Party, agree to any material modification or amendment of any such obligation or agree to any subordination or cancellation of any such obligation.

l.   All tangible Collateral shall be located at the Debtor's address(es) set forth at the beginning of this Agreement or as disclosed in writing to the Secured Party. No such Collateral shall be located at any other address without the prior written consent of the Secured Party. The Debtor shall provide the Secured Party with the location of all farm products, machinery and equipment on a quarterly basis so long as the obligations remained unpaid.[11]

m.   The Debtor shall: (1) keep all tangible Collateral in good condition and repair, normal depreciation excepted; (2) from time to time replace any worn, broken or defective parts thereof; (3) promptly notify the Secured Party of any loss of or material damage to any Collateral or of any adverse change in the prospect of payment of any account, instrument, chattel paper, other right to payment or general intangible constituting Collateral; (4) not permit any Collateral to be used or kept for any unlawful purpose or in violation of any federal, state or local law; (5) keep all tangible Collateral insured in such amounts, against such risks and in such companies as shall be acceptable to the Secured Party, with loss payable clauses in favor of the Secured Party to the extent of its interest in form acceptable to the Secured Party (including without limitation a provision for at least ten (10) days' prior written notice to the Secured Party of any cancellation or modification of such insurance), and deliver polices or certificates of such insurance to the

---

10.  Section 2.j restricts the debtor from storing, transferring, or consigning any farm products without the prior consent of secured party and without first obtaining an acknowledgment from the bailee relating to several matters. A form of bailee acknowledgment (farm products) appears as Form 3.5.2. Bailments of collateral create several risks for the secured party. If goods are subject to a negotiable warehouse receipt, the rights of a holder to which a negotiable document of title has been duly negotiated may have priority over an earlier perfected security interest in the goods to the extent provided in UCC Article 7. *See* Rev. § 9-331(a); UCC § 7-502(1) (setting forth rights acquired upon negotiation of a negotiable document of title). *Compare* UCC § 7-503(1) (setting forth certain cases in which holder of document of title will not have priority). If the debtor consigns collateral to a third party, Revised Article 9 treats the transaction as a security interest. Rev. § 9-109(a)(4). And any such transaction in the goods may give rise to "agricultural liens" (defined in Rev. § 9-102(a)(9)) which could obtain priority over the secured party under. Rev. § 9-322(g).

11.  In order to enable the secured party to monitor its collateral, Section 2.l requires the debtor to advise the secured party as to the location of its collateral. Should the collateral be moved to another state, Revised Article 9 provides that the law of the state in which farm products are located governs perfection, the effect of perfection or nonperfection and the priority of an *agricultural lien*. Rev. § 9-302. Choice of law as to perfection, the effect of perfection or nonperfection, and priority of the *security interest* in the same collateral will, however, be governed by Rev. § 9-301.

Secured Party; (6) at the Debtor's chief executive office, keep accurate and complete records pertaining to the Collateral and the Debtor's financial condition, business and property, and submit to the Secured Party such periodic reports concerning the Collateral and the Debtor's financial condition, business and property as the Secured Party may from time to time request; (7) at all reasonable times permit the Secured Party and its representatives to examine and inspect any Collateral, and to examine, inspect and copy the Debtor's records pertaining to the Collateral and the Debtor's financial condition, business and property; (8) at the Secured Party's request, promptly execute, endorse and deliver such financing statements and other instruments, documents, chattel paper and writings and take such other actions deemed by the Secured Party to be necessary or desirable to establish, protect, perfect or enforce the Security Interest and the rights of the Secured Party under this Agreement and applicable law, and pay all costs of filing financing statements and other writings in all public offices where filing is deemed by the Secured Party to be necessary or desirable.

n.   Debtor will cooperate with Secured Party in obtaining control with respect to Collateral consisting of deposit accounts, investment property, letter-of-credit rights, and electronic chattel paper. Debtor will not create any chattel paper without placing a legend on the chattel paper acceptable to the Secured Party indicating that Secured Party has a security interest in the chattel paper.

o.   To the extent Debtor uses the proceeds of loan(s) extended by Secured Party to purchase Collateral, Debtor's repayment of said loan(s) shall apply on a "first-in-first-out" basis so that the portion of the loan(s) used to purchase a particular item of Collateral shall be paid in the chronological order the Debtor purchased the Collateral.

p.   The Debtor shall comply with the provisions of all federal or state government programs, agreements and contracts to which it is a party, and shall not engage in activities which contribute to excessive erosion of highly erodible land or the conversion of wetlands to produce an agricultural commodity.[12]

3.    COLLECTION RIGHTS. At any time before or after an Event of Default, the Secured Party may, and at the request of the Secured Party the Debtor shall, promptly notify any account debtor or obligor of any account, instrument, chattel paper, other right to payment or general intangible constituting Collateral that the same has been assigned to the Secured Party and shall direct such account debtor or obligor to make all future payments to the Secured Party.

4.    LIMITED POWER OF ATTORNEY. If the Debtor at any time fails to perform or observe any agreement herein, the Secured Party, in the name and on behalf of the Debtor

---

12.  Section 2.p restricts the debtor from engaging in environmentally damaging activities. Federal farm program benefits may be denied to debtors who fail to comply with the applicable highly erodible land ("sodbuster") and wetland conservation ("swampbuster") provisions of the Food Security Act of 1985. *See* 7 U.S.C. § 7211(a)(1) & (2); *see also*, 16 U.S.C. §§ 3801-3814 & 16 U.S.C. §§ 3821-3824.

or, at its option, in its own name, may perform or observe such agreement and take any action which the Secured Party may deem necessary or desirable to cure or correct such failure. The Debtor irrevocably authorizes Secured Party and grants the Secured Party a limited power of attorney in the name and on behalf of the Debtor or, at its option, in its own name, to collect, receive, receipt for, create, prepare, complete, execute, endorse, deliver, and file any and all financing statements, insurance applications, remittances, instruments, documents, chattel paper, and other writings, to grant an extension to, compromise, settle, waive, notify, amend, adjust, change, and release any obligation of any account debtor, obligor, insurer, or other person pertaining to any Collateral, and take any other action deemed by the Secured Party to be necessary or desirable to establish, perfect, protect, or enforce the Security Interest. All of the Secured Party's advances, charges, costs, and expenses, including without limitation reasonable attorneys' fees, in connection with the Obligations and in the protection and exercise of any rights or remedies hereunder, together with interest thereon at the highest rate then applicable to any of the Obligations, shall be secured hereunder and shall be paid by the Debtor to the Secured Party on demand.

5.    EVENTS OF DEFAULT. The occurrence of any of the following events shall constitute an "Event of Default":[13] (a) any default in the payment or performance of any of the Obligations; or (b) any default under the terms of this Agreement or any other note, obligation, agreement, mortgage, or other writing heretofore, herewith or hereafter given to or acquired by the Secured Party to which the Debtor or any maker, endorser, guarantor, or surety of any of the obligations or any other person providing security for any of the Obligations or for any guaranty of any of the Obligations is a party; or (c) the insolvency, death, dissolution, liquidation, merger, or consolidation of the Debtor or any such maker, endorser, guarantor, surety, or other person; or (d) any appointment of a receiver, trustee, or similar officer of any property of the Debtor or any such maker, endorser, guarantor, surety, or other person; or (e) any assignment for the benefit of creditors of the Debtor or any such maker, endorser, guarantor, surety, or other person; or (f) any commencement of any proceeding under any bankruptcy, insolvency, dissolution, liquidation, or similar law by or against the Debtor or any such maker, endorser, guarantor, surety, or other person; or (g) the sale, lease or other disposition (whether in one transaction or in a series of transactions) to one or more persons other than in the ordinary course of business of all or a substantial part of the assets of the Debtor or any such maker, endorser, guarantor, surety, or other person; or (h) the death, dissolution, or liquidation of any partner of the Debtor or any such maker, endorser, guarantor, surety, or other person; or (i) the entry of any judgment against the Debtor or any such maker, endorser, guarantor, surety, or any other person which is not discharged in a manner acceptable to the Secured Party within thirty (30) days after such entry; or (j) the issuance of levy of any writ, warrant, attachment, garnishment, execution, or other process against any property of the Debtor or any such maker, endorser, guarantor, surety, or any other person; or (k) the attachment of any tax lien to any property of the Debtor or any such maker, endorser, guarantor, surety, or other person; or (l) any statement, representation, or warranty made by Debtor or any such maker, endorser, guarantor, surety, or other person (or any representative

---

13. Under Rev. § 9-606, a default occurs with respect to an *agricultural lien* at the time the secured party becomes entitled to enforce the lien in accordance with the statute under which the lien was created.

of the Debtor or any such maker, endorser, guarantor, surety, or other person) to the Secured Party at any time shall be incorrect or misleading in any material respect when made; or (m) there is a material adverse change in the condition (financial or otherwise), business, or property of the Debtor or any such maker, endorser, guarantor, surety, or other person; or (n) the Secured Party shall in good faith believe that the prospect for due and punctual payment or performance of any of the Obligations, this Agreement or any other note, obligation, agreement, or mortgage heretofore, herewith or hereafter given to or acquired by the Secured Party in connection with any of the Obligations is impaired.

6.    REMEDIES. Upon the occurrence of any Event of Default and at any time thereafter, the Secured Party may exercise any one or more of the following rights and remedies: (a) declare all Obligations to be immediately due and payable, and the same shall thereupon be immediately due and payable, without presentment or other notice or demand, all of which are hereby waived by the Debtor; (b) require the Debtor to assemble all or any part of the Collateral and make it available to the Secured Party at a place to be designated by the Secured Party which is reasonably convenient to both parties; (c) exercise and enforce any and all rights and remedies available upon default under this Agreement, the Uniform Commercial Code, and any other applicable agreements and laws. If notice to the Debtor of any intended disposition of Collateral or other action is required, such notice shall be deemed reasonably and properly given if mailed by regular or certified mail, postage prepaid, to the Debtor at the address stated at the beginning of this Agreement or at the most recent address shown in the Secured Party's records, at least ten (10) days prior to the action described in such notice. The Debtor consents to the personal jurisdiction of the state and federal courts located in the State of _____ in connection with any controversy related to this Agreement, the Collateral, the Security Interest, or any of the Obligations, waives any argument that venue in such forums is not convenient, and agrees that any litigation initiated by the Debtor against the Secured Party in connection with this Agreement, the Collateral, the Security Interest, or any of the Obligations shall be venued in either the _____ Court of _____ County, _____, or the United States District Court, _____ District of _____.[14]

7.    MISCELLANEOUS. All terms in this Agreement that are defined in the Uniform Commercial Code, as enacted in the state of _____ and as amended from time to time (the "UCC"), shall have the meanings set forth in the UCC and such meanings shall automatically change at the time that any amendment to the UCC which such meanings shall become effective. A carbon, photographic, or other reproduction of this Agreement is sufficient as a financing statement. This Agreement cannot be waived, modified, amended, abridged, supplemented, terminated, or discharged, and the Security Interest cannot be released or terminated, except by a writing duly executed by the Secured party. A waiver shall be effective only in the specific instance and for the specific purpose given. No delay or failure to act shall preclude the exercise or enforcement of any of the Secured Party's rights or remedies. All rights and remedies of the Secured Party shall be cumulative and may be exercised singularly, concurrently, or successively at the Secured Party's

---

14. Rev. § 9-603(a) permits the parties to determine by agreement the standards measuring the "fulfillment of the rights of a debtor or obligor and the duties of a secured party" so long as such standards are not "manifestly unreasonable." It may be appropriate to provide some such standards in this farm products security agreement.

option, and the exercise or enforcement of any one such right or remedy shall not be a condition to or bar the exercise or enforcement of any other. This Agreement shall be binding upon and inure to the benefit of the heirs, legatees, executors, administrators, successors and assigns of Secured Party and shall bind all persons and parties who become bound as a debtor to this Security Agreement. If any provision or application of this Agreement is held unlawful or unenforceable in any respect, such illegality or unenforceability shall not affect other provisions or applications which can be given effect, and this Agreement shall be construed as if the unlawful or unenforceable provision or application had never been contained herein or prescribed hereby. All representations and warranties contained in this Agreement shall survive the execution, delivery, and performance of this Agreement and the creation, payment, and performance of the Obligations. This Agreement shall be governed by and construed in accordance with the laws of the State [insert choice of law].

8.  WAIVER OF JURY TRIAL. DEBTOR WAIVES ITS RIGHT TO A JURY TRIAL WITH RESPECT TO ANY ACTION OR CLAIM ARISING OUT OF ANY DISPUTE IN CONNECTION WITH THIS AGREEMENT, ANY RIGHTS, REMEDIES, OBLIGATIONS, OR DUTIES HEREUNDER, OR THE PERFORMANCE OR ENFORCEMENT HEREOF OR THEREOF. Except as prohibited by law, Debtor waives any right which it may have to claim or recover in any litigation referred to in the preceding sentence any special, exemplary, punitive or consequential damages or any damages other than, or in addition to, actual damages. Debtor (i) certifies that neither Secured Party nor any representative, agent or attorney of Secured Party has represented, expressly or otherwise, that Secured Party would not, in the event of litigation, seek to enforce the foregoing waivers or other waivers contained in this Agreement, and (ii) acknowledges that, in entering into this Agricultural Security Agreement [and documents to which the Secured Party is a party], Secured Party is relying upon, among other things, the waivers and certifications contained in this section 8.[15]

THE DEBTOR REPRESENTS, CERTIFIES, WARRANTS, AND AGREES THAT THE DEBTOR HAS READ THIS ENTIRE AGREEMENT AND UNDERSTANDS ALL OF ITS PROVISIONS.

IN WITNESS WHEREOF, intending to be legally bound, the Debtor has caused this Agreement to be duly executed as of the date first above written.

\*\*\*

By: _____

Title: _____


DEBTOR:

By: _____

---

15.  There may be other standard provisions the parties wish to include on, *e.g.*, marshalling, waiver of suretyship rights, enforceability, and so on, which appear in the all personal property assets security agreement (Form 2.1 of this book).

# PART 3

# Perfecting the Security Interest

# Where to File Financing Statements under Revised Article 9[1]

**Basic Rule:** With few exceptions, in order to perfect a security interest by filing, a financing statement must be filed in the jurisdiction where the debtor[2] is "located."[3]

**First question:** Does the transaction involve **collateral** that is subject to one of the exceptions to the Basic Rule?

---

1.   This checklist is intended to be used as a guide in determining where to file a financing statement to perfect a security interest. As discussed elsewhere in this book, filing a financing statement may not be an effective or appropriate means of perfecting a security interest. A security interest in a deposit account as original collateral, for example, can be perfected only by control. Rev. §§ 9-312(b)(1), 9-314 & 9-104. Even where a security interest may be perfected by filing, the security interest so perfected may nevertheless be junior as to a security interest in the same collateral perfected by another method. For example, while a security interest in an instrument may be perfected by filing a financing statement, a purchaser of the same instrument will have priority if the purchaser takes possession of the instrument, and has satisfied the other requirements of Rev. § 9-330(d).

2.   Rev. § 9-102(a)(28) defines a debtor as "(A) a person having an interest, other than a security interest or other lien, in the collateral, whether or not the person is an obligor; (B) a seller of accounts, chattel paper, payment intangibles or promissory notes; or (C) a consignee." *See also* § 9-102(a)(59) (defining obligor) Rev. § 9-102 cmt. 2.a (distinguishing debtor and obligor).

3.   As discussed below, the debtor's "location" will be determined for most purposes related to the filing of a financing statement by Rev. §§ 9-301 (choice of law governing perfection and priority of security interests) & 9-307 (location of debtor).

The exceptions (and proper jurisdiction for filing with respect to such collateral) are:

| Type of Collateral | Where to File | Code Section |
|---|---|---|
| Goods[4] subject to a fixture filing[5] | Jurisdiction where the goods are located | Rev. § 9-301(3)(A) |
| Goods consisting of timber to be cut[6] | Jurisdiction where the goods are located | Rev. § 9-301(3)(B) |
| As-extracted collateral[7] | Jurisdiction in which the wellhead or minehead is located | Rev. § 9-301(4) |
| Farm products[8] (with respect to perfection of an agricultural lien[9]) | Jurisdiction in which the farm products are located | Rev. § 9-302 |

**Second question**: Where is the debtor "located"[10] for purposes of the Basic Rule?

The debtor's location depends upon the debtor's category for purposes of Rev. § 9-307. The possible categories (and related "location") are:

| Type of Debtor | "Location" of the Debtor | Code Section |
|---|---|---|
| Individual (which will include a sole proprietorship[11]) whose principal residence is in the United States,[12] whether assets are business or personal assets | Jurisdiction of the individual's principal residence[13] | Rev. § 9-307(b)(1) |

*Continued*

---

4.    "Goods" are "all things that are movable when a security interest attaches" and includes fixtures. Rev. § 9-102(a)(44).

5.    "Fixtures" are "goods that have become so related to particular real property that an interest in them arises under real property law." Rev. § 9-102((41). *See also* Rev. § 9-102(a)(40) (defining fixture filing).

6.    *See* Rev. § 9-301 cmt. 5.c (discussing choice-of-law rules applicable to timber to be cut, as distinct from timber that has been cut).

7.    *See* Rev. § 9-102(a)(6) (defining as-extracted collateral).

8.    *See* Rev. § 9-102(a)(34) (defining farm products).

9.    Rev. § 9-102(a)(5) (defining agricultural lien).

10.    Note that this definition of location differs from that used in F. § 9-103(3).

11.    A sole proprietorship is not within the definition of "organization" because it is not a "legal or commercial entity." UCC § 1-201(28).

12.    *See* Rev. § 9-307 cmt. 3. A jurisdiction that has not enacted Revised Article 9 or an earlier version of Article 9 should be treated as not being in the United States for purposes of applying the rules in this portion of the checklist.

13.    *See* Rev. § 9-307 cmt. 2 (noting that "principal residence" is not defined).

| Type of Debtor<br>*Continued* | "Location" of the Debtor | Code Section |
|---|---|---|
| Individual whose principal residence is *not* in the United States, whether the assets are business or personal assets | • If the debtor's principal residence is located in a jurisdiction whose law affords public notice of security interests,[14] the law of the jurisdiction of the individual's principal residence will govern (*and the secured party must comply with "perfection" requirements in that jurisdiction rather than file a financing statement under the UCC*)[15]<br>• If the foregoing is not applicable, the District of Columbia | Rev. § 9-307(b)(1) & (c) |
| "Registered organization"[16] organized under the law of a single state[17] | The registered organization's state of organization | Rev. § 9-307(e) |
| "Registered organization" organized under the law of the United States | 1. In the state that the law of the United States designates, if the law designates a state of location<br>2. In the state that the registered organization designates, if the law of the United States authorizes the registered organization to designate its state of location<br>3. In the District of Columbia, if neither paragraph (1) nor (2) applies | Rev. § 9-307(f) |

*Continued*

---

14.   The law of a jurisdiction affords public notice of a security interest if it generally requires information concerning the existence of a nonpossessory security interest to be made generally available in a filing, recording, or registration system as a condition or result of the security interest's obtaining priority over the rights of a lien creditor with respect to the collateral (*i.e.* being "perfected"). *See* Rev. § 9-307(c) & cmt. 3.

15.   *See* Rev. § 9-307 cmt. 3 (regarding choice of law as to non-U.S. debtors).

16.   A "registered organization" is defined in Rev. § 9-102(a)(70) as "an organization organized solely under the laws of a single State or the United States and as to which the State or the United States must maintain a public record showing the organization to have been organized." Rev. § 9-102 cmt. 11 explains that corporations, limited liability companies, and limited partnerships generally are registered organizations, and that general partnerships generally are not registered organizations. For any other type of domestic organization, it will be necessary to check the laws of the applicable state or of the United States to determine whether the entity is a registered organization within the meaning of the definition. An organization organized under the laws of a non-U.S. jurisdiction will *not* be a registered organization, but ordinarily will be considered an "organization" under the UCC. *See* UCC § 1-201(28).

17.   "State" is defined in Rev. § 9-102(a)(76) as "a State of the United States, the District of Columbia, Puerto Rico, the United States Virgin Islands, or any territory or insular possession subject to the jurisdiction of the United States."

| Type of Debtor<br>*Continued* | "Location" of the Debtor | Code Section |
|---|---|---|
| Organization[18]<br>(other than a<br>registered organi-<br>zation organized<br>under the law of<br>a State or of the<br>United States) | Unless covered by any of the<br>specialized rules below:<br>• If the debtor has only one place of<br>  business,[19] the jurisdiction of its<br>  place of business<br>• If the debtor has more than one place<br>  of business, the jurisdiction of its<br>  chief executive office[20] | Rev. § 9-307(b)(2)<br>& (3) |
| Organization (other<br>than a registered<br>organization<br>organized under<br>the law of a state or<br>the United States)<br>whose sole place<br>of business or<br>chief executive<br>office is not in the<br>United States | • If the debtor's place of business or<br>  chief executive office, as applicable,<br>  is located in a jurisdiction whose law<br>  affords public notice of security<br>  interests[21], the law of the jurisdiction<br>  of the organization's sole place of<br>  business or chief executive office, as<br>  applicable, will govern (*and the<br>  secured party must comply with<br>  "perfection" requirements in that<br>  jurisdiction rather than filing a<br>  financing statement under the UCC*)[22]<br>• If the foregoing is not applicable,<br>  the District of Columbia | Rev. § 9-307(b)(2)<br>& (3), & (c) |
| A branch or agency<br>in the United States<br>of a bank that is not<br>organized under the<br>law of the United<br>States or a state | • In the state in which the branch or<br>  agency is licensed, if all branches and<br>  agencies of the bank are licensed in<br>  only one state<br>• If not all branches and agencies of<br>  the bank are licensed in only one state:<br>  1. In the state that the law of the<br>     United States designates, if such<br>     law designates a state of location | Rev. § 9-307(f)<br>& (i) |

*Continued*

---

18.   "Organization" is defined in UCC § 1-201(28) to include "a corporation, government or governmental subdivision or agency, business trust, estate, trust, partnership, or association, two or more persons having a joint or common interest, or any other legal or commercial entity" and "person" is defined in UCC § 1-201(30) to include "an individual or an organization." *See also* UCC § 1-102(5) (rules of construction regarding number and gender).

19.   "Place of business" is defined in Rev. § 9-307(a) as "a place where a debtor conducts its affairs" for purposes of Rev. § 9-307. *See also* Rev. § 9-307 cmt. 2 (discussing "place of business"). Revised Article 9 does not define "chief executive office." Rev. § 9-307 cmt. 2 explains that chief executive office means "the place from which the debtor manages the main part of its business operations or other affairs."

20.   Revised Article 9 does not define "chief executive office;" Rev. § 9-307 cmt. 2 explains that chief executive office means "the place from which the debtor manages the main part of its business operations or other affairs."

21.   *See* note 14, above.

22.   *See* note 15, above.

23.   49 U.S.C. §§ 40101, *et seq.* (1994).

| Type of Debtor | "Location" of the Debtor | Code Section |
|---|---|---|
| *Continued* | 2. In the state that the branch or agency designates, if the law of the United States authorizes the branch or agency to designate its state of location<br>3. In the District of Columbia, if neither paragraph (1) nor (2) applies | |
| Foreign air carrier under the Federal Aviation Act of 1958, as amended[23] | The jurisdiction of the designated office of the agent upon which service of process may be made on behalf of the carrier[24] | Rev. § 9-307(j) |
| United States | In the District of Columbia | Rev. § 9-307(h) |
| Unusual Situations | A person that ceases to exist, have a residence, or have a place of business continues to be located in the jurisdiction specified by Rev. § 9-307(b) & (c) (*i.e.*, the general rules on location of debtor)<br><br>A registered organization continues to be located in the jurisdiction specified by Rev. § 9-307(e) or (f) notwithstanding (1) the suspension, revocation, forfeiture, or lapse of the registered organization's status as such in its jurisdiction of organization, or (2) the dissolution, winding up, or cancellation of the existence of the registered organization[25] | Rev. § 9-307(d) & (g) |

**Caveat**: A non-U.S. forum may not be bound by the Revised Article 9 choice of law requirements outlined above. Although the Revised Article 9 choice of law provisions may result in the choice of the law of a state in the United States to govern the issue of how to perfect a security interest, including place of filing, a non-U.S. forum may reach a different conclusion and not recognize as effective perfection under the UCC or other law of a state or the United States.[26] In addition, a transaction or debtor may not have sufficient contacts with any state or the United States to make the application of Revised Article 9

---

24.   *See* Rev. § 9-307 cmt. 7 (indicating that this provision is superceded by the Convention on the International Recognition of Rights in Aircraft (Geneva Convention) to the extent the Convention is applicable).

25.   *See* Rev. § 9-307 cmt. 4 (events affecting status of registered organization, "such as dissolution," do not affect its location for purposes of Rev. § 9-307(e)).

26.   *See* Rev. §§ 9-307 cmt. 3 & 9-109 cmt. 9 (including Example 4).

appropriate.[27] Therefore, in a transaction with contacts to a non-U.S. jurisdiction (*e.g.*, a debtor or property located outside the United States) the requirements (including choice of law provisions) of the law of the other jurisdiction should also be reviewed.

**Third question:** In what office in the applicable state should the financing statement be filed?

**General Rule:** File in the central office designated for that state (Rev. § 9-501(a)(2)).

**Exceptions:**

- File in the office designated for the filing or recording of a record of a mortgage[28] on the related real property if:

    - the collateral is as-extracted collateral or timber to be cut (Rev. § 9-501(a)(1)(A))[29]
    - the financing statement is filed as a fixture filing and the collateral is goods that are or are to become fixtures (Rev. § 9-501(a)(1)(B))[30]

- If the debtor is a transmitting utility,[31] file in the office specified by that state for filings with respect to this type of debtor (including for collateral that is fixtures) (Rev. § 9-501(b))[32]

---

27.    *See* Rev. §§ 9-307 cmt. 3 & 9-109 cmt. 4 (Example 4).
28.    Rev. § 9-102(a)(55) (defining mortgage).
29.    Rev. § 9-501 cmt. 3.
30.    Rev. § 9-501 cmt. 4. The central office is the appropriate place for filing if the collateral is goods that are or are to become fixtures and the financing statement is not filed as a fixture filing. Rev. § 9-501(a)(2).
31.    Rev. § 9-102(a)(80) (defining transmitting utility).
32.    Rev. § 9-501 cmt. 5.

# "In Lieu"
# Initial Financing Statement

As discussed in the Summary of Revised Article 9, if a financing statement filed before Revised Article 9's effective date, whether or not effective under former Article 9, would, if filed in that jurisdiction and office on Revised Article 9's effective date, be effective to perfect a security interest under Revised Article 9, the filing is given effect under Revised Article 9. Rev. § 9-705(b). If, instead, a financing statement filed before Revised Article 9's effective date that is effective to perfect a security interest under former Article 9 would, if filed on Revised Article 9's effective date, be *ineffective* to perfect that security interest under Revised Article 9, the filing is nevertheless given effect under Revised Article 9 until the earlier to occur of the financing statement's normal lapse (without regard to any continuation statement filed after Revised Article 9's effective date) and June 30, 2006. Rev. § 9-705(c). (Note that certain states (Alabama, Connecticut, Florida and Mississippi) have delayed the effective date of Revised Article 9. The cutoff date for financing statements filed under former Article 9 may also be extended.).

To avoid lapse, and in order to continue the original financing statement, an initial financing statement (often called an *"in lieu" initial financing statement*), referring to the original financing statement to be continued, must be filed under Rev. § 9-706 in the jurisdiction and office required by Revised Article 9. This Form may be used for such purpose. For a detailed discussion of the contents of the various Items in this Form, see Form 3.2.3 (Paper Financing Statement) and the accompanying notes.

**UCC FINANCING STATEMENT***

FOLLOW  INSTRUCTIONS (front and back) CAREFULLY

A. NAME & PHONE OF CONTACT AT FILER [optional]

B. SEND ACKNOWLEDGMENT TO:  (Name and Address)

⌐Lending Bank
  987 State Street
  Anytown, MA 00000
  Attention: UCC Department
  └

THE ABOVE SPACE IS FOR FILING OFFICE USE ONLY

1. DEBTOR'S EXACT FULL LEGAL NAME - insert only one debtor name (1a or 1b) - do not abbreviate or combine names

| | | | | |
|---|---|---|---|---|
| 1a. ORGANIZATION'S NAME **Debtor Corporation** | | | | |
| OR 1b. INDIVIDUAL'S LAST NAME | FIRST NAME | MIDDLE NAME | | SUFFIX |
| 1c. MAILING ADDRESS **123 South Charles Street** | CITY **Baltimore** | STATE **MD** | POSTAL CODE **21201** | COUNTRY **USA** |

| 1d. TAX ID #:  SSN OR EIN | ADD'L INFO RE ORGANIZATION DEBTOR | 1e. TYPE OF ORGANIZATION **Corporation** | 1f. JURISDICTION OF ORGANIZATION **Maryland** | 1g. ORGANIZATIONAL ID #, if any ☐NONE |
|---|---|---|---|---|

2. ADDITIONAL DEBTOR'S EXACT FULL LEGAL NAME - insert only one debtor name (2a or 2b) - do not abbreviate or combine names

| | | | | |
|---|---|---|---|---|
| 2a. ORGANIZATION'S NAME | | | | |
| OR 2b. INDIVIDUAL'S LAST NAME | FIRST NAME | MIDDLE NAME | | SUFFIX |
| 2c. MAILING ADDRESS | CITY | STATE | POSTAL CODE | COUNTRY |

| 2d. TAX ID #:  SSN OR EIN | ADD'L INFO RE ORGANIZATION DEBTOR | 2e. TYPE OF ORGANIZATION | 2f. JURISDICTION OF ORGANIZATION | 2g. ORGANIZATIONAL ID #, if any ☐NONE |
|---|---|---|---|---|

3. SECURED PARTY'S NAME (or NAME of TOTAL ASSIGNEE of ASSIGNOR S/P) - insert only one secured party name (3a or 3b)

| | | | | |
|---|---|---|---|---|
| 3a. ORGANIZATION'S NAME **Lending Bank** | | | | |
| OR 3b. INDIVIDUAL'S LAST NAME | FIRST NAME | MIDDLE NAME | | SUFFIX |
| 3c. MAILING ADDRESS **987 State Street, Attention: UCC Department** | CITY **Anytown** | STATE **MA** | POSTAL CODE **00000** | COUNTRY **USA** |

4. This FINANCING STATEMENT covers the following collateral:  THOSE ASSETS INDICATED ON ITEM 16 OF THIS FINANCING STATEMENT. This initial financing statement continues each financing statement (a "pre-effective-date financing statement") identified below. Each identified pre-effective-date financing statement remains  effective.

| Office in which the pre-effective-date financing statement was filed | Date of filing of the pre-effective-date financing statement | File number of the pre-effective-date financing statement | Date of filing of most recent continuation statement relating to the pre-effective-date financing statement | File number of the most recent continuation statement relating to the pre-effective-date financing statement |
|---|---|---|---|---|
| Secretary of State, New York | October 1, 1994 | 12345 | August 1, 1999 | 161718 |
| Secretary of State, Connecticut | May 1, 1999 | 1112131415 | Not applicable | Not applicable |

| 5. ALTERNATIVE DESIGNATION [if applicable]: | ☐ LESSEE/LESSOR | ☐ CONSIGNEE/CONSIGNOR | ☐ BAILEE/BAILOR | ☐ SELLER/BUYER | ☐ AG. LIEN | ☐ NON-UCC FILING |
|---|---|---|---|---|---|---|

| 6. ☐ This FINANCING STATEMENT is to be filed [for record] (or recorded) in the REAL ESTATE RECORDS.    Attach Addendum    [if applicable] | 7. Check to REQUEST SEARCH REPORT(S) on Debtor(s) [ADDITIONAL FEE]    [optional] | ☐ All Debtors | ☐ Debtor 1 | ☐ Debtor 2 |
|---|---|---|---|---|

8. OPTIONAL FILER REFERENCE DATA

## UCC FINANCING STATEMENT **ADDENDUM**

FOLLOW INSTRUCTIONS (front and back) CAREFULLY

**9. NAME OF FIRST DEBTOR (1a or 1b) ON RELATED FINANCING STATEMENT**

9a. ORGANIZATION'S NAME

Debtor Corporation

OR

9b. INDIVIDUAL'S LAST NAME | FIRST NAME | MIDDLE NAME,SUFFIX

10. MISCELLANEOUS:

THE ABOVE SPACE IS FOR FILING OFFICE USE ONLY

**11. ADDITIONAL DEBTOR'S EXACT FULL LEGAL NAME** - insert only one name (11a or 11b) - do not abbreviate or combine names

11a. ORGANIZATION'S NAME

OR

11b. INDIVIDUAL'S LAST NAME | FIRST NAME | MIDDLE NAME | SUFFIX

11c. MAILING ADDRESS | CITY | STATE | POSTAL CODE | COUNTRY

11d. TAX ID #: SSN OR EIN | ADD'L INFO RE ORGANIZATION DEBTOR | 11e. TYPE OF ORGANIZATION | 11f. JURISDICTION OF ORGANIZATION | 11g. ORGANIZATIONAL ID #, if any | □ NONE

**12. □ ADDITIONAL SECURED PARTY'S or □ ASSIGNOR S/P'S NAME** - insert only one name (12a or 12b)

12a. ORGANIZATION'S NAME

OR

12b. INDIVIDUAL'S LAST NAME | FIRST NAME | MIDDLE NAME | SUFFIX

12c. MAILING ADDRESS | CITY | STATE | POSTAL CODE | COUNTRY

**13.** This FINANCING STATEMENT covers □ timber to be cut or □ as-extracted collateral, or is filed as a □ fixture filing.

**14.** Description of real estate:

**16.** Additional collateral description:

All equipment, inventory, documents, accounts, instruments, chattel paper and general intangibles. All commercial tort claims arising out of Tort M. Feasor's interference with Debtor Corporation's business.

**15.** Name and address of a RECORD OWNER of above-described real estate (if Debtor does not have a record interest):

**17.** Check only if applicable and check only one box.

Debtor is a □ Trust or □ Trustee acting with respect to property held in trust or □ Decedent's Estate

**18.** Check only if applicable and check only one box.

□ Debtor is a TRANSMITTING UTILITY

□ Filed in connection with a Manufactured-Home Transaction — effective 30 years

□ Filed in connection with a Public-Finance Transaction — effective 30 years

**Form 3.2.2**

# Information Request

Rev. § 9-523 requires all filing offices to respond to requests for filed records regarding a debtor. This form may be used to make such requests. For a detailed discussion of the Items to be completed herein, see the corresponding notes in Form 3.2.3, (Paper Financing Statement).

FOLLOW INSTRUCTIONS (front and back) CAREFULLY[1]

| A. NAME & PHONE OF CONTACT AT REQUESTOR |
| --- |

B. RETURN TO: (Name and Address)

> Lending Bank
> 987 State Street
> Anytown, MA 00000
> Attention: UCC Department

**THE ABOVE SPACE IS FOR FILING OFFICE USE ONLY**

1.    DEBTOR S EXACT FULL LEGAL NAME insert only one Debtor name (1a or 1b)     .

OR

| 1a. ORGANIZATION S NAME |  |  |  |
| --- | --- | --- | --- |
| Debtor Corporation |  |  |  |
| 1b. INDIVIDUAL S LAST NAME | FIRST NAME | MIDDLE NAME | SUFFIX |

2.    INFORMATION OPTIONS RELATING TO UCC FILINGS AND OTHER NOTICES FILED IN YOUR OFFICE THAT INCLUDE AS A DEBTOR THE DEBTOR NAME INDICATED IN ITEM 1:

2a. ☒   SEARCH CERTIFICAT E  Please furnish a certi cate/report listing ALL (regardless of Debtor s address and Social Security or Tax ID#) presently effective  nancing statements, related subsequent  lings including statements of assignment, and other notices, showing the date and time of  ling and the name and address of each Secured Party named therein.

2b. ☒   SEARCH CERTIFICATE and ALL COPIES Please furnish search certi cate/report (as described in 2a above) and exact copies of each page of ALL financing statements, related subsequent  lings including statements of assignment, and other notices, including ALL attachment pages.

2c. ☒   SPECIFIED COPIES ONLY Please furnish exact copies of each page of the  nancing statements, related subsequent  lings including statements of assignment, or other notices (including all attachments) that are identified below by document locator number. Certain  ling of ces require additional identifying information please complete if required.

| Document Locator # | Date Document Filed | Additional Identifying Information (if required) |
| --- | --- | --- |
|  |  |  |
|  |  |  |
|  |  |  |

2d. ☒   SEARCH CERTIFICATE and PARTIAL COPIES (ALL FILINGS FIRST PAGES ONLY) Please furnish search certi cate/report (as described in 2a above) and exact copies of the FIRST PAGE ONLY of ALL  nancing statements, related subsequent  ling including statements of assignment, and other notices.

3.    DELIVERY INSTRUCTIONS (request will be  lled by mail to address shown in item B unless otherwise instructed here)[2]

☒  Pick Up   ☒  Other

Specify other desired method here verify that desired method is available in this state and include other pertinent delivery information (*e.g.*, courier name, addressee s account number with courier, addressee s telephone number, etc.)

[This area of national form reserved for options available in particular state.]

1. This form is not included on the CD-ROM accompanying this book, but may be obtained from your state's official government web site.

2. **Item 3:** Unless otherwise instructed, a filing office will mail information to the name and mailing address in item B. If information will be picked up from the filing office, check the "Pick Up" box. For other than mail or pick up, check the "Other" box and specify other delivery method. If specifying courier delivery, include courier name and account number to bill for delivery charge. Filing office will not deliver by courier unless prepaid waybill or account number for billing is provided. Contact the filing office concerning availability of fax service or other delivery options.

# Paper Financing Statement and Addendum

Like former Article 9, Revised Article 9 permits a security interest in many types of collateral to be perfected by the filing of a financing statement. *See* Rev. §§ 9-310 & 9-312 (setting forth types of collateral as to which financing statement may or must be filed). Rev. § 9-521 creates a form of financing statement and addendum which a filing office must accept, if properly completed and accompanied by the appropriate filing fee. This Form is identical in all material respects to the statutory form.

Revised Article 9—unlike former Article 9—does not require a debtor's signature on a financing statement. The secured party may not, however, file a financing statement against the debtor unless the filing is "authorized" by the debtor. Rev. § 9-509(a)(1). If the debtor has authenticated a security agreement, the authorization is automatic, at least to the extent of the collateral described in the security agreement. Rev. § 9-509(b). *See also* § 3 of Form 2.1 (All Personal Property Assets Security Agreement). Absent an authenticated security agreement, however, a secured party will need an authorization authenticated by the debtor to pre-file a financing statement, or to file a financing statement with a collateral description broader than that contained in the debtor's authenticated security agreement. A debtor may ratify the filing of a financing statement after it has been filed. *See* Rev. § 9-502 cmt. 3. A secured party that files a financing statement without the debtor's authorization may be liable to the debtor for actual or statutory damages. *See* Rev. § 9-625(b) & (e)(3). A form of pre-filing authorization letter appears as Form 1.3.

Please note that some filing offices have idiosyncratic formatting and similar requirements. This paper financing statement and addendum does not reflect or account for these idiosyncrasies. A useful guide to actual local filing requirements appears in *The UCC Filing Guide*, Ernst Publishing Company (Carl R. Ernst, ed.), which is updated frequently, and is supplemented by *The Revised UCC Alert*, by the same publisher.

**UCC FINANCING STATEMENT** *

FOLLOW INSTRUCTIONS (front and back) CAREFULLY

A. NAME & PHONE OF CONTACT AT FILER [optional] 1

B. SEND ACKNOWLEDGMENT TO: (Name and Address) 2

Lending Bank
987 State Street
Anytown, MA 00000
Attention: UCC Department

THE ABOVE SPACE IS FOR FILING OFFICE USE ONLY 3

1. DEBTOR'S EXACT FULL LEGAL NAME - insert only one debtor name (1a or 1b) - do not abbreviate or combine names 4

| 1a. ORGANIZATION'S NAME 5 | | | | |
|---|---|---|---|---|
| Debtor Corporation | | | | |

OR

| 1b. INDIVIDUAL'S LAST NAME 6 | FIRST NAME | MIDDLE NAME | SUFFIX |
|---|---|---|---|
| | | | |

| 1c. MAILING ADDRESS 7 | CITY | STATE | POSTAL CODE | COUNTRY |
|---|---|---|---|---|
| 123 South Charles Street | Baltimore | MD | 21201 | USA |

| 1d. TAX ID #: 8 SSN OR EIN | ADD'L INFO RE ORGANIZATION DEBTOR | 1e. TYPE OF ORGANIZATION 9 | 1f. JURISDICTION OF ORGANIZATION | 1g. ORGANIZATIONAL ID #, if any | |
|---|---|---|---|---|---|
| | | Corporation | Maryland | | ☐ NONE |

2. ADDITIONAL DEBTOR'S EXACT FULL LEGAL NAME - insert only one debtor name (2a or 2b) - do not abbreviate or combine names 10

| 2a. ORGANIZATION'S NAME | | | | |
|---|---|---|---|---|
| | | | | |

OR

| 2b. INDIVIDUAL'S LAST NAME | FIRST NAME | MIDDLE NAME | SUFFIX |
|---|---|---|---|
| | | | |

| 2c. MAILING ADDRESS | CITY | STATE | POSTAL CODE | COUNTRY |
|---|---|---|---|---|
| | | | | |

| 2d. TAX ID #: SSN OR EIN | ADD'L INFO RE ORGANIZATION DEBTOR | 2e. TYPE OF ORGANIZATION | 2f. JURISDICTION OF ORGANIZATION | 2g. ORGANIZATIONAL ID #, if any | |
|---|---|---|---|---|---|
| | | | | | ☐ NONE |

3. SECURED PARTY'S NAME (or NAME of TOTAL ASSIGNEE of ASSIGNOR S/P) - insert only one secured party name (3a or 3b) 11

| 3a. ORGANIZATION'S NAME | | | | |
|---|---|---|---|---|
| Lending Bank | | | | |

OR

| 3b. INDIVIDUAL'S LAST NAME | FIRST NAME | MIDDLE NAME | SUFFIX |
|---|---|---|---|
| | | | |

| 3c. MAILING ADDRESS | CITY | STATE | POSTAL CODE | COUNTRY |
|---|---|---|---|---|
| 987 State Street, Attention: UCC Department | Anytown | MA | 00000 | USA |

4. This FINANCING STATEMENT covers the following collateral: 12

All equipment, inventory, documents, accounts, instruments, chattel paper and general intangibles. All commercial tort claims arising out of Tort M. Feasor's interference with Debtor Corporation's business.[13]

| 5. ALTERNATIVE DESIGNATION [if applicable]: | ☐ LESSEE/LESSOR | ☐ CONSIGNEE/CONSIGNOR | ☐ BAILEE/BAILOR | ☐ SELLER/BUYER | ☐ AG. LIEN | ☐ NON-UCC FILING 14 |
|---|---|---|---|---|---|---|

6. ☐ This FINANCING STATEMENT is to be filed [for record] (or recorded) in the REAL ESTATE RECORDS. 15 Attach Addendum [if applicable]   7. Check to REQUEST SEARCH REPORT(S) on Debtor(s) 16 [ADDITIONAL FEE] [optional]   ☐ All Debtors   ☐ Debtor 1   ☐ Debtor 2

8. OPTIONAL FILER REFERENCE DATA 17

# UCC FINANCING STATEMENT ADDENDUM

FOLLOW INSTRUCTIONS (front and back) CAREFULLY

**9. NAME OF FIRST DEBTOR (1a or 1b) ON RELATED FINANCING STATEMENT** [18]

OR

9a. ORGANIZATION'S NAME

Debtor Corporation

9b. INDIVIDUAL'S LAST NAME | FIRST NAME | MIDDLE NAME,SUFFIX

**10. MISCELLANEOUS:** [19]

**THE ABOVE SPACE IS FOR FILING OFFICE USE ONLY**

**11. ADDITIONAL DEBTOR'S EXACT FULL LEGAL NAME** - insert only one name (11a or 11b) - do not abbreviate or combine names [20]

11a. ORGANIZATION'S NAME

OR

| 11b. INDIVIDUAL'S LAST NAME | FIRST NAME | MIDDLE NAME | SUFFIX |
|---|---|---|---|
| 11c. MAILING ADDRESS | CITY | STATE | POSTAL CODE | COUNTRY |

| 11d. TAX ID #:  SSN OR EIN | ADD'L INFO RE ORGANIZATION DEBTOR | 11e. TYPE OF ORGANIZATION | 11f. JURISDICTION OF ORGANIZATION | 11g. ORGANIZATIONAL ID #, if any |
|---|---|---|---|---|
| | | | | ☐ NONE |

**12.** ☐ **ADDITIONAL SECURED PARTY'S** or ☐ **ASSIGNOR S/P'S  NAME** - insert only one name (12a or 12b) [21]

12a. ORGANIZATION'S NAME

OR

| 12b. INDIVIDUAL'S LAST NAME | FIRST NAME | MIDDLE NAME | SUFFIX |
|---|---|---|---|
| 12c. MAILING ADDRESS | CITY | STATE | POSTAL CODE | COUNTRY |

**13.** This FINANCING STATEMENT covers ☐ timber to be cut or ☐ as-extracted [22] collateral, or is filed as a ☐ fixture filing.

**14.** Description of real estate:

**15.** Name and address of a RECORD OWNER of above-described real estate (if Debtor does not have a record interest):

**16.** Additional collateral description: [23]

**17.** Check only if applicable and check only one box. [24]

Debtor is a ☐ Trust  or ☐ Trustee acting with respect to property held in trust  or ☐ Decedent's Estate

**18.** Check only if applicable and check only one box. [25]

☐ Debtor is a TRANSMITTING UTILITY

☐ Filed in connection with a Manufactured-Home Transaction — effective 30 years

☐ Filed in connection with a Public-Finance Transaction — effective 30 years

1. **Item A**: To assist filing offices that might wish to communicate with the filer, the filer may wish to provide the information in Item A. This Item is optional.

2. **Item B**: Complete Item B if the filer wants to receive an acknowledgment from the filing office. If filing in a filing office that returns an acknowledgment copy furnished by filer, present simultaneously with this completed form a carbon or other copy that the filing office can use as an acknowledgment copy.

3. Do not insert anything in the open space in the upper portion of this form; it is reserved for filing office use.

4. **Item 1—Debtor name: Enter only one debtor name in Item 1,** an organization's name (1a) *or* an individual's name (1b). To add a debtor, complete Item 2, below. Enter the debtor's exact full legal name. Do not abbreviate.

5. **Item 1a—Organization debtor**: "Organization" means any legal or commercial entity. UCC § 1-201(28). For example, a partnership is an entity, and therefore an organization, while a sole proprietorship is not, even if it does business under a trade name. If the debtor is a partnership, enter the exact full legal name of the partnership. Individual partners need not be named as additional debtors. If the debtor is a registered organization, as defined in Rev. § 9-102(a)(70) (*e.g.*, corporation, limited partnership, limited liability company), it is advisable to examine the debtor's current filed formation documents (*e.g.*, articles or certificate of incorporation) to determine the debtor's correct name, organization type, and jurisdiction of organization. A financing statement that fails sufficiently to provide the exact legal name of a debtor that is a registered organization will be is "seriously misleading" and may be ineffective to perfect a security interest. *See* Rev. §§ 9-506(b) & 9-503(a)(1).

6. **Item 1b—Individual debtor**: "Individual" means a natural person;, and includes a sole proprietorship, whether or not operating under a trade name. Do not use prefixes (Mr., Mrs., Ms.). Use suffix box only for titles of lineage (Jr., Sr., III) and not for other suffixes or titles (*e.g.*, M.D.). Use a married woman's personal name (Mary Smith, not Mrs. John Smith). Enter an individual debtor's family name (surname) in Last Name box, first given name in First Name box, and all additional given names in Middle Name box.

   Whether the debtor is an individual or an organization, *do not* use a debtor's trade name, (*e.g.*, "doing-business-as" name) a/k/a, f/k/a, division name, etc. in place of or combined with the debtor's legal name. Such other names may be added as additional debtors, but doing so is neither required nor recommended.

7. **Item 1c**: An address is always required for the debtor named in Item 1a or 1b. Rev. § 9-520(a) provides that a filing office "shall refuse" to accept a financing statement for filing if, among other things, it lacks an address for the debtor, as required by Rev. § 9-516(b)(5). If a financing statement containing an incorrect address for a debtor is nevertheless accepted for filing, and is otherwise complete (and the appropriate filing fee was paid), the financing statement will be legally sufficient to perfect the subject security interest (Rev. § 9-502(a)), but may not assure the secured party priority. *See* Rev. § 9-338

8. **Item 1d**: The debtor's taxpayer identification number, social security number or employer identification number, may be required in some states. Only North Dakota and South Dakota require this item.

9. **Item 1e**: "Additional information re organization Debtor" (Items 1e, f, g) is always required. The debtor's type and jurisdiction of organization, as well as the debtor's exact legal, name can be determined from the debtor's current filed formation documents (*e.g.*, certificate or articles of incorporation). An organizational identification number, if any, is assigned by the agency where the formation documents were filed. This is different from a tax identification number. The organizational identification number should be entered preceded by the 2-character U.S. Postal identification of state of organization if one of the United States (*e.g.*, CA12345, for a California corporation whose organizational ID # is 12345). If the agency does not assign organizational identification numbers, check the box in Item 1g indicating "none."

   Note that, if the debtor is a trust or a trustee acting with respect to property held in trust, enter the debtor's name in Item 1 and attach an addendum (Form UCC1Ad) and check the appropriate box in Item 17. If the debtor is a decedent's estate, enter name of the deceased individual in Item 1b and attach addendum (Form UCC1Ad) and check the appropriate box in Item 17. If the debtor is a transmitting utility or this financing statement is filed in connection with a "manufactured-home transaction" (as defined in Rev. § 9-102(a)(54)) or a "public-finance transaction" (as defined in Rev. § 9-102(a)(67)), attach addendum (Form UCC1Ad) and check the appropriate box in Item 18.

10. **Item 2**: If an additional debtor is to be included, complete Item 2, determined and formatted as provided in the notes to Item 1. To include further additional debtors, or one or more additional secured parties, attach either addendum (Form UCC1Ad) or other additional page(s), using the correct name format. A form of financing statement addendum (Form UCC1Ad) appears immediately below.

11. **Item 3**: Enter information for the secured party or total assignee of the secured party assignor, determined and formatted per the notes to Item 1. If there is more than one secured party, see the notes to Item 2. If there has been a

total assignment of the secured party's interest prior to the filing of this form, one may either (1) enter name and address of the assignor/secured party in Item 3 and file an amendment (Form UCC3) [*see* Item 5 of that form] (a form of financing statement amendment (UCC3) appears as Form 3.2.4); *or* (2) enter the name and address of the total assignee in Item 3 and, if you wish, also attach an addendum (Form UCC1Ad) giving the name and address of the assignor/secured party in Item 12. A form of financing statement addendum appears at the end of the Form. Some states, *e.g.,* Utah, require the use of the addendum.

12. **Item 4**: Indicate here the collateral covered by the financing statement. If space in Item 4 is insufficient, put the entire collateral description or continuation of the collateral description on either an addendum (Form UCC1Ad) (Form 3.2.5) or other attached additional page(s). If additional pages are attached, they should be 8-1/2 X 11 inch sheets and set forth at the top of each sheet the name of the first debtor, formatted exactly as it appears in Item 1 of this Form. Filers are, however encouraged to use addendum (Form UCC1Ad), which appears immediately below.

13. Although commercial tort claims are similar in many respects to general intangibles, listing "general intangibles" as a type of collateral will not perfect a security interest in a commercial tort claim. Indeed, listing "commercial tort claims" in a financing statement will be insufficient to perfect a security interest in a particular commercial tort claim. Rev. § 9-108(e). Comment 5 to Rev. § 9-108 explains that a commercial tort claim must be described with greater specificity than is required of other types of collateral under the UCC. The description need not be highly specific, however: "a description such as 'all tort claims arising out of the explosion of debtor's factory' would suffice, even if the exact name of the claim, the theory on which it may be based, and the identity of the tortfeasor(s) are not described." *See* Rev. § 9-108, cmt. 5.

14. **Item 5**: If the filer desires (at filer's option) to use titles of lessee and lessor, or consignee and consignor, or seller and buyer (in the case of accounts or chattel paper), or bailee and bailor instead of "debtor" and "secured party", check the appropriate box in Item 5. If the interest perfected is an agricultural lien (as defined in Rev. § 9-102(a)(5)) filing, or is otherwise not a UCC security interest filing (*e.g.,* is a tax lien, judgment lien, etc.), check the appropriate box in Item 5, complete Items 1-7 , as applicable, and attach any other items required under other law.

15. **Item 6**: If this financing statement is filed as a fixture filing or if the collateral consists of timber to be cut or as-extracted collateral, complete Items 15, check the box in Item 6, and provide the required information (Items 13, 14 and/or 15) on addendum (Form UCC1Ad), which appears immediately below.

16. **Item 7**: This Item is optional. Check the appropriate box in Item 7 to request search report(s) on all or some of the debtors named in this financing statement. The report will list all financing statements on file against the designated debtor on the date of the report, including this financing statement. There is an additional fee for each report. If the filer has checked a box in Item 7, file a search report copy together with filing officer copy (and acknowledgment copy). Note that not all states will conduct searches and not all states will honor a search request made via this Form. Some states require a separate request form, *e.g.,* the information request, appearing as Form 3.2.2.

17. **Item 8**: This Item is optional and is for the filer's use only. For the filer's convenience of reference, filer may enter in Item 8 any identifying information (*e.g.,* secured party's loan number, law firm file number, the debtor's name or other identification, state in which form is it being filed, etc.) that filer may find useful.

18. **Item 9**: Insert name of first debtor shown in Item 1 of paper financing statement to which this addendum is related, exactly as shown in Item 1.

19. **Item 10**: Under certain circumstances, additional information not provided in a financing statement may be required or appropriate. In addition, some states may have non-uniform requirements. Use this space to provide such additional information or to comply with such requirements. If none, leave it blank.

20. **Item 20**: If this addendum adds an additional debtor, complete Item 11 in accordance with the instruments to Item 1 on the paper financing statement. To add more than one additional debtor, either use an additional addendum form for each additional debtor or replicate for each additional debtor the formatting of financing statement Item 1 on an 8-1/2 X 11 inch sheet of paper (showing at the top of the sheet the name of the first debtor shown in Item 1 of the paper financing statement). In either case, give complete information for each additional debtor in accordance with the instructions for Item 1 in the paper financing statement. All additional debtor information, especially the name, must be presented in proper format exactly identical to the format of Item 1 of the paper financing statement.

21. **Item 12**: If this addendum adds an additional secured party, complete Item 12 in accordance with the instructions for Item 3 on the paper financing statement. In the case of a total assignment of the secured party's interest before the filing of the paper financing statement, if the filer has given the name and address of the total assignee in Item 3 of the paper financing statement, the filer may give the name and address of the assignor/secured party in Item 12.

22. **Item 13**: If the collateral is timber to be cut or as-extracted collateral, or if the paper financing statement to which this addendum relates is filed as a fixture filing, check the appropriate box in Item 13; provide description of the real estate in Item 14; and, if the debtor is not a record owner of the described real estate, also provide, in Item 15, the name and address of the record owner of the real estate. Also provide a collateral description in Item 4 of the related paper financing statement, and check the box in Item 6 thereof. The description of real estate must be sufficient under the applicable law of the jurisdiction where the real estate is located.

23. **Item 16**: Use this space to provide continued description of collateral, if you cannot complete description in Item 4 of the related paper financing statement. If the debtor is a transmitting utility (as defined in Rev. § 9-102(a)(80)) or if the related paper financing statement pertains to a manufactured-home transaction (defined in Rev. § 9-102(a)(54) or a public-finance transaction (as defined in Rev. § 9-102(a)(67)), check the appropriate box in the related paper financing statement.

24. **Item 17**: If the debtor is a trust or a trustee acting with respect to property held in trust or is a decedent's estate, check the appropriate box.

25. **Item 18**: If the debtor is a transmitting utility (as defined in Rev. § 9-102(a)(80)) or if the related paper financing statement pertains to a manufactured-home transaction (defined in Rev. § 9-102(a)(54) or a public-finance transaction (as defined in Rev. § 9-102(a)(67)), check the appropriate box.

# Paper Financing Statement Amendment and Addendum

An initial financing statement may be amended for a number of purposes, including (if authorized) to add or release collateral or a debtor (Rev. § 9-509(a)), to change the name of the secured party (Rev. § 9-514(b), or to reflect a change in the debtor's name (Rev. § 9-507(c)(2)). The filer may use this amendment form to accomplish at one time both data changes (Items 4, 5, and/or 8) and a continuation of the initial financing statement (Item 3), although in some states filer may have to pay a separate fee for each purpose. Note that if the debtor's location changes, a new initial financing statement—not an amendment—must be filed in the appropriate jurisdiction and office. Rev. § 9-316(b). A form of paper financing statement appears as Form 3.2.3. As with the paper financing statement, the debtor need not and cannot sign an amendment. Nevertheless, as with the paper financing statement, an amendment cannot be filed unless authorized ratified by the debtor or otherwise permitted by Revised Article 9.

Rev. § 9-521 creates a form of financing statement amendment which a filing office must accept, if properly completed and accompanied by the appropriate filing fee. This Form is identical in all material respects to the statutory form.

## UCC FINANCING STATEMENT AMENDMENT*

FOLLOW INSTRUCTIONS (front and back) CAREFULLY

A. NAME & PHONE OF CONTACT AT FILER [optional] 1

B. SEND ACKNOWLEDGMENT TO: (Name and Address) 2

Lending Bank
987 State Street
AnyCity, MA 00001
Attention: UCC Department

THE ABOVE SPACE IS FOR FILING OFFICE USE ONLY 3

| 1a. INITIAL FINANCING STATEMENT FILE # 4 | 1b. This FINANCING STATEMENT AMENDMENT is to be filed [for record] (or recorded) in the REAL ESTATE RECORDS. 5 |
|---|---|
| 03040210 | |

2. ☐ TERMINATION: 6 Effectiveness of the Financing Statement identified above is terminated with respect to security interest(s) of the Secured Party authorizing this Termination Statement.

3. ☐ CONTINUATION: 7 Effectiveness of the Financing Statement identified above with respect to security interest(s) of the Secured Party authorizing this Continuation Statement is continued for the additional period provided by applicable law.

4. ☐ ASSIGNMENT (full or partial) 8 Give name of assignee in item 7a or 7b and address of assignee in item 7c; and also give name of assignor in item 9.

5. AMENDMENT (PARTY INFORMATION): 9 This Amendment affects ☒ Debtor or ☐ Secured Party of record. Check only one of these two boxes.

Also check one of the following three boxes and provide appropriate information in items 6 and/or 7.

☒ CHANGE name and/or address: Give current record name in item 6a or 6b; also give new name (if name change) in item 7a or 7b and/or new address (if address change) in item 7c. ☐ DELETE name: Give record name to be deleted in item 6a or 6b. ☐ ADD name: Complete item 7a or 7b, and also item 7c; also complete items 7d-7g (if applicable).

6. CURRENT RECORD INFORMATION:

| 6a. ORGANIZATION'S NAME | | | |
|---|---|---|---|
| Debtor Corporation | | | |

OR

| 6b. INDIVIDUAL'S LAST NAME | FIRST NAME | MIDDLE NAME | SUFFIX |
|---|---|---|---|
| | | | |

7. CHANGED (NEW) OR ADDED INFORMATION:

| 7a. ORGANIZATION'S NAME | | | |
|---|---|---|---|
| New Debtor Corporation | | | |

OR

| 7b. INDIVIDUAL'S LAST NAME | FIRST NAME | MIDDLE NAME | SUFFIX |
|---|---|---|---|
| | | | |

| 7c. MAILING ADDRESS | CITY | STATE | POSTAL CODE | COUNTRY |
|---|---|---|---|---|
| | | | | |

| 7d. TAX ID #: SSN OR EIN | ADD'L INFO RE ORGANIZATION DEBTOR | 7e. TYPE OF ORGANIZATION | 7f. JURISDICTION OF ORGANIZATION | 7g. ORGANIZATIONAL ID #, if any |
|---|---|---|---|---|
| | | | | ☐ NONE |

8. AMENDMENT (COLLATERAL CHANGE): check only one box 10

Describe collateral ☐ deleted or ☐ added, or give entire ☐ restated collateral description, or describe collateral ☐ assigned.

9. NAME OF SECURED PARTY OF RECORD AUTHORIZING THIS AMENDMENT (name of assignor, if this is an Assignment) 11 If this is an Amendment authorized by a Debtor which adds collateral or adds the authorizing Debtor, or if this is a Termination authorized by a Debtor, check here ☐ and enter name of DEBTOR authorizing this Amendment.

| 9a. ORGANIZATION'S NAME | | | |
|---|---|---|---|
| Lending Bank | | | |

OR

| 9b. INDIVIDUAL'S LAST NAME | FIRST NAME | MIDDLE NAME | SUFFIX |
|---|---|---|---|
| | | | |

10. OPTIONAL FILER REFERENCE DATA 12

**UCC FINANCING STATEMENT AMENDMENT ADDENDUM**

FOLLOW INSTRUCTIONS (front and back) CAREFULLY

11. INITIAL FINANCING STATEMENT FILE # (same as item 1a on Amendment form) [13]

12. NAME OF PARTY AUTHORIZING THIS AMENDMENT (same as item 9 on Amendment form) [14]

| 12a. ORGANIZATION'S NAME |  |  |
|---|---|---|

OR

| 12b. INDIVIDUAL'S LAST NAME | FIRST NAME | MIDDLE NAME,SUFFIX |
|---|---|---|

13. Use this space for additional information [15]

THE ABOVE SPACE IS FOR FILING OFFICE USE ONLY

—

—

1. **Item A**: To assist filing offices that might wish to communicate with the filer, the filer may wish to provide the information in Item A. This Item is optional.

2. **Item B**: Complete Item B if the filer wants to receive an acknowledgment from the filing office. If filing in a filing office that returns an acknowledgment copy furnished by filer, present simultaneously with this completed form a carbon or other copy that the filing office can use as an acknowledgment copy.

3. Do not insert anything in the open space in the upper portion of this form; it is reserved for filing office use.

4. **Item 1a.—File number:** Enter the file number of the initial financing statement to which this amendment relates. Enter only one file number. An amendment may relate to only one financing statement. Do not enter more than one file number in Item 1a. In some states, the file number is not unique; in those states, also enter in Item 1a, after the file number, the date that the initial financing statement was filed.

5. **Item 1b:** Only if this amendment is to be filed or recorded in the real estate records, check box 1b and also, in Item 13 of amendment addendum, enter the debtor's name, in proper format exactly identical to the format of Item 1 of financing statement, and name of the record owner if the debtor does not have a record interest.

6. **Items 2–5:** Show the purpose of this amendment by checking box 2, 3, 4, 5 (in Item 5 you must check two boxes) or 8; also complete Items 6, 7 and/or 8 as appropriate. The filer may use this amendment form to accomplish at one time data changes (Items 4, 5, and/or 8) and a continuation (Item 3), although in some states the filer may have to pay a separate fee for each purpose.

To **terminate** the effectiveness of the identified financing statement with respect to security interest(s) of authorizing secured party, check box 2. *See also* Instructions to Item 9 below. A completed form of termination statement appears as Form 3.2.7.

7. **Item 3:** To continue the effectiveness of the identified financing statement with respect to security interest(s) of an authorizing secured party, check box 3. *See also* Instructions to Item 9 below.

8. **Item 4:** To assign (i) all of assignor's interest under the identified financing statement, or (ii) a partial interest in the security interest covered by the identified financing statement, or (iii) assignor's full interest in some (but not all) of the collateral covered by the identified financing statement: Check box in Item 4 and enter the name of the assignee in Item 7a if assignee is an organization, or in Item 7b, formatted as indicated, if the assignee is an individual. Complete Item 7a or 7b, but not both. Also enter the assignee's address in Item 7c and the name of the assignor in Item 9. If a partial assignment affects only some (but not all) of the collateral covered by the identified financing statement, the filer may check the appropriate box in Item 8 and indicate the affected collateral in Item 8. A completed form of assignment of financing statement appears as Form 3.2.5.

9. **Items 5, 6, 7:** To **change the name and/or address** of a party: Check the box in Item 5 to indicate whether this amendment amends information relating to a debtor or a secured party; also check the box in Item 5 to indicate that this is a name and/or address change; also enter the name of the affected party (current record name, in the case of name change) in Items 6a or 6b as appropriate; and also give the new name (in Item 7a or 7b) and/or new address (Item 7c).

To **delete** a party: Check the box in Item 5 to indicate whether the filer is deleting a debtor or a secured party; also check the box in Item 5 to indicate that this is a deletion of a party; and also enter name (6a or 6b) of the deleted party.

To **add** a party: Check the box in Item 5 to indicate whether the filer is adding a debtor or secured party; also check box in Item 5 to indicate that this is an addition of a party; also enter all required information in Item 7: name (7a or 7b) and address (7c); also, if the filer is adding a debtor, provide a tax identification number for the debtor in those states where required, and additional organization debtor information (7e-g) if the added debtor is an organization. Note further that the preferred method for filing against a new debtor (an individual or organization not previously of record as a debtor under this file number) is to file a new financing statement (UCC1) (Form 3.2.3) and not an amendment (UCC3).

10. **Item 8:** To **change the collateral** covered by the identified financing statement, describe the change in Item 8. This may be accomplished either by describing the collateral to be added or deleted, or by setting forth in full the collateral description as it is to be effective after the filing of the amendment, indicating clearly the method chosen (check the appropriate box). If the space in Item 8 is insufficient, use Item 13 of amendment addendum (Form UCC3Ad), set forth below. A partial release of collateral is a deletion. A completed form of partial release of collateral appears as Form 3.2.6. If, due to a full release of its security interest on all collateral, the filer no longer claims a security interest under the identified financing statement, check box 2 (Termination) and not box 8 (Collateral Change). If a partial assignment consists of the assignment of some (but not all) of the collateral covered by the identified financing state-

ment, the filer may indicate the assigned collateral in Item 8, check the appropriate box in Item 8, and also comply with the instructions to Item 4 above.

11. **Item 9**: Always enter the name of the party of record authorizing this amendment. In most cases, this will be a secured party of record. *See* Rev. § 9-513. Note, however, that under Rev. § 9-509(d)(2) a debtor may file an amendment terminating the initial financing statement under certain circumstances.

If there is more than one authorizing secured party, give the name(s) of the additional secured parties, properly formatted, in Item 13 of the amendment addendum (Form UCC3Ad), set forth below. If the indicated financing statement refers to the parties as lessee and lessor, or consignee and consignor, or seller and buyer, instead of debtor and secured party, references in this amendment shall be deemed likewise so to refer to the parties. If this is an assignment, enter assignor's name. If this is an amendment authorized by a debtor that adds collateral or adds a debtor, or if this is a termination authorized by a debtor, check the box in Item 9 and enter the name, properly formatted, of the debtor authorizing this amendment, and, if this amendment or termination is to be filed or recorded in the real estate records, also enter, in Item 13 of the amendment addendum, the name of owner of record of the real estate

12. **Item 10**: This Item is optional and is for the filer's use only. For the filer's convenience of reference, filer may enter in Item 10 any identifying information (*e.g.*, secured party's loan number, law firm file number, the debtor's name or other identification, state in which form is it being filed, etc.) that filer may find useful.

13. **Item 11**: Enter information exactly as given in Item 1a on amendment form.

14. **Item 12**: Enter information exactly as given in Item 9 on amendment form.

15. **Item 13**: If space on amendment form is insufficient or you must provide additional information, enter additional information in Item 13.

# Assignment of Financing Statement

As discussed in the notes to Form 3.2.4 (Financing Statement Amendment and Addendum), an initial financing statement may be amended for a number of purposes, including (if authorized) to effect an assignment of the rights of a secured party thereunder. Rev. § 9-521 creates a form of financing statement amendment which a filing office must accept, if properly completed and accompanied by the appropriate filing fee. This Form is identical in all material respects to the statutory form. For detailed discussions of the Items within this Form, see the corresponding Items and their notes in Form 3.2.4.

UCC FINANCING STATEMENT **AMENDMENT***

FOLLOW INSTRUCTIONS (front and back) CAREFULLY

A. NAME & PHONE OF CONTACT AT FILER [optional]

B. SEND ACKNOWLEDGMENT TO:  (Name and Address)

⌐                                                                ⌐
  Great Bank
  987 State Street
  AnyCity, MA 00001
  Attention: UCC Department
└                                                                ┘

THE ABOVE SPACE IS FOR FILING OFFICE USE ONLY

| 1a. INITIAL FINANCING STATEMENT FILE # | 1b. This FINANCING STATEMENT AMENDMENT is to be filed [for record] (or recorded) in the REAL ESTATE RECORDS. |
|---|---|
| 03040210 | ☐ |

2. ☐ **TERMINATION:** Effectiveness of the Financing Statement identified above is terminated with respect to security interest(s) of the Secured Party authorizing this Termination Statement.

3. ☐ **CONTINUATION:** Effectiveness of the Financing Statement identified above with respect to security interest(s) of the Secured Party authorizing this Continuation Statement is continued for the additional period provided by applicable law.

4. ☒ **ASSIGNMENT** (full or partial):  Give name of assignee in item 7a or 7b and address of assignee in item 7c; and also give name of assignor in item 9.

5. **AMENDMENT (PARTY INFORMATION):** This Amendment affects ☐ Debtor _or_ ☐ Secured Party of record.  Check only _one_ of these two boxes.

Also check _one_ of the following three boxes _and_ provide appropriate information in items 6 and/or 7.

☐ CHANGE name and/or address:  Give current record name in item 6a or 6b; also give new name (if name change) in item 7a or 7b and/or new address (if address change) in item 7c.  ☐ DELETE name: Give record name to be deleted in item 6a or 6b.  ☐ ADD name: Complete item 7a or 7b, and also item 7c; also complete items 7d-7g (if applicable).

6. CURRENT RECORD INFORMATION:

| 6a. ORGANIZATION'S NAME | | | |
|---|---|---|---|

OR

| 6b. INDIVIDUAL'S LAST NAME | FIRST NAME | MIDDLE NAME | SUFFIX |
|---|---|---|---|

7. CHANGED (NEW) OR ADDED INFORMATION:

| 7a. ORGANIZATION'S NAME | | | |
|---|---|---|---|
| Great Bank | | | |

OR

| 7b. INDIVIDUAL'S LAST NAME | FIRST NAME | MIDDLE NAME | SUFFIX |
|---|---|---|---|

| 7c. MAILING ADDRESS | CITY | STATE | POSTAL CODE | COUNTRY |
|---|---|---|---|---|
| 987 State Street | AnyCity | MA | 00001 | USA |

| 7d. TAX ID #:  SSN OR EIN | ADD'L INFO RE ORGANIZATION DEBTOR | 7e. TYPE OF ORGANIZATION | 7f. JURISDICTION OF ORGANIZATION | 7g. ORGANIZATIONAL ID #, if any |
|---|---|---|---|---|
| | | | | ☐ NONE |

8. **AMENDMENT (COLLATERAL CHANGE):** check only _one_ box.

Describe collateral ☐ deleted  or  ☐ added,  or give entire ☐ restated collateral description, or  describe collateral ☐ assigned.

9. NAME OF SECURED PARTY OF RECORD AUTHORIZING THIS AMENDMENT (name of assignor, if this is an Assignment).  If this is an Amendment authorized by a Debtor which adds collateral or adds the authorizing Debtor,  or if this is a Termination authorized by a Debtor, check here ☐ and enter name of DEBTOR authorizing this Amendment.

| 9a. ORGANIZATION'S NAME | | | |
|---|---|---|---|
| Lending Bank | | | |

OR

| 9b. INDIVIDUAL'S LAST NAME | FIRST NAME | MIDDLE NAME | SUFFIX |
|---|---|---|---|

10. OPTIONAL FILER REFERENCE DATA

# Partial Release of Collateral

As discussed in the notes to Form 3.2.4 (Financing Statement Amendment and Addendum), an initial financing statement may be amended for a number of purposes, including (if authorized) to release collateral. Rev. § 9-521 creates a form of financing statement amendment which a filing office must accept, if properly completed and accompanied by the appropriate filing fee. This Form is identical in all material respects to the statutory form. For detailed discussions of the Items within this Form, see the corresponding Items and their notes in Form 3.2.4.

## UCC FINANCING STATEMENT **AMENDMENT***

FOLLOW INSTRUCTIONS (front and back) CAREFULLY

A. NAME & PHONE OF CONTACT AT FILER [optional]

B. SEND ACKNOWLEDGMENT TO:  (Name and Address)

⌐ Great Bank
   987 State Street
   AnyCity, MA 00001
   Attention: UCC Department ⌐

**THE ABOVE SPACE IS FOR FILING OFFICE USE ONLY**

| 1a. INITIAL FINANCING STATEMENT FILE # | 1b. This FINANCING STATEMENT AMENDMENT is |
|---|---|
| 03040210 | ☐ to be filed [for record] (or recorded) in the REAL ESTATE RECORDS. |

**2.** ☐ **TERMINATION:** Effectiveness of the Financing Statement identified above is terminated with respect to security interest(s) of the Secured Party authorizing this Termination Statement.

**3.** ☐ **CONTINUATION:** Effectiveness of the Financing Statement identified above with respect to security interest(s) of the Secured Party authorizing this Continuation Statement is continued for the additional period provided by applicable law.

**4.** ☐ **ASSIGNMENT** (full or partial): Give name of assignee in item 7a or 7b and address of assignee in item 7c; and also give name of assignor in item 9.

**5. AMENDMENT (PARTY INFORMATION):** This Amendment affects ☐ Debtor _or_ ☐ Secured Party of record. Check only _one_ of these two boxes.

Also check _one_ of the following three boxes _and_ provide appropriate information in items 6 and/or 7.

☐ CHANGE name and/or address: Give current record name in item 6a or 6b; also give new name (if name change) in item 7a or 7b and/or new address (if address change) in item 7c.   ☐ DELETE name: Give record name to be deleted in item 6a or 6b.   ☐ ADD name: Complete item 7a or 7b, and also item 7c; also complete items 7d-7g (if applicable).

**6. CURRENT RECORD INFORMATION:**

| 6a. ORGANIZATION'S NAME | | | |
|---|---|---|---|
| Good Debtor Corporation | | | |

OR

| 6b. INDIVIDUAL'S LAST NAME | FIRST NAME | MIDDLE NAME | SUFFIX |
|---|---|---|---|
| | | | |

**7. CHANGED (NEW) OR ADDED INFORMATION:**

| 7a. ORGANIZATION'S NAME | | | |
|---|---|---|---|
| | | | |

OR

| 7b. INDIVIDUAL'S LAST NAME | FIRST NAME | MIDDLE NAME | SUFFIX |
|---|---|---|---|
| | | | |

| 7c. MAILING ADDRESS | CITY | STATE | POSTAL CODE | COUNTRY |
|---|---|---|---|---|
| | | | | |

| 7d. TAX ID #:   SSN OR EIN | ADD'L INFO RE ORGANIZATION DEBTOR | 7e. TYPE OF ORGANIZATION | 7f. JURISDICTION OF ORGANIZATION | 7g. ORGANIZATIONAL ID #, if any |
|---|---|---|---|---|
| | | | | ☐ NONE |

**8. AMENDMENT (COLLATERAL CHANGE):** check only _one_ box.

Describe collateral ☒ deleted  or ☐ added,  or give entire ☐ restated collateral description, or describe collateral ☐ assigned.

Investment property credited to securities account numbered 0192837465 at Investment Brothers.

**9. NAME** OF **SECURED PARTY** OF RECORD AUTHORIZING THIS AMENDMENT (name of assignor, if this is an Assignment).  If this is an Amendment authorized by a Debtor which adds collateral or adds the authorizing Debtor,  or if this is a Termination authorized by a Debtor, check here ☐ and enter name of DEBTOR authorizing this Amendment.

| 9a. ORGANIZATION'S NAME | | | |
|---|---|---|---|
| Great Bank | | | |

OR

| 9b. INDIVIDUAL'S LAST NAME | FIRST NAME | MIDDLE NAME | SUFFIX |
|---|---|---|---|
| | | | |

**10.** OPTIONAL FILER REFERENCE DATA

# Termination Statement

As discussed in the notes to Form 3.2.4 (Financing Statement Amendment and Addendum), an initial financing statement may be amended for a number of purposes, including (if authorized) to terminate the filed financing statement. Rev. § 9-521 creates a form of financing statement amendment which a filing office must accept, if properly completed and accompanied by the appropriate filing fee. This Form is identical in all material respects to the statutory form. For detailed discussions of the Items within this Form, see the corresponding Items and their notes in Form 3.2.4.

**UCC FINANCING STATEMENT AMENDMENT***

FOLLOW INSTRUCTIONS (front and back) CAREFULLY

A. NAME & PHONE OF CONTACT AT FILER [optional]

B. SEND ACKNOWLEDGMENT TO:  (Name and Address)

Great Bank
987 State Street
AnyCity, MA 00001
Attention: UCC Department

THE ABOVE SPACE IS FOR FILING OFFICE USE ONLY

| 1a. INITIAL FINANCING STATEMENT FILE #  03040210 | 1b. This FINANCING STATEMENT AMENDMENT is ☐ to be filed [for record] (or recorded) in the REAL ESTATE RECORDS. |

2. ☒ **TERMINATION**: Effectiveness of the Financing Statement identified above is terminated with respect to security interest(s) of the Secured Party authorizing this Termination Statement.

3. ☐ **CONTINUATION**: Effectiveness of the Financing Statement identified above with respect to security interest(s) of the Secured Party authorizing this Continuation Statement is continued for the additional period provided by applicable law.

4. ☐ **ASSIGNMENT** (full or partial):  Give name of assignee in item 7a or 7b and address of assignee in item 7c; and also give name of assignor in item 9.

5. **AMENDMENT (PARTY INFORMATION):** This Amendment affects ☐ Debtor _or_ ☐ Secured Party of record. Check only _one_ of these two boxes.
Also check _one_ of the following three boxes _and_ provide appropriate information in items 6 and/or 7.

☐ CHANGE name and/or address: Give current record name in item 6a or 6b; also give new name (if name change) in item 7a or 7b and/or new address (if address change) in item 7c.  ☐ DELETE name: Give record name to be deleted in item 6a or 6b.  ☐ ADD name: Complete item 7a or 7b, and also item 7c; also complete items 7d-7g (if applicable).

6. CURRENT RECORD INFORMATION:

| 6a. ORGANIZATION'S NAME | | | |
|---|---|---|---|
| OR  6b. INDIVIDUAL'S LAST NAME | FIRST NAME | MIDDLE NAME | SUFFIX |

7. CHANGED (NEW) OR ADDED INFORMATION:

| 7a. ORGANIZATION'S NAME | | | |
|---|---|---|---|
| OR  7b. INDIVIDUAL'S LAST NAME | FIRST NAME | MIDDLE NAME | SUFFIX |
| 7c. MAILING ADDRESS | CITY | STATE  POSTAL CODE | COUNTRY |

| 7d. TAX ID #:  SSN OR EIN | ADD'L INFO RE ORGANIZATION DEBTOR | 7e. TYPE OF ORGANIZATION | 7f. JURISDICTION OF ORGANIZATION | 7g. ORGANIZATIONAL ID #, if any ☐ NONE |

8. **AMENDMENT (COLLATERAL CHANGE)**: check only _one_ box.
Describe collateral ☐ deleted  or ☐ added, or give entire ☐ restated collateral description, or describe collateral ☐ assigned.

9. NAME OF SECURED PARTY OF RECORD AUTHORIZING THIS AMENDMENT (name of assignor, if this is an Assignment). If this is an Amendment authorized by a Debtor which adds collateral or adds the authorizing Debtor,  or if this is a Termination authorized by a Debtor, check here ☐ and enter name of DEBTOR authorizing this Amendment.

| 9a. ORGANIZATION'S NAME  Great Bank | | | |
|---|---|---|---|
| OR  9b. INDIVIDUAL'S LAST NAME | FIRST NAME | MIDDLE NAME | SUFFIX |

10. OPTIONAL FILER REFERENCE DATA

Form 3.3.1

# Deposit Account Control Agreement[1]

CONTROL AGREEMENT, dated as of [date], by and among [Name of Secured Party], with an address at [address of Secured Party] ("Secured Party"); [Name of Debtor], with an address at [address of Debtor] ("Debtor"); and [Name of Bank] with an address at [address of Bank] ("Bank").[2]

---

1.   A security interest in a deposit account that is original collateral (as opposed to proceeds) may be perfected only by "control." Rev. §§ 9-312(b)(1) & 314(a). Under Rev. § 9-104(a)(2), the secured party will have "control" of a deposit account if, among other things, the debtor, the secured party, and the bank have agreed that the bank will comply with instructions originated by the secured party directing disposition of the funds in the deposit account without further consent of the debtor. The secured party may also have "control" of a deposit account under Rev. § 9-104(a) if (i) it is the bank with which the deposit account is maintained or (ii) the secured party becomes the bank's "customer" with respect to the deposit account. *See* Rev. § 9-104(a)(1)&(3). *See also* UCC § 4-104 (defining "customer"). This form is intended to be used to create control under the first alternative.

If the deposit account is not original collateral, but instead contains identifiable cash proceeds, the security interest may be perfected by a means other than "control" if the security interest in the original collateral was perfected. *See* Rev. § 9-315(c) & (d)(2). However, a security interest in a deposit account perfected by control will have priority over a security interest perfected by other means, including as to proceeds, even if control arose after perfection by the other means. Rev. § 9-327(1). As between two secured parties claiming to be perfected by control, priority ranks according to priority in time of obtaining control. Rev. § 9-327(2). The bank that is also the secured party will always have priority regardless of when it obtained control. Rev. § 9-327(3).

Control agreements are voluntary. A bank is not required to enter into a control agreement. *See* Rev. § 9-342 ("This article does not require a bank to enter into a [control] agreement of the kind described in [Rev. §] 9-104(a)(2), even if its customer so requests or directs"). The term "account control agreement," while descriptive, is not a term used in Revised Article 9.

This form contains an unusually large number of bracketed provisions, indicating that there may be a number of matters for negotiation by the parties. The securities account control agreement (Form 3.3.2) shares certain, but not all, features with this form. The forms are not intended to be interchangeable.

2.   The "bank" is defined in Rev. § 9-102(a)(8) as "an organization that is engaged in the business of banking. The term includes savings banks, savings and loan associations, credit unions, and trust companies." *See also* UCC §§ 1-201(4) (defining the bank under UCC Article 1) & 4-105(1) (defining the bank under UCC Article 4). Article 4 of the UCC and other law, not Article 9, governs the relationship of the bank and customer.

## PREAMBLE:

Debtor has granted Secured Party a security interest[3] in a deposit account[4] maintained by Bank for Debtor. The parties are entering into this agreement to perfect Secured Party's security interest in that account.

## TERMS:

SECTION 1. **The Account.** Bank maintains a deposit account for Debtor, currently numbered [_____] and titled [_____] (as such account may be renumbered[5] or retitled, the "Account"). All parties agree that the Account is a "deposit account" within the meaning of Article 9 of the Uniform Commercial Code of the State of [_____] (the "UCC").[6]

SECTION 2. **Control.** Bank will comply with instructions originated by Secured Party directing disposition of the funds in the Account without further consent by Debtor.[7] [*Except as provided below, Bank will not permit the withdrawal or other disposition*[8] *of any*

---

3.    The creation of the security interest must be "pursuant to agreement" which, when control exists, does not need to be in writing, although written agreements are recommended. *Cf.* Rev. § 9-203(b)(3)(D) (permitting attachment via control agreement in lieu of authenticated record security agreement). This form deposit account control agreement is not a security agreement. A form of security agreement—all personal property assets security agreement, that could be used in connection with this form, appears in this book as Form 2.1. The security agreement should, but need not, be specifically identified in the control agreement. The bank need not, and normally will not, be a party to the security agreement, unless it also the secured party. If the bank *is* also the secured party, this form would have to be modified. Unlike the treatment of securities accounts, there is no statutory distinction between the deposit account and the funds credited to it. *See* Rev. § 9-203(h) (regarding treatment of securities accounts and securities entitlements).

4.    A "deposit account" is defined in Rev. § 9-102(a)(29) as "a demand, time, savings, passbook, or similar account maintained with a bank."

5.    The definition of "Account" allows for possible renumbering, which may happen automatically under certain circumstances (such as when the account is moved to a different branch), or for retitling, as when the secured party wishes its own name or other indication of its security interest added to the account title.

6.    The fact that the parties agree that an account is a deposit account is not necessarily controlling. A court or regulatory authority may determine that the account is not a deposit account.

7.    This language tracks Rev. § 9-104(a)(2). Under this agreement, the secured party's right to give instructions with respect to the account is not conditioned on the debtor's default under any agreement between the debtor and the secured party. If the secured party's rights were conditioned on the debtor's default, it would still have "control." Rev. § 9-104 cmt. 3 (the bank has control "even if the bank's agreement is subject to specified conditions, *e.g.*, that the secured party's instructions are accompanied by a certification that the debtor is in default.") It is not likely, however, that the bank will want to be put in the position of having to decide whether the condition has been satisfied—that is, whether the secured party has become entitled to give a "Notice of Exclusive Control," as defined in this § 2.

         Some may be concerned that conditioning the secured party's ability to originate instructions upon the occurrence (or the allegation) of an event of default under the underlying security agreement could be viewed as delaying the secured party's acquisition of control, and thus perfection, of its security interest. That concern should be unfounded. Comment 3 to Rev. § 9-104 anticipates and solves these problems by explaining that "[a]n agreement to comply with the secured party's instructions suffices for "control" of a deposit account under this section even if the bank's agreement is subject to specified conditions, *e.g.*, that the secured party's instructions are accompanied by a certification that the debtor is in default."

8.    The secured party may have "control" of the deposit account even if it permits the debtor to withdraw or otherwise dispose of funds in the deposit account. *See* Rev. § 9-104(b) & cmt. 3.

*funds in the Account by Debtor without Secured Party's prior* [written] *consent.*][9] [*Bank may also comply with instructions directing the disposition of funds in the Account originated by Debtor or its authorized representatives until such time as Secured Party delivers a* [written][10] *notice to Bank that Secured Party is thereby exercising exclusive control over the Account.*][11] Such notice is referred to herein as the "Notice of Exclusive Control." After Bank receives a Notice of Exclusive Control [*and has had reasonable opportunity to comply*],[12] it will cease complying with instructions concerning the Account or funds on deposit therein originated by Debtor or its representatives. Bank has not and will not agree with any third party to comply with instructions or other directions concerning the Account or the disposition of funds in the Account originated by such third party without the prior [*written*][13] consent of Secured Party and Debtor.[14]

SECTION 3. **Subordination of Bank's security interest.** Bank hereby subordinates all security interests, encumbrances, claims and rights of setoff it may have, now or in the future, against the Account or any funds in the Account other than in connection with the payment of Bank's customary fees and charges pursuant to its agreement with Debtor and for the reversal of provisional credits.[15]

SECTION 4. **Statements, confirmations and notices of adverse claims.** Bank will send copies of all statements concerning the Account to each of Debtor and Secured Party at the address set forth in the heading of this Agreement. Upon receipt of written notice of any lien, encumbrance or adverse claim against the Account or any funds credited thereto, Bank will make reasonable efforts promptly to notify Secured Party and Debtor thereof.

---

9.   The extent and nature of the debtor's access to the account is a business point to be negotiated by the parties. The secured party may feel comfortable allowing the debtor and the bank to withdraw or dispose of funds in the ordinary course of business. Alternatively, some collateral monitoring or maintenance provisions may be added, which may impose administrative costs on the bank.

10.   The parties may wish to permit oral or electronic instructions. As noted above, best practice would dictate that oral instructions be complemented by a written or authenticated electronic confirmation of the oral instruction.

11.   As noted above, the debtor may withdraw or otherwise dispose of funds in the deposit account without impairing the secured party's control, Rev. § 9-104(b) & cmt. 3. The notice of exclusive control performs some, but not all, of the functions of the "entitlement order" contemplated in the securities account control agreement. *Compare* § 2, Form 3.3.2.

12.   In the securities account context, UCC § 8-115(1) explicitly affords a securities intermediary a "reasonable opportunity" to act on an injunction, restraining order or other legal process before incurring liability to adverse claimants, prompting the drafters of some securities account control agreements to include such an opportunity to act on notices of exclusive control in that context. *See* § 7.1, Form 3.3.2. No similar statutory provision applies to deposit accounts, but a specific contractual provision to this effect may be desirable from the bank's perspective.

13.   The parties may wish to permit oral or electronic consent. Best practice would dictate that oral consent be supplemented by a written or authenticated electronic confirmation of the oral instruction. When this form deposit account control agreement refers to "written" consent or instructions or notifications, it should be understood that oral and/or electronic alternatives may be acceptable. Of course, the control agreement itself must be either written or electronic. *See* Rev. § 9-104(a)(2) (the bank must agree in "authenticated record" to control agreement).

14.   This provision ensures that the bank does not comply with a later request by the debtor that it enter into a control agreement with another secured party. Although the bank would still have priority over a later secured party perfected by control under Rev. § 9-327(2), the secured party would likely be uncomfortable with a junior security interest in the deposit account. *See* Rev. § 9-332.

15.   Absent subordination under this control agreement, the bank has priority as a matter of law under Rev. §§ 9-327(3) & 9-340.

SECTION 5. **Bank's responsibility.** Except for acting on Debtor's instructions in violation of Section 2 above, Bank shall have no responsibility or liability to Secured Party for complying with instructions concerning the Account from Debtor or Debtor's authorized representatives which are received by Bank before Bank receives a Notice of Exclusive Control and has had reasonable opportunity to act on it. Bank shall have no responsibility or liability to Debtor for complying with a Notice of Exclusive Control or complying with instructions concerning the Account originated by Secured Party, and shall have no responsibility to investigate the appropriateness of any such instruction or Notice of Exclusive Control, even if Debtor notifies Bank that Secured Party is not legally entitled to originate any such instruction or Notice of Exclusive Control.

SECTION 7. **Indemnity.** Debtor and Secured Party hereby agree to indemnify[16] and hold harmless Bank, its directors, officers, agents and employees against any and all claims, causes of action, liabilities, lawsuits, demands and damages, including without limitation, any and all court costs and reasonable attorney's fees, in any way related to or arising out of or in connection with this Agreement or any action taken or not taken pursuant hereto, except to the extent caused by Bank's gross negligence or willful misconduct or Bank's breach of any of the provisions hereof.

SECTION 8. **Customer agreement.** In the event of a conflict between this Agreement and any other agreement between the Bank and the Debtor relating to the Account, the terms of this Agreement will prevail[; *provided, however, that this Agreement shall not alter or affect any mandatory arbitration provision currently in effect between Bank and Debtor pursuant to a separate agreement*].[17]

SECTION 9. **Termination.**[18] [*Unless earlier terminated by Bank pursuant to this section,*] this Agreement shall continue in effect until Secured Party has notified Bank in writing that this Agreement, or its security interest in the Account, is terminated. Upon receipt of such notice the obligations of Bank hereunder with respect to the operation and maintenance of the Account after the receipt of such notice shall terminate, Secured Party shall have no further right to originate instructions concerning the Account and any previous Notice of Exclusive Control delivered by Secured Party shall be deemed to be of no further force and effect. [*Bank reserves the right, unilaterally, to terminate this Agreement, such termination to be effective* [insert number] *business days' after written notice thereof is given to Debtor and Secured Party.*[19]]

---

16.    The willingness of either the secured party or the debtor to indemnify the bank may be a subject for negotiation. Such indemnities, although not uncommon, are by no means universal.

17.    At least anecdotally, it appears that arbitration is a more common feature of securities accounts than deposit accounts. *Compare* § 10, Form 3.3.2.

18.    Section 9 of the form of securities account control agreement (Form 3.3.2) contains a somewhat simpler provision on termination.

19.    The bank will ordinarily expect to be able to cease acting in connection with the account, although permitting the bank to terminate the control agreement while the security interest remains in effect poses a significant risk to the secured party. If the bank does not have the unilateral right to terminate (with notice), the terms and conditions of any bank-initiated termination will need to be negotiated.

SECTION 10. **Complete agreement; amendments.** This Agreement and the instructions and notices required or permitted to be executed and delivered hereunder set forth the entire agreement of the parties with respect to the subject matter hereof, and, subject to § 8 above supersede any prior agreement and contemporaneous oral agreements of the parties concerning its subject matter. No amendment, modification or (except as otherwise specified in § 9 above) termination of this Agreement, nor any assignment of any rights hereunder (except to the extent contemplated under § 13 below), shall be binding on any party hereto unless it is in writing and is signed by each of the parties hereto, and any attempt to so amend, modify, terminate or assign except pursuant to such a writing shall be null and void. No waiver of any rights hereunder shall be binding on any party hereto unless such waiver is in writing and signed by the party against whom enforcement is sought.

SECTION 11. **Governing law.** This Agreement [and the agreement governing the Account] shall be governed by and construed in accordance with the law of the State of [_____].[20] [*The parties agree that* [_____] *is the "bank's jurisdiction" for purposes of the UCC.*][21]

SECTION 12. **Severability.** To the extent a provision of this Agreement is unenforceable, this Agreement will be construed as if the unenforceable provision were omitted.

SECTION 13. **Successors and assigns.**[22] The terms of this Agreement shall be binding upon, and shall inure to the benefit of, the parties hereto and their respective [corporate] successors or heirs and personal representatives. This Agreement may be assigned by Secured Party to any successor of Secured Party under its security agreement with Debtor, provided that written notice thereof is given by Secured Party to Bank.

SECTION 14. **Notices.**[23] Except as otherwise expressly provided herein, any notice, order, instruction, request or other communication required or permitted to be given under this Agreement shall be in writing and deemed to have been properly given when delivered in person, or when sent by telecopy or other electronic means and electronic confirmation of error-free receipt is received or upon receipt of notice sent by certified or registered United States mail, return receipt requested, postage prepaid, addressed to the

---

20.   This choice of law provision establishes the bank's jurisdiction under Rev. § 9-304. This may or may not be different from the choice of law provision in the underlying account agreement, if any. Best practice may dictate using the same law for some (or all) purposes. Revised Article 9 recognizes a contractual choice of law by the bank and its customer. *See* Rev. § 9-304(b)(2).

21.   The parties may choose governing law without necessarily agreeing as to the "bank's jurisdiction" under Rev. § 9-304. If the parties wish to choose the bank's jurisdiction, as provided in Rev. § 9-304, they may use the bracketed language.

22.   Section 13 of the form of securities account control agreement (Form 3.3.2) contains a somewhat simpler provision on successors and assigns.

23.   Section 14 of the form of securities account control agreement (Form 3.3.2) contains a somewhat simpler provision on notices.

party at the address set forth next to such party's name at the heading of this Agreement.[24] Any party may change its address for notices in the manner set forth above.

SECTION 15. **Jury Waiver.**[25] THE DEBTOR WAIVES ITS RIGHT TO A JURY TRIAL WITH RESPECT TO ANY ACTION OR CLAIM ARISING OUT OF ANY DISPUTE IN CONNECTION WITH THIS AGREEMENT, ANY RIGHTS, REMEDIES, OBLIGATIONS, OR DUTIES HEREUNDER, OR THE PERFORMANCE OR ENFORCEMENT HEREOF OR THEREOF.

SECTION 16. **Counterparts.** This Agreement may be executed in any number of counterparts, all of which shall constitute one and the same instrument, and any party hereto may execute this Agreement by signing and delivering one or more counterparts.

SIGNATURES:

SECURED PARTY:

By:_____
Title:_____

DEBTOR:

By:_____
Title:_____

BANK:

By:_____
Title:_____

---

24.    If the parties elect to give notice electronically, they should provide both an email address and a telecopy number at the beginning of this agreement. Parties using electronic communications may wish to use the electronic mail protocol, set forth as Form 1.2.

25.    A jury waiver may not be appropriate or enforceable in a consumer context, and may be irrelevant if disputes under the agreement are subject to binding arbitration. *See* § 8 of this form.

Form 3.3.2

# Securities Account Control Agreement[1]

CONTROL AGREEMENT, dated as of [date], by and among [Name of Secured Party], with an address at [address of Secured Party] ("Secured Party"); [Name of Debtor], with an address at [address of Debtor] ("Debtor"); and [Name of Securities Intermediary] with an address at [address of Securities Intermediary] ("Intermediary").[2]

---

1    A security interest in investment property (*e.g.*, securities) may be perfected by control or filing a financing statement. Rev. § 9-312(a) & 9-314(a). A security interest in investment property perfected by control will have priority over a security interest in the same investment property perfected by filing. Rev. § 9-328. This form is intended to be used to create control of investment property for the benefit of the secured party. For the most part, "control" of investment property is the same under Revised Article 9 as it is under the 1994 version of UCC Article 8 and includes delivery, with indorsements, of certificated securities to the secured party, an agreement by the issuer of uncertificated securities that the issuer will honor orders from the secured party without further consent of the debtor, and an agreement by a securities intermediary maintaining a securities account that it will honor instructions from the secured party without further consent of the debtor. Control also includes registering the securities in the name of the secured party, having the secured party become the security entitlement holder, or having another person acknowledge that it has control on behalf of the secured party. Where the secured party is the debtor's securities intermediary, the securities intermediary automatically has control. Rev. § 9-106 & UCC § 8-106.

Like the deposit account control agreement, set forth as Form 3.3.1 in this book, a securities account control agreement is voluntary. The intermediary is not required to enter into such an agreement even if the debtor so directs, and cannot enter into such an agreement without the debtor's consent. UCC § 8-106(g). For the secured party to have control, the intermediary must be a party to the agreement. UCC § 8-106 cmt. 5. The term "account control agreement," while descriptive, is not a term used in UCC Articles 8 or 9.

The deposit account control agreement (Form 3.3.1) shares certain, but not all, features with this form. The forms are not intended to be interchangeable.

2.    A "securities intermediary" is defined in UCC § 8-102(a)(14) as "(i) a clearing corporation; or (ii) a person, including a bank or broker, that in the ordinary course of its business maintains accounts for others and is acting in that capacity." A "broker" is defined in UCC § 8-102(a)(3) as "a person defined as a broker or dealer under the federal securities laws, but without excluding a bank acting in that capacity."

## PREAMBLE:

Debtor has granted Secured Party a security interest[3] in a securities account[4] maintained by Intermediary for Debtor. The parties are entering into this agreement to perfect Secured Party's security interest in that account.

## TERMS:

SECTION 1. **The Account.** Intermediary represents and warrants to Secured Party that:

1.1    Intermediary maintains a securities account number [_____] for Debtor, and titled [_____] (as such account may be renumbered[5] or retitled, the "Account").

1.2    **Exhibit A** is a statement produced by Intermediary in the ordinary course of its business regarding the property credited to the Account at the statement's date. Intermediary does not know of any inaccuracy in the statement.[6]

---

3.    The creation of the security interest must be "pursuant to agreement", which in this case does not need to be in writing, although written agreements are recommended. *Cf.* Rev. § 9-203(b)(3)(D) (permitting attachment via control agreement in lieu of authenticated record security agreement). This form securities account control agreement is not a security agreement. A form of all personal property assets security agreement, that could be used in connection with this form, appears in this book as Form 2.1. The security agreement should, but need not, be specifically identified in the control agreement. The intermediary need not, and normally will not, be a party to the security agreement, unless it is also the secured party. If the intermediary *is* also the secured party, this form would have to be modified. Unlike the treatment of deposit accounts, there is a statutory distinction between the securities account and the "security entitlements" carried in that account. *See* Rev. § 9-203(h) (regarding treatment of securities accounts and securities entitlements).

4.    A "securities account" is "an account to which a financial asset is or may be credited in accordance with an agreement under which the person maintaining the account [here, the intermediary] undertakes to treat the person for whom the account is maintained [the debtor] as entitled to exercise the rights that comprise the financial asset." UCC § 8-501(a). ("Account" is obviously not used in the definition of securities account (or in this form) in its Article 9 sense of a right to payment of certain monetary obligations. *Cf.* Rev. § 9-102(a)(2)). "Financial assets" include (i) securities, (ii) obligations of or interests in a person or property or an enterprise that is of a type traded on financial markets or recognized as a medium for investment, and (iii) property held by the intermediary in the account *if* the intermediary agrees that the property is to be treated as a financial asset under Article 8. UCC § 8-102(a)(9). Once the property in the account is a "financial asset," the debtor will have a "security entitlement" with respect to it (UCC § 8-102(a)(17)). the debtor's security entitlement with respect to a financial asset will be "investment property," and the secured party will be able to perfect a security interest in such investment property by this investment property account control agreement. "Investment property" is comprised of certificated and uncertificated securities, securities accounts and security entitlements, all of which are defined in UCC Article 8. Rev. § 9-102(a)(49); *see also* UCC §§ 8-102(a)(15)(defining "security"), 8-501(a)(defining "securities account") & 8-102(a)(17)(defining "security entitlement"). Investment property also includes commodity contracts (Rev. § 9-102(a)(15)) and commodity accounts. Rev. § 9-102(a)(14). *See also* Rev. § 9-102(a)(49), although this form is not intended to be used to create control of a commodity contract, which is subject to different rules set forth in Rev. § 9-106(b).

5.    The definition of "account" allows for possible renumbering, which may happen automatically under certain circumstances (such as when the account is moved to a different branch), or for retitling, as when the secured party wishes its own name or other indication of its security interest added to the account title.

6.    The intermediary does not represent or warrant the accuracy of the account statement, only that it was produced in the ordinary course of business and that the intermediary does not know that the statement is inaccurate. The intermediary "knows" of an inaccuracy if it has actual knowledge of the inaccuracy. UCC § 1-201(25). Note that the deposit account control agreement, Form 3.3.1, contains no comparable provision.

1.3    Intermediary does not know of any claim to or interest in the Account, except for claims and interests of the parties referred to in this agreement [, *except that property noted as* [...] *or* [...] *on* **Exhibit A** *is not property credited to the Account*].[7]

1.4    All property credited to the Account, and all other rights of Debtor against Intermediary arising out of the Account, including any free credit balances, will be treated as "financial assets" under Article 8 of the [jurisdiction] Uniform Commercial Code.[8]

SECTION 2. **Control by Secured Party.** Intermediary will comply with all notifications it receives directing it to transfer or redeem any financial assets in the Account (each an "entitlement order"[9]) originated by Secured Party without further consent by Debtor.[10]

---

7.    The intermediary's representation and warranty in § 103 will provide the secured party with some comfort that the debtor has a "clean" title to the financial assets in the account. For example, it will provide comfort that the account is not a joint account. (Sections 4, "priority of the secured party's security interest," and 5, "no third party control," will give the secured party comfort as to the priority of its security interest.). Note that the deposit account control agreement, Form 3.3.1, contains no comparable provision.

Financial assets registered in the debtor's name, payable to her order or specially endorsed to her (and that have not been endorsed to the intermediary or in blank) are not part of the account. UCC § 8-501(d). Therefore, the secured party cannot perfect its security interest in such assets by using an account control agreement. To avoid listing any such assets, the intermediary may want to set up a separate "clean" account that does not contain such assets. Alternatively, the intermediary may include the bracketed language identifying those assets that may be listed in the account statement but are not part of the account. (Some intermediaries mark these assets as "certificated" or "in safekeeping.")

8.    This paragraph assures that the secured party will have a perfected security interest in all property credited to the account, even if the property is not a security.

A commodity contract cannot be a "financial asset." UCC § 8-103(f). Accordingly, the debtor cannot have a security entitlement with respect to a commodity contract. Commodity contracts and commodity accounts are, however, investment property (Rev. § 9-102(a)(49)) in which a security interest can be perfected by control conferred by an appropriate agreement between a commodity intermediary, its debtor and the secured party. Rev. § 9-106(b)(2). This form would have to be modified to perfect a security interest in such assets.

9.    An "entitlement order" is a notice to the intermediary directing it to transfer or redeem a financial asset to which the debtor has a security entitlement. UCC § 8-102(a)(8). It performs some, but not all, of the functions of the "notice of exclusive control" contemplated in the deposit account control agreement. *Compare* § 2, Form 3.3.1.

This form contemplates that entitlement orders be oral. *See* § 14, *infra.* Best practice may dictate that oral entitlement orders be confirmed by a written or authenticated electronic confirmation of the oral instruction. When this form securities account control agreement refers to "written" consent or instructions or notifications, it should be understood that oral and/or electronic alternatives may be acceptable.

10.    This § 2 perfects the secured party's security interest in both the account and the financial assets in the account. An agreement that provides that the intermediary will, without the debtor's consent, honor instructions from the secured party concerning the account will give the secured party control over the security entitlements carried in the account. Rev. § 9-106 cmt. 4. If the secured party obtains control over all security entitlements carried in the account, the secured party will also have control over the account (Rev. § 9-106(c)), and therefore will have perfected its security interest in the account. Rev. § 9-314(a).

Under this agreement, the secured party's right to give an entitlement order is not conditioned on the debtor's default under any agreement between the debtor and secured party. If the secured party's right to give an entitlement order was conditioned on the debtor's default, it would still have "control." UCC § 8-106 cmt. 7. It is not likely, however, that the intermediary will want to be put in the position of having to decide whether the condition has been satisfied—that is, whether the secured party has become entitled to give an entitlement order.

Some may be concerned that conditioning the secured party's ability to originate instructions upon the occurrence (or the allegation) of an event of default under the underlying security agreement could be viewed as delaying the secured party's acquisition of control, and thus perfection, of its security interest. That concern should be unfounded. Comment 7 to Rev. § 9-106 anticipates and solves these problems by explaining that "There is no implication that retention by the debtor of powers other than those [set forth UCC § 9-106(f)] is inconsistent with the [secured party] having control."

SECTION 3. **Subordination of Intermediary's security interest.**[11] Intermediary subordinates in favor of Secured Party any security interest, lien or right of setoff Intermediary may have, now or in the future, against the Account or financial assets in the Account, *except* that Intermediary will retain its prior lien on financial assets in the Account to secure payment for financial assets purchased for the Account and normal commissions and fees for the Account.[12]

SECTION 4. **Debtor's rights in Account.** Except as otherwise provided in this § 4 Intermediary will comply with entitlement orders originated by Debtor without further consent by Secured Party.[13] If Secured Party notifies Intermediary that Secured Party will exercise exclusive control over the Account (a "notice of exclusive control"), Intermediary will cease[14] (i) complying with entitlement orders or other directions concerning the Account originated by Debtor, and (ii) distributing to Debtor interest and/or dividends on financial assets in the Account. Until Intermediary receives a notice of exclusive control, Intermediary may distribute to Debtor all interest and regular cash dividends on financial assets in the Account.[15] Intermediary will not comply with any entitlement order originated by Debtor that would require Intermediary to make a free delivery[16] to Debtor or any other person.[17]

---

11.    This Section and the truth of the representation contained in § 5 ensure that the secured party has priority over any other security interests in the account that are perfected under the UCC.

12.    Without this subordination, any security interest in the securities account held by the intermediary would have priority over the secured party. Rev. § 9-328(3). A practical consequence of the intermediary's subordination is that the account must be a cash account, not a margin account. The intermediary's junior security interest may be useful to the intermediary if the debtor has a debit in a separate margin account with the intermediary. This provision protects the intermediary's margin claim.

13.    Unless otherwise agreed, the intermediary has a duty to comply with the debtor's entitlement orders. Rev. UCC § 9-507(a). The importance of the first sentence in the text of § 3 lies, therefore, in its introductory proviso. The debtor's right to give entitlement orders does not preclude the secured party from having control over the account. UCC § 8-106(f). The secured party might want to limit the kinds of investment that the debtor can make. Such a provision would, however, require a degree of monitoring that the intermediary may be unable or unwilling to provide.

Note that UCC § 8-115(1) explicitly affords a securities intermediary a "reasonable opportunity" to act on an injunction, restraining order or other legal process before incurring liability to adverse claimants. No similar statutory provision applies to deposit accounts, but a specific contractual provision to this effect may be desirable from the bank's perspective. *See* § 3, Form 3.3.1.

14.    The intermediary's duty to obey the debtor's entitlement orders can be modified by agreement. UCC § 8-507 cmt. 3. The control agreement should specify whether, and under what circumstances, the debtor can continue to give entitlement orders. If the debtor is to be permitted to originate entitlement orders—for example, if the account is a trading account—the control agreement must provide a mechanism for extinguishing this right. The term "notice of exclusive control" is not used in Revised Article 9. The security agreement, rather than the control agreement, should state the circumstances (*e.g.*, events of default) under which the secured party can deliver a notice of exclusive control. If the debtor is not given access to the account, this agreement can so provide.

15.    The debtor's right to receive dividends and other distributions would not defeat the secured party's control. UCC § 8-106 cmt. 4 (Example 7).

16.    A "free delivery" refers to a transfer of a security or other financial asset from a securities account other than in connection with trading activities. *See* Sandra M. Rocks & Robert A. Wittie, *Getting Control of Control Agreements*, 283, n. 18 in AMERICAN LAW INSTITUTE—AMERICAN BAR ASSOCIATION CONTINUING LEGAL EDUCATION, ALI-ABA COURSE OF STUDY, SF80 ALI-ABA 275 (March 8, 2001) ("The use of the term "withdrawal" appears to be understood in the market to refer to "free deliveries" or other instructions by a customer to deliver to a named recipient, as opposed to "trading" in an account, which is accomplished by the Broker executing a trade with a third party.")

17.    The secured party will have control even without this provision. However, allowing the debtor to withdraw property or make free deliveries from the account would undermine the economic value of the secured party's security interest. If the secured party wants to allow the debtor to make a specific withdrawal or free delivery, the secured party can give the appropriate entitlement order. A more complicated alternative would be for the securities account control agreement to allow the debtor to give the entitlement order if the secured party gives the intermediary a certificate permitting the withdrawal or delivery.

SECTION 5. **No third party control.** Intermediary represents and warrants that no third party has a right to give an entitlement order regarding financial assets in the Account.[18] Intermediary will not agree with any third party that Intermediary will comply with entitlement orders originated by the third party.[19]

SECTION 6. **Statements, confirmations and notices of adverse claims.** Intermediary will send copies of all statements and confirmations for the Account simultaneously to Debtor and Secured Party.[20] Intermediary will use reasonable efforts to promptly notify Secured Party and Debtor if any other person claims that it has a property interest in a financial asset in the Account and that it is a violation of that person's rights for anyone else to hold, transfer or deal with the financial asset.[21]

SECTION 7. **Intermediary's responsibility.**

7.1  Except for permitting a withdrawal, delivery or payment in violation of Section 3, Intermediary will not be liable to Secured Party for complying with entitlement orders from Debtor that are received by Intermediary before Intermediary receives and has a reasonable opportunity to act on a notice of exclusive control.[22] Intermediary will not be liable to Debtor for complying with a notice of exclusive control or with entitlement orders originated by Secured Party, even if Debtor notifies Intermediary[23] that Secured Party is not legally entitled to issue the entitlement order or notice of exclusive control, unless (i) Intermediary takes the action after it is served with an injunction, restraining order or other legal process enjoining it from doing so, issued by a court of competent jurisdiction, and had a reasonable opportunity to act on the injunction, restraining order or other legal process, or (ii) Intermediary acts in collusion with Secured Party in violating Debtor's rights.

---

18.  If a third party had a prior agreement that permitted it to give such an order without the debtor's further consent, the third party would have "control." UCC § 8-106(d)(2). If it also had a security interest in property in the account, that security interest would be prior to the secured party's. Rev. § 9-328(2)(B)(ii). Even if the third party did not have a security interest, it could transfer property out of the account, which could destroy perfection of the secured party's security interest in the transferred property.

19.  The intermediary has represented (in the immediately preceding sentence) that no third party has the right to give entitlement orders. If the intermediary and the debtor subsequently enter into an account control agreement with a third party, the secured party's security interest will be prior to the third party's security interest. Rev. § 9-328(2)(B)(ii). Nonetheless, the secured party will still want to prevent any third party from acquiring the right to transfer property out of the account.

20.  This provision will assist the secured party in monitoring the account.

21.  The claims referred to in this sentence are "adverse claims." UCC § 8-102(a)(1). The secured party will want to be informed of such claims, which would likely constitute a default under the related security agreement.

22   This § 7.1 treats the secured party's delivery of a notice of exclusive control like an adverse claimant's obtaining of an injunction or other legal process. Under Revised Article 9, if the intermediary transfers a financial asset pursuant to an effective entitlement order, the intermediary is not liable to an adverse claimant unless the intermediary "took the action after being served with an injunction, restraining order or other legal process enjoining it from doing so...and had a reasonable opportunity to act on the injunction, restraining order or legal process." UCC § 8-115(1).

23.  If the debtor gives such a notice, *it* is an adverse claimant. UCC § 8-102(a)(1). This sentence states the rule of UCC § 8-115, as preserved by Rev. § 9-331(b).

7.2    This agreement does not create any obligation of Intermediary except for those expressly set forth in this agreement. In particular, Intermediary need not investigate whether Secured Party is entitled under Secured Party's agreements with Debtor to give an entitlement order or a notice of exclusive control. Intermediary may rely on notices and communications it believes given by the appropriate party.

SECTION 8. **Indemnity.** Secured Party and Debtor will indemnify Intermediary, its officers, directors, employees, and agents against claims, liabilities and expenses arising out of this agreement (including reasonable attorneys' fees and disbursements), except to the extent the claims, liabilities, or expenses are caused by Intermediary's gross negligence or willful misconduct.[24] Secured Party's and Debtor's liability under this Section is joint and several.[25]

SECTION 9. **Termination.**[26] Secured Party may terminate this agreement by notice to Intermediary and Debtor. Intermediary may terminate this agreement on [insert number] days' notice to Secured Party and Debtor. If Secured Party notifies Intermediary that Secured Party's security interest in the Account has terminated, this agreement will immediately terminate. Sections 7, "Intermediary's responsibility," and 8, "indemnity," will survive termination of this agreement.[27]

SECTION 10. **Complete agreement; amendments.** This agreement is the entire agreement, and supersedes any prior agreements and contemporaneous oral agreements, of the parties concerning its subject matter[; *provided, however, that this agreement shall not alter or affect any mandatory arbitration provision currently in effect between Bank and Debtor pursuant to a separate agreement*].[28] No amendment of, or waiver of a right under, this agreement will be binding unless it is in writing and signed by the party to be charged.

---

24.    The intermediary is not likely to charge a fee for entering into a securities account control agreement but may enter into the agreement as an accommodation to the debtor. The intermediary will therefore not want to take additional material risks, and will want to be indemnified against claims.

25.    Joint and several liability of the debtor and the secured party on the indemnity is common, though not universal, in pledged account agreements governed by pre-1994 Article 9.

26.    Section 9 of the deposit account control agreement (Form 3.3.1 in this book) contains a somewhat more elaborate version of this § 9.

27.    The intermediary should have the right to terminate the account control agreement or the account. However, simply permitting the intermediary to terminate the control arrangement would pose too great a risk to the secured party unless the secured party has enough time to move the collateral to another account subject to the secured party's perfected security interest. The steps the secured party can take in this situation should be set out in the security agreement.

28.    The bracketed language in § 10 should be negotiated by the parties. Arbitration is often a feature of agreements governing securities accounts.

SECTION 11. **Governing law.** This agreement will be governed by the laws of the State of [jurisdiction].[29]

SECTION 12. **Severability.** To the extent a provision of this agreement is unenforceable, this agreement will be construed as if the unenforceable provision were omitted.

SECTION 13. **Successors and assigns.**[30] A successor to or assignee of Secured Party's rights and obligations under the security agreement between Secured Party and Debtor will succeed to Secured Party's rights and obligations under this agreement.

SECTION 14. **Notices.**[31] A notice or other communication to a party under this agreement will be in writing (except that entitlement orders may be given orally),[32] will be sent to the party's address set forth below or to such other address as the party may notify the other parties and will be effective on receipt.

SECTION 15. **Jury Waiver.**[33] THE DEBTOR WAIVES ITS RIGHT TO A JURY TRIAL WITH RESPECT TO ANY ACTION OR CLAIM ARISING OUT OF ANY DISPUTE IN CONNECTION WITH THIS AGREEMENT, ANY RIGHTS, REMEDIES, OBLIGATIONS, OR DUTIES HEREUNDER, OR THE PERFORMANCE OR ENFORCEMENT HEREOF OR THEREOF.

---

29.    Perfection and priority of the secured party's security interest will be governed by the local law of the intermediary's "jurisdiction." Rev. § 9-305(a)(3). The local law of the intermediary's jurisdiction also governs issues concerning the indirect holding system that are dealt with in Article 8. UCC § 8-110(b) cmt. 3. If an agreement between the intermediary and the debtor specifies a particular jurisdiction as the intermediary's jurisdiction, that is the intermediary's jurisdiction for purposes of Revised Article 9. Rev. § 9-305(a)(3); UCC § 8-110(e)(1). This type of specification would most likely appear in the control agreement. If the parties have not have availed themselves of that option, but an agreement between the intermediary and its entitlement holder governing the account selects a governing law, such law is the "securities intermediary's jurisdiction." UCC § 8-110(e)(2). This type of specification would most likely appear in the agreement between the intermediary and the debtor that governs the account. If so, it would prevail over the standard governing law clause in a control agreement unless a specific override is provided for. If, however, there is no agreement between the debtor and the intermediary governing the account (as frequently happens for cash accounts), or if the agreement does not specify the intermediary's jurisdiction, then either a specification as to "the intermediary's jurisdiction," a specific statement that the maintenance of the account is to be governed by the law of a chosen jurisdiction, or the governing law specification in the control agreement will be effective to determine the intermediary's jurisdiction. UCC § 8-110(e)(1) & (2). The validation of the parties' selection of governing law by agreement is not conditioned upon a determination that the jurisdiction whose law is chosen bear a "reasonable relation" to the transaction. UCC § 8-110 cmt. 3. *See also* UCC § 1-105(2). UCC § 8-110(e)(3)-(53) sets forth other rules that will determine governing law in the event that UCC § 8-110(e)(1) or (2), discussed immediately above, do not apply.
30.    A somewhat more elaborate version of this § 13 appears in the deposit account control agreement (Form 3.3.1), providing that the secured party shall give written notice of an assignment to the bank, the equivalent of the intermediary in this form.
31.    A somewhat more elaborate notice provision appears as § 14 of the form of deposit account control agreement (Form 3.3.1).
32.    Note that § 2 of the deposit account control agreement, Form 3.3.1, is written so that the parties may require that notice of exclusive control (comparable to an entitlement order in this form) is written, not oral.
33.    A jury waiver may not be appropriate or enforceable in a consumer context, and may be irrelevant if disputes under the agreement are subject to binding arbitration. *See* § 10 of this Form.

SECTION 16. **Counterparts.** This agreement may be executed in any number of counterparts, all of which shall constitute one and the same instrument, and any party hereto may execute this Agreement by signing and delivering one or more counterparts.

SIGNATURES:

SECURED PARTY:

By:_____

Title:_____


DEBTOR:

By:_____

Title:_____


INTERMEDIARY:

By:_____

Title:_____

Form 3.4

# Assignment of Proceeds of Letter of Credit and Request for Issuer's Consent[1]

---

1.    Revised Article 9 provides new—and exclusive—means by which the secured party may perfect a security interest in "letter-of-credit rights" (the proceeds of a letter of credit)—"control." This form is to be used to confer such control. It is designed for use in states where *both* Revised Articles 5 and 9 are in effect; it is *not* designed for use in states where only Revised Article 9 (and not Revised 5) is in effect (*e.g.* Georgia and Wisconsin). For a list of states that have adopted Revised Article 5, see <http://www.nccusl.org/nccusl/uniformact_factsheets/uniformacts-fs-ucca5.asp> (last visited 12/17/01). Under Rev. § 9-102(a)(51), a "letter-of-credit right" is "a right to payment or performance under a letter of credit" exclusive of the right of the beneficiary to demand payment or performance under a letter of credit. Filing a financing statement will not perfect a security interest in a letter-of-credit right. Rev. §§ 9-312(b)(2); 9-310(b)(8). Nor under Rev. § 9-313 can the assignee's security interest in a letter-of-credit right be perfected by possession as it could under F. §§ 9-305 and 5-116(2)(a). Rather, the secured party seeking to perfect a security interest in a letter-of-credit right as original collateral may do so only by "control," which arises under Rev. § 9-107 when the issuer or any nominated person "has consented to the assignment of proceeds of the letter of credit under [UCC Revised] Section 5-114(c) or otherwise applicable law or practice." Note that where the letter-of-credit right is a "supporting obligation" (Rev. § 9-102(a)(77)), the attachment and perfection of a security interest in collateral is also the attachment and perfection of a security interest in a supporting obligation for the collateral. Rev. § 9-203(f); Rev. § 9-308(d). A security interest in letter-of-credit rights perfected by control has priority over a conflicting security interest in the same letter-of-credit rights held by a party that does not have control. *See* Rev. § 9-329(1). Conflicting security interests in letter-of-credit rights perfected by control rank according to priority in time of obtaining control. Rev. § 9-329(2).

This form can be used for *commercial* or *standby* letters of credit. It is compatible with the *Uniform Customs and Practice for Documentary Credits*, 1993 Revision, *International Chamber of Commerce Publication* No. 500 (UCP 500), and the *International Standby Practices 1998, International Chamber of Commerce Publication* No. 590 (ISP98). *See* UCP 500, Art. 49 and ISP 98 Rules 6.06–6.10.

_____ , 20 ____

[Insert Name and Address of Issuer of Letter of Credit][2]

Re:    Your Letter of Credit No.

Ladies/Gentlemen:

The undersigned beneficiary of the captioned letter of credit issued by you (the "Credit") hereby assigns[3] to the Assignee named below the proceeds[4] of the undersigned's drawing(s) payable to the undersigned under the Credit, and instructs you to remit the proceeds of such drawing(s) presented to you, if and when hereafter honored under the Credit, as follows:

Exact Name of Assignee: _____

Complete Address of Assignee: _____

_____

_____

---

2.    This form is designed for presentation to the *issuer* of the letter of credit. It is *not* designed for presentation to a "confirmer" (Rev. § 5-102(a)(4)) of the letter of credit or any other "nominated person" (Rev. § 5-102(a)(11)) under the letter of credit. The form can be modified to cover proceeds payable by a confirmer or other nominated person. Note that, "[a] confirmer is directly obligated on a letter of credit and has the rights and obligations of an issuer to the extent of its confirmation." Rev. § 5-107(a). However, "[a] nominated person who is not a confirmer is not obligated to honor or otherwise give value for a presentation." Rev. § 5-107(b). Accordingly, a consent to an assignment of proceeds from a nominated person other than a confirmer may be of less value than a consent from the issuer or a confirmer because the nominated person is not obligated (unless it otherwise agrees) to make any payment under the letter of credit.

3.    This form may be used for an *outright* assignment or for an assignment as *security*. See Rev. § 1-201(37) (definition of "security interest"). However, Revised Article 9 applies to the assignment only if the assignment creates a security interest. Rev. § 9-109(a)(1); Rev. § 5-114(f). Assuming that Revised Article 9 applies, in order for the security interest to be enforceable, the assignee (*i.e.*, the secured party) must be the secured party under a security agreement authenticated by the debtor, or have a security interest in the letter-of-credit rights as proceeds, or as a supporting obligation, or pursuant to a control agreement. Rev. § 9-203(b)(3)(D) and (f). The security agreement need not be in writing, although it should be an authenticated record (*i.e.* written or electronic. Rev. §§ 9-102(a)(73) ("security agreement") & 1-201(3) ("agreement") & 9-102(a)(7) ("authenticated") & 9-102(a)(69) ("record"). The security agreement need not be identified in this form. The issuer need not, and normally will not, be a party to the security agreement.

4.    Letter of credit law and practice draw a sharp distinction between *transfer* of the beneficiary's *right to draw* under a letter of credit and *assignment* of the *proceeds* of a letter of credit. An assignment of proceeds of a letter of credit does not include the beneficiary's drawing rights, and can be made even where the letter of credit is not transferable. *Compare* Rev. § 5-112 (transfer) *with* Rev. § 5-114 (assignment of proceeds). Rev. § 9-102(a)(51) reflects this distinction in the definition of a "letter-of-credit right," which, as noted above, is "a right to payment or performance under a letter of credit, whether or not the beneficiary has demanded or is at the time entitled to demand payment or performance. The term does not include the right of a beneficiary to demand payment or performance under a letter of credit. *Compare also* UCP 500, Art. 48 (transfer) *with* UCP 500. Art. 49 (assignment of proceeds), and ISP98 Rules 6.01–6.05 (transfer of drawing rights) *with* ISP 98 Rules 6.06–6.10 (assignment of proceeds).

The amounts or portions assigned and to be paid to Assignee are as follows (*check/complete only one*):

☐ All drawings under the Credit, without limit.

☐ The sum of _____ in the aggregate of the next drawing(s) under the Credit until such sum has been paid.

☐ _____% of the amount of each of the next drawing(s) under the Credit, but not exceeding _____ in the aggregate.

☐ At the rate of _____ per (*insert applicable unit:*) shipped (as evidenced in the documents presented to you under the Credit), but not exceeding _____ in the aggregate.

☐ Other (*specify*): _____.

In the event that this Assignment does not apply to the full proceeds of the Credit, pay the balance of the proceeds, if any, to the undersigned.

The undersigned requests your consent[5] to this Assignment, and in consideration thereof, the undersigned agrees that this Assignment is irrevocable and cannot be cancelled or amended without the written agreement of the Assignee and you.

The undersigned transmits to you herewith the original Credit,[6] including any and all accepted amendments, and requests that you endorse thereon the foregoing Assignment and dispose of the Credit as follows (*check/complete only one*):

☐ Return it to the undersigned.

☐ Send it to _____.

☐ Retain it in your records.

---

5.   As noted above, the issuer's or nominated person's consent to the assignment of proceeds constitutes "control" under Rev. § 9-107. Where Revised Article 5 applies, an issuer need not recognize an assignment of proceeds of a letter of credit until it consents to the assignment. Rev. § 5-114(c). "An issuer … has no obligation to give or withhold its consent to an assignment of proceeds of a letter of credit, but consent may not be unreasonably withheld if the assignee possesses and exhibits the letter of credit and presentation of the letter of credit is a condition to honor." Rev. § 5-114(d). Rev. § 9-409(a) makes ineffective a term in a letter of credit or an applicable law, regulation, custom or practice applicable to the letter of credit to the extent that it would impair the creation, attachment, or perfection of a security interest in the letter-of-credit right or provides that the creation, attachment or perfection of such security interest gives rise to a default, breach, right of recoupment, claim, defense, termination, right of termination, or remedy under the letter-of-credit right.

6.   An assignee that is relying upon an assignment of proceeds of a letter of credit will normally want to see the letter of credit, any amendments thereto, and any indorsements thereon. This form therefore contemplates that the original letter of credit will be presented to the issuer. Presenting the original letter of credit may lessen the possibilities for fraud and facilitate tracking multiple assignments, especially if each assignment is noted on the original. The assignee may also ask the issuer to certify the terms and conditions of the letter of credit and any amendments (including the undrawn amount thereof) and to certify that there are no prior assignments of the proceeds in question.

In the event of multiple assignments, the undersigned authorizes you to pay in order of your receipt of or consent to such assignments.[7]

To cover your assignment of proceeds fee of _____, the undersigned (*check/complete only one*):

☐ Encloses a certified check or bank check payable to your order.

☐ Authorizes you to debit the undersigned's account number _____.

☐ Has arranged for a funds transfer in your favor, referencing the Credit by number.

This Assignment, and your consent thereto, (i) is not a transfer or assignment of the Credit, (ii) does not give the Assignee any interest in the Credit or any documents presented thereunder or any right to draw on the Credit or to consent or to refuse to consent to amendments to the Credit or to the cancellation thereof, (iii) does not affect whether the undersigned can transfer its right to draw on the Credit, and (iv) does not affect the undersigned's right to draw on the Credit or the undersigned's or your right to consent or to refuse to consent to amendments to the Credit or to the cancellation thereof.[8]

The undersigned represents and warrants to you that: (i) other than as set forth above, the undersigned has not and will not, by transfer or assignment of the Credit, by negotiation of drafts, by drawing drafts to a third party, or otherwise, assign the right to receive the whole or any portion of the above proceeds of the Credit or give any other authorization or direction to make any payment thereof to any other party; (ii) the undersigned has not and will not, without your prior written consent, present to anyone but you any documents under the Credit; (iii) the undersigned's execution, delivery, and performance of this Assignment (a) are within the undersigned's powers, (b) have been duly authorized, (c) do not contravene any charter provision, by-law, resolution, contract, or other undertaking binding on or affecting the undersigned or any of the undersigned's properties, (d) do not violate any applicable domestic or foreign law, rule, or regulation, and (e) do not require any notice, filing, or other action to, with, or by any governmental authority; (iv) this Assignment has been duly executed and delivered by the undersigned and is the undersigned's legal, valid, and binding obligation; and (v) the transactions underlying the Credit (including any shipment of goods or provision of services and any related financial arrangements) and this Assignment do not violate any applicable United States or other law, rule, or regulation.

The undersigned agrees to immediately return to you any assigned proceeds of the Credit inadvertently paid to the undersigned.

The undersigned agrees to indemnify[9] you and hold you harmless from and against any and all claims, liabilities, and expenses (including reasonable attorney's fees) in any

---

7.   The general rule is that conflicting perfected security interests rank according to priority in time of filing or perfection. Rev. § 9-322(a)(1). However, a security interest in a letter-of-credit right perfected by control has priority over a conflicting security interest held by a party that does not have control. Rev. § 9-329(1) (*i.e.*, as a supporting obligation). Conflicting security interests in letter-of-credit rights perfected by control rank according to priority in time of obtaining control. Rev. § 9-329(2).

8.   This paragraph highlights the limited rights of an assignee of proceeds of a letter of credit. Note that, "Rights of a transferee beneficiary or nominated person are independent of the beneficiary's assignment of the proceeds of a letter of credit and are superior to the assignee's right to the proceeds." Rev. § 5-114(e); Rev. § 9-109(c)(4).

9.   The willingness of the beneficiary to indemnify the issuer may be a subject for negotiation. ISP 98 Rule 6.08(d) recognizes that an issuer may require an indemnity as a condition to consenting to an assignment of proceeds.

way related to or arising out of or in connection with this Assignment or any action taken or not taken pursuant hereto (except to the extent caused by your gross negligence or willful misconduct),[10] and the undersigned agrees to pay you, on demand, for any such liability or expense.

[Remainder of page intentionally left blank]

---

10. Consideration should be given to the appropriate standard for the issuer's loss of indemnification, *e.g.*, ordinary negligence, gross negligence, etc.

This Assignment is made subject to the practice rules (*e.g.*, UCP 500 or ISP 98 to which the Credit is subject) and shall be governed by the laws of the State of _____.[11] [The undersigned waives the right to trial by jury in any action or proceeding relating to or arising out of this Assignment.][12]

SIGNATURE GUARANTEED:*     Very truly yours,

_____  _____
*(Name of Bank Guaranteeing*     *(Name of Beneficiary)*
*Beneficiary's Signature)*

_____  _____
*(Authorized Signature)*       *(Authorized Signature)*

_____  _____
*(Print or Type Signer's Name and Title)*  *(Print or Type Signer's Name and Title)*

_____  _____
*(Address of Bank)*        *(Address of Beneficiary)*

_____  _____
*(Telephone Number of Bank)*    *(Telephone Number of Beneficiary)*


*The beneficiary's signature, with title as stated herein, conforms with that on file with us, and is authorized for the execution of this Assignment.

---

11.   Under Rev. § 9-306(a), "the local law of the issuer's jurisdiction … governs perfection, the effect of perfection or nonperfection and the priority of a security interest in a letter-of-credit right if the issuer's jurisdiction … is a State." Rev. § 9-306(b) specifies that, "For purposes of this part [3 of Revised Article 9], an issuer's jurisdiction … is the jurisdiction whose law governs the liability of the issuer … with respect to the letter-of-credit right as provided in [Rev.] Section 5-116." Rev. § 5-116 provides that the law governing the liability of the issuer of a letter of credit may be chosen pursuant to Rev. § 5-116(a); in the absence of such a choice, Rev. § 5-116(b) specifies the governing law. Here, the law has been chosen in this form of Assignment, and so the default rules do not apply.

12.   Certain issuers may insist upon a waiver of the right to trial by jury in the event of litigation relating to the assignment. Neither Revised Article 5 nor Revised Article 9 requires or prohibits a jury waiver.

## CONSENT TO ASSIGNMENT OF
## PROCEEDS OF LETTER OF CREDIT:

The undersigned, as issuer of the captioned letter of credit, hereby consents to the foregoing Assignment of Proceeds of Letter of Credit as of (insert date and time): _____ , 20 ____ .[13]

Very truly yours,

_____

*(Name of Issuer)*

_____

*(Authorized Signature)*

_____

*(Print or Type Signer's Name and Title)*

---

13. Noting a time of day as well as a date may facilitate determining the priority of conflicting perfected security interests under Rev. § 9-329(2).

Form 3.5.1

# Bailee Acknowledgment
# (Non-Farm Products)[1]

_____, 20___

Blanket Security Interest Holder
Anytown, USA

   Re:  Bay Lore, Inc. ("Debtor")

Dear Sir or Madam:

   We hereby acknowledge that the Debtor has entered into a Security Agreement with you and has granted to you a first priority security interest in [*insert description of collat-*

---

1.   This form is intended to enable the secured party to perfect a security interest in collateral in possession of a third party, such as a bailee. Former Article 9 permitted perfection of a security interest by notification to a bailee in possession of collateral. *See* F. § 9-305. Revised Article 9 does not. Perfection by "possession" of collateral in the possession of a third party is possible under Revised Article 9 only when the third party acknowledges that it holds the collateral for the secured party's benefit. *See* Rev. § 9-313(c)(1). Revised Article 9 permits perfection by third-party possession only if the third party in possession is not the debtor, the secured party, or a lessee of the collateral from the debtor in the ordinary course of the debtor's business. Rev. § 9-313(c). Revised Article 9 thus rejects the reasoning of *In re Atlantic Computer Sys., Inc.*, 135 B.R. 463 (Bankr. S.D.N.Y. 1992), which held that notification to a debtor-lessor's lessee in possession of collateral sufficed to perfect a security interest in the leased collateral.

    In any such transaction between a bailor and a bailee, there is a risk that the transaction may be characterized as a "consignment" under Rev. § 9-102(a)(20). Revised Article 9 brings consignments, even true consignments, within its scope. Rev. § 9-109(a)(2) & (4). Under Rev. § 9-102(a)(20), a "consignment" is defined as "a transaction, regardless of its form, in which a person delivers goods to a merchant for the purpose of sale" where several other criteria are satisfied. Revised Article 9 treats all consignments, whether "true" consignments or security consignments, as purchase-money security interests and requires consignors to comply with Revised Article 9 rules applicable to purchase-money secured parties in order to obtain priority. *See* Rev. §§ 1-201(37) & 9-103(d). A form of purchase-money security interest notification, for use in connection with inventory subject to a purchase-money security interest, appears as Form 3.5.3.

*eral*] and proceeds thereof (the "Collateral"). We further acknowledge that, pursuant to our agreements with the Debtor, from time to time we receive and maintain possession of certain of the Collateral of the Debtor, which are presently kept at our premises located at: [*Insert address of facilities*]. We further acknowledge that we have received and hold possession of the Collateral for your benefit and that we shall continue to hold possession of the Collateral for your benefit until we receive notice (in an authenticated record) from you that your security interest has been terminated.

We hereby waive, surrender and relinquish any rights in or to the Collateral, including, without limitation, any security interests, liens or agricultural liens provided by applicable law to which we may otherwise be entitled. We further acknowledge and agree that no negotiable warehouse receipts or documents of title will be issued covering the Collateral. We further acknowledge that we have not acquired any rights in the Collateral sufficient to transfer an interest or grant a security interest in or to the Collateral.[2]

We further acknowledge that, according to the terms of your Security Agreement with the Debtor, you have the right to inspect the Collateral and, upon default, the right to remove and take possession of the Collateral after paying in full all storage charges incurred by the Debtor and owing to us. We agree to permit you access to the Collateral for these purposes at your request without first receiving the consent or permission of the Debtor.

Sincerely,


Bay Lee, LLC

cc: Debtor
[DEBTOR] CONFIRMS AND AGREES TO THE FOREGOING

---

2.    In any such acknowledgment it may also be advisable for the secured party to obtain an acknowledgment from the bailee that it has not acquired sufficient rights in the collateral so as to be legally capable of transferring an interest in the collateral in order to limit rights of the bailee's creditors in the collateral.

Form 3.5.2

# Bailee Acknowledgment
# (Farm Products)[1]

_____, 20____

Blanket Security Interest Holder
Anytown, USA

    Re:  Eagle Farms, Ltd ("Debtor")

Dear Sir or Madam:

    We hereby acknowledge that the Debtor has entered into a Security Agreement with you and has granted to you a first priority security interest in all of its inventory and farm products and all products and proceeds thereof (the "Collateral"). We hereby acknowl-

---

    1.    This form is intended to enable the secured party to perfect a security interest in farm products in possession of a third party, such as a bailee. Former Article 9 permitted perfection of a security interest by notification to a bailee in possession of collateral. *See* F § 9-305. Revised Article 9 does not. Perfection by "possession" of collateral in the possession of a third party is possible under Revised Article 9 only when the third party acknowledges that it holds the collateral for the secured party's benefit. *See* Rev. § 9-313(c)(1).
    In any such transaction between a bailor and a bailee, there is a risk that the transaction may be characterized as a "consignment" under Rev. § 9-102(a)(20). While traditional livestock contracts may not be consignments under Revised Article 9, the line between a consignment and a bailment in such arrangements is not always clear. *See, e.g., Rohweder v. Aberdeen PCA*, 765 F.2d 109 (8th Cir. 1985); *Germany v. Farmers Home Administration*, 73 B.R. 19 (Bankr. S.D. Miss. 1986); and *Porter v. Michigan Livestock Credit Corp.*, 202 B.R. 109 (N.D. Ind. 1996). Thus, the secured party should also consider complying with the provisions of Rev. § 9-324 in order to obtain purchase money priority status as against the bailee/consignee. A form of purchase-money security interest notification, for use in connection with livestock subject to a purchase-money security interest, appears as Form 3.5.4.

edge that, pursuant to our agreements with the Debtor, from time to time we receive and maintain possession of certain of the Collateral of the Debtor, which are kept at our premises located at: [*Insert address of facilities*]. We further acknowledge that we have received and hold possession of the Collateral for your benefit and that we shall continue to hold possession of the Collateral for your benefit until we receive notice (in an authenticated record) from you that your security interest has been terminated.

We hereby waive, surrender and relinquish any rights in or to the Collateral, including, without limitation, any security interests, liens or agricultural liens provided by applicable law to which we may otherwise be entitled.[2] We further acknowledge and agree that no negotiable warehouse receipts or documents of title will be issued covering the Collateral. We further acknowledge that we have not acquired any rights in the Collateral sufficient to transfer an interest or grant a security interest in or to the Collateral.[3]

We further acknowledge that, according to the terms of your Security Agreement with the Debtor, you have the right to inspect the Collateral and, upon default, the right to remove and take possession of the Collateral after paying in full all storage charges incurred by the Debtor and owing to us. We agree to permit you access to the Collateral for these purposes at your request without first receiving the consent or permission of the Debtor.

Sincerely,

Livestock Feeders, LLC

cc: Debtor

[DEBTOR] CONFIRMS AND AGREES TO THE FOREGOING

---

2. In the context of agricultural financing, bailees may enjoy the benefit of a statutory lien on the collateral to secure obligations owed by the debtor, known under Rev. § 9-102(a)(5) as an "agricultural lien." *See, e.g.,* Iowa Code §§ 579A.2, sub. 1; 579B.3. A waiver of such statutory liens may be unenforceable. *See, e.g.,* Iowa Code § 579A.4. As a result, many bailees may be reluctant to concede the priority of the secured party's security interest.

3. In any such acknowledgment it may also be advisable for the secured party to obtain an acknowledgment from the bailee that it has not acquired sufficient rights in the collateral so as to be legally capable of transferring an interest in the collateral in order to limit rights of the bailee's creditors in the collateral.

# Inventory Purchase-Money Security Interest Notice[1]

_____, 20____[2]

Blanket Security Interest Holder
Anytown, USA

    Re:  Inventory RetailCo. (the "Debtor")

Dear Sir or Madam:

    We note your financing statement filed on _____, 20____, with the office of _____ against the Debtor (the "Financing Statement"). Based upon the contents of

---

    1.    Revised Article 9 continues the general approach of former Article 9 regarding purchase-money security interests in inventory. *See* F. § 9-312(3). As with former Article 9, the holder of a perfected purchase-money security interest, who has taken certain applicable steps, achieves "super priority," *i.e.*, its security interest in the purchase-money collateral will rank ahead of any security interest which would otherwise be entitled to priority under the first-to-file-or-perfect priority rule. To achieve super priority in inventory, the purchase-money the secured party must (i) perfect its security interest before the debtor receives possession of the inventory, and (ii) notify existing holders of a security interest of record in the same type of inventory that the purchase-money lender expects to acquire a purchase-money security interest in the inventory, and describes the inventory, in advance of the debtor receiving possession of the inventory. The notice is effective for a period of five years. Rev. § 9-324(b). This form is intended to be used as such a notification.

    A "purchase-money security interest" is a security interest in collateral which is taken by either (a) a vendor of that collateral to finance the purchase price of the collateral, or (b) a lender in the collateral that secures a loan that enables the debtor to acquire the collateral. Rev. § 9-103. The purchase-money collateral must generally be goods (*e.g.*, inventory). It may, however, also be software sold or licensed with goods which are themselves purchase-money collateral, if the software is acquired principally for use with the goods. Rev. § 9-103(b)(3) & (c).

    2.    Rev. § 9-324 contains two important temporal requirements. First, the purchase-money security interest

the Financing Statement, it appears that you may assert a security interest in the Debtor's inventory.[3]

Please be advised that we have or expect to acquire a purchase-money security interest in the following property: [*insert description of inventory*][4] (the "Inventory"), together with the identifiable proceeds of the Inventory.[5]

Sincerely,

Inventory Lender

cc: DEBTOR

---

must be perfected when the debtor receives possession of the inventory. Rev. § 9-324(b)(1). Thus, the purchase-money the secured party will have to have filed a financing statement against the inventory *before* the debtor receives possession of it, and cannot rely on the twenty-day grace period provided by Rev. § 9-324(a) for non-purchase-money collateral. *See* Rev. § 9-324 cmt. 4 ("The twenty-day grace period of subsection (a) does not apply."). Second, the purchase-money the secured party must send the holder of the conflicting security interest notice of its purchase-money security interest within *five years before* the debtor receives possession of the inventory. Rev. § 9-324(b)(2).

　　3.　"Inventory" is defined in Rev. § 9-102(a)(48) as "goods, other than farm products, which: (a) are leased by a person as lessor; (b) are held by a person for sale or lease or to be furnished under a contract of service; (c) are furnished by a person under a contract of service; or (d) consist of raw materials, work in process, or materials used or consumed in a business."

　　4.　The notice must contain a "description" of the inventory. Rev. § 9-324(b)(4). Under Rev. § 9-108(a) a description of collateral is sufficient "if it reasonably identifies what is described" by, for example, specific listing, category, UCC type, quantity, and so on, as set forth in Rev. § 9-108(b).

　　5.　A perfected purchase-money security interest in inventory will have priority over a conflicting security interest in chattel paper constituting proceeds of the inventory (or proceeds of such chattel paper, to the extent provided in Rev. § 9-330), an instrument constituting proceeds of the inventory, and in identifiable cash proceeds of the inventory received on or before the delivery of the inventory. Rev. § 9-324(b).

**Form 3.5.4**

# Livestock Purchase-Money Security Interest Notice[1]

_____, 20\_\_\_\_[2]

Blanket Security Interest Holder
Anytown, USA

 Re: Lowing Cattle Farms, Inc. (the "Debtor")

Dear Sir or Madam:

 We note your financing statement filed on _____, 20\_\_\_\_, with the office of _____ against the Debtor (the "Financing Statement"). Based upon the contents of the Financing Statement, it appears that you may assert a security interest in the Debtor's livestock.

---

 1. Revised Article 9 creates a new purchase-money priority rule for livestock that are farm products. Rev. § 9-324(d) & (e). These rules are patterned on the purchase-money priority rules for inventory, set forth in Rev. § 9-324(b) & (c), and described in the notes to Form 3.5.3. Among other things, a lender seeking purchase-money priority in livestock that are farm products must send an authenticated notification to the holder of any conflicting security interest. Rev. § 9-324(2). This form is intended to be used as such a notification.

Please be advised that we have or expect to acquire a purchase-money security interest in the following property: [*insert description of livestock*][2] (the "Livestock"), together with the identifiable proceeds of the Livestock.[3]

Sincerely,

Livestock Lender

cc: DEBTOR

---

2.    The notice must contain a "description" of the livestock. Rev. § 9-324(d)(4). Under Rev. § 9-108(a) a description of collateral is sufficient "if it reasonably identifies what is described" by, for example, specific listing, category, UCC type, quantity, and so on, as set forth in Rev. § 9-108(b). Special care in describing livestock may be advisable in order to identify the subject livestock.

3.    The holder of the conflicting security interest must receive this notification within six months before the debtor receives "possession" of the livestock. Rev. § 9-324(d)(3). What constitutes possession for such purposes is not always clear. *See, e.g., Kunkel v. Sprague National Bank (In re Morken)*, 128 F.3d 636 (8th Cir. 1997) (owner of livestock lacked "possession" of livestock which never left feedlot operated by seller).

# Form 3.6

# Pledge Agreement[1]

THIS PLEDGE AGREEMENT (this "Agreement"), dated as of _____, is entered into between _____, a _____ ("Pledgor"), and _____, a _____ ("Secured Party"), with reference to the following:

WHEREAS, Pledgor and Secured Party are parties to that certain Credit Agreement (as amended, restated, or otherwise modified from time to time, the "Credit Agreement"),

---

1.    A security interest in a certificated security may be perfected by filing, possession or control. Rev. § 9-312(a), 9-313(a) & 9-314(a). This form permits the secured party to create and perfect a security interest in a certificated security by possession. If the parties wish to perfect a security interest in an *un*certificated security by control, a form of securities account control agreement appears as Form 3.3.2.

The secured party's perfection of a security interest in a certificated security by possession is accomplished by the secured party's taking delivery of the certificated security under UCC § 8-301. Rev. § 9-313(a). *See also* Rev. § 9-106(a)(the secured party has control of certificated security as provided in UCC § 8-106). Delivery generally means that the secured party obtains possession of the security certificate even if lacking a necessary indorsement. *See* § 8-301. Under UCC § 8-102(a)(4), a "certificated security" is defined as "a security that is represented by a security certificate." A security certificate is defined in UCC § 8-102(a)(16) as "a certificate representing a security," and is intended to refer to the paper certificates that have traditionally been used to embody the underlying intangible interest, *i.e.*, the "security" itself. *See* UCC § 8-102 cmt. 16.

A security interest in a certificated security perfected by possession will generally be superior to a security interest perfected other than by control. The secured party's possession by agreement of a security certificate in registered form, without any necessary indorsements, results in the secured party's security interest in the certificated security being superior to another secured party's security interest in the certificated security perfected by filing. Rev. § 9-328(5). Where certificated security collateral is transferred to a person protected under UCC Article 8's adverse claim cutoff rules, however, the transferee remains protected under UCC Article 8. Rev. § 9-331(b).

This form is designed principally with the non-consumer pledgor in mind. Special rules may apply to the pledgor that is a consumer, under both Revised Article 9 and other applicable law. *See, e.g.,* Rev. §§ 9-626 (actions in which deficiency or surplus in issue); 9-201(b)("A transaction subject to this article is subject to any applicable rule of law which establishes a different rule for consumers . . . .").

of even date herewith, pursuant to which Secured Party has agreed to make certain financial accommodations to Pledgor;

WHEREAS, Pledgor beneficially owns the Equity Interests (as hereinafter defined) in the Issuers (as hereinafter defined);

WHEREAS, to induce Secured Party to make the financial accommodations provided to Pledgor pursuant to the Credit Agreement, Pledgor desires to pledge, grant, transfer, and assign to Secured Party a security interest in the Collateral (as hereinafter defined) to secure the Secured Obligations (as hereinafter defined), as provided herein.

NOW, THEREFORE, in consideration of the mutual promises, covenants, representations, and warranties set forth herein and for other good and valuable consideration, the parties hereto agree as follows:

1. **Definitions and Construction.**

    (a)    Definitions.

    All initially capitalized terms used herein and not otherwise defined herein shall have the meaning ascribed thereto in the Credit Agreement. As used in this Agreement:

    "Bankruptcy Code" means United States Bankruptcy Code (11 U.S.C. § 101 *et seq.*), as in effect from time to time, and any successor statute thereto.

    "Business Day" means any day that is not a Saturday, Sunday, or other day on which national banks are authorized or required to close.

    [*If Pledgor is neither a Registered Organization nor an individual*: "Chief Executive Office" shall mean where Pledgor manages the main part of its business operations or other affairs as contemplated by § 9-307 of the Code.]

    "Code" means the Uniform Commercial Code as in effect in the State of _____ from time to time.

    "Credit Agreement" shall have the meaning ascribed thereto in the recitals to this Agreement.

    "Credit Documents" shall mean the Credit Agreement and all other agreements, instruments, or other documents entered into or executed in connection therewith, in each case, as amended, restated, or otherwise modified from time to time.

    "Collateral" shall mean the Pledged Interests, the Future Rights, and the Proceeds, collectively.

    "Equity Interests" means all securities, shares, units, options, warrants, interests, participations, or other equivalents (regardless of how designated) of or in a corporation, partnership, limited liability company, or similar entity, whether voting or nonvoting, certificated or uncertificated, including general partner partnership interests, limited partner partnership interests, common stock, preferred stock, or any other "equity security" (as such term is defined in Rule 3a11-1 of the General Rules and Regulations promulgated by the Securities and Exchange Commission under the Securities Exchange Act of 1934).[2]

"Event of Default" shall have the meaning ascribed thereto in the Credit Agreement.

"Future Rights" shall mean: (a) all Equity Interests (other than Pledged Interests) of the Issuers, and all securities convertible or exchangeable into, and all warrants, options, or other rights to purchase, Equity Interests of the Issuers; and (b) the certificates or instruments representing such Equity Interests, convertible or exchangeable securities, warrants, and other rights and all dividends, cash, options, warrants, rights, instruments, and other property or proceeds from time to time received, receivable, or otherwise distributed in respect of or in exchange for any or all of such Equity Interests.

"Holder" and "Holders" shall have the meanings ascribed thereto in § 3 of this Agreement.

"Issuers" shall mean each of the Persons identified as an Issuer on **Schedule 1** attached hereto (or any addendum thereto), and any successors thereto, whether by merger or otherwise.

"Lien" shall mean any lien, mortgage, pledge, assignment (including any assignment of rights to receive payments of money), security interest, charge, or encumbrance of any kind (including any conditional sale or other title retention agreement, any lease in the nature thereof, or any agreement to give any security interest).

"Pledged Interests" shall mean (a) all Equity Interests of the Issuers identified on **Schedule 1**; and (b) the certificates or instruments representing such Equity Interests.

"Pledgor" shall have the meaning ascribed thereto in the preamble to this Agreement.

"Proceeds" shall mean all proceeds (including proceeds of proceeds) of the Pledged Interests and Future Rights including all: (a) rights, benefits, distributions, premiums, profits, dividends, interest, cash, instruments, documents of title, accounts, contract rights, inventory, equipment, general intangibles, payment intangibles, deposit accounts, chattel paper, and other property from time to time received, receivable, or otherwise distributed in respect of or in exchange for, or as a replacement of or a substitution for, any of the Pledged Interests, Future Rights, or proceeds thereof (including any cash, Equity Interests, or other securities or instruments issued after any recapitalization, readjustment, reclassification, merger or consolidation with respect to the Issuers and any security entitlements, as defined in § 8-102(a)(17) of the Code, with respect thereto); (b) "proceeds," as such term is defined in § 9-102(a)(64) of the Code; (c) proceeds of any insurance, indemnity, warranty, or guaranty (including guaranties of delivery) payable from time to time with respect to any of the Pledged Interests, Future Rights, or proceeds

---

2. Although characterized as "equity interests," there is no reason that the collateral could not also be debt securities, in which event a modification of the definition may be appropriate.

thereof; (d) payments (in any form whatsoever) made or due and payable to Pledgor from time to time in connection with any requisition, confiscation, condemnation, seizure or forfeiture of all or any part of the Pledged Interests, Future Rights, or proceeds thereof; and (e) other amounts from time to time paid or payable under or in connection with any of the Pledged Interests, Future Rights, or proceeds thereof.

"Registered Organization" shall have the meaning ascribed thereto in § 9-102(a)(7) of the Code.

"Secured Obligations" shall mean all liabilities, obligations, or undertakings owing by Pledgor to Secured Party of any kind or description arising out of or outstanding under, advanced or issued pursuant to, or evidenced by the Credit Agreement, this Agreement, or the other Credit Documents, irrespective of whether for the payment of money, whether direct or indirect, absolute or contingent, due or to become due, voluntary or involuntary, whether now existing or hereafter arising, and including all interest (including interest that accrues after the filing of a case under the Bankruptcy Code) and any and all costs, fees (including attorneys fees), and expenses which Pledgor is required to pay pursuant to any of the foregoing, by law, or otherwise.

"Secured Party" shall have the meaning ascribed thereto in the preamble to this Agreement, together with its successors or assigns.

"Securities Act" shall have the meaning ascribed thereto in § 9(c) of this Agreement.

(b)    Construction.

(i)    Unless the context of this Agreement clearly requires otherwise, references to the plural include the singular and to the singular include the plural, the part includes the whole, the term "including" is not limiting, and the term "or" has, except where otherwise indicated, the inclusive meaning represented by the phrase "and/or." The words "hereof," "herein," "hereby," "hereunder," and other similar terms in this Agreement refer to this Agreement as a whole and not exclusively to any particular provision of this Agreement. Article, section, subsection, exhibit, and schedule references are to this Agreement unless otherwise specified. All of the exhibits or schedules attached to this Agreement shall be deemed incorporated herein by reference. Any reference to any of the following documents includes any and all alterations, amendments, restatements, extensions, modifications, renewals, or supplements thereto or thereof, as applicable: this Agreement, the Credit Agreement, or any of the other Credit Documents.

(ii)    Neither this Agreement nor any uncertainty or ambiguity herein shall be construed or resolved against Secured Party or Pledgor, whether under any rule of construction or otherwise. On the contrary, this Agreement has been reviewed by both of the parties and their respective counsel and shall be construed and interpreted according to the ordinary meaning of the words used so as to fairly accomplish the purposes and intentions of the parties hereto.

(iii)    In the event of any direct conflict between the express terms and provisions of this Agreement and of the Credit Agreement, the terms and provisions of the Credit Agreement shall control.

2.   **Pledge.**[3]

As security for the prompt payment and performance of the Secured Obligations in full by Pledgor when due, whether at stated maturity, by acceleration or otherwise (including amounts that would become due but for the operation of the provisions of the Bankruptcy Code), Pledgor hereby pledges, grants, transfers, and assigns to Secured Party a security interest in all of Pledgor's right, title, and interest in and to the Collateral.

3.   **Delivery and Registration of Collateral.**

(a)   All certificates or instruments representing or evidencing the Collateral shall be promptly delivered by Pledgor to Secured Party or Secured Party's designee pursuant hereto at a location designated by Secured Party and shall be held by or on behalf of Secured Party pursuant hereto, and shall be in suitable form for transfer by delivery, or shall be accompanied by duly executed indorsement certificate in the form attached hereto as **Exhibit A** or other instrument of transfer or assignment in blank, in form and substance satisfactory to Secured Party.

(b)   Upon the occurrence and during the continuance of an Event of Default, Secured Party shall have the right, at any time in its discretion and without notice to Pledgor, to transfer to or to register on the books of the Issuers (or of any other Person maintaining records with respect to the Collateral) in the name of Secured Party or any of its nominees any or all of the Collateral. In addition, Secured Party shall have the right at any time to exchange certificates or instruments representing or evidencing Collateral for certificates or instruments of smaller or larger denominations.

(c)   If, at any time and from time to time, any Collateral (including any certificate or instrument representing or evidencing any Collateral) is in the possession of a Person other than Secured Party or Pledgor (a "Holder"), then Pledgor shall immediately, at Secured Party's option, either cause such Collateral to be delivered into Secured Party's possession, or cause such Holder to enter into a control agreement, in form and substance satisfactory to Secured Party, and take all other steps deemed necessary by Secured Party to perfect the security interest of Secured Party in such Collateral, all pursuant to §§ 9-106 & 9-313 of the Code or other applicable law governing the perfection of Secured Party's security interest in the Collateral in the possession of such Holder.

(d)   Any and all Collateral (including dividends, interest, and other cash distributions) at any time received or held by Pledgor shall be so received or held in trust for Secured Party, shall be segregated from other funds and property of Pledgor and shall be forthwith delivered to Secured Party in the same form as so received or held, with any necessary indorsements; *provided* that cash dividends or distributions received by Pledgor, may be retained by Pledgor in accordance with § 4 and used in the ordinary course of Pledgor's business.

---

3.   There need not be a separate security agreement pursuant to which the security interest in the certificated securities is granted. This pledge agreement (and, in particular, this Section 2) grants the security interest in the collateral, which grant will be effective to satisfy the attachment element of Rev. § 9-203(b)(3)(C).

(e)    If at any time, and from time to time, any Collateral consists of an uncertificated security or a security in book entry form, then Pledgor shall immediately cause such Collateral to be registered or entered, as the case may be, in the name of Secured Party, or otherwise cause Secured Party's security interest thereon to be perfected in accordance with applicable law.

4.    **Voting Rights and Dividends.**

(a)    So long as no Event of Default shall have occurred and be continuing, Pledgor shall be entitled to exercise any and all voting and other consensual rights pertaining to the Collateral or any part thereof for any purpose not inconsistent with the terms of the Credit Documents and shall be entitled to receive and retain any cash dividends or distributions paid or distributed in respect of the Collateral.

(b)    Upon the occurrence and during the continuance of an Event of Default, all rights of Pledgor to exercise the voting and other consensual rights or receive and retain cash dividends or distributions that it would otherwise be entitled to exercise or receive and retain, as applicable pursuant to § 4(a), shall cease, and all such rights shall thereupon become vested in Secured Party, who shall thereupon have the sole right to exercise such voting or other consensual rights and to receive and retain such cash dividends and distributions. Pledgor shall execute and deliver (or cause to be executed and delivered) to Secured Party all such proxies and other instruments as Secured Party may reasonably request for the purpose of enabling Secured Party to exercise the voting and other rights which it is entitled to exercise and to receive the dividends and distributions that it is entitled to receive and retain pursuant to the preceding sentence.

5.    **Representations and Warranties.**

Pledgor represents, warrants, and covenants as follows:

(a)    Pledgor has taken all steps it deems necessary or appropriate to be informed on a continuing basis of changes or potential changes affecting the Collateral (including rights of conversion and exchange, rights to subscribe, payment of dividends, reorganizations or recapitalization, tender offers and voting and registration rights), and Pledgor agrees that Secured Party shall have no responsibility or liability for informing Pledgor of any such changes or potential changes or for taking any action or omitting to take any action with respect thereto.

(b)    [*If Pledgor is a Registered Organization:* Pledgor is a Registered Organization, organized under the laws of the state set forth on **Schedule 2**. Pledgor's type of organization is set forth on **Schedule 2**.]

[*If Pledgor is an individual:* Pledgor is an individual. The address of Pledgor's principal residence is set forth on **Schedule 2**.]

[*If Pledgor is neither a Registered Organization nor an individual:* Pledgor is not a Registered Organization. Pledgor's type of organization is set forth on **Schedule 2**. The addresses of all of Pledgor's places of business are set forth on **Schedule 2**.]

(c)    All information herein or hereafter supplied to Secured Party by or on behalf of Pledgor in writing with respect to the Collateral is, or in the case of information hereafter supplied will be, accurate and complete in all material respects.

(d)    Pledgor is and will be the sole legal and beneficial owner of the Collateral (including the Pledged Interests and all other Collateral acquired by Pledgor after the date hereof) free and clear of any adverse claim, Lien, or other right, title, or interest of any party, other than the Liens in favor of Secured Party.

(e)    This Agreement, and the delivery to Secured Party of the Pledged Interests representing Collateral (or the control agreements referred to in Section 3 of this Agreement), creates a valid, perfected, and first priority security interest in one hundred percent (100%) of the Pledged Interests in favor of Secured Party securing payment of the Secured Obligations, and all actions necessary to achieve such perfection have been duly taken.[4]

(f)    **Schedule 1** to this Agreement is true and correct and complete in all material respects. Without limiting the generality of the foregoing: (i) except as set forth on **Schedule 1**, all the Pledged Interests are in certificated form, and, except to the extent registered in the name of Secured Party or its nominee pursuant to the provisions of this Agreement, are registered in the name of Pledgor; and (ii) the Pledged Interests as to each of the Issuers constitute at least the percentage of all the fully diluted issued and outstanding Equity Interests of such Issuer as set forth in **Schedule 1** to this Agreement.

(g)    There are no presently existing Future Rights or Proceeds owned by Pledgor.

(h)    The Pledged Interests have been duly authorized and validly issued and are fully paid and nonassessable.

(i)    Neither the pledge of the Collateral pursuant to this Agreement nor the extensions of credit represented by the Secured Obligations violates Regulation T, U or X of the Board of Governors of the Federal Reserve System.

6.    **Further Assurances.**

(a)    Pledgor agrees that from time to time, at the expense of Pledgor, Pledgor will promptly execute and deliver all further instruments and documents, and take all further action that may be necessary or reasonably desirable, or that Secured Party may request, in order to perfect and protect any security interest granted or purported to be granted hereby or to enable Secured Party to exercise and enforce its rights and remedies hereunder with respect to any Collateral. Without limiting the generality of the foregoing, Pledgor will: (i) at the request of Secured Party, mark conspicuously each of its records pertaining to the Collateral with a legend, in form and substance reasonably satisfactory

---

4.    As observed in footnote 1, a security interest in a certificated security perfected by possession will generally be superior to a security interest perfected other than by control.

to Secured Party, indicating that such Collateral is subject to the security interest granted hereby; (ii) execute and such instruments or notices, as may be necessary or reasonably desirable, or as Secured Party may request, in order to perfect and preserve the first priority security interests granted or purported to be granted hereby; (iii) allow inspection of the Collateral by Secured Party or Persons designated by Secured Party; and (iv) appear in and defend any action or proceeding that may affect Pledgor's title to or Secured Party's security interest in the Collateral.

(b)    Pledgor hereby authorizes Secured Party to file one or more financing or continuation statements, and amendments thereto, relative to all or any part of the Collateral. A carbon, photographic, or other reproduction of this Agreement or any financing statement covering the Collateral or any part thereof shall be sufficient as a financing statement where permitted by law.

(c)    Pledgor will furnish to Secured Party, upon the request of Secured Party: (i) a certificate executed by an authorized officer of Pledgor, and dated as of the date of delivery to Secured Party, itemizing in such detail as Secured Party may request, the Collateral which, as of the date of such certificate, has been delivered to Secured Party by Pledgor pursuant to the provisions of this Agreement; and (ii) such statements and schedules further identifying and describing the Collateral and such other reports in connection with the Collateral as Secured Party may request.

7.    **Covenants of Pledgor.**

Pledgor shall:

(a)    Perform each and every covenant in the Credit Documents applicable to Pledgor;

(b)    [*For Pledgor that is Registered Organization:* Neither change its jurisdiction of organization nor cease to be a Registered Organization, in each case, without giving Secured Party at least thirty (30) days prior written notice thereof;]

[*For Pledgor that is an individual:* Not change its principal residence without giving Secured Party at least thirty (30) days prior written notice thereof;]

[*For Pledgor that is neither an individual nor a Registered Organization:* Not change the location of its Chief Executive Office, establish any new places of business, change the address of any of its places of business, or become a Registered Organization, in each case, without giving Secured Party at least thirty (30) days prior written notice thereof;]

(c)    To the extent it may lawfully do so, use its best efforts to prevent the Issuers from issuing Future Rights or Proceeds, except for cash dividends and other distributions to be paid by any Issuer to Pledgor; and

(d)    Upon receipt by Pledgor of any material notice, report, or other communication from any of the Issuers or any Holder relating to all or any part of the Collateral, deliver such notice, report or other communication to Secured Party as soon as possible, but in no event later than five (5) days following the receipt thereof by Pledgor.

### 8. Secured Party as Pledgor's Attorney-in-Fact.

(a)   Pledgor hereby irrevocably appoints Secured Party as Pledgor's attorney-in-fact, with full authority in the place and stead of Pledgor and in the name of Pledgor, Secured Party or otherwise, from time to time at Secured Party's discretion, to take any action and to execute any instrument that Secured Party may reasonably deem necessary or advisable to accomplish the purposes of this Agreement, including: (i) upon the occurrence and during the continuance of an Event of Default, to receive, indorse, and collect all instruments made payable to Pledgor representing any dividend, interest payment or other distribution in respect of the Collateral or any part thereof to the extent permitted hereunder and to give full discharge for the same and to execute and file governmental notifications and reporting forms; (ii) to enter into any control agreements Secured Party deems necessary pursuant to Section 3 of this Agreement; or (iii) to arrange for the transfer of the Collateral on the books of any of the Issuers or any other Person to the name of Secured Party or to the name of Secured Party's nominee.

(b)   In addition to the designation of Secured Party as Pledgor's attorney-in-fact in subsection (a), Pledgor hereby irrevocably appoints Secured Party as Pledgor's agent and attorney-in-fact to make, execute and deliver any and all documents and writings which may be necessary or appropriate for approval of, or be required by, any regulatory authority located in any city, county, state or country where Pledgor or any of the Issuers engage in business, in order to transfer or to more effectively transfer any of the Pledged Interests or otherwise enforce Secured Party's rights hereunder.

### 9. Remedies upon Default.

Upon the occurrence and during the continuance of an Event of Default:

(a)   Secured Party may exercise in respect of the Collateral, in addition to other rights and remedies provided for herein or otherwise available to it, all the rights and remedies of a secured party on default under the Code (irrespective of whether the Code applies to the affected items of Collateral), and Secured Party may also without notice (except as specified below)[5] sell the Collateral or any part thereof in one or more parcels at public or private sale, at any exchange, broker's board or at any of Secured Party's offices or elsewhere, for cash, on credit or for future delivery, at such time or times and at such price or prices and upon such other terms as Secured Party may deem commercially reasonable, irrespective of the impact of any such sales on the market price of the Collateral. To the maximum extent permitted by applicable law, Secured Party may be the purchaser of any or all of the Collateral at any such sale and shall be entitled, for the purpose of bidding and making settlement or payment of the purchase price for all or any portion of the Collateral sold at any such public sale, to use and apply all or any part of the Secured Obligations as a credit on account of the purchase price of any Collateral payable at such sale.[6] Each pur-

---

5.   Note that Rev. § 9-611(d) does not require notification to a debtor, secondary obligor or other persons (as set forth in Rev. § 9-611(c)) where the collateral is disposed of after default and "is of a type customarily sold on a recognized market."

6.   Rev. § 9-610(c) permits the secured party to purchase collateral after default at a public disposition, or at a private disposition, "only if the collateral is of a kind that is customarily sold on a recognized market or the subject of widely distributed standard price quotations."

chaser at any such sale shall hold the property sold absolutely free from any claim or right on the part of Pledgor, and Pledgor hereby waives (to the extent permitted by law) all rights of redemption, stay, or appraisal that it now has or may at any time in the future have under any rule of law or statute now existing or hereafter enacted. Pledgor agrees that, to the extent notice of sale shall be required by law, at least ten (10) calendar days notice to Pledgor of the time and place of any public sale or the time after which a private sale is to be made shall constitute reasonable notification. Secured Party shall not be obligated to make any sale of Collateral regardless of notice of sale having been given. Secured Party may adjourn any public or private sale from time to time by announcement at the time and place fixed therefor, and such sale may, without further notice, be made at the time and place to which it was so adjourned. To the maximum extent permitted by law, Pledgor hereby waives any claims against Secured Party arising because the price at which any Collateral may have been sold at such a private sale was less than the price that might have been obtained at a public sale, even if Secured Party accepts the first offer received and does not offer such Collateral to more than one offeree.

(b)    Pledgor hereby agrees that any sale or other disposition of the Collateral conducted in conformity with reasonable commercial practices of banks, insurance companies, or other financial institutions in the city and state where Secured Party is located in disposing of property similar to the Collateral shall be deemed to be commercially reasonable.

(c)    Pledgor hereby acknowledges that the sale by Secured Party of any Collateral pursuant to the terms hereof in compliance with the Securities Act of 1933 as now in effect or as hereafter amended, or any similar statute hereafter adopted with similar purpose or effect (the "Securities Act"), as well as applicable "Blue Sky" or other state securities laws, may require strict limitations as to the manner in which Secured Party or any subsequent transferee of the Collateral may dispose thereof. Pledgor acknowledges and agrees that in order to protect Secured Party's interest it may be necessary to sell the Collateral at a price less than the maximum price attainable if a sale were delayed or were made in another manner, such as a public offering under the Securities Act. Pledgor has no objection to sale in such a manner and agrees that Secured Party shall have no obligation to obtain the maximum possible price for the Collateral. Without limiting the generality of the foregoing, Pledgor agrees that, upon the occurrence and during the continuation of an Event of Default, Secured Party may, subject to applicable law, from time to time attempt to sell all or any part of the Collateral by a private placement, restricting the bidders and prospective purchasers to those who will represent and agree that they are purchasing for investment only and not for distribution. In so doing, Secured Party may solicit offers to buy the Collateral or any part thereof for cash, from a limited number of investors reasonably believed by Secured Party to be institutional investors or other accredited investors who might be interested in purchasing the Collateral. If Secured Party shall solicit such offers, then the acceptance by Secured Party of one of the offers shall be deemed to be a commercially reasonable method of disposition of the Collateral.

(d)    If Secured Party shall determine to exercise its right to sell all or any portion of the Collateral pursuant to this Section, Pledgor agrees that, upon request of Secured Party, Pledgor will, at its own expense:

(i)    use its best efforts to execute and deliver, and cause the Issuers and the directors and officers thereof to execute and deliver, all such instruments and documents, and to do or cause to be done all such other acts and things, as may be necessary or, in the opinion of Secured Party, advisable to register such Collateral under the provisions of the Securities Act, and to cause the registration statement relating thereto to become effective and to remain effective for such period as prospectuses are required by law to be furnished, and to make all amendments and supplements thereto and to the related prospectuses which, in the opinion of Secured Party, are necessary or advisable, all in conformity with the requirements of the Securities Act and the rules and regulations of the Securities and Exchange Commission applicable thereto;

(ii)   use its best efforts to qualify the Collateral under the state securities laws or "Blue Sky" laws and to obtain all necessary governmental approvals for the sale of the Collateral, as requested by Secured Party;

(iii) cause the Issuers to make available to their respective security holders, as soon as practicable, an earnings statement which will satisfy the provisions of § 11(a) of the Securities Act;

(iv)  execute and deliver, or cause the officers and directors of the Issuers to execute and deliver, to any person, entity or governmental authority as Secured Party may choose, any and all documents and writings which, in Secured Party's reasonable judgment, may be necessary or appropriate for approval, or be required by, any regulatory authority located in any city, county, state or country where Pledgor or the Issuers engage in business, in order to transfer or to more effectively transfer the Pledged Interests or otherwise enforce Secured Party's rights hereunder; and

(v)   do or cause to be done all such other acts and things as may be necessary to make such sale of the Collateral or any part thereof valid and binding and in compliance with applicable law.

Pledgor acknowledges that there is no adequate remedy at law for failure by it to comply with the provisions of this Section and that such failure would not be adequately compensable in damages, and therefore agrees that its agreements contained in this Section may be specifically enforced.

(e)   PLEDGOR EXPRESSLY WAIVES TO THE MAXIMUM EXTENT PERMITTED BY LAW: (i) ANY CONSTITUTIONAL OR OTHER RIGHT TO A JUDICIAL HEARING PRIOR TO THE TIME SECURED PARTY DISPOSES OF ALL OR ANY PART OF THE COLLATERAL AS PROVIDED IN THIS SECTION; (ii) ALL RIGHTS OF REDEMPTION, STAY, OR APPRAISAL THAT IT NOW HAS OR MAY AT ANY TIME IN THE FUTURE HAVE UNDER ANY RULE OF LAW OR STATUTE NOW EXISTING OR HEREAFTER ENACTED; AND (iii) EXCEPT AS SET FORTH IN SUBSECTION (a) OF THIS § 9, ANY REQUIREMENT OF NOTICE, DEMAND, OR ADVERTISEMENT FOR SALE.

## 10.  **Application of Proceeds.**

Upon the occurrence and during the continuance of an Event of Default, any cash held by Secured Party as Collateral and all cash Proceeds received by Secured Party in respect of any sale of, collection from, or other realization upon all or any part of the Collateral pursuant to the exercise by Secured Party of its remedies as a secured creditor as provided in § 9 shall be applied from time to time by Secured Party as provided in the Credit Agreement.

### 11. Indemnity and Expenses.

Pledgor agrees:

(a)    To indemnify and hold harmless Secured Party and each of its directors, officers, employees, agents and affiliates from and against any and all claims, damages, demands, losses, obligations, judgments and liabilities (including, without limitation, reasonable attorneys' fees and expenses) in any way arising out of or in connection with this Agreement or the Secured Obligations, except to the extent the same shall arise as a result of the gross negligence or willful misconduct of the party seeking to be indemnified; and

(b)    To pay and reimburse Secured Party upon demand for all reasonable costs and expenses (including, without limitation, reasonable attorneys' fees and expenses) that Secured Party may incur in connection with (i) the custody, use or preservation of, or the sale of, collection from or other realization upon, any of the Collateral, including the reasonable expenses of re-taking, holding, preparing for sale or lease, selling or otherwise disposing of or realizing on the Collateral, (ii) the exercise or enforcement of any rights or remedies granted hereunder, under the Credit Agreement, or under any of the other Credit Documents or otherwise available to it (whether at law, in equity or otherwise), or (iii) the failure by Pledgor to perform or observe any of the provisions hereof. The provisions of this Section shall survive the execution and delivery of this Agreement, the repayment of any of the Secured Obligations, the termination of the commitments of Secured Party under the Credit Agreement and the termination of this Agreement or any other Credit Document.

### 12. Duties of Secured Party.

The powers conferred on Secured Party hereunder are solely to protect its interests in the Collateral and shall not impose on it any duty to exercise such powers. Except as provided in § 9-207 of the Code, Secured Party shall have no duty with respect to the Collateral or any responsibility for taking any necessary steps to preserve rights against any Persons with respect to any Collateral.[7]

### 13. Choice of Law and Venue; Submission to Jurisdiction; Service of Process.

(a)    THE VALIDITY OF THIS AGREEMENT, ITS CONSTRUCTION, INTERPRETATION, AND ENFORCEMENT, AND THE RIGHTS OF THE PARTIES HERETO SHALL BE DETERMINED UNDER, GOVERNED BY, AND CONSTRUED IN ACCORDANCE WITH THE LAWS OF THE STATE OF _____ (WITHOUT REFERENCE

---

7.    Rev. § 9-207(a) provides that the secured party shall use "reasonable care in the custody and preservation of the collateral in the secured party's possession."

TO THE CHOICE OF LAW PRINCIPLES THEREOF). THE PARTIES AGREE THAT ALL ACTIONS OR PROCEEDINGS ARISING IN CONNECTION WITH THIS AGREEMENT SHALL BE TRIED AND LITIGATED ONLY IN THE STATE AND FEDERAL COURTS LOCATED IN THE COUNTY OF _____, STATE OF _____ OR, AT THE SOLE OPTION OF SECURED PARTY, IN ANY OTHER COURT IN WHICH SECURED PARTY SHALL INITIATE LEGAL OR EQUITABLE PROCEEDINGS AND WHICH HAS SUBJECT MATTER JURISDICTION OVER THE MATTER IN CONTROVERSY.

(b) PLEDGOR HEREBY SUBMITS FOR ITSELF AND IN RESPECT OF ITS PROPERTY, GENERALLY AND UNCONDITIONALLY, TO THE JURISDICTION OF THE AFORESAID COURTS AND WAIVES, TO THE EXTENT PERMITTED UNDER APPLICABLE LAW, ANY RIGHT IT MAY HAVE TO ASSERT THE DOCTRINE OF FORUM NON CONVENIENS OR TO OBJECT TO VENUE TO THE EXTENT ANY PROCEEDING IS BROUGHT IN ACCORDANCE WITH THIS SECTION.

(c) PLEDGOR HEREBY WAIVES PERSONAL SERVICE OF THE SUMMONS, COMPLAINT, OR OTHER PROCESS ISSUED IN ANY ACTION OR PROCEEDING AND AGREES THAT SERVICE OF SUCH SUMMONS, COMPLAINT, OR OTHER PROCESS MAY BE MADE BY REGISTERED OR CERTIFIED MAIL ADDRESSED TO PLEDGOR AT ITS ADDRESS FOR NOTICES IN ACCORDANCE WITH THIS AGREEMENT AND THAT SERVICE SO MADE SHALL BE DEEMED COMPLETED UPON THE EARLIER OF PLEDGOR'S ACTUAL RECEIPT THEREOF OR THREE DAYS AFTER DEPOSIT IN THE UNITED STATES MAILS, PROPER POSTAGE PREPAID.

(d) NOTHING IN THIS AGREEMENT SHALL BE DEEMED OR OPERATE TO AFFECT THE RIGHT OF SECURED PARTY TO SERVE LEGAL PROCESS IN ANY OTHER MANNER PERMITTED BY LAW, OR TO PRECLUDE THE ENFORCEMENT BY SECURED PARTY OF ANY JUDGMENT OR ORDER OBTAINED IN SUCH FORUM OR THE TAKING OF ANY ACTION UNDER THIS AGREEMENT TO ENFORCE SAME IN ANY OTHER APPROPRIATE FORUM OR JURISDICTION.

### 14. **Amendments; etc.**

No amendment or waiver of any provision of this Agreement nor consent to any departure by Pledgor herefrom shall in any event be effective unless the same shall be in writing and signed by Secured Party, and then such waiver or consent shall be effective only in the specific instance and for the specific purpose for which given. No failure on the part of Secured Party to exercise, and no delay in exercising any right under this Agreement, any other Credit Document, or otherwise with respect to any of the Secured Obligations, shall operate as a waiver thereof; nor shall any single or partial exercise of any right under this Agreement, any other Credit Document, or otherwise with respect to any of the Secured Obligations preclude any other or further exercise thereof or the exercise of any other right. The remedies provided for in this Agreement or otherwise with respect to any of the Secured Obligations are cumulative and not exclusive of any remedies provided by law.

15. **Notices.**

Unless otherwise specifically provided herein, all notices shall be in writing addressed to the respective party as set forth below: and may be personally served, faxed, telecopied or sent by overnight courier service or United States mail:

If to Pledgor:                   _____

                                 _____

                                 _____

                                 Fax No.:_____

                                 Attn:_____

with a copy to:                  _____

                                 _____

                                 _____

                                 Fax No.:_____

                                 Attn:_____

If to Secured Party:             _____

                                 _____

                                 _____

                                 Fax No.:_____

                                 Attn:_____

Any notice given pursuant to this section shall be deemed to have been given: (a) if delivered in person, when delivered; (b) if delivered by fax, on the date of transmission if transmitted on a Business Day before 4:00 p.m. at the place of receipt or, if not, on the next succeeding Business Day; (c) if delivered by overnight courier, two (2) days after delivery to such courier properly addressed; or (d) if by United States mail, four (4) Business Days after depositing in the United States mail, with postage prepaid and properly addressed. Any party hereto may change the address or fax number at which it is to receive notices hereunder by notice to the other party in writing in the foregoing manner.

16. **Continuing Security Interest.**

This Agreement shall create a continuing security interest in the Collateral and shall: (a) remain in full force and effect until the indefeasible payment in full of the Secured Obligations, including the cash collateralization, expiration, or cancellation of all Secured Obligations, if any, consisting of letters of credit, and the full and final termination of any commitment to extend any financial accommodations under the Credit Agreement; (b) be binding upon Pledgor and its successors and assigns; and (c) inure to the benefit of Secured Party and its successors, transferees, and assigns. Upon the indefeasible payment in full of the Secured Obligations, including the cash collateralization, expiration, or cancellation of all Secured Obligations, if any, consisting of letters of credit, and the full and final termination of any commitment to extend any financial accommodations under the Credit Agreement, the security interests granted herein shall automatically terminate and all rights to the Collateral shall revert to Pledgor. Upon any such termination, Secured Party will, at Pledgor's expense, execute and deliver to Pledgor such documents as Pledgor shall reasonably request to evidence such termination. Such documents shall be prepared by Pledgor and shall be in form and substance reasonably satisfactory to Secured Party.

17. **Security Interest Absolute.**

To the maximum extent permitted by law, all rights of Secured Party, all security interests hereunder, and all obligations of Pledgor hereunder, shall be absolute and unconditional irrespective of:

(a)  any lack of validity or enforceability of any of the Secured Obligations or any other agreement or instrument relating thereto, including any of the Credit Documents;

(b)  any change in the time, manner, or place of payment of, or in any other term of, all or any of the Secured Obligations, or any other amendment or waiver of or any consent to any departure from any of the Credit Documents, or any other agreement or instrument relating thereto;

(c)  any exchange, release, or non-perfection of any other collateral, or any release or amendment or waiver of or consent to departure from any guaranty for all or any of the Secured Obligations; or

(d)  any other circumstances that might otherwise constitute a defense available to, or a discharge of, Pledgor.

18. **Headings.**

Section and subsection headings in this Agreement are included herein for convenience of reference only and shall not constitute a part of this Agreement or be given any substantive effect.

19. **Severability.**

In case any provision in or obligation under this Agreement shall be invalid, illegal or unenforceable in any jurisdiction, the validity, legality and enforceability of the remaining provisions or obligations, or of such provision or obligation in any other jurisdiction, shall not in any way be affected or impaired thereby.

20. **Counterparts; Telefacsimile Execution.**

This Agreement may be executed in one or more counterparts, each of which shall be deemed an original and all of which together shall constitute one and the same Agreement. Delivery of an executed counterpart of this Agreement by telefacsimile shall be equally as effective as delivery of an original executed counterpart of this Agreement. Any party delivering an executed counterpart of this Agreement by telefacsimile also shall deliver an original executed counterpart of this Agreement but the failure to deliver an original executed counterpart shall not affect the validity, enforceability, or binding effect hereof.

### 21.  Waiver of Marshaling.

Each of Pledgor and Secured Party acknowledges and agrees that in exercising any rights under or with respect to the Collateral: (a) Secured Party is under no obligation to marshal any Collateral; (b) may, in its absolute discretion, realize upon the Collateral in any order and in any manner it so elects; and (c) may, in its absolute discretion, apply the proceeds of any or all of the Collateral to the Secured Obligations in any order and in any manner it so elects. Pledgor and Secured Party waive any right to require the marshaling of any of the Collateral.

### 22.  Waiver of Jury Trial.

PLEDGOR AND SECURED PARTY HEREBY WAIVE THEIR RESPECTIVE RIGHTS TO A JURY TRIAL OF ANY CLAIM OR CAUSE OF ACTION BASED UPON OR ARISING OUT OF THIS AGREEMENT OR ANY OF THE TRANSACTIONS CONTEMPLATED HEREIN, INCLUDING CONTRACT CLAIMS, TORT CLAIMS, BREACH OF DUTY CLAIMS, AND ALL OTHER COMMON LAW OR STATUTORY CLAIMS. PLEDGOR AND SECURED PARTY REPRESENT THAT EACH HAS REVIEWED THIS WAIVER AND EACH KNOWINGLY AND VOLUNTARILY WAIVES ITS JURY TRIAL RIGHTS FOLLOWING CONSULTATION WITH LEGAL COUNSEL. IN THE EVENT OF LITIGATION, A COPY OF THIS AGREEMENT MAY BE FILED AS A WRITTEN CONSENT TO A TRIAL BY THE COURT.

[Signature page to follow.]

IN WITNESS WHEREOF, Pledgor and Secured Party have caused this Agreement to be duly executed and delivered by their officers thereunto duly authorized as of the date first written above.

[PLEDGOR],

a _____

By _____

Title: _____

[SECURED PARTY],

a _____

By _____

Title: _____

# Schedule 1

# Pledged Interests

| Name of Issuer | Jurisdiction of Organization | Type of Interest | Number of Shares/Units (if applicable) | Certificate Number(s) (if any) | Percentage of Outstanding Interests in Issuer |
|---|---|---|---|---|---|
| ———— | ———— | ———— | ———— | ———— | ———— |
| ———— | ———— | ———— | ———— | ———— | ———— |
| ———— | ———— | ———— | ———— | ———— | ———— |
| ———— | ———— | ———— | ———— | ———— | ———— |
| ———— | ———— | ———— | ———— | ———— | ———— |
| ———— | ———— | ———— | ———— | ———— | ———— |
| ———— | ———— | ———— | ———— | ———— | ———— |
| ———— | ———— | ———— | ———— | ———— | ———— |
| ———— | ———— | ———— | ———— | ———— | ———— |
| ———— | ———— | ———— | ———— | ———— | ———— |
| ———— | ———— | ———— | ———— | ———— | ———— |
| ———— | ———— | ———— | ———— | ———— | ———— |
| ———— | ———— | ———— | ———— | ———— | ———— |
| ———— | ———— | ———— | ———— | ———— | ———— |
| ———— | ———— | ———— | ———— | ———— | ———— |
| ———— | ———— | ———— | ———— | ———— | ———— |
| ———— | ———— | ———— | ———— | ———— | ———— |
| ———— | ———— | ———— | ———— | ———— | ———— |
| ———— | ———— | ———— | ———— | ———— | ———— |
| ———— | ———— | ———— | ———— | ———— | ———— |
| ———— | ———— | ———— | ———— | ———— | ———— |
| ———— | ———— | ———— | ———— | ———— | ———— |
| ———— | ———— | ———— | ———— | ———— | ———— |
| ———— | ———— | ———— | ———— | ———— | ———— |

# Schedule 2

## Pledgor Information

*For Pledgor That Is a Registered Organization:*
Jurisdiction of Organization:

Type of Organization:

Organizational ID Number (if any):

*For Pledgor That Is An Individual:*
Address of Principal Residence:

*For Pledgor That Is Neither a Registered Organization nor an Individual:*
Type of Organization:

Address of Chief Executive Office:

Address of all Places of Business:

# Exhibit A

## Indorsement Certificate

FOR VALUE RECEIVED, the undersigned does hereby sell, assign and transfer unto ————, [———— (———) shares of the ———— Stock [or other securities of]] [a ———— percent (———%) interest in ] ———— (the "Issuer") standing in the undersigned's name on the books of the Issuer represented by Certificate No(s). ————, and does hereby irrevocably constitute and appoint ———— as the undersigned's attorney-in-fact to transfer the said stock [or other securities] on the books of the Issuer with full power of substitution in the premises.

Date:                              [PLEDGOR]


By: _____

Name:_____

Title:_____

*PART 4*

# Enforcing the Security Interest

Form 4.1.1

# Notification of Proposal of Full Strict Foreclosure[1] (Non-Consumer Transaction)[2]

_____, 20____

[Name and address of person entitled to notice under § 9-621(a)][3]

Re:  Notification of Proposal to Accept Collateral in [Full] Strict Foreclosure
Debtor: [Debtor, address] (the "Debtor")
Secured Party: [Secured Party, address] (the "Secured Party")
Collateral: [collateral description] (the "Collateral")[4]

---

1.  As with former Article 9, Revised Article 9 permits a secured party to accept collateral in full satisfaction of an obligation. Rev. § 9-620 is based on F. § 9-505, and sets forth the procedure for strict foreclosure. This form is intended to be used to give notice to a debtor or other party entitled to notice under Rev. § 9-621 that the secured party intends to accept collateral in full satisfaction of an obligation. If the secured party sends this notice to the appropriate persons, and receives no timely objection, it will be entitled to retain ("accept") the collateral in full satisfaction of the outstanding obligations, as proposed in this notification.

2.  As under F. § 9-505, strict foreclosure in a consumer transaction is much more difficult than is the case in a non-consumer transaction. If the collateral is consumer goods, Rev. § 9-620(a)(3) prohibits the secured party from accepting the collateral in strict foreclosure if the collateral is in the debtor's possession. Rev. § 9-620(g) forbids a secured party from accepting collateral in partial satisfaction of an obligation secured in a consumer transaction. Rev. § 9-620(e) sets forth limits on when a secured party may accept consumer goods in satisfaction of an obligation, and Rev. § 9-620(f) sets deadlines for the secured party's subsequent disposition of consumer goods so accepted. A secured party seeking to accept collateral in a consumer transaction should take care to research the requirements under Rev. §§ 9-620(b) and (e) and, if applicable, other state and federal. Note that Rev. § 9-201(b) & (c) provides that conflicting consumer laws will control over Revised Article 9.

3.  The secured party wishing to accept collateral in satisfaction of an obligation must send notice to the parties identified in Rev. § 9-621: (i) any party from whom the secured party has received notice of an interest in the collateral; (ii) holders of certain security interests and liens who have filed a financing statement against the debtor; and (iii) holders of certain security interests who perfected by compliance with a statute (_e.g._, a certificate-of-title statute). Note that, unlike "partial" strict foreclosure, the secured party wishing to conduct a _full_ strict foreclosure need not send notice to secondary obligors. Rev. § 9-621(b).

4.  Revised Article 9 differs significantly from former Article 9 in that the secured party may now accept collateral in satisfaction of the obligation even if the secured party does not have possession of the collateral. Rev. § 9-620 cmt. 7. Indeed, Revised Article 9 now permits the secured party to accept intangible collateral in satisfaction of an obligation. Former Article 9 allowed retention only if the secured party already had possession of the collateral. F. § 9-505.

Dear [Name of person receiving notice]:

The Debtor is in default under a security agreement dated [date] entered into between the Debtor and the Secured Party, granting a security interest in the Collateral. The outstanding balance due from the Debtor to the Secured Party as of [date] is [$ amount] (the "Balance").

The Secured Party shall accept[5] the Collateral in full satisfaction of the Balance, and the obligations due shall be deemed fully discharged as a result.[6]

If you have any objection to the Secured Party's proposal to accept the Collateral in full satisfaction of the Balance, you must send us an authenticated statement of your objection within twenty (20) days[7] from the date this notice was sent. If we have not received an authenticated objection within that time period, you will be deemed to have consented to this proposal and will have no further right to object,[8] and the Secured Party will retain the Collateral in full satisfaction of the Debtor's obligation, as described in this letter.

[SECURED PARTY]

By:_____

Name:_____

Title:_____

---

5.    A secured party's acceptance of collateral cannot be "implied." Rev. § 9-620(b). This provision is designed to prevent the debtor from unilaterally proclaiming the secured party's "acceptance" of collateral, thereby eliminating the secured party's deficiency claim. Rev. § 9-620 cmt. 5. This form of notice expressly informs the debtor of the secured party's intentions and is contrary to decisions under former Article 9 that permitted an implied acceptance. *See, e.g., In re Boyd,* 73 B.R. 122 (Bankr. N.D. Tex. 1987); *Schmode's, Inc. v. Wilkinson,* 219 Neb. 209 (1985). Revised Article 9 eliminates the possibility that a secured party's delay in disposition will be construed as an implied strict foreclosure. Nevertheless, if the secured party ultimately does not retain the collateral, and instead disposes of it, the secured party's delay may affect a determination of whether the disposition was "commercially reasonable." *See* Rev. § 9-610(b) ("[e]very aspect of a disposition of collateral . . . must be commercially reasonable . . . ."); Rev. § 9-627 (setting forth standards for determining whether disposition is commercially reasonable).

6.    Revised Article 9 reflects the view that "strict foreclosures should be encouraged [as they will] often produce better results than a disposition [of collateral] for all concerned." Rev. § 9-620 cmt. 2. Further, Rev. § 9-620 eliminates the fiction (of F. § 9-505) that the secured party will *always* present a strict foreclosure "proposal" to the debtor and that the debtor will respond within a fixed period of time. Instead, a proposal is permitted, but not necessary. *See* Rev. § 9-620 cmt. 2.

7.    Under Rev. § 9-620(d), a debtor or other recipient of this notice has twenty days to object to the proposed acceptance Under F. § 9-505, the objection period lasted twenty-one days. F. § 9-505(2). Third parties who are not entitled to notice may object at any time within twenty days after the last notification was sent or, if no such notice was sent out, before the debtor agrees to the acceptance in writing. *See* Rev. § 9-620 cmt. 8.

8.    Revised Article 9 expands the number of parties to whom the secured party must send notice, and the grounds for objections to strict foreclosure. Under Rev. § 9-620 the debtor, any person identified in Rev. § 9-621 (including secondary obligors), or any other person holding an interest subordinate to the security interest that is the subject of the proposal may object to the proposed acceptance within twenty days of the date the notice is sent. Rev. § 9-620(a)(2) & (d).

# Notification of Proposal of Partial Strict Foreclosure[1] (Non-Consumer Transaction)[2]

_____, 20___

[Name and address of person entitled to notice under § 9-621(a)][3]

Re:   Notification of Proposal to Accept Collateral in Partial Strict Foreclosure
Debtor: [Debtor, address] (the "Debtor")
Secured Party: [Secured Party, address] (the "Secured Party")
Collateral: [collateral description] (the "Collateral")

---

1.   Former Article 9 did not explicitly contemplate "partial strict foreclosure." Revised Article 9 does, in Rev. § 9-620(a). This form is intended to be used to give notice to a debtor, obligor or other party entitled to notice under Rev. § 9-621 (e.g., a "secondary obligor") that the secured party intends to accept collateral in partial satisfaction of an obligation. If the secured party sends this notice to the appropriate persons, and receives no timely objection, it will be entitled to retain ("accept") the collateral in partial satisfaction of the outstanding obligations, as proposed in this notice.

2.   Rev. § 9-620(g) prohibits a secured party from accepting collateral in partial satisfaction of an obligation in a "consumer transaction," defined in Rev. § 9-102(a)(26) as "a transaction in which (i) an individual incurs an obligation primarily for personal, family or household purposes, (ii) a security interest secures the obligation, and (iii) the collateral is held or acquired primarily for personal, family, or household purposes."

3.   The secured party wishing to accept collateral in partial satisfaction of an obligation must send notice to the parties identified in Rev. § 9-621: (i) any party from whom the secured party has received notice of an interest in the collateral; (ii) holders of certain security interests and liens who have filed a financing statement against the debtor; and (iii) holders of certain security interests who perfected by compliance with a statute (e.g., a certificate-of-title statute). Note that, unlike "full" strict foreclosure, the secured party wishing to conduct a _partial_ strict foreclosure must also send notice to secondary obligors. Rev. § 9-621(b).

Dear [Name of person receiving notice]:

The Debtor is in default under a security agreement dated [date] entered into between the Debtor and the Secured Party, granting a security interest in the Collateral. The outstanding balance due from the Debtor to the Secured Party as of [date] is [$amount] (the "Balance").

The Secured Party shall accept[4] the Collateral in satisfaction of [$collateral value] of the total debt of [$ total amount of debt] due from the Debtor.[5]

If you have any objection to Secured Party's proposal to accept the Collateral in satisfaction of [$ collateral value] of the Balance, you must send us a signed, written statement of your objection within twenty (20) days[6] from the date of this letter. If we have not received a signed, written objection within that time period, you will be deemed to have consented to this proposal and will have no further right to object[7], and the Secured Party will retain the Collateral in partial satisfaction of the Balance, as described in this letter.

[SECURED PARTY]

By:_____

Name:_____

Title:_____

---

4.   A secured party's acceptance of collateral cannot be "implied." Rev. § 9-620(b). This provision is designed to prevent the debtor from unilaterally causing an "acceptance" of collateral, thereby eliminating the secured party's deficiency claim. Rev. § 9-620 cmt. 5. This form of notice expressly informs the debtor of the secured party's intentions and is contrary to decisions under former Article 9 that permitted an implied acceptance. *See, e.g., In re Boyd*, 73 B.R. 122 (Bankr. N.D. Tex. 1987); *Schmode's, Inc. v. Wilkinson*, 219 Neb. 209 (1985). Revised Article 9 seeks to eliminate the possibility that a secured party's delay in disposition will be construed as an implied strict foreclosure. Nevertheless, delay by the secured party may affect a determination of whether the secured party disposed of the collateral in a commercially reasonable manner. *See* Rev. § 9-610(b) ("[e]very aspect of a disposition of collateral . . . must be commercially reasonable . . . ."); Rev. § 9-627 (setting forth standards for determining whether disposition is commercially reasonable).

5.   Revised Article 9 reflects the view that "strict foreclosures should be encouraged [as they will] often produce better results than a disposition [of collateral] for all concerned." Rev. § 9-320 cmt. 2. Further, Rev. § 9-620 eliminates the fiction (of F. § 9-505) that the secured party will *always* present a strict foreclosure "proposal" to the debtor and that the debtor will respond within a fixed period of time. Instead, a proposal is permitted, but not necessary. *See* Rev. § 9-620 cmt. 2.

6.   Under Rev. § 9-620(d), a debtor or other recipient of this notice has twenty days to object to the proposed acceptance. Under F. § 9-505, the objection period lasted twenty-one days. *See* F. § 9-505(2).

7.   Revised Article 9 expands the number of parties to whom the secured party must send notice, and the grounds for objections to strict foreclosure. Under Rev. § 9-620 the debtor, any person identified in § 9-621 (including secondary obligors), or any other person holding an interest subordinate to the security interest that is the subject of the proposal may object to the proposed acceptance within 20 days of the date the notice is sent. Rev. § 9-620(a)(2) & (d).

# Notification of Private Disposition of Collateral[1] (Non-Consumer Transaction)[2]

_____, 20___

To:     [Name of Debtor, obligor or other person to whom the notification is sent][3]

From:     [Name, address, and telephone number of secured party]

Name of Debtor(s):     [Include only if debtor(s) is (are) not the addressee(s)]

---

1.  As under former Article 9, Revised Article 9 permits the secured party to dispose of collateral following a default. Rev. § 9-601. A secured party is generally required to give the debtor notice of a disposition of collateral following default (_e.g.,_ by sale, lease, license, etc.). _See_ Rev. § 9-611(b)(secured party disposing of collateral required to send notice to debtor and other parties with interest in collateral); Rev. § 9-612 (timing of notice). Notification of disposition is not required where collateral is perishable, threatens to decline speedily in value or is of a type customarily sold on a "recognized market." Rev. § 9-613(5) provides a statutory form that will be deemed to provide "sufficient information" of a disposition of collateral under 9-611(b). This form is modeled after the statutory form contained in Rev. § 9-613(5), and will, when properly completed, contain the information required in a notification of disposition.

2.  Rev. § 9-614 sets forth a different form of notice for use in disposing of collateral in a "consumer transaction," defined in Rev. § 9-102(a)(26) as "a transaction in which (i) an individual incurs an obligation primarily for personal, family or household purposes, (ii) a security interest secures the obligation, and (iii) the collateral is held or acquired primarily for personal, family, or household purposes."

3.  Rev. § 9-611(c) sets forth the parties to whom notice must be sent: (i) the debtor, (ii) any "secondary obligor," (iii) other persons from whom the secured party has received notification of a claim of an interest in collateral (if not consumer goods), and (iv) secured parties that have filed financing statements in the proper offices (or otherwise perfected a security interest under Rev. § 9-311(a)) as of ten days before the date the secured party gives the debtor notice of disposition of the collateral (if not consumer goods).

Rev. § 9-611 continues the requirement of F. § 9-504 that the secured party send notice to any person who has notified the secured party claiming an interest in the collateral. Unlike former Article 9, Revised Article 9 also requires the secured party to send notice of the disposition to any other secured party that, as of ten days before the notice is sent, had a financing statement on file covering the same collateral (so long as the collateral is not consumer goods). Rev. § 9-611(c)(3)(B). Notice must also be given to holders of security interests perfected by compliance with a statute, regulation or treaty (_i.e.,_ a certificate-of-title statute).

# NOTIFICATION OF PRIVATE DISPOSITION

We will sell [or *lease* or *license*, as applicable][4] the [describe collateral] privately some-time after [day and date].[5]

You are entitled to an accounting of the unpaid indebtedness[6] secured by the property that we intend to sell [or *lease* or *license*, as applicable] [for a charge of $_____].[7] You may request an accounting by calling us at [telephone number].

[SECURED PARTY]

By:_____

Name:_____

Title:_____

---

4.   The secured party may sell, lease, license or otherwise dispose of the collateral. Rev. § 9-610(a).

5.   Revised Article 9 follows former Article 9's requirements for notice of private sale: the secured party need only inform the relevant parties of the time *after which* disposition is to be made. *See* F. § 9-504; Rev. § 9-613(1)(E).

6.   The debtor is entitled to an accounting of a surplus, if any, arising out of the sale of the property. Rev. § 9-608(a)(4). According to Official Comment 3, Article 9 omits any references to agreements which vary the rules on surplus and deficiency; the parties are free to agree that an obligor will or will not be liable for a deficiency. Rev. § 9-608(a)(4) cmt. 3; *see also* § 9-615(d) & (e). Rev. § 9-603(a) also provides that the parties may determine by agreement the standards measuring the fulfillment of the rights and duties of a secured party under a variety of circumstances, so long as such standards are not "manifestly unreasonable."

7.   The requirement that the secured party notify the debtor that it is entitled to an accounting is new, and appears in Rev. § 9-613(1)(D). A debtor is entitled without charge to one accounting response during any six-month period. Rev. § 9-616(e). The secured party may not charge more than $25.00 for each additional response. *Id.* Although Revised Article 9 does not appear to entitle parties other than the debtor to an accounting, best practice may suggest that it is appropriate to share the accounting with other parties asserting an interest in the collateral, *e.g.* junior secured parties or secondary obligors.

# Form 4.1.4

# Notification of Public
# Disposition of Collateral[1]
# (Non-Consumer Transaction)[2]

_____ , 20 ____

To:     [Debtor, obligor or other person to whom the notification is sent][3]

From:     [Name, address, and telephone number of secured party]

Name of Debtor(s):     [Include only if debtor(s) is (are) not addressee(s)]

---

1.  As under former Article 9, Revised Article 9 permits the secured party to dispose of collateral following a default. Rev. § 9-601. A secured party is generally required to give the debtor notice of a disposition of collateral following default (*e.g.*, by sale, lease, license, etc.). *See* Rev. § 9-611(b)(secured party disposing of collateral required to send notice to debtor and other parties with interest in collateral); Rev. § 9-612 (timing of notice). Notification of disposition is not required where collateral is perishable, threatens to decline speedily in value or is of a type customarily sold on a "recognized market." Rev. § 9-611(d). When notification is appropriate, Rev. § 9-613(5) provides a statutory form that will be deemed to provide "sufficient information" of a disposition of collateral under 9-611(b). This form is modeled after the statutory form contained in Rev. § 9-613(5), and will, when properly completed, contain the information required in a notification of disposition.

2.  Rev. § 9-614 sets forth a different form of notice for use in disposing of collateral in a "consumer transaction," defined in Rev. § 9-102(a)(26) as "a transaction in which (i) an individual incurs an obligation primarily for personal, family or household purposes, (ii) a security interest secures the obligation, and (iii) the collateral is held or acquired primarily for personal, family, or household purposes."

3.  Rev. § 9-611(c) sets forth the parties to whom notice must be sent: (i) the debtor, (ii) any "secondary obligor," (iii) other persons from whom the secured party has received notification of a claim of an interest in collateral (if not consumer goods), and (iv) secured parties that have filed financing statements in the proper offices (or otherwise perfected a security interest under Rev. § 9-311(a)) as of ten days before the date the secured party gives the debtor notice of disposition of the collateral (if not consumer goods).

Rev. § 9-611 continues the requirement of F. § 9-504 that the secured party send notice to any person who has notified the secured party claiming an interest in the collateral. Unlike former Article 9, Revised Article 9 also requires the secured party to send notice of the disposition to any other secured party that, as of ten days before the notice is sent, had a financing statement on file covering the same collateral (so long as the collateral is not consumer goods). Rev. § 9-611(c)(3)(B).

# NOTIFICATION OF PUBLIC DISPOSITION

We will sell [or *lease* or *license,* as applicable][4] the [describe collateral] [to the highest qualified bidder][5] in public as follows:

Day and Date: _____ [6]

Time: _____ [7]

Place: _____

You are entitled to an accounting of the unpaid indebtedness[8] secured by the property that we intend to sell [or lease or license, as applicable] [for a charge of $_____ ].[9] You may request an accounting by calling us at [telephone number].

[SECURED PARTY]

By: _____

Name: _____

Title: _____

---

4.   The secured party may sell, lease, license, or otherwise dispose of the collateral. Rev. § 9-610(a).

5.   Revised Article 9 does not require the secured party to dispose of the collateral to the "highest qualified bidder." Of course, "[e]very aspect of a disposition of collateral, including the method, manner, time, place, and other terms, must be commercially reasonable." Rev. § 9-610(b). "While not of itself sufficient to establish a violation of [Part 6 of Revised Article 9], a low price suggests that a court should scrutinize carefully all aspects of a disposition to ensure that each aspect was commercially reasonable." Rev. § 9-610 cmt. 10. A commercially reasonable sale may or may not include a sale to the highest qualified bidder; as always, whether a disposition is "commercially reasonable" is a question of fact. *See* Rev. § 9-627.

6.   As under F. § 9-504, Rev. § 9-613(1)(E) requires the secured party to give the debtor notification of the time and place of a public disposition. Rev. § 9-611 generally contemplates that a secured party will send notification of a disposition before the disposition occurs. *See* Rev. § 9-611 cmt. 2 (reasonable notification will be given "a reasonable time before the disposition is to take place . . . ."). Notification of disposition in a non-consumer transaction is deemed to be given in "reasonable time" if given after default and at least ten days before the earliest date of the intended disposition set forth in the notification. Rev. § 9-612(b).

7.   Revised Article 9 does not specify a deadline by which the secured party must dispose of collateral in a non-consumer transaction. *See* Rev. § 9-610 cmt. 3 ("This Article does not specify a period within which the secured party must dispose of collateral."). It may, for example, be imprudent to dispose of collateral when the market for that type of collateral has collapsed. *Id.* Alternatively, some types of collateral must be disposed of more quickly than others, or during a specific seasons, in order to maximize sale price. As with the giving of the notification of disposition, the secured party must act in a "commercially reasonable" manner in disposing of the collateral. Rev. § 9-610(b).

8.   The debtor is entitled to an accounting of a surplus, if any, arising out of the sale of the property. Rev. § 9-608(a)(4). According to Official Comment 3 to Rev. § 9-608(a)(4), Article 9 intentionally omits any references to agreements which vary the rules of surplus and deficiency; the parties remain free to agree that an obligor will or will not be liable for a deficiency. Rev. § 9-608(a)(4) cmt. 3; *see also* § 9-615(d) & (e). Rev. § 9-603(a) also provides that the parties may determine by agreement the standards measuring the fulfillment of the rights and duties of a secured party under a variety of circumstances, so long as such standards are not "manifestly unreasonable."

9.   The requirement that the secured party notify the debtor that it is entitled to an accounting is new, and appears in Rev. § 9-613(1)(D). A debtor is entitled to obtain one accounting response during any six-month period free of charge by the secured party. Rev. § 9-617(e). The secured party may not charge more than $25.00 for each additional response. *Id.* Although Revised Article 9 does not appear to entitle parties other than the debtor to an accounting, best practice may suggest that it is appropriate to share the accounting with other parties asserting an interest in the collateral, *e.g.* junior secured parties or secondary obligors.

# Form of Complaint Enforcing Security Interest[1] (Non-Consumer Transaction)

IN THE DISTRICT COURT OF _____, _____

| | | |
|---|---|---|
| Secured Party | ) | |
| | ) | |
| Plaintiff | ) | |
| | ) | |
| v. | ) | Case No.:_____ |
| | ) | |
| Debtor | ) | |
| Defendant | ) | |

## COMPLAINT ON A NOTE, TO ENFORCE SECURITY INTEREST AND FOR DECLARATORY JUDGMENT

[Secured party] a [entity] ("Secured Party"), as and for its Complaint against [Debtor], a [entity] (the "Debtor"), states and alleges as follows:

1. Secured Party is [describe], with an office at [address].

2. Debtor's is [describe], with a principal [place of business, residence select one] at [address].

---

1. Although a secured party need not use judicial process to enforce a security interest, it may be advisable to do so. For example, where the secured party is unable to obtain possession of collateral without "breach of the peace," or is concerned that a proposed disposition may not be commercially reasonable (thus exposing the secured party to reduction of its deficiency claim under Rev. § 9-626), the secured party may wish to seek judicial approval of its enforcement of its rights arising under and in connection with the security agreement. This form is intended to be used where the secured party seeks judicial approval of its enforcement of such rights. Rev. § 9-627(c)(1).

3.  This Court has subject matter jurisdiction over this matter pursuant to [describe].

4.  Venue is proper in this Court pursuant to [describe].

5.  Debtor is subject to personal jurisdiction in this Court because [describe].

# COUNT I
# SUIT ON PROMISSORY NOTE[2]

6.  Secured Party incorporates by reference and realleges paragraphs 1 through 5 of its Complaint, as though fully set forth herein.

7.  On or about _____, ____ in consideration of a loan of $_____ from Secured Party, Debtor [, by its authorized signatory if applicable] signed and delivered to Secured Party a promissory note dated [insert] (the "Promissory Note"). A true and accurate copy of the Promissory Note is attached hereto, and incorporated herein by reference, as **Exhibit A**.

8.  Under the Promissory Note, Debtor promised to repay [describe terms of obligation].

9.  The Promissory Note also provides that [describe remedies, *e.g.*, if Debtor defaulted in its payments, Secured Party would be entitled to declare the entire amount of principal and interest owed on the Note to be immediately due, to increase the interest rate to a "default rate" of _____ (the "Default Rate") , and to recover its attorneys' fees and costs if legal action was required to collect Debtor's debt.]

10. Debtor failed to make payments under the Promissory Note due [missed payment], which failures constitute an "Event of Default" under the Promissory Note.

11. By letter dated [date of default letter] (the "Default Letter") Secured Party demanded payment of all amounts due under the Promissory Note. A true and accurate copy of the Default Letter is attached hereto, and incorporated herein by reference, as **Exhibit B**. Debtor has refused, and continues to refuse, to make the payments due under the Promissory Note.

12. Secured Party advised Debtor in the Default Letter that the interest rate has been increased to the Default Rate and that late charges and other fees are due and owing, and continue to accrue. *See* **Exhibit B**.

13. As of the date of this Complaint, $[insert total amount due as of date of complaint] is due and owing on the Note, with interest continuing to accrue at the Default Rate.

14. Under the Note, Secured Party is entitled to recover its reasonable attorneys' fees and costs incurred herein. Such costs and fees continue to accrue.

---

2.  Count 1 of this form complaint establishes the debtor's liability for all principal, interest (including default interest), costs and fees due and owing as provided in the debtor's promissory note. Rev. § 9-601(a)(1) provides that, after default, a secured party "may reduce a claim to judgment, foreclose, or otherwise enforce, the claim . . . by any available judicial procedure." There is no election of remedies by the secured party's taking any of these actions. *See* Rev. § 9-601(c) cmt. 5.

WHEREFORE, Secured Party requests that the Court enter judgment against Debtor and in favor of Secured Party in the amount of $[insert total amount due as of date of complaint], for such interest as accrues between the date of this Complaint and the date judgment is satisfied, for attorneys' fees and costs incurred herein, and for such further relief as the Court deems just and proper.

## COUNT II
## ACTION TO ENFORCE SECURITY INTEREST[3]

15. Secured Party incorporates by reference and realleges paragraphs 1 through 14 of its Complaint, as though fully set forth herein.

16. To secure Debtor's performance of the Promissory Note and in consideration of Secured Party's loan in the amount of $_____, Debtor executed and delivered to Secured Party that certain Security Agreement dated _____, ____ (the "Security Agreement"). A true and accurate copy of the Security Agreement is attached hereto, and incorporated herein by reference, as **Exhibit C**.

17. Pursuant to the Security Agreement and Article 9 of the Uniform Commercial Code as enacted in [state] (the "UCC"), Debtor granted Secured Party a security interest in _____ (the "Collateral"). *See* **Exhibit C**, § [insert].

18. Secured Party perfected its security interest in the Collateral by [filing a financing statement with the [state][set forth filing office] on _____, ____][or insert alternatives means of perfection, *e.g.*, compliance with certificate-of-title statute].[4]

19. Under Section _____ of the Security Agreement and § 9-601 of the UCC, Debtor's default under the Note also constitutes a default under the Security Agreement. Under the Security Agreement and §§ 9-601 and 9-609 of the UCC, the Secured Party is entitled to enforce its security interest in the Collateral, including by taking immediate possession of the Collateral.

WHEREFORE, Secured Party respectfully requests that the Court enter judgment against Debtor and in favor of Secured Party declaring that Secured Party is entitled to immediate possession of the Collateral and for such further relief as the Court deems just and proper.

---

3.    Count 2 of this form complaint seeks judicial enforcement of the security interest by, among other things, giving the secured party possession of the collateral. Rev. § 9-601(a)(1) provides that, after default, a secured party "may . . . foreclose, or otherwise enforce the . . . security interest . . . by any available judicial procedure." Rev. § 9-609(a)(1) permits a secured party to take possession of collateral. It may do so without judicial process only if it proceeds without "breach of the peace." Rev. § 9-609(b)(2).

4.    The security interest need not be perfected to be enforceable against the debtor. The security interest need only have attached. *See* Rev. § 9-201.

## COUNT III
## DECLARATORY JUDGMENT[5]

20. Secured Party incorporates by reference and realleges paragraphs 1 through 19 of its Complaint, as though set forth herein.

21. On or about _____, 20____, Secured Party sent notice of its intent to dispose of the Collateral by [insert proposed method of disposition][6] to be held [ _____ ], 20____ (the "Proposed Disposition") to the Debtor [and other parties entitled to notification[7] (the "Notice of Proposed Disposition"). A true and accurate copy of the Notice of Proposed Disposition is attached hereto, and incorporated herein by reference, as **Exhibit D**.

22. The Notice of Proposed Disposition comports with Section 9-613 of the UCC because it (a) describes the Debtor and Secured Party, (b) describes the Collateral subject to the Proposed Disposition, (c) identifies the Proposed Disposition as the intended method of disposition of the Collateral, (d) states the Debtor's entitlement to an accounting of the unpaid indebtedness [and the charge, if any, for an accounting], and (e) states the time and place of the Proposed Disposition [or the time after which any other disposition is to be made].[8]

23. The Proposed Disposition is scheduled for [or after] _____, 20____, [which shall allow a prompt disposition of the Collateral taking into account the trends and developments of the market applicable to the Collateral and potential diminution in the Collateral's value if the Sale is further delayed.][9]

---

5.  Count 3 of this form complaint seeks judicial appoval of the secured party's disposition of the collateral, as contemplated by Rev. § 9-627(c)(1). *Compare* F. § 9-507(2) (disposition approved in "judicial proceeding" deemed commercially reasonable). Rev. § 9-627(c)(1) provides that a disposition "is commercially reasonable if it has been approved . . . in a judicial proceeding." Although the term "judicial proceeding" is not defined in the UCC, it would certainly include a proceeding in a state or United States district court of competent jurisdiction.

6.  A secured party that disposes of collateral under Rev. § 9-610 must provide reasonable notification of the disposition unless the collateral is perishable or threatens to decline speedily in value or is of a type customarily sold on a recognized market. Rev. § 9-611(b) & (d). Rev. § 9-613(1) provides that a notification of disposition must (i) describe the debtor and the secured party, (ii) describe the collateral that is the subject of the intended disposition; (iii) state the method of the intended disposition; (iv) state that the debtor is entitled to an accounting; and (v) state the time and place of a public disposition or the time after which any other disposition is to be made. Forms of notice of proposed disposition appear as Forms 4.1.3 & 4.1.4.

7.  Rev. § 9-611(c) sets forth the parties to whom notice of the intended disposition must be sent: (i) the debtor, (ii) any "secondary obligor" (iii) other persons from whom the secured party has received notification of a claim of an interest in collateral (if not consumer goods) and (iv) secured parties with financing statements filed before the date the secured party gives the debtor notice of disposition of the collateral (if not consumer goods). A "secondary obligor" is defined in Rev. § 9-102(a)(71) as "an obligor [a person that "owes payment or other performance of the obligation," Rev. § 9-102((a)(59)] to the extent that: (A) the obligor's obligation is secondary; or (B) the obligor has a right of recourse with respect to an obligation secured by collateral against the debtor, another obligor, or property of either."

8.  The bracketed language is to be used in the event the Proposed Disposition is not a "public" disposition. *See* Rev. § 9-613(1)(e).

9.  Rev. § 9-610(b) provides that every aspect of a disposition of collateral, including the method, manner, time, place, and other terms, must be commercially reasonable. The bracketed language is intended to indicate that the secured party has proposed a disposition that the court will find to be commercially reasonable. The secured party should be sensitive to local practice as to what is considered commercially reasonable.

24. [Prior to the Proposed Disposition, Secured Party will take the following measures to prepare the Collateral for the Proposed Disposition: _____ ].[10]

25. [Public notice of the Proposed Disposition, including its time and place will be published and advertised in the [name of publication], a recognized publication for such public notices for this type of Collateral, commencing on _____20____ and running for ____ consecutive days including the date of the Sale.][if a public disposition]

[26. [In accordance with the published notice and in conformity with reasonable commercial practices among dealers of [type of collateral], the Proposed Disposition will be conducted as follows: [describe public disposition].[11]]

[26A [In accordance with the Notice of Proposed Disposition, the Proposed Disposition Disposition will be conducted as follows: [describe non-public disposition][if a non-public disposition].[12]]

27. Following the conclusion of the Proposed Disposition, the [purchaser, or lessee or licensee, as applicable] of the Collateral will acquire any and all of the debtor's right, title and interest in and to the Collateral. The Secured Party shall not make, and shall not be deemed to have made, any warranties, express or implied, including no warranties relating to title, possession, quite enjoyment or the like,[13] with respect to the Collateral except as expressly stated in writing by the Secured Party at the Proposed Disposition.[14]

WHEREFORE, Secured Party respectfully requests this Court to enter judgment (i) declaring the Notice of Proposed Disposition to be sufficient under §§ 9-611(b) and 9-613 of the UCC; (ii) authorizing and approving the Proposed Disposition; (iii) declaring the Proposed Disposition to be commercially reasonable in all respects; and (iv) granting such other relief as the Court deems just and proper.[15]

_____
COUNSEL TO SECURED PARTY

---

10. Under Rev. § 9-610(a), the secured party is entitled to dispose of collateral in its present condition or "following any commercially reasonable preparation or processing." The bracketed language is intended to enable the secured party to prepare or process collateral and insure that such action will be found commercially reasonable.

11. Use this ¶ 26 if the disposition is a "public" disposition.

12. Use this ¶ 26A if the disposition is not a "public" disposition.

13. Rev. § 9-610(e) permits the secured party to disclaim or modify disposition warranties otherwise given to a foreclosure transferee.

14. Under Rev. § 9-610(d), and unless disclaimed under Rev. § 9-610(e), a contract for the sale, lease, license, or other disposition of collateral "includes the warranties relating to title, possession, quiet enjoyment, and the like which by operation of law accompany a voluntary disposition of property of the kind subject to the contract."

15. Under Rev. § 9-617(a), a secured party's disposition of collateral transfers to a transferee for value all of the debtor's rights in the collateral, discharges the security interest under which the disposition is made and "discharges any subordinate security interest or other subordinate lien." This form complaint does not expressly contemplate the discharge of subordinate security interests. If a secured party wishes to do so, it should consider modifying this form to explain the nature of the subordinate security interest.

# PART 5

# Miscellaneous Forms

# Form of Secured Credit Facility– Closing Checklist[1]

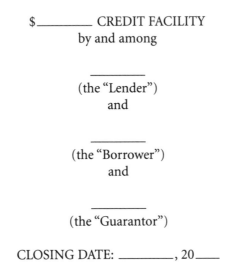

$_____$ CREDIT FACILITY
by and among

$_____$
(the "Lender")
and

$_____$
(the "Borrower")
and

$_____$
(the "Guarantor")

CLOSING DATE: $_____$, 20$\_\_\_$

## A. LOAN COMMITMENT:

1. Pre-Filing Authorization Letter[2]

2. Electronic Transaction Protocols

---

1. This form of closing checklist is intentionally over-inclusive. It lists all the documents that would be expected at a closing in connection with the secured lending portion of a variety of different kind of transactions in which a secured loan would play a central part, including an asset or stock acquisition. As with all of the forms in this book, special care will have to be taken to tailor it to particular transactions.

2. Rev. § 9-509(a)(1) authorizes a secured party to "pre-file" an initial financing statement if, among other things, "the debtor authorizes the filing." Best practice will suggest that the authority to file the financing statement be evidenced by a document or record authenticated by the debtor. A form of pre-filing authorization letter is set forth as Form 1.3.

3. Loan Approval

4. Authenticated Loan Commitment Letter

5. Review of Organizational Documents, Supporting Documentation, Loan Documentation, Insurance, Opinions, Certificates and Records Searches

6. Satisfactory Field Examination by Lender

## B. ORGANIZATIONAL DOCUMENTS (To be provided by Borrower and its Counsel):

**Corporate Borrower:**

7. Certificate of Good Standing dated as of [a date no later than 30 days before closing]

8. Certificate of Qualification to do Business in each jurisdiction in which the Borrower conducts business dated as of [a date no later than 10 days before closing]

9. Certificate of Secretary of Borrower as to:
   (a) Filed Articles [Certificates] of Incorporation and Amendments
   (b) By Laws
   (c) Resolutions (certified copies)
   (d) Incumbency of Officers Authorized to Execute Loan Documents and Authorized to Attest Loan Documents
   (e) Current Directors, Common Stock Holders and other equity holders, as well as their respective percentage ownership interests

**General Partnership Borrower:**

10. Partnership Agreement (as amended)

11. Authenticated Consents of Partners

12. Name of Partner Authorized to Execute Loan Documents

**Limited Liability Company:**

13. Operating Agreement (as amended)

14. Articles of Organization

15. Authenticated Consents of Members

16. Name of Member/Manager Authorized to Execute Loan Documents

**Limited Partnership Borrower:**

17. Partnership Agreement (as amended)

18. Authenticated Consents of Partners

19. Name of Partner Authorized to Execute Loan Documents

**Corporate Guarantor:**

**Limited Liability Company Guarantor:**

**General Partnership Guarantor:**

**Limited Partnership Guarantor:**

C. **SUPPORTING DOCUMENTATION—(Personal Property Collateral) (To be provided by Borrower and its Counsel):**

20. Collateral Disclosure List[3]

21. Copies of all licenses, patents, trademark, copyright, trade secret and intellectual property documentation

22. Current Financial Statements for the Borrower

23. Pro forma Financial Statements for the Borrower

24. Business Plans of the Borrower

25. Current Financial Statements for the Guarantors

26. Original life insurance policy

27. Original credit insurance policy

28. Original certificated security

29. Original instruments, duly endorsed

30. Original letter of credit

31. Original non-electronic chattel paper or evidence of notation

32. Motor Vehicles:
    (a) Certificates of title with notation of lender's security interest
    (b) Certificates of title with motor vehicle security interest filing statements

33. Description of aircraft and avionics

34. Landlord's Acknowledgement and Agreement

35. Mortgagee's Acknowledgement and Agreement

36. Bailee's Acknowledgement and Agreement

37. Equipment Appraisal

38. Notice of Inventory Purchase Money Security Interest

D. **INSURANCE (To be provided by Borrower and its Counsel):**

39. Processor's Acknowledgment

40. Duplicate original Hazard Insurance Policy with paid receipt on the Borrower's real property and business contents (including equipment and inventory),

---

3. The document contemplated is a comprehensive questionnaire regarding the borrower's personal property. The information received will be the basis for record searches and documentation. The document may be a separate certificate authenticated by a responsible officer of the borrower or the form of exhibit to be attached to the all assets personal property security agreement (Form 2.1).

together with *Evidence of Property Insurance (Form ACORD-27)* naming Lender as mortgagee, additional insured and loss payee and providing 30 days notice of cancellation

41. Duplicate original Public Liability and Property Damage Insurance with paid receipt, together with *Evidence of Property Insurance (Form ACORD-25)* naming Lender as additional insured and loss payee and providing 30 days notice of cancellation

42. Comprehensive General Liability Insurance Policy with paid receipt

43. Workers' Compensation Insurance Policy with paid receipt

44. Rent Loss/Business Interruption Insurance Policy/Endorsement with paid receipt

45. Flood Hazard Insurance Policy with paid receipt

**E.   OPINIONS AND CERTIFICATES (To be provided by Borrower and its Counsel):**

46. Opinion of Borrower's Counsel[4]

47. Opinion of Other Obligor's/Guarantor's Counsel

**F.   RECORD SEARCHES (To be obtained by Lender):**

48. UCC, Judgement, Tax Lien, Litigation and Bankruptcy Court search reports

49. Copyright and Patent and search reports

50. Trademark search reports

51. United States Federal Aviation Administration search reports

**G.   LOAN DOCUMENTATION:**

52. Credit Agreement

53. $_____ Revolving Credit Note

54. $_____ Term Note

55. $_____ Time Note

56. All Personal Property Assets Security Agreement[5]

57. Copyright Security Agreement[6]

58. Patent Security Agreement[7]

59. Trademark Security Agreement[8]

---

4.   A form of borrower's counsel perfection opinion letter appears as Form 5.2.1.
5.   A form of all personal property assets security agreement is set forth as Form 2.1.
6.   A form of copyright security agreement is set forth as Form 2.2.
7.   A form of patent security agreement is set forth as Form 2.3.
8.   A form of trademark security agreement is set forth as Form 2.4.

60. Assignment of Certificate of Deposit

61. Assignment of Government Contract
    (a)  Notice to contracting office
    (b)  Notice to disbursing officer
    (c)  Transmittal letters

62. Guaranty of Payment Agreement

63. Conditional Guaranty

64. Assignment and Security Agreement (General Partner's Interests)

65. Assignment and Security Agreement (Limited Partner's Interests)

66. UCC-1 Financing Statement:[9] _____ Secretary of State

67. Deposit Account Control Agreement[10]

68. Securities Account Control Agreement[11]

69. Pledge Agreement[12]
    • Irrevocable blank stock (or bond) power for each certificated security in registered form

70. Control Agreement—electronic chattel paper

71. Aircraft Chattel Mortgage, Security Agreement, and Assignment of Rents

72. Assignment of Life Insurance Policy as Collateral (executed in duplicate)

73. Assignment of Credit Insurance Policy as Collateral (executed in duplicate)

74. Payout Agreement (from existing creditors)

75. UCC Termination Statements[13]

76. Recording Instructions Letter

77. Intercreditor Agreement

78. Subordination Agreement

79. Participation Agreement

80. Letters of Credit Documents:
    (a)  Letter of Credit Agreement
    (b)  Letter of Credit
    (c)  Assignment of Letter of Credit Proceeds[14]

---

9.  Forms of financing statements, amendments and related forms are set forth as Forms 3.2.1–3.2.7.
10. A form of deposit account control agreement appears as Form 3.3.1.
11. A forms of securities account control agreement appears as Form 3.3.2.
12. A forms of pledge agreement is set forth as Form 3.6.
13. A form of termination statement is set forth as Form 3.2.7.
14. A form of assignment of proceeds of letter of credit is set forth as Form 3.4.

81. Eagle 9 UCC Insurance Policy

82. Certificate of Sources and Uses of Funds

83. Post Closing Agreement

## H.  FEES AND EXPENSES:

84. Commitment Fees

85. Field Examination Fee

86. Lender's Counsel Fee

87. Record Search Expenses

88. UCC/Lien Search Expenses

# Borrower's Counsel Perfection Opinion Letter[1]

[Borrower's counsel letterhead]

_____, 20____

[Secured Party/Lender's name and address]

Re:   Loan to [name of Borrower]

Ladies and Gentlemen:

We have acted as counsel for [name of Borrower], a [name of state and type of Borrower] (the "Borrower") in connection with the [name of agreement] dated _____, 20____ (the "Loan and Security Agreement") by Borrower in favor of [name of secured party/lender] ("Lender"). Each initially capitalized term used, but not otherwise defined, in this letter shall have the meaning ascribed to such term in the Loan and Security Agreement. Terms defined in the Uniform Commercial Code of any applicable state ("UCC") shall have the meanings set forth in the UCC. The following terms shall have the following meanings:

1.    "Filing Collateral" means Collateral that constitutes accounts, equipment, inventory, general intangibles, investment property, instruments, or tangible chattel paper as defined in the UCC.[2]

2.    "Filing Office" means [*if the Borrower is a registered organization:* the office of the Secretary of State of the State in which Borrower was organized or formed] [*if*

---

1.   This form of opinion covers many of the issues likely to arise in the course of opinion-giving on security interests under Revised Article 9.

2.   Revised Article 9 has not only expanded the coverage of the definition of accounts, but also expanded the types of collateral that can be perfected by filing to include instruments, a subcategory of which is promissory notes. Rev. § 9-310(a).

*the Borrower is not a registered organization, such as a general partnership:* the office of the secretary of state for the state in which Borrower has its principal place of business, if it only has one place of business or its chief executive office, if such trust has more than one place of business] [*if the Borrower is an individual:* the office of the secretary of state for the state in which Borrower maintains his/her principal residence.][3]

3.    "Control Collateral" means Collateral that is [investment property, deposit accounts, electronic chattel paper and letter-of-credit rights] as defined in the UCC.[4]

4.    "Intermediary" means the depositary bank for a deposit account, the securities intermediary for a security entitlement, the commodity intermediary for a commodity account, the issuer of uncertificated securities or the issuer or nominated person of a letter of credit.[5]

5.    "Possessory Collateral" means Collateral that is money, instruments, certificated securities, tangible chattel paper, and negotiable documents as defined in the UCC.[6]

In our capacity as counsel to the Borrower, we have reviewed [drafts/final execution copies/executed copies] of the following documents (the "Loan Documents"):

1.    Promissory Note made by Borrower in favor of Lender in the original principal amount of $_____, (the "Note");

2.    The Loan and Security Agreement;

3.    Perfection Certificate;

4.    Control Agreement (Deposit Accounts);[7]

---

3.    Under Revised Article 9, perfection by filing is generally accomplished by filing a financing statement in the debtor's "location." Rev. §§ 9-301(1) & 9-307. For registered organizations (Rev. §§ 9-102(a)(70)) which would typically include corporations, limited liability companies and most limited partnerships, the debtor is "located" in the state in which it is organized. Rev. § 9-307(e). If the borrower is not a registered organization, but still an "organization (Rev. §§ 1-201(28) and 9-102(a)(70)), it will be "located" at its "place of business" (if it has only one) or its "chief executive office," if it has more than one place of business. An individual is located at the individual's principal residence. *See* Rev. §§ 9-307(b). A checklist setting forth where to file a financing statement to perfect a security interest is set forth at Form 3.1.

4.    Certain types of collateral, such as deposit accounts and letter-of-credit rights, can only be perfected by "control." Rev. § 9-312. *See also* Rev. §§ 9-104 (defining "control" of deposit account); 9-107 (defining control of letter-of-credit rights). Control is also available for investment property (UCC § 8-106 & Rev. § 9-106) and electronic chattel paper. Rev. § 9-105.

5.    Certain methods of perfection by control require agreements with the third-party holder or issuer (*i.e.*, "Intermediary") as to certain collateral. UCC § 8-106; Rev. §§ 9-104, 9-106 & 9-107.

6.    A security interest in money can be perfected only by possession. Rev. § 9-312(b)(3). Security interests in negotiable documents, goods, instruments or tangible chattel paper may be perfected by filing or possession. Rev. §§ 9-310 & 9-313. A security interest in certificated securities may only be perfected by possession or control of the certificates (UCC § 8-106(a) &(b)) or by filing a financing statement. Rev. § 9-310(a).

7.    A control agreement is not needed to perfect a security interest in a deposit account where the lender is the borrower's depository bank or where the lender is the borrower's depository bank's customer. Rev. § 9-104(a)(i) & (3). A form of deposit account control agreement is contained as Form 3.3.1.

5.  Control Agreement (Investment Property);[8]

6.  Control Agreement (Letter-of-Credit Rights);[9]

7.  Bailee Acknowledgment (Possessory Collateral);[10] and

8.  UCC-1 Financing Statement.[11]

Items 4–6, inclusive are collectively the "Control Agreements."

We have reviewed and relied on the following documents:

1.  Certificate of [Good Standing/Existence/Status] of Borrower issued by the Secretary of State of _____ dated _____, 20____ ("Certificate of Status");

2.  Certificate of foreign [Good Standing/Existence/Status] of Borrower issued by the Secretary of State of _____ dated _____, 20____ ("Certificate of Foreign Status")

3.  [Articles/Certificate] of [Incorporation/Organization] of Borrower certified by the Secretary of State of _____ dated _____, 20____;

4.  [Bylaws/Operating Agreement/Limited Liability Company Agreement] of Borrower certified by Borrower;

5.  Borrower's Certificate identifying certain agreements and other matters applicable to Borrower ("Borrower's Certificate");[12] and

6.  The agreements and other matters identified and attached to the Borrower's Certificate

Items 1–4 are collectively, the "Organizational Documents."

In rendering this Opinion, we have assumed that:[13]

1.  each Loan Document, was duly executed and delivered by the parties thereto [other than Borrower] by the duly authorized representatives of such parties;

2.  Value has been given to the Borrower pursuant to the Loan Documents;[14]

---

8.  "Investment property" is defined in Rev. § 9-102(a)(49) as "a security, whether certificated or uncertificated, security entitlement, securities account, commodity contract, or commodity account." A security interest in investment property may be perfected by "control" of the investment property via a control agreement (among other methods). *See* Rev. §§ 9-106, 9-314. A form of securities account control agreement appears as Form 3.3.2.

9.  A form of assignment of proceeds of letter of credit appears as Form 3.4.

10.  Former Article 9 merely required lender to notify a third party holding collateral in which lender had a security interest. F. § 9-305. Under Revised Article 9, lender may perfect a possessory security interest in collateral in possession of a third party (*e.g.*, a bailee) only if the third party acknowledges in an authenticated record that it possesses the collateral for the benefit of the lender. Rev. § 9-313(c). A form of bailee acknowledgement (non-farm products) appears as Form 3.5.1.

11.  Various forms of UCC financing statement and addenda appear as Forms 3.2.1–3.2.7.

12.  A form of perfection certificate that may be used for this purpose is attached to the all personal property assets security agreement (Form 2.1).

13.  For the most part, this opinion is based on the reports of the TriBar Opinion Committee. *See* THE COLLECTED TRIBAR LEGAL OPINION REPORTS 1979-1998, SECTION OF BUSINESS LAW, AMERICAN BAR ASSOCIATION (1999). These reports have streamlined the opinion giving process and have become an outline of customary practice throughout most of the United States. In certain situations, however, it may be appropriate to make additional assumptions, to take additional exceptions and to make additional qualifications.

14.  Value given remains a requirement for attachment. Rev. § 9-203(b).

3.   Borrower has rights in the Collateral or the power to transfer rights in the Collateral to a secured party;[15]

4.   the Possessory Collateral is located, within the meaning of §§ 9-301 and 9-305(a)(1), only in the States of _____ (the "Possessory Collateral States"); and

5.   the Intermediaries are located, within the meaning of §§ 9-304, 9-305 and 9-306 of the UCC only in the States of _____ , (the "Control Collateral States").

Subject to the foregoing assumptions, and the exceptions and qualifications hereinafter contained, we are of the opinion that, under applicable law in effect on the date of this Opinion:

1.   Based solely on the Certificate of Status, Borrower is a [corporation/limited liability company/limited partnership] under the [name of corporation/limited liability company/limited partnership act of the state in which Borrower is organized]. Based solely on the Certificate of Foreign Status, Borrower is qualified to do business as a foreign [corporation/limited liability company/limited partnership] under the laws of the State of _____. Borrower has the [entity] power to enter into and perform its obligations under the Loan Documents to which it is a party.

2.   The execution, delivery, and performance of the Loan Documents to which Borrower is a party have been duly authorized by all necessary entity action on the part of Borrower. The Loan Documents to which Borrower is a party have been duly executed and delivered on behalf of Borrower.

3.   No further governmental or judicial consents, approvals, authorizations, registrations, declarations, or filings are required to be made by Borrower in order to execute, deliver, or perform its obligations under the Loan Documents or to consummate the transactions contemplated by the Loan Documents, except for any filings, consents or acknowledgments required to perfect Lender's security interests.

4.   The Loan Documents to which Borrower is a party constitute the valid and binding obligations of Borrower enforceable against Borrower in accordance with their respective terms.

5.   The execution and delivery by Borrower of the Loan Documents to which it is a party do not, and the performance by Borrower of its obligations thereunder will not violate or contravene or conflict with any provision of the Organizational Documents, or any law of the State of _____ applicable to Borrower, or result in a breach of or default under any agreement, indenture, or instrument identified in the Borrower's Certificate; or violation of any order, judgment, or decree of any court or other agency identified in the Borrower's Certificate.[16]

6.   The Loan and Security Agreement is effective to create a security interest in the Collateral in favor of the Lender in those items of Collateral consisting of personal property in which a security interest can be created under Article 9 of the UCC.

---

15. The borrower need not have "rights in the collateral" for a security interest to attach under Revised Article 9 so long as it has the "power to transfer rights to a secured party." Rev. § 9-203(b)(2).

16. Note that the opinion rendered in this paragraph is limited to those items listed in the borrower's certificate. If this opinion is not so limited, knowledge qualifiers may be appropriate for certain of these opinions.

7.  The Financing Statement is in proper form for filing with the Filing Office, and upon filing of the Financing Statement in the Filing Office, Lender will have a perfected security interest in the Filing Collateral.

8.  The security interest in the Possessory Collateral will be perfected upon: (i) execution of the Loan and Security Agreement by all parties thereto; and (ii) the Lender taking possession of the Possessory Collateral [*alternative*: (ii) the bailee or third party under the Bailee Acknowledgment taking possession of the Possessory Collateral].

9.  The security interest in the Control Collateral described in the Control Agreements will be perfected upon: (i) execution of the Loan and Security Agreement by all parties thereto; and (ii) the execution of the Control Agreements by all parties thereto [(ii) the Lender becoming the depository bank's customer with respect to deposit accounts,[17] (iii) the Lender becoming the entitlement holder with respect to security entitlements,[18] (iv) the Lender becoming the commodity intermediary with which the commodity contract is carried,[19] and/or (v) with respect to uncertificated securities, such securities being registered in the name of the Lender by the issuer[20]].

The opinions expressed above are subject to the following qualifications and limitations:

1.  Our opinion on any Loan Document may be limited by bankruptcy, insolvency, or similar laws affecting the rights and remedies of creditors' generally and by general principles of equity. [*in addition, the following is sometimes used:* Certain of the provisions in the Loan Documents may be further limited or rendered unenforceable by applicable law, but in our opinion such law does not make the remedies afforded by the Loan Documents inadequate for the practical realization of the principal benefits intended to be provided (except as otherwise limited by this Opinion and except for the economic consequences of any judicial, administrative, or other procedural delay which may result from such laws)].

2.  We express no opinion as to any of the following to the extent relevant to the Loan Documents:

    a)  The enforceability of any provision in the Loan Documents making irrevocable a power of attorney, whether or not coupled with an interest;

    b)  The enforceability of any provision in the Loan Documents that excludes, waives or limits the liability of any party (a) for its own gross fault, intentional fault or for causing physical injury to the other party, (b) for the released or indemnified party's negligence, where the release or indemnity does not expressly include liability arising out of such negligence, or (c) for

---

17. Rev. § 9-104(a)(3). If the lender is the borrower's depository bank, or the customer of the borrower's depositary bank with respect to the deposit account, it automatically has control. Rev. § 9-104(a)(1), (3). These methods and those that follow are alternative methods of obtaining "control" without a control agreement.

18. Rev. § 9-106(a); UCC § 8-106(c).

19. Rev. § 9-106(b)(1).

20. Rev. § 9-106(a); UCC §§ 8-106(c)(1), & 8-301(b)(1).

matters set forth in § 9-602, or (d) that requires indemnification for the indemnified party's failure to comply with limitations or requirements of applicable law;

c)  The enforceability of any provision in the Loan Documents prohibiting the non-written modification of such documents;

d)  As to whether or not Borrower is in compliance with any financial covenants, representations or warranties contained in the Loan Documents;

e)  The enforceability of any provision in the Loan Documents waiving the right to a jury trial, the objection of improper venue, unknown rights or defenses or any agreement granting subject matter and personal jurisdiction in any court;

f)  The enforceability of any provision requiring the payment of attorneys' fees and expenses, in an amount in excess of reasonable attorneys' fees and expenses actually incurred;

g)  The enforceability of any provision purporting to shorten any statute of limitations, or waiving in advance any defense with respect to any statute of limitations;

h)  The enforceability of any provision of the Loan Documents granting the secured party or obligee the unilateral right or discretion to determine standards or requirements for performance not expressly enumerated in the Loan Documents, or to establish standards or requirements that are not commercially (or manifestly) reasonable;[21]

i)  Any waivers of rights of setoff, or any agreement to set off debts that are not liquidated and payable; and

j)  Any provision providing for the right to injunctive relief without a showing of irreparable harm or injury.

The opinions rendered herein are limited to the federal law of the United States, and the laws of the State of _____, the Possessory Collateral States and the Control Collateral States. We are licensed to practice law only in the state of [_____]. As to other states covered by this opinion, we have based our opinion on our review of the Uniform Commercial Code of such other states as reported in [*identify compilation*]. This opinion letter is delivered only to you in connection with the transactions contemplated by the Loan Documents, may not be relied upon for any other purpose and may not be relied on by or furnished to any other person without our prior written consent.

Very truly yours,

[Name of Firm]

---

21.  The lender and borrower may agree under Rev. § 9-603 to the "standards" that will determine whether the rights of the Borrower (as debtor) and the duties of the Lender (as secured party) have been satisfied, so long as such standards are not "manifestly unreasonable." The parties may not agree to such standards for purposes of determining whether a secured party has fulfilled its duty under Rev. § 9-609 to refrain from breaching the peace.

# Perfection Opinion for Asset Securitization[1]

_____, 20____

To: [The Addressees Listed on Schedule 1 Attached Hereto]

---

1. This form is intended to be used in an asset securitization. "Securitizations" are generally defined as "the sale of equity or debt instruments, representing ownership interests in [an], ... income-producing asset or pool of assets ... structured to reduce or reallocate certain risks inherent in owning or lending against the underlying assets." _See_ TAMAR FRANKEL, SECURITIZATION: STRUCTURED FINANCING, FINANCIAL ASSET POOLS, AND ASSET-BACKED SECURITIES (1991 & Supp. 1995). A securitization typically involves at least three parties: (i) the originator of the debt or equity instruments, typically defined as the "originator," (ii) the "special purpose entity" that is the initial purchaser of these assets (typically defined as the "SPE"), and (iii) a trust or other entity (typically defined as the "trust") that purchases these assets from the SPE and issues the securities backed by the assets. In theory, securitizations place the assets sold by the Originator beyond the reach of the creditors (or bankruptcy trustee) of the originator.

Financial institutions that provide asset securitizations typically require that counsel for the originator issue two opinions in connection with the securitization: (i) an opinion that the trustee for the trust will obtain a perfected security interest in the assets sold, and (ii) an opinion that the sale of such assets from the originator to the SPE is a "true" sale (and thus the assets may not be recaptured by a bankruptcy trustee of the originator through doctrines of, _e.g._, "recharacterization" or "substantive consolidation"). The former opinion squarely involves Revised Article 9, and this form is an example of such an opinion. It is a generic opinion in that it does not address special issues that may arise with respect to specific types of assets (_e.g._, credit card receivables, residential real property mortgages, equipment leases, etc). Special care should be taken to determine whether the use of such assets requires modifications to this form. This form does not address issues of true sale or substantive consolidation.

This form has not been approved by agencies that rate asset-backed securities issued in asset securitizations.

259

Ladies and Gentlemen:

We have acted as special counsel to _____ ("Originator"), a [_____ _____],[2] and _____, a _____ _____ (the "SPE")[3] in connection with the execution and delivery of the following documents:

1.  [*identify the purchase and sale agreement whereby the Originator of the securitized assets (the "Receivables") sells those assets to the SPE*] (the "Receivables Purchase Agreement");

2.  [*identify second-step sale agreement or pooling and servicing agreement whereby the SPE transfers the Receivables or interests therein to investors or to a trust for the benefit of certificateholders and/or noteholders*] (the "Sale and Servicing Agreement") with [_____], as [trustee] (the "Trustee") for the [_____ Receivables Owner Trust] (the "Trust").[4]

The Receivables Purchase Agreement and the Sale and Servicing Agreement are hereby referred to collectively as the "Transfer Documents." Capitalized terms used herein and not otherwise defined shall have the meanings ascribed to those terms in [*identify agreement*].

This opinion is being delivered to you pursuant to Section _____ of [*identify agreement*].

In rendering the opinions set forth herein, we have examined and relied on originals or copies of the following:

(a)  the Transfer Documents;

(b)  a Uniform Commercial Code financing statement naming the Originator, as debtor or seller, the SPE, as secured party or buyer,[5] and the Trustee, as assignee, filed with the Secretary of State of _____ (the "Originator Financing Statement"), a copy of which is attached hereto as **Exhibit A**; and

---

2.    This opinion assumes, as will be true for most securitizations, that the originator and the SPE are "registered organizations" under the laws of a single state and that perfection will therefore be governed by the laws of that state. *See* Rev. § 9-301 (law governing perfection of a security interest is the law of the debtor's location as determined under Rev. § 9-307). *See also* Rev. § 9-307(e) (a debtor which is a registered organization organized under the laws of a state (*e.g.*, a corporation, limited liability company or limited partnership) is deemed located in that state). Rev. § 9-307(b) sets forth separate rules for determining the location of entities which are not registered organizations. In addition, there are special rules for determining the location of certain other debtors, such as national banks and registered organizations organized under the law of the United States. *See* Rev. § 9-307(f).

3.    As observed in footnote 1, the term "SPE" is a common term for referring to a "special-purpose entity", *i.e.*, a transferee of assets that is intentionally designed to be "bankruptcy-remote" through limitations in its charter documents on the scope of business activities in which it may engage.

4.    This opinion assumes that the securitization is comprised of two steps: The first step will be a sale from the originator to the SPE, which is designed to be a "true sale" for bankruptcy purposes. The second step will be a sale from the SPE to a trust. For convenience of reference, the second step in this opinion is described as a transfer to a Trust that issues certificates to investors. This second-step may instead consist of a pledge or a sale of undivided interests directly to investors in which event appropriate changes in terminology will be required. Additionally, many securitization transactions may involve a third-step whereby the trust issues notes and pledges the purchased assets to an indenture trustee for the benefit of noteholders. In the latter situation, additional security interest opinions would need to be given to address the perfection of the indenture trustee's security interest.

5.    Rev. § 9-505(a) provides that a buyer of a payment intangible or promissory note may use the term "buyer" instead of the term "secured party" in a financing statement.

(c)   a Uniform Commercial Code financing statement filed with the Secretary of State of [_____] (the "SPE Financing Statement" and together with the Originator Financing Statement, the "Financing Statements") naming the SPE, as debtor or seller, and the Trustee as secured party or buyer, a copy of which is attached hereto as **Exhibit B.**

In rendering the opinions set forth herein, we have also examined and relied on originals, or copies certified or otherwise identified to our satisfaction, of such (i) certificates of public officials, (ii) certificates and representations of officers and representatives of the Originator and the SPE, and (iii) other documents and records, and we have made such inquiries of officers and representatives of the Originator and the SPE, as we have deemed relevant or necessary as the basis for such opinions. We have relied upon, and assumed the accuracy of, all such certificates and representations, documents and records and the representations and warranties made by the Originator and the SPE in the Agreements, in each case with respect to the factual matters set forth therein. We have assumed the genuineness of all signatures, the authenticity of all documents submitted to us as originals, the conformity to original documents of all copies submitted to us as certified or photostatic copies and the legal capacity of all natural persons.

Unless otherwise indicated, references in this opinion to the "UCC" shall mean the Uniform Commercial Code as in effect on the date hereof in the State of _____.

We have also reviewed copies of the reports of [*describe applicable UCC search service*] described on **Exhibit C** hereto (the "Search Reports") with respect to financing statements on file listing the Originator or the SPE as debtor under their current names and the names listed in **Schedule 2** in offices of the Secretar[y][ies] of State of _____ [and _____] (the "Filing Offices").[6] We have assumed that each such Search Report is accurate and complete as of the date hereof and that, since the stated effective date of such reports, no filings or notices have been made with respect to the Originator or the SPE with the Filing Offices other than the filing of the Financing Statements. We have assumed, based on representations made in the Agreements, that (i) neither the Originator nor the SPE has had any [trade names, assumed names and/or] prior corporate names within the [last five years][7] other than those set forth in **Schedule 2** attached

---

6.   Some rating agencies (*e.g.*, Moody's) that rate asset-backed securities will typically require counsel to give a limited priority opinion in order, among other things, to relieve the agencies of the need to review UCC searches. This opinion includes a sample priority discussion based on specified search reports. Until at least July 1, 2006, it may be necessary to obtain searches in the appropriate filing offices under both former and Revised Article 9. In addition, note that attorneys searching in jurisdictions with delayed effective dates (*e.g.*, Alabama) should review Revised Article 9 as adopted in those states to determine whether the July 1, 2006 cutoff date for financing statements filed under former Article 9 was extended due to the delayed effective date of the Revision. Similarly, although Arizona used the uniform effective date (July 1, 2001), it extended the cutoff for financing statements filed under former Article 9 to July 1, 2007.

7.   Rev. § 9-507(c), like former Article 9, provides that a change in the name of the debtor which results in the financing statement being seriously misleading under Rev. § 9-506, renders the financing statement ineffective only as to collateral acquired more than four months after the change. Attorneys giving priority opinions should therefore typically search UCC records under all names going back to the full five-year period during which a financing statement may remain effective. A shorter time period may suffice in certain circumstances (*e.g.*, if the documents provide that all the financial assets were originated on or after a set date, the attorney would need to search only through the earliest date of origination). Conversely, a longer time period may be required if some of the securitized assets are more than five years old at the time of the securitization.

hereto;[8] (ii) neither the SPE nor the Trustee has knowledge of the contents of any financing statement or lien not disclosed in such Search Reports; (iii) *[except as noted in clause (v) below]* the Originator did not acquire the Receivables directly or indirectly from any person *[other than such persons whose names were searched for filings in the Search Reports]*, (iv) each of the Originator and the SPE is a _____ organized under the laws of the State of _____ and neither has changed its corporate structure or jurisdiction of organization in the past four months;[9] and (v) that, to the extent the Originator acquired its interest in the Receivables directly or indirectly from any other person *[whose name is not searched in the Search Reports,]* the Originator acquired such Receivables free and clear of any security interest or lien created by such person.[10] *[For opinions issued within four months following effectiveness of Revised Article 9 only: In addition, we have assumed that neither the SPE nor the Originator nor the SPE has changed the location of its [chief executive office] [sole place of business] in the past four months.[11]]*

---

8. Rev. § 9-503(c) rejects certain decisions under former Article 9 that considered a debtor's trade name—rather than its corporate or similar name—sufficient for a financing statement. Such decisions are widely considered to have been incorrect and have been rejected by many courts. Nevertheless, because most states have not ruled on the issue, it has been a common practice for attorneys representing secured parties to search for possible trade name filings. Rev. § 9-503 should generally eliminate the need for this practice, and should also eliminate the need in opinions for qualifications concerning the absence of trade or assumed names. Rev. § 9-705(c), however, expressly validates financing statements that were effective under former Article 9 until the earlier of the date such financing statements would have lapsed under former Article 9 or the applicable cutoff date under the Revision (usually June 30, 2006; *see* note 6, *supra*). Accordingly, absent express authority in the relevant former Article 9 jurisdiction rejecting the effectiveness of trade name filings, a trade name filing could continue to be effective through the applicable cutoff date. Attorneys issuing priority opinions through the applicable cutoff date may therefore wish to retain assumptions as to the absence of trade or assumed names. The assumption on the absence of prior corporate (or similar) names will continue to be revelant even after the applicable cutoff date (*e.g.*, June 30, 2006).

9. Note that this qualification reflects a change from former Article 9 consistent with the changes in filing rules under Rev. § 9-301 and Rev. § 9-307 based on a debtor's state of organization. *See* Rev. § 9-316(a)(2).

10. A security interest continues in collateral notwithstanding sale, exchange or other disposition unless the secured party authorized the disposition free of its security interest. *See* Rev. § 9-315(a)(1). The continuity of interest rule largely tracks the language of F. § 9-306. If the transferee becomes the debtor, however, and the transferee is located in another jurisdiction, the security interest becomes unperfected one year after the transfer unless re-perfected prior to that time. *See* Rev. § 9-316(a)(3). In most securitization transactions, the "originator" will have represented and warranted that it is the original creator (hence its name) of the receivables, in which event the bracketed language in clause (iii) above can be stricken and reliance on clause (iii) as reworded should eliminate the need for the assumption in clause (v) regarding predecessor transferors. Alternatively, the originator may represent, in the case of chattel paper and instruments, that it took possession thereof and acquired such receivables for value and in good faith without knowledge of any prior security interests, in which event the originator's title would be prior to any security interest created by its transferor. If, however, the originator otherwise acquired receivables from a predecessor transferor, opining counsel will need to search for filings against the predecessor transferor or, alternatively, include an assumption along the lines of the one suggested here.

11. Under former Article 9, financing statements as to intangible collateral and chattel paper must be filed where the debtor maintains its place of business, if it has only one, or otherwise its chief executive office. If a debtor relocated its chief executive office to another jurisdiction, the financing statement became ineffective as to accounts (other than accounts relating to minerals), chattel paper, general intangibles and mobile goods four months after the change. Counsel issuing priority opinions during the first four months after the effective date of Revised Article 9 as to collateral for which filing is effective under former Article 9 (*e.g.*, accounts (other than accounts relating to minerals), chattel paper and general intangibles) will want to include express assumptions that the locations of the originator and SPE under former Article 9 (*i.e.*, its sole place of business or chief executive office) are the same locations searched in the search reports.

In rendering the opinions set forth herein, we have assumed that:

(i)    [all parties to the Agreements (other than the Originator and the SPE) are duly organized, validly existing, and in good standing under the laws of their respective jurisdictions of organization and have the requisite corporate or banking power (as applicable) to enter into such Agreements;][12]

(ii)   the execution and delivery of the Agreements have been duly authorized by all necessary corporate or banking action (as applicable) and proceedings on the part of all such parties (other than the Originator and the SPE); the Transaction Documents have been duly executed and delivered by all such parties (other than the Originator and the SPE) and the Agreements constitute the valid and binding obligations of such parties, enforceable against such parties in accordance with their respective terms; the respective terms and provisions of each of the Agreements do not, and the execution, delivery and performance of its obligations thereunder by each of such parties (other than the Originator and the SPE) will not, violate the articles or certificate of incorporation or other charter document or by-laws of any such party or any law, order or decree of any court, administrative agency or other governmental authority binding on any such party, or result in a breach of or cause a default under any contract or indenture to which it is a party or by which it is bound;

(iii)  the exact legal names of the Originator and the SPE are as set forth in the copies of the organizational documents certified to us by the _____ Secretary of State;[13]

(iv)   the name and mailing address of the Trustee, the mailing addresses for the Originator and the SPE, and the organizational identification numbers of the Originator and the SPE are as set forth on the Financing Statements;[14] and

(v)    the SPE has paid the purchase price to the Originator in accordance with the terms of the Receivables Purchase Agreement and the Trustee has paid to the SPE the proceeds from the sales of the [Certificates] in accordance with the terms of the Sale and Servicing Agreement.

Based upon the foregoing and subject to the limitations, qualifications, exceptions and assumptions set forth herein, we are of the opinion that:

1.     The provisions of the Receivables Purchase Agreement are effective under the UCC to create in favor of the SPE a valid security interest in the Receivables constituting [accounts, chattel paper, payment intangibles and/or promissory notes],[15] and in any

---

12. This assumption may be viewed as implicit, and so need not be stated.

13. Whether or not counsel is separately opining on the due existence and validity of the transferors, review of the relevant corporate documents will be necessary to confirm each entity's name, that each entity is a "registered organization," and the state under which each entity is organized.

14. *See* Rev. § 9-516 (items to be included on financing statements). Errors in, or omissions of, some of these items will not render a financing statement seriously insufficient so as to prevent perfection, but could nonetheless cause a loss in priority as against a subsequent perfected secured party who reasonably relied on the erroneous information. Rev. § 9-338.

15. Insert applicable types of property. Counsel should be aware that this opinion assumes a one-time transfer of Receivables occurring contemporaneously with the issuance of the opinion. For so-called "revolving" transactions involving a series of transfers, the opinion language may need to be redrafted to reflect such ongoing sales, in which event the need for forward-looking assumptions and/or qualifications concerning the giving of value and the cut-off of liens under § 552 of the Bankruptcy Code should also be considered. *See, e.g.*, 11 U.S.C. § 552 (limiting security interests in property acquired by debtor after commencement of case).

identifiable proceeds thereof. (We note that a "security interest" as defined in § 1-201(37) of the UCC includes the interests of a buyer of [accounts, chattel paper, payment intangibles and/or promissory notes] and we refer you to [our other opinion] of even date herewith with respect to whether the security interest of the SPE should be characterized as an ownership interest or solely as a collateral interest held to secure a loan made to the Originator.)[16]

2.    The provisions of the Sale and Servicing Agreement are effective to create in favor of the Trustee a valid security interest in the Receivables constituting [accounts, chattel paper, payment intangibles and/or promissory notes], and in any identifiable proceeds thereof. [*We express no opinion as to whether the security interest of the Trustee would be characterized as an ownership interest or solely as a collateral interest held to secure a loan made to the SPE.*][17]

3.    Under the UCC (including the conflict of laws provisions thereof), the internal laws of the State of _____ govern the perfection by the filing of financing statements of the SPE's security interest in the Receivables sold by the Originator pursuant to the Receivables Purchase Agreement and the internal laws of the State of _____ govern the perfection by the filing of financing statements of the Trust's security interest in the Receivables transferred by the SPE pursuant to the Sale and Servicing Agreement.[18]

4.    Upon the filing of the Originator Financing Statement in the Office of the Secretary of State of _____, the SPE's security interest in the Receivables constituting [accounts, chattel paper, payment intangibles and/or promissory notes],[19] and in identifiable cash proceeds thereof, will be perfected. According to the provisions of the UCC, such perfected security interest is prior to any other security interest granted by the Originator that is perfected solely by the filing of financing statements under the UCC after the date of the filing of the Financing Statements. Based solely on our review of the Search Reports, [*and assuming the accuracy and completeness of such Search Reports,*][20] as

---

16. The bracketed language refers to the so-called "true sale" opinion whereby counsel opines that the transfer from the originator to the SPE would be characterized as a "true sale" for bankruptcy purposes. Such opinion is based on numerous assumptions and qualifications, most of which would not be repeated in a UCC perfection opinion.

17. In most transactions, the second-step sale from SPE to the trust would not qualify as a true sale because the SPE retains a residual interest in the assets transferred.

18. Insert the applicable location of the originator and the SPE in the respective blanks as determined under Rev. § 9-301. So long as the originator is a registered organization and its jurisdiction of organization has been confirmed by a certified charter document, counsel can conclude that the law of the originator's jurisdiction of organization governs perfection by filing. This opinion assumes that counsel is giving an opinion solely on perfection by filing. Under Rev. § 9-301, the law of physical location of instruments or chattel paper would apply to the effect of perfection or nonperfection, priority or to perfection of a possessory security interest in such assets. Note also that sales of payment intangibles and of promissory notes are perfected automatically when they attach under Rev. § 9-309 without filing of a financing statement. Counsel may still wish to rely on filing of financing statements for opinion purposes in the event that the underlying transaction is held not to be a true sale.

19. The above-described assets generally comprise property in which a security interest can be perfected by the filing of a financing statement under the UCC. Therefore, the opining counsel should not need an express limitation that the opinion addresses only collateral in which a security interest can be perfected by filing, such as would be customary under former Article 9 in an opinion covering a broad range of types of collateral.

20. The bracketed assumption may be viewed as implicit, and so need not be stated.

of each of the dates set forth therein, there were no UCC financing statements of record in the Filing Offices other than the Originator Financing Statement which name the Originator as debtor or seller and purport to cover any of the Receivables and the Filing Offices constitute all of the offices in which searches must be made to determine whether a security interest has been perfected by filing in such Receivables.[21] The conclusions expressed in this paragraph 4 are subject to the accuracy of the personnel in the filing offices referred to above with regard to the filing, indexing and recording of financing statements and notices of liens, and to the correctness of the Search Reports. We have further assumed that none of you has knowledge of the contents of any financing statement not disclosed in such reports.

5.    Upon the filing of the SPE Financing Statement in the Office of the Secretary of State of _____, the Trustee's security interest in the Receivables constituting [accounts, chattel paper, payment intangibles and/or promissory notes], and in identifiable cash proceeds thereof, will be perfected. According to the provisions of the UCC, such perfected security interest is prior to any other security interest granted by the SPE that is perfected solely by the filing of financing statements under the UCC after the date of the filing of the Financing Statements. Based solely on our review of the Search Reports, and assuming the accuracy and completeness of such Search Reports, as of each of the dates set forth therein, there were no UCC financing statements of record in the Filing Offices other than the SPE Financing Statement which name the SPE as debtor or seller and purport to cover any of the Receivables and the Filing Offices constitute all of the offices in which searches must be made to determine whether a security interest has been perfected by filing in such Receivables. The conclusions expressed in this paragraph 5 are subject to the accuracy of the personnel in the filing offices referred to above with regard to the filing, indexing and recording of financing statements and notices of liens, and to the correctness of the Search Reports. We have further assumed that none of you has knowledge of the contents of any financing statement not disclosed in such reports.

The opinions expressed herein are subject to the following assumptions, qualifications, exceptions and limitations:

(a)    We have assumed that the Originator has sufficient rights in the Receivables in order for the security interest of the SPE to attach thereto, and we express no opinion as to the nature or extent of the rights or title of the Originator in or to any of the Receivables.[22]

(b)    The perfection and priority of any security interest in proceeds is limited to the extent set forth in §§ 9-315 & 9-322 of the UCC.

---

21. It is common in securitization transactions for counsel to be asked to review search reports for the existence of federal tax and ERISA liens. If so, opining counsel should check the appropriate filing rules under § 6323 of the Internal Revenue Code and § 4068 of ERISA and make appropriate revisions in this and the next paragraph. As of the date of this publication, the filing locations specified under these sections for liens on intangible collateral are governed by a debtor's chief executive office, rather than its state of organization, and will therefore often require additional searches.

22. Counsel may need or want to include a similar assumption that the SPE has sufficient rights in the receivables for the trust's security interest to attach thereto and that no opinion is expressed as to the SPE's title. This opinion contains no such assumption because of the express assumptions concerning the enforceability of the transfer agreements and the giving of value to the originator by the SPE.

(c)     We call to your attention that the security interest of the SPE or the Trust in any Receivables may be subject to the rights of account debtors in respect of such Receivables, claims and defenses of such account debtors and the terms of agreements with such account debtors.[23]

(d)     The rights of the Originator and/or the SPE to assign any Receivables consisting of claims against any government or governmental agency (including, without limitation, the United States of America or any state thereof or any agency or department thereof or of any state) may be limited by the Federal Assignment of Claims Act or similar state or local statute.

(e)     In the case of any Receivable payment of which is secured by an interest in other property, we express no opinion with respect to the rights of the SPE and/or the Trust in and to such interest or underlying property.

(f)     [*We express no opinion as to any actions that may be required to be taken periodically under the UCC or other applicable law in order for the effectiveness of the Financing Statements, or the validity or perfection of any security interest, to be maintained.*][24] [*We call to your attention (i) that perfection of any security interest in the Receivables by filing will lapse (x) four months after the Originator or the SPE, as applicable, changes its location to another jurisdiction or (y) one year after the Originator or SPE transferred the Receivables to a person who thereby becomes a debtor under the Transfer Agreements and who is located in another jurisdiction, unless, in either case, appropriate steps are taken to perfect such security interest in such other jurisdiction before the expiration of such four-month or one-year period, as applicable;*[25] [*(ii) if the Originator or the SPE changes its name so as to make the Financing Statement filed against it seriously misleading, then perfection will lapse as to any Receivables acquired by such party more than four months after such change unless new appropriate financing statements indicating the new name of the Originator or the SPE are properly filed before the expiration of such four-month period*[26]], [*(iii) if the Originator or the SPE changes its jurisdiction of organization or otherwise transfers Receivables to a person who thereby becomes a debtor under the Transfer Agreements and who is located in another jurisdiction, the Financing Statements will not be effective to perfect any security interest in Receivables acquired by the Originator or the SPE or such other debtor, as applicable, after such change or transfer,*[27]] *and (iv) § 9-515 of the UCC requires the filing of continuation statements within the period of six months to the expiration of five years from the date of the filing of the original Financing Statements or the filing of any continuation statements in order to maintain the effectiveness of the Financing Statements.*]

---

23. *See* Rev. § 9-404.

24. Note the two bracketed alternatives: The first sentence is suggested as an abbreviated way of addressing the issues described in more detail in the second sentence.

25. *See* Rev. § 9-316(a)(2) & (3).

26. Because name changes only invalidate financing statements as to after-acquired collateral, clause (ii) is unnecessary for transactions that involve a one-time transfer but is inserted since it would be required for any transaction involving future transfers.

27. The qualification in this paragraph 5(f)(iii) is necessary only if the securitization provides for the ongoing sale of receivables by the originator to the SPE.

(g)   Except as provided in paragraphs 5 and 6, we express no opinion as to the priority of any security interest. Without limiting the foregoing, we express no opinion as to the priority as against any security interests or other liens as to which a UCC filing in the Filing Offices is not required, including, without limitation, (i) liens for the payment of federal, state or local taxes or charges which are given priority by operation of law, including, without limitation, under §§ 6321 and 6323(c)(2) & (d) of the Internal Revenue Code; (ii) claims of the United States of America under the federal priority statutes (31 U.S.C. § 3713 *et seq.*); (iii) liens in favor of the United States of America, any state or local governmental authority or any agency or instrumentality thereof, including, without limitation, liens arising under Title IV of ERISA; (iv) liens of a collecting bank under § 4-210 of the UCC; (v) the rights of a "lien creditor" as defined in § 9-102(52) of the UCC which is entitled to priority under § 9-323(b) of the UCC: (vi) security interests in respect of proceeds of collateral other than Receivables in which a security interest was properly perfected other than by filing in the Filing Offices, to the extent that the applicable secured party has a perfected security interest in such proceeds under § 9-315 and such interest is entitled to priority under § 9-322 of the UCC; (vii) the rights of a "purchaser" of chattel paper who is entitled to priority under § 9-330 of the UCC; (viii) the rights of a "purchaser" of instruments, documents, and securities who is entitled to priority under § 9-331 of the UCC; (ix) any other liens, claims or other interests that arise by operation of law and do not require any filing or possession in order to take priority over security interests perfected through the filing of a financing statement; (x) a security interest which was perfected automatically upon attachment pursuant to § 9-309 of the UCC; (xi) a security interest temporarily perfected without filing or possession under § 9-312(e), (f) or (g) of the UCC; (xii) a security interest perfected by taking possession or the taking of delivery under § 9-313; (xiii) a security interest in deposit accounts, electronic chattel paper, investment property or letter-of-credit rights which is perfected by control under § 9-314 of the UCC; and (xiv) the rights of any person to whom Receivables have been released or reassigned or in whose favor the security interest of the SPE or the Trust, as applicable, have been subordinated.

(h)   Our opinions herein are limited to the UCC and do not address the laws of any jurisdiction other than the laws of the State of _____. Without limiting the foregoing, we note that, (i) if any of the Receivables is or becomes evidenced by instruments or tangible chattel paper or any other property in which a security interest may be perfected by taking possession, the local law of the jurisdiction where such property is located will govern the priority of a possessory security interest in such property and the effect of perfection or nonperfection of a non-possessory security interest in such property, and (ii) if and to the extent that the Receivables are converted into deposit accounts, investment property, letter-of-credit rights, or goods covered by a certificate of title, perfection and the effect of perfection or non-perfection of a security interest in such property may be governed by other law in accordance with Rev. §§ 9-303 through 9-306.

We express no opinion as to the laws of any jurisdiction other than the laws of the State of _____ and the federal laws of the United States of America to the extent specifically referred to herein.

This opinion is being furnished only to you, is solely for your benefit, and is not to be used, quoted, relied upon or otherwise referred to by any other person or for any other purposes without our prior written consent. This opinion is based on factual matters in existence as of the date hereof and laws and regulations in effect on the date hereof, and we assume no obligation to revise or supplement this opinion should such factual matters change or should such laws or regulations be changed by legislative or regulatory action, judicial decision or otherwise.

Very truly yours,

[name of firm]